DATE		

The Blind Boss and His City

Christopher Augustine Buckley.

The Blind Boss & His City

Christopher Augustine Buckley and
Nineteenth-Century San Francisco

William A. Bullough

University of California Press

Berkeley · Los Angeles · London

University of California Press

Berkeley and Los Angeles, California

University of California Press, Ltd.

London, England

© 1979 by The Regents of the University of California

ISBN 0-520-03797-9

Library of Congress Catalog Card Number: 78-64468

Printed in the United States of America

1   2   3   4   5   6   7   8   9

For Pat and Greg

CONTENTS

Contents

ILLUSTRATIONS

All illustrations are reproduced through the courtesy of The Bancroft Library, University of California, Berkeley, unless otherwise noted.

Illustrations

PREFACE

Despite tactical similarities to other potentates ruling at different times and places in history, the urban saloon boss constitutes a phenomenon unique to the nineteenth-century American city. I first became acquainted with these arrogant, autocratic practitioners of the art and science of political chicanery, including Christopher Augustine Buckley, as a graduate student in history at the University of California, Santa Barbara. Professor Alexander B. Callow, Jr.—a scholar whose knowledge of these masters of municipal manipulation encompasses Buckey and William Marcy Tweed as well as a host of their contemporaries and successors[1]—performed the introductory rites and inspired an abiding curiosity about the San Francisco statesman in particular, bosses in general, and the relationship between municipal politics and other facets of urban development. Subsequent encounters with the Blind Boss occurred almost incidentally in the course of research into other topics, and interest in him and his city grew with each meeting. It peaked with the fortuitous discovery of his son, Christopher

Augustine Buckley, Jr., who provided important insights into otherwise obscure aspects of his father's character and career.[2]

Recurrent encounters with the Blind Boss precipitated numerous questions about him and about the history of San Francisco in the last quarter of the nineteenth century. Some of them, such as whether or not Chris Buckley was a "typical" boss, have relatively apparent and straightforward answers. Insofar as typical bosses existed, Buckley was one. Like many of his counterparts in other cities, he was the son of recent Irish immigrants. He also possessed a unique sense of the city, its people, and its strengths and weaknesses, and he employed his understandings to capitalize upon disorganized urban conditions for his own profit and that of his party. Buckley professed allegiance to the Democracy (although he entered San Francisco politics as a Republican), but like most nineteenth-century bosses, personal leadership rather than partisan ideology constituted his principal stock in trade. In typical fashion, also, he commenced his public life as the keeper of saloons which doubled as his political headquarters in the lower wards of the city. He later broadened his economic interests to include a variety of profitable enterprises as his career progressed, and in the process he accumulated a substantial personal fortune. Finally, like many contemporary municipal politicos, Buckley learned his profession in the streets and neighborhoods of the city, climbed to the pinnacle of local power, extended his influence to state and even national affairs, and ultimately succumbed to the onslaughts of preprogressive municipal reformers in the closing decade of the nineteenth century.[3]

Answers to other questions about Buckley and his city are substantially more complex and elusive. How, for example, did an individual who was sightless for most of his adult life manage to capture and retain political authority in the city, despite the fact that he never held or even sought an elective office? To what degree was the Blind Boss a uniquely local phenomenon? If Buckley was as unprincipled and corrupt as he has been portrayed and the public was aware of his tactics, how did he manage to maintain his position for a decade? How were his career and his political style related to specific conditions in his city? Did urbanization in Buckley's San Francisco recapitulate concurrent developments in other United States cities? Or did it evolve as an isolated social, economic, political, and demographic entity, a provincial outpost on the fringes of urban-industrial America? Were the forces which finally dethroned Buckley related to the process of urbanization? Did reformers redeem San Francisco from a demonic, unscrupulous regime, or did they too have personal interests in the acquisition of political power? Did the Blind Boss's hegemony make any positive contributions to the history of San Francisco? Or was his reign an entirely negative interlude?

This book was written neither to convict nor to exonerate Chris Buckley but rather to seek answers to these and other questions and to share them with those interested in the phenomenon of the saloon boss and in the history of nineteenth-century San Francisco. To whatever degree success has been attained, there have been numerous contributors.

Mr. and Mrs. Christopher Augustine Buckley, Jr. acted as gracious hosts, gave generously of their time, added important human dimensions to my understanding of the Blind Boss, and became good friends. Without their interest, the book might not have been written.

Alec Callow—mentor, friend, and occasional boss in his own right—will disagree with some of my interpretations and conclusions. Nevertheless, he pointed the way and my debts to him are countless.

Encouragement and insights came from my colleagues in the Department of History at California State University, Hayward, especially from Professors José A. Fernández-Santamaria, Gerald S. Henig, and Richard J. Orsi. This trio of exemplary scholars and teachers generously took time from their own pursuits in order to read the entire manuscript; their editorial skills and historical expertise certainly prevented numerous factual, stylistic, and interpretive blunders.

Professors R. Hal Williams of Southern Methodist University, Martin Shefter of Cornell University and the Institute for Advanced Study at Princeton, William Issel of San Francisco State University, and James P. Walsh of San Jose State University added perspective at various stages of the work. William F. Heintz of Glen Ellen, California, eased the task by making available his own research notes and unpublished manuscripts.

Numerous libraries and archives provided the essential raw materials: the local history collection at San Francisco Public Library, the Bender Room at Stanford University Library, the California State Library and Archive in Sacramento, the library of the California Historical Society in San Francisco, the resources of the California State University Library at Hayward, and the Bancroft Library at the University of California,

Berkeley. At these institutions, three individuals in particular facilitated research and eliminated much of the routine drudgery which often accompanies it. At the San Francisco Public Library, archivist Gladys Hansen located obscure resources and provided a congenial setting for concentrated work. At California State University, Hayward, reference librarians Carol A. Castagnozzi and Ruth M. Jaeger demonstrated genuine interest in the study and extended themselves far beyond normal expectations to respond to occasionally peculiar requests and to tolerate frequent impositions.

Janet Newton of the Livermore Heritage Guild extended her hospitality and furnished important materials and insights relating to Buckley's life and career at his Ravenswood estate.

The editors of *California Historical Quarterly* and *Pacific Historical Review* have granted permission for previously published material to be included.

A sabbatical leave from California State University, Hayward, and grants from the institution's Research Foundation expedited matters substantially.

Finally, my wife Pat and my son Greg, to whom the book is dedicated, deserve first place rather than last in the hierarchy of my gratitude. They gave what they alone could provide: love, patience, and encouragement in sufficient quantities to see the work through to its completion. My debts to them are both infinite and incalculable.

CHAPTER

1

Prologue:
Chris Buckley and
San Francisco,
1862–1873

*W*hen Christopher Augustine Buckley migrated to San Francisco in 1862, he was the poor and obscure son of one of the multitude of Irishmen who thronged to the city during its formative years. When he died in 1922, he was neither poor nor obscure. Indeed, his renown as the Blind Boss of the city's Democracy had sufficed, during his lifetime, not only to spread his fame (or notoriety) throughout the state and the nation but also to warrant his inclusion in works by authors of international literary standing. In 1889, for example, Rudyard Kipling observed that

Today the city of San Francisco is governed by the Irish vote, . . . under the rule of a gentleman whose sight is impaired and who requires a man to lead him about the streets. He is called officially "Boss Buckley," and unofficially the "Blind White Devil."

A decade later, Robert Louis Stevenson gave Buckley a place in popular fiction in *The Wrecker*, a novel partially set on the San Francisco Barbary

Coast. Stevenson's narrator recalls an experience in a local waterfront saloon:

I remember one day, not long before an election, seeing a blind man, very well dressed up, led up to the counter and remain a long while in consultation with a negro [Black Tom, the proprietor of the place]. The pair looked so ill-assorted, and the awe with which the drinkers fell back and left them in the midst of an impromptu privacy was so unusual in such a place, that I turned to my next neighbor with a question. He told me that the blind man was a distinguished party boss, called by some the King of San Francisco, but perhaps better known by his picturesque Chinese nickname of the Blind White Devil.[1]

Both characterizations, however, involve not only insights but also misconceptions concerning the boss and nineteenth-century San Francisco politics.

Buckley was blind and had been since his early thirties, he did employ a series of bodyguards—including former prizefighter Alex Greggains—to guide and protect him, and he did frequent the city's waterfront saloons as well as its more elegant hostelries. But the Irish, who were deeply involved in local politics, never developed sufficient cohesiveness to exercise a control comparable to that of their compatriots in New York City's Tammany Hall, and black San Franciscans remained adherents of the "party of Lincoln" in the 1880s, not of Buckley's Democracy. Similarly, the sinister implications of both authors' references—and those of contemporary critics and more recent historians—to the sobriquet Blind White Devil *(Maang Pâak Kwái)* are erroneous; the Chinese in San Francisco habitually referred to all Caucasians as Pâak Kwái, a virtually untranslatable phrase which approximates "pale spirit."[2] Still, the observations by Kipling and Stevenson do illustrate the reality of Buckley's authority and the extent of his reputation.

He had earned his reputation while still in his early forties, principally within San Francisco itself and as the epitome of the "self-made man" in its political, business, and social affairs. The city's economic potential permitted him to leave a substantial legacy—nearly 1 million dollars—despite the loss of several previous fortunes. From 1882 until 1891 when he was deposed, allies and enemies alike recognized him as the true authority in local government and the single most powerful individual in state politics, a status which he had attained principally by his responses to the chaos of urbanization. Although Buckley never held elective public office, his power enabled him to make mayors, judges, governors, and legislators—including United States Senator George Hearst—and to unmake others. His social and economic standing allowed him to travel the world and to consort with millionaires, presidents, and other heads of state, some as exotic as King Kalakaua of Hawaii. Buckley's power also drew the fire of a basically hostile press which, while he was alive, vilified him with accusations of bribery, corruption, and even felonious crime but, after his death, hailed him as a "great leader" who had "ruled San Francisco with a powerful but kindly hand." In contrast to his public image, his family, friends, and the numerous recipients of his charity consistently regarded him as a warm, intelligent, generous human being whose "word was his bond." And even in 1922, more than three decades after his reign ended, he still retained sufficient private and public respect to close San Francisco courts on the day of his funeral; most of the judges served as his honorary pallbearers, joining with throngs of citizens to bring to a fitting end a long and remarkable career.[3]

While that career lasted, it constituted an integral part of the history of Buckley's San Francisco. Indeed, the life of the man and the history of the city paralleled one another in numerous ways. When Buckley disembarked in 1862, San Francisco, like the sixteen-year-old youth, was leaving its adolescence behind and entering a vigorous maturity, emerging from the chaos of the gold rush and Vigilance Committee episodes and moving into the initial phase of metropolitan development. Already, permanent buildings of brick, stone, and iron were displacing the temporary structures—including derelict ships—which had provided shelter for the city's early settlers and fuel for its perennial conflagrations. A polyglot population of some 60,000—European and Latin American immigrants, Chinese, and a smattering of blacks, as well as native-born seekers of wealth—sprawled from North Beach and Telegraph Hill to the tent, tenement, and factory districts south of Market Street and the elegant residential neighborhoods on Rincon Hill. Economic diversification had commenced with factories, foundries, shipyards, tanneries, grain mills, and gas works joining traditional commercial and speculative enterprises and helping to produce extremes of poverty and affluence in the city. Like social and economic conditions, political arrangements were constantly changing and little short of chaotic. Ostensibly, the municipality conducted its business under the provisions of the Consolidation Act of 1856, a relatively progressive organic law when it was written for a town of some 30,000 but already, by the 1860s, inadequate for the government of a growing and changing city. In reality, a coterie of interests, the People's Party (political descendants of the Vigilance Committee of 1856), and a host of political bosses, many headquartered among the thousands of saloons in the city, directed San Francisco's affairs.[4]

During Buckley's public lifetime, the already established dynamics of urban growth continued and even accelerated. A persistently cosmopolitan population increased to nearly a third of a million and, with the advent of cable cars and other transportation innovations, dispersed to cover the city's heights and the level districts to the west. It would include even greater extremes of wealth, ranging from the ostentatious affluence of the railroad barons and silver kings to the poverty of the ever-present Chinese and the denizens of the Barbary Coast. Moreover, socioeconomic fragmentation of the city's neighborhoods, exemplified by elegant Nob Hill and impoverished Tar Flat south of Market Street, clearly reflected the distinctions. And the city's skyline, although not yet "Manhattanized" at the turn of the century, attested to continuing social and economic development with its palatial hotels and multistoried business edifices.

Clearly, by 1900 San Francisco had become a metropolis, and throughout the final third of the nineteenth century its citizens had struggled to adjust confused political arrangements to the exigencies of change. Repeated amendments to the Consolidation Act proved futile and perhaps even added to the political perplexity. Indeed, the sole effective response to urbanization emerged in the form of a succession of political potentates—including Chris Buckley and his Republican counterpart Martin Kelly—who employed their personal authority and not inconsiderable talents to resolve the conflicts of the city. By 1900, however, all that had changed. The archaic Consolidation Act and its unwieldy amendments had yielded to the modern, efficient, and businesslike City Charter of 1898, the final product of recurrent good-government movements in the late 1880s and 1890s. The saloon boss had apparently outlived his utility to the city, and his place was occupied by a new breed of politician, personified in San Francisco by yet another son

4

of Irish immigrants: Mayor James Duval Phelan—banker, business and civic leader, and father of the city's reform charter of 1898.[5]

The city had been radically transformed in the interval between Buckley's arrival on the scene and the opening of the twentieth century. What had been a chaotic, brawling, and often violent instant city became a modern, sophisticated, and progressive metropolis. And both political rearrangements and the Blind Boss's career mirrored the social, economic, and demographic change which urbanization precipitated.

The culmination of the process of urban change, however, remained a generation away in 1862, and nothing in the circumstances of Chris Buckley's arrival in California presaged his ultimately critical involvement in its history or that of San Francisco. His father, John, was simply another immigrant Irishman who had left his homeland and settled in New York City during the early 1840s. In that city, he pursued his stonemason's trade, and there, too, Christopher was born on Christmas Day, 1845, and grew up in the notorious Fourteenth Ward where his contemporaries—and perhaps even his playmates—included future Tammany chieftains Richard Croker and "Honest" John Kelly. The extent of John Buckley's participation in the political hurly-burly of his Irish Democratic ward remains essentially speculative. But the demand for his skills in a constantly expanding city apparently did contribute to significantly greater economic success than that experienced by the majority of his foreign-born contemporaries in New York City or other urban centers in the United States.

In this instance, success proved to be a decidedly mixed blessing; it permitted John Buckley to pursue his preoccupation with instant wealth. Like so many others in the United States and elsewhere during the 1840s and 1850s, he had been almost incurably infected by the sting of the California gold bug, and whenever he accumulated a sufficiently substantial stake, he would leave home and family and depart for the western mines. His persistent efforts proved futile and resulted principally in the dissipation of resources which rendered an already marginal family status even more precarious and perhaps minimized Christopher's opportunity for more than a rudimentary formal education. Still, the sporadic pattern of solitary sojourns persisted until 1862 when the elder Buckley embarked upon his final migration, probably by way of

Panama, to the Golden State. Leaving his older sons John, Jr. and William behind, he took his wife Ellen, young Christopher, and probably two grandchildren, John (age eight) and Ellen (age six) Parrotte, with him to pursue what Kevin Starr has aptly called the "California dream."[6] None of them would ever return permanently to New York.

Considerations other than the lure of gold also may have prompted the Buckley's final departure from the East. By the 1860s, in fact, hydraulic mining and other extractive processes requiring sophisticated equipment, corporate organization, and substantial capital had all but displaced the individual prospector in the California gold fields. But a new source of mineral wealth, the Comstock Lode discovered in Nevada in 1859, had generated a speculative mania for silver analogous to the fury of the gold rush a decade earlier. And a new wave of Argonauts, perhaps including the Buckleys, headed west in response to the news of the most recent bonanza. It is possible, also, that the impact of the Civil War influenced the decision to migrate. Even by mid-1862, well before the Conscription Act of the following March, it had become apparent that some form of mandatory military service would be essential in order to maintain the strength of Union armies, and rumors of impending legislation precipitated comment as far away as London. In New York City, moreover, immigrant Irish Democrats harbored little sympathy for service in the Union cause, a fact to which the riots of 1863 would attest. Thus, John Buckley's final migration westward may have involved an effort to shield both himself and his youngest son from service by joining the estimated 100,000 refugees who flocked to California during the first year of the conflict. Finally, the Buckleys may have responded to a peculiarly Irish version of the California dream. Irishmen in the East most frequently found themselves congested in cities, involved in menial kinds of labor, and persecuted for their religion by Know-Nothings and other nativists, and they saw the West as an escape. Although the dream materialized for very few, California represented an opportunity to escape the constraints of the city, to acquire land of their own, and to maintain their religious and cultural identities free from the harassment of bigots.[7]

Whatever the motivation for the Buckleys' journey, upon their arrival in San Francisco the family established residence together in the city's working class neighborhoods, first on Tehama Street in the South of

Market area and later on Pacific Street at the foot of Telegraph Hill. But neither immediately nor eventually did the California or Nevada mines provide John Buckley's livelihood; instead, his craft once again furnished employment in yet another burgeoning city. Urban growth necessitated new buildings of every description—up to a thousand in a single year—and created numerous jobs for skilled craftsmen. The senior Buckley (city directories list him as "builder" or "contractor") may well have participated in the construction of such elegant hostelries as the Lick House, Russ House, Occidental Hotel, or Cosmopolitan Hotel, all completed within a year of his arrival in the city. Or he may have been involved in the erection of the scores of public and private buildings which altered the San Francisco skyline in the 1860s. Christopher—a youngster not yet seventeen, without a marketable skill to offer—also secured employment related to expanding urban needs; he became a conductor on the Omnibus Railway Company's North Beach and South Park Line, traversing the varied and already specialized districts of the city.[8]

Like other urban Americans of the period, San Franciscans optimistically regarded their horsedrawn street railway systems—several minor operations and the major Market Street and Omnibus Railway Companies—as modern, efficient modes of travel capable of unifying the community and bringing the benefits of suburban life to members of the working classes and their families. Although the street railways never fulfilled their apparent promise and public approval would turn to vehement hostility in the 1880s, for the moment at least they served residents of the city well, transporting citizens of all classes over frequently miserable streets with reasonable regularity and reliability. And for Chris Buckley, the running board of a horsecar provided a platform from which he might observe the diversity and excitement of life in his adopted city.[9]

In the 1860s, Buckley's San Francisco remained a relatively compact urban center. The principal region of settlement extended from the Golden Gate on the north to the foot of Potrero Hill approximately three miles to the south and from the bay westward roughly two and a half miles to present Van Ness Avenue and the Western Addition. The young conductor's daily excursions through this cramped and congested community originated in its northern working class districts near Tele-

7

South Park and North Beach Line horsecar in the 1860s.

graph Hill, a height already being reduced by "vaporiphic patricks," the local sobriquet for the steam shovels which had replaced Irish laborers. In these areas, once referred to as Little Chile or the Latin Quarter, he encountered increasingly amorphous colonies of immigrants who occupied numerous boarding houses and hotels; Latin Americans, the largest single group there, joined Italians in North Beach (which once was a beach), a gathering of French settlers near Clark's Point at the end of Broadway, and a smattering of Irish and remnants of the Sydney Duck settlement of the 1850s. Slightly to the south, and west of Montgomery Street, the omnibus skirted enclaves of the city's most segregated ethnic groups: the approximately 2000 blacks employed as cooks, laborers, porters, and barbers, and the Chinese, mainly servants and laundry operators. Still farther south, at the end of Montgomery Street, Buckley's route turned southwestward along Market Street where it bisected neighborhoods of German merchants, artisans, and laborers. When the line turned southward once again, through the region across Market Street and extending toward Potrero Hill, the young man found himself among members of the city's largest single immigrant group, the Irish, many of whom congregated around Old Saint Patrick's Church where they demonstrated their own version of the Italians' *campanilismo,* the desire to live in the shadow of one's church steeple.[10]

Daily rounds through the city's working-class districts familiarized Buckley with the seemingly endless variety of San Francisco society, but there was more to be seen. For when the railway line looped around Rincon Hill and South Park, it terminated in sharp contrast to its beginning. At a site which is now the western abutment of the transbay bridge from Oakland, the homes and gardens of the city's elite nestled on gentle slopes overlooking the bay. Respectable middle-class neighborhoods existed elsewhere in the city, especially along Stockton Street a few blocks west of the central district, but for aristocratic San Franciscans of the 1860s, wooded charm, superior climate, and remoteness from urban bustle and congestion made Rincon Hill the favored place to live. And the residents of its elegant Old English and antebellum style estates included the cream of the city's society: industrialist Peter Donahue, leading clerics like Bishop William I. Kip and the Reverend William Anderson Scott, financiers William C. Ralston and later Asbury Harpending, Senator William Gwin, and author Gertrude Atherton who was born there in 1857.[11] It is likely that many of them handed their streetcar fares to Chris Buckley, permitting him yet another brief glimpse of the diversity and potential which characterized urban society.

Despite the apparent contrast among the various districts which the young conductor traversed, and the seeming homogeneity within them, the controlling dynamic of urban settlement remained socioeconomic rather than ethnic considerations; individuals of all nationalities and races lived in close proximity to one another in all areas of the city, with the possible exception of Rincon Hill. Nevertheless, the clustering and associational life of the neighborhoods gave Buckley clear evidence of the necessity for social contact and identity among isolated citizens of an equally isolated city. Indeed, even on Rincon Hill displaced southerners and New Englanders attempted to perpetuate the familiar lifestyles and values of their former homes, and less secure individuals exhibited similar needs, albeit in different ways. In areas where a particular nationality perdominated, associations based upon common origins appeared: the *Turner Gesang Verein,* the *Campagnia Bersaglieri,* the Hibernian Society, or church-affiliated sodalities and societies. Nearly all national groups sponsored benevolent and burial associations, ethnic theaters, native language newspapers, and other institutions which lined the streets of their communities. These were not entirely private activities. Because the supply of family residences constantly lagged substantially behind the demand for them, San Franciscans of all origins and social strata tended to live publicly in the 1860s, gathering in their favorite hotels, lodging houses, restaurants, theaters, and saloons, and frequently spilling their activities into the congested streets of their own neighborhoods and those of the central district itself.[12]

The city's street life made its society an open book for an ambitious and observant youngster, but the volume contained still more pages to be read and lessons to be absorbed, especially concerning the economic potential of San Francisco. Buckley's journeys between the principal residential areas to the north and south carried him along the approximately one-mile length of Montgomery Street from the foot of Telegraph Hill to its intersection with Market Street. And that short thoroughfare, with the adjacent blocks of its cross-streets, constituted the artery through which flowed the lifeblood of the city. In the words of one contemporary habitué of the street: "During the busy hours of the day you could meet there every man worth knowing . . . and in the afternoon every woman with a pretty face or a handsome gown to show."[13]

San Franciscans of all classes flocked to Montgomery Street, called the "Broadway of the Pacific" in 1862, for entertainment ranging from grand opera productions to presentations capable of shocking all but the most jaded audiences. They also went to eat and imbibe in scores of equally varied establishments: fine French restaurants, elegant saloons, cheap diners, and the seamy dives called "blind tigers." But more importantly, the activities, institutions, and individuals which in 1862 made San Francisco the commercial and financial capital of California, Nevada, and perhaps the Pacific focused upon the Montgomery district. Along the street, speculators openly made—and lost—great fortunes daily, perhaps even on Buckley's horsecar. Entrepreneurs like William Ralston, William Sharon, Isaac Friedlander, George Hearst, and the elder James Phelan conducted their affairs and established business headquarters there. The newly-formed San Francisco Stock and Exchange Board attempted to rationalize transactions in volatile silver mining shares, while the older Merchants' Exchange informed local investors of shipping activities and guided profits from the waterfront a few blocks away into their coffers. Simultaneously, a dozen American and European banking houses furnished the capital and credit for transactions which attracted speculators from the Comstock region, the eastern United States, and even overseas to risk their fortunes in California while residing in one of the district's fine hotels. In short, Montgomery Street fairly hummed with an energy which—especially after news of the Civil War and the impending transcontinental railroad added to its intensity—clearly evidenced the economic maturity and vitality of San Francisco.[14] It is unlikely that Buckley missed the implications of scenes observed daily on his rounds through the business district and the rest of the city; nor were the lessons learned as a horsecar conductor in 1862 forgotten or ignored during the balance of his career.

But even though guiding an omnibus through San Francisco's varied streets and districts furnished an invaluable opportunity to glean and store away a harvest of observations concerning the many elements comprising its cosmopolitan society and the realities, exigencies, and potential of urban life, it was not the sort of enterprise capable of satisfying a young Argonaut's aspirations for very long. Buckley later commented that in the 1860s,

it was the laudable ambition of aspiring youth [including himself] to secure a portfolio as a mixologist in one of the great saloons . . . not so much for the sake of the salary but for the opportunity of meeting the great in their hours of relaxation and good humor, whereby connections were possible that often proved stepping stones to fortune.[15]

The observation may have been premised upon personal experience, for the future boss took his own first step on the path to fortune while still driving a horsecar. He met his future employer and partner, the impresario Thomas Maguire, then "at the peak of his affluence and power." In his early association with the theatrical promoter, Buckley began to acquire not only a mixologist's portfolio but also an intimate familiarity with aspects of San Francisco society and politics not ordinarily exposed to the sons of immigrants. Within a year of his arrival in the city, he found himself not collecting fares behind a horse but dispensing Pisco Punch behind the elegant sixty-five foot bar of Maguire's popular establishment, The Snug Saloon.[16]

Tom Maguire, Buckley's employer and partner in The Snug Saloon.

When the news of gold lured Maguire, still in his twenties, to California in 1849—to promote entertainment, not to grub in the mines—he had already dabbled successfully in hack-driving, saloon-keeping, theatrical management, and Tammany politics in New York City. In San Francisco during the early 1850s, he managed several saloons and theaters before building a series of three Jenny Lind Theaters. The first two were destroyed by the fires which recurrently swept the city and the last was sold in 1852—amidst charges of corruption hurled at both Maguire and his comrade from the New York days, Senator David C. Broderick—to the municipality for a new city hall.[17]

Despite the scandal surrounding the sale, Maguire did provide quality entertainment for San Franciscans, including performances by nationally recognized artists, and he would continue to pursue a similar policy in his subsequent ventures. During the local business depression of the 1850s, he purchased San Francisco Hall which he operated, remodeled, and reopened in March 1856 as the luxurious Maguire's New Opera House.[18] He could not have selected a more propitious location for the new enterprise; at 612 Washington Street, it was adjacent to the Montgomery Block (contemporaries called it the "Monkey Block") which constituted the heart of the city's commercial, financial, and quality entertainment district. Indeed, when Buckley first entered Maguire's employ in 1863, the Opera House, the equally sumptuous Snug Saloon presided over by Tom's brother John and future senator Tim McCarthy, and the adjoining Diana gambling hall had become the

clearing house of all Bohemia, the favorite haunt of actors, artists, writers, journalists and wits; of the great lawyers and other distinguished professionals; of stock brokers and financiers, of the beaux who existed in plenty.[19]

In the setting of The Snug, Buckley acquired a "fine judgment of high-priced tobacco, a delicate taste for the rarest vintage, and a sincere love of good company."[20]

But that is not all he acquired. The years at The Snug represented a substitute for the formal education otherwise absent from his early life and a continuation of his schooling on a streetcar. His post behind the bar was his postgraduate classroom, and from there he could observe the passing scene and cultivate acquaintances and associations which would not only influence his life profoundly but also prove invaluable in later years in politics and business. Just who Buckley's "good company" at The Snug included is impossible to determine with certainty. It is entirely possible, however, that—given the atmosphere of San Francisco in the 1860s and the nature of Maguire's clientele—many of the great and near-great literary figures of the era frequented the place. For the city was alive with representatives of the world of letters; "during the generation following the gold-rush San Francisco was the focal point, and to an unparalleled degree the literary capital, of a huge frontier territory."[21] Maguire had located his establishment at the heart of life in a city which attracted a truly remarkable array of talent. Samuel Clemens—recently self-christened Mark Twain and disenchanted with life in Washoe and the Comstock region—arrived in 1864 to write for the *Morning Call* and for Bret Harte's literary weekly, *The Californian.* Simultaneously, Harte managed the journal with his associate C. H. Webb, wrote, and earned a respectable living at the United States Mint on Montgomery Street, a few blocks from The Snug.[22]

And there were more. During Buckley's tenure with Maguire, Henry George, not yet the champion of the single-tax, wrote essays on the spirit world for *The Californian* and, with Daniel O'Connell, co-owned the *Evening Post.* Joaquin Miller published his work—albeit sporadically—in yet another literary journal, the *Golden Era,* and Ina Coolbrith, subsequently California's poet laureate, contributed to *The Californian* and other publications and after 1868, with Bret Harte, edited *The Overland Monthly.* In 1866, Ambrose Bierce—still untainted by the cynicism which would produce unkind comments about Buckley (and nearly everyone else) in the satirical *Wasp* and the aphorisms of *The Devil's Dictionary*—joined these luminaries and a host of lesser literati who flocked to San Francisco in the 1860s and established a Bohemian colony at the foot of Russian Hill. And while they made their contributions to the literature of the West and the nation, Hubert Howe Bancroft tended his thriving bookseller's business at the corner of Montgomery and Merchant Streets and assembled his ultimately formidable collection of Californiana.[23] The presence of these individuals and many others like them undoubtedly created a heady climate of ideas in the city and a stimulating experience for a bright young son of an Irish immigrant.

It is not likely, however, that Buckley formed intimate acquaintances with the more eminent writers, but his memoirs suggest that he observed them—including Clemens leaning against a billiard table in Grimm's Beer Hall—as they frequented The Snug and other nearby haunts and that he did learn from them. Indeed, it may have been this early, vicarious association with the world of letters and ideas which stimulated the love of literature he retained throughout his life, even after he lost his sight in the 1870s and could no longer read the books which he avidly collected.[24] Moreover, he developed an interest in drama as a consequence of association with the performers who regularly appeared at the Opera House and Maguire's other theaters during the decade. From the galleries of various halls—kept full in early San Francisco by two-bit admissions—Buckley witnessed opera as well as performances by the Booth family, Adelaide Neilsen, Lotta Crabtree, Christy's Minstrels, and a variety of other players who found attentive and appreciative audiences in the West. He heard Artemus Ward lecture in Platt's Hall in 1864, an event for which Maguire darkened his own

Opera House. And occasionally, as his employer's agent, Buckley formed close acquaintances with performers. These included the diminutive and dynamic poet-actress Adah Isaacs Menken who startled even San Francisco audiences with her appearance (apparently nude but actually in flesh-colored tights) in *Mazeppa* in 1863.[25]

Associations with such individuals unquestionably made a substantial and enduring impression upon young Buckley and had important implications for his subsequent years, but other contacts and observations made in Maguire's service would have even greater ultimate significance. To be sure, San Francisco's perennial eccentrics passed through The Snug's swinging doors: Norton I, self-styled Emperor of the United States and Protector of Mexico; phrenologist George Washington, arrayed in colonial garb and whispering market tips to all; the mysteriously anonymous Great Unknown, a creature attired in once-elegant rags and guarding the secret of a hidden fortune.[26] But there were others, too, including the business and political leaders of the city and the state.

Buckley arrived in San Francisco too late to meet Maguire's close friend from New York and the Tammany days, Senator David C. Broderick; he had been killed in his notorious duel with David Terry nearly three years earlier. There were, however, numerous habitués of The Snug—including Maguire himself and his partner Tim McCarthy —who early on began to direct their young protégé's interests toward other aspects of life, especially business and politics. A list of the leaders in both fields whose paths may have crossed Buckley's during these years and whose influence he may have felt would itself fill a volume. The potential for great wealth—and the political authority which accompanied it—based upon commerce, finance, and speculation in railroad and mining enterprises attracted countless entrepreneurs to the city in the 1850s and 1860s, and many conducted their ventures in close proximity to Maguire's establishment. Future Bonanza Kings James Flood and William O'Brien, for example, had parlayed the profits from their Auction Lunch Saloon, just blocks from The Snug, into substantial fortunes in silver stock. And they would soon join with James Fair and John W. Mackay (whose home Buckley would one day own) to control the Comstock Silver Lode. Even nearer, William C. Ralston founded his ill-fated Bank of California in 1864, and simultaneously other notables—George Hearst, the senior James Phelan, Leland Stanford,

William Sharon, Charles Crocker, and William T. Coleman, to name but a few—frequented the financial and entertainment district of San Francisco.[27] Many of them would subsequently form close political or business affiliations with the young man who observed them from behind the bar at The Snug, but for the moment their influence remained principally in the realm of example.

One of Maguire's patrons did have an immediate, concrete, and perhaps more profound impact upon Chris Buckley. William Higgins was a personality of considerably less renown than Ralston, the Railroad Barons, or the Silver Kings, but he would, nevertheless, shape Buckley's future more emphatically than either the writers, the entertainers, or the entrepreneurs who frequented The Snug. In the early 1860s, Higgins was just emerging as the Republican boss of San Francisco's Fifth Ward, a district which he managed from his own saloon beneath the Metropolitan Theater, another of Maguire's properties, on Montgomery Street near Jackson. But his earlier years included a background in some respects unique for a budding municipal politico. Born in Ireland about 1830, Higgins arrived in Boston in 1835, and there his parents became moderately successful hatmakers. In about 1843, they sent their son back to Ireland where he was enrolled in a Jesuit seminary in Dublin. The clerical life was not for him, however; as one contemporary observed, Higgins was "intended for Holy Orders, but being addicted to the fleshpots of Egypt and of a jovial nature, he marked out a different course." The first steps taken along that new itinerary in 1849 involved marriage to an Irish lass and a return to the United States—not to Boston as a priest but to Sierra County in California as a miner. A year later, Higgins migrated to Sacramento where he operated a small sawmill and, in the later 1850s, entered active politics as a Douglas Democrat and a supporter of David C. Broderick.[28]

Higgins may have spent sufficient time in San Francisco in 1851 to become involved in that year's Vigilance Committee movement, but he did not move permanently to the city until 1860. Then he opened his saloon in the business district and, with future Democratic mayor Andrew Jackson Bryant and nativist publisher of the San Francisco *Argonaut* Frank M. Pixley, participated in Republican efforts to elect Abraham Lincoln and in the campaigns of the People's Party in municipal politics. For the remainder of his career, Higgins would remain consistently an active Republican, despite a brief defection to the abortive Independent Taxpayers' ("Dolly Varden") schism of the early 1870s. Indeed, by the mid-1860s, he had become a recognized leader in the local party and a factor in the tumult of San Francisco partisan politics, and by 1875 he dominated Republican city and state organizations. During his climb to supremacy, Higgins took Chris Buckley under his wing, probably in 1864 or 1865, and began to tutor him in the fine art of municipal politics and to introduce him to Richard Chute, Mike Conroy, and the rest of the corps of sub-bosses who managed the party's affairs in the city.

Whether or not Buckley—still several years short of his majority—had evolved a political philosophy of his own during this period is uncertain. It is probable that he had not, for nowhere in his memoirs does he discuss his views of even the momentous issue of the Civil War. Nevertheless, he proved to be an adept student of political technique, mastering not only the subtleties of partisan organization but also the more physical aspects of factional struggle. According to Republican boss Martin Kelly, Buckley "developed a knack for colonizing the boarding houses and turning tricks in the rough work of the primaries," and Higgins is quoted as describing the youngster as "a handy man behind the ballot box." Buckley apparently found the experiences intriguing, exhilarating, and potentially rewarding, for he would later credit the interlude under Higgins' guidance as a major factor influencing his decision to make politics his chosen profession. At the time, however, he still regarded himself as a neophyte: "I was purely in the amateur class and it greatly amused me when some of the well-known professional[s] seriously asked me for advice."[29]

After the apprenticeship, master and pupil remained friends—although not always political allies—until Higgins' death in 1889. Nevertheless, even while under Higgins' tutelage Buckley decided to strike out on his own in both business and politics. His reasons are not entirely clear, but they may have involved principally the apparent desire to satisfy his own obviously substantial abilities and ambitions. In any case, Buckley left Tom Maguire's employ in 1866 and became his competitor. With his partner Jack Mannix, a Democratic sub-boss later among Buckley's rivals for control of the party, he opened a groggery at 711 Montgomery Street, just around the corner from the Opera House and The Snug. For approximately a year and a half, Buckley operated the new enterprise and, in the process, became familiar with another facet of San Francisco politics and with the leaders of the local Democracy: Owen Brady, Sam Rainey, and Al Fritz whose eventual influence on Buckley's career would rival that of Bill Higgins himself.[30]

The association with Mannix, Fritz, and the others did not flourish in the 1860s, and early in 1868 Buckley returned to The Snug. Several possible explanations for the change present themselves. The partnership with Mannix may have begun to sour, or the business itself may have proved unsuccessful. On the other hand, it may have succeeded only too well in its competition with Maguire, for the promoter himself extended to his former employee a surprisingly generous proposal. He requested that Buckley return to his previous post not as a mere bartender but as a partner with the Maguire brothers and Tim McCarthy in the management and operation of the saloon. Buckley accepted, leaving Mannix to do his own business at the Monkey Block address. Perhaps he was impressed by Maguire's apparently liberal proposition, or perhaps he simply found the atmosphere of The Snug more congenial. He certainly found the remarkable turn of affairs impressive and memorable. Barely twenty-two years old and little more than five years from a penurious arrival in the city, he was now the coproprietor of one of San Francisco's most successful and prestigious watering holes. A half-century later, he would still recall his emotion at seeing his name beside the door of The Snug: "I felt the dignity and the power of an independent prince."[31]

Buckley records few additional details of his experiences during the last years of the 1860s, and neither his memoirs nor other sources provide insights into yet another change in his career in the spring of 1871.[32] At that time, following an apparently satisfactory interlude spent expanding his acquaintance with the city and its residents from his vantage point in The Snug, he left Maguire's establishment for good, departed from San Francisco, and with his father temporarily settled in Vallejo.

It is possible that the motivation for this sudden shift in the course of Buckley's career involved his major partner's financial problems. Toward the end of the decade, Tom Maguire's fortunes underwent a temporary decline resulting from several factors. Eleven theaters in San Francisco, Sacramento, and Virginia City demanded constant capital reinvestment

Maguire's Opera House.
The entrance to The Snug Saloon and a barely legible sign
reading "Buckley's" are visible at the lower right.

for talent and general operations and severely taxed the impresario's resources. Therefore, when the recessions which recurrently troubled California's speculative economy (a particularly severe decline began in 1869)
reduced patronage at theaters, Maguire felt the pinch sharply. In addition, in 1869 and 1870 William C. Ralston opened his sumptuous California Theater and Grand Hotel, and the competition unquestionably
cut into Maguire's profits. But even more significant were the locations
of these new enterprises on lower Kearny and Market Streets respectively, signaling the impending southward shift of the center of urban
life away from the site of the Opera House and many of Maguire's current interests. Finally, in mid-1870 the state legislature approved a
long-sought law, championed by Ralston, mandating the extension and
improvement of Montgomery Street and threatening the very existence
of the Opera House and The Snug.[33] Thus, Maguire's apparently

gloomy prospects (which may explain his willingness to take Buckley into partnership in the first place) as well as changing urban conditions may have prompted the younger man to alter both his business affiliation and his residence.

Buckley's decision to leave San Francisco quite likely also involved his own pragmatic response to a depressed economy. Both Maguire's adversities and those which generally afflicted the city emanated from the same principal sources: overspeculation and declining productivity on the Comstock Lode and the adverse effects of the transcontinental railroad. Between 1864 and the big bonanza of 1873, the flood of mining profits slowed to a trickle, and the city seemed to languish. Real estate sales and values dwindled, commerce and retail business deteriorated, construction activity diminished, unemployment increased, and the population growth rate stabilized. Moreover, by early 1870 it had become abundantly clear that the anticipated immediate recovery based upon completion of the transcontinental railroad in the previous May simply was not to be. On the one hand, optimistic San Francisco merchants who had overstocked warehouses to the bursting point now found themselves in sharp competition with eastern firms for the business of the state, and many of them closed their doors. On the other hand, Sacramento—not San Francisco as expected—became the line's western terminus, and several additional cities entered the race for the lucrative secondary prize: designation as the railway's Pacific entrepôt. Although numerous bay area centers involved themselves in the context, Oakland and Vallejo emerged as the principal rivals, and both had apparent advantages over San Francisco, including potentially better deep water ports, superior fog-free weather, and far easier maritime and overland access to the interior. In response to the situation, editors of San Francisco newspapers and commercial publications, formerly complacent about the future, commenced a litany of lamentation about currently dismal prospects and warned that "the fate of Venice" awaited their city if direct rail connections to the East were not secured.[34]

The jubilation of Oakland and Vallejo promoters contrasted sharply with the gloom prevalent in San Francisco. In the spring of 1870, Oakland boosters were "perfectly astounded" by the building boom and population increase resulting from expected railroad connections.[35] The outlook for smaller Vallejo (population about 5000), located farther north on the Carquinez Strait, appeared even brighter, for it had not only the already-established Mare Island Navy Yard and unobstructed access to the interior but also its own railroad, the California Pacific Company's line completed to Sacramento in February 1869. Moreover, rumors added to the optimism there. Some residents expected that the Central Pacific might build its railbed through Beckwourth's Pass along the Feather River some forty miles north of Theodore Judah's proposed route, and thence southward through the Sacramento Valley. If that did not happen, it was anticipated that the California Pacific might construct its own competitive route through the valley and Beckwourth's Pass and eastward to the mining regions. A third possibility—and the one which ultimately transpired in September 1871—involved the absorption of the local railroad and its Vallejo-Sacramento link by the Central Pacific Company.[36]

Any of the three alternatives could make Vallejo—not Sacramento, San Francisco, or Oakland—the logical Pacific terminus for the transcontinental rail line and provide a tremendous potential for the building of a "great city." Boosters quickly responded to the possibilities, touting their community's virtues not only in the local press but also in San Francisco and other regional centers. Simultaneously, they formed organizations such as the Vallejo City Homestead Association and the Vallejo Land and Improvement Company (capitalized at $4,000,000 and including Leland Stanford among its officers) to disseminate propaganda, develop the area, and lure settlers and investors to the town. As Henry George observed, "Vallejo talks of her coming foreign commerce, and is preparing to load the grain of the Sacramento and Napa Valleys for all parts of the world." Even historian John S. Hittell, an owner of Solano County property, became involved in the effort to promote the town as the commercial and perhaps even political capital of the state.[37]

Thus, Buckley's departure from San Francisco quite probably involved a response to the sort of city boosterism and promotion which typified nineteenth-century urban rivalries as well his own declining fortunes as an associate of Tom Maguire and depressed conditions in San Francisco. To be sure, the Vallejo boom proved ephemeral and the Central Pacific Railroad Company rather than the cities themselves determined the ultimate outcome of municipal competition in California.[38] Nevertheless, in the early 1870s the city on the Carquinez Strait seemed to hold substantial potential for the pursuit of both financial and political rewards which would surely accompany metropolitan expansion. And it is unlikely that an alert, ambitious youth who had already sampled the fruits of both and found them appealing would allow the opportunity to pass. Finally, personal tragedy may have eliminated any lingering doubts about leaving San Francisco; on July 31, 1870, Ellen Buckley died.[39] Since their arrival in the state, the closely-knit family had lived as a unit, and Christopher had been a willing mainstay of support for his parents when periodic declines in construction activity diminished his father's income. Now, with the young man's fortunes on the wane, his father's opportunities simultaneously reduced by local depression and advancing age, and apparent prosperity beckoning from another quarter, grief over their personal loss may have provided the final motivation for both Buckleys to depart from their adopted city.

The decision to move to Vallejo and the interlude spent there may represent one of the few errors of judgment which Buckley made during his long career, for the town's anticipated role in the economic and political history of California never materialized. When he and his father arrived in the spring of 1871, however, the dream of urban prominence remained alive, and Buckley threw himself into the community's energetic effort to capitalize upon it. He began by utilizing the approach most familiar to him, opening the X-Change Saloon—formerly Lowden's Grocery Store—on West Georgia Street near the central business district, the waterfront, and the navy yard. His associate in the venture, James Nevins, had been an acquaintance in San Francisco politics, and he preceded Buckley to Vallejo by approximately two years and perhaps influenced him to move there. Nevins had involved himself in the politics of the Republican party—then dominant in Vallejo and Solano County—and worked at his shipwright's trade at Mare Island between 1869 and 1870.[40] In association with Nevins—and with General John B. Frisbie, one of the area's social, political, and business leaders and an officer in the Vallejo Land and Improvement Company—Buckley participated in the successful campaigns for Governor Newton Booth in 1871 and President Ulysses S. Grant in 1872 and became an active member of the Solano County Republican Central Committee.[41]

At the same time, he acquainted himself with yet another aspect of nineteenth-century municipal life. Like many other American cities,

Vallejo suffered from recurrent and costly fires, and in just one week in November 1871, two major conflagrations of suspected incendiary origins swept its business district and revealed the local fire department's gross inadequacy. In response to the disaster, Sam Brannan dispatched a surplus fire engine from Calistoga, freighted by courtesy of the Central Pacific Railroad Company, to bolster Vallejo's ability to protect itself from fire. Around Brannan's apparatus formed a new volunteer fire unit, Engine Company Number Two (formerly the Frisbie Hose Company and subsequently known as Frisbie Number Two in honor of its sponsor) with Christopher A. Buckley as a charter member.[42] And like similar organizations in other cities, Engine Company Number Two spent as much time dabbling in politics as it did in fighting fires.

Despite his efforts in business, politics, and community affairs, Buckley did not prosper in Vallejo, principally because his prospects—like those of the city itself—remained closely tied to a pair of external influences: the Mare Island Navy Yard and especially the Central Pacific Railroad Company. Throughout the period of Buckley's sojourn in Vallejo, the navy yard provided a major source of employment for the town's residents and an important ingredient in its economy. It was an inconsistent factor, however, and subject to the exigencies of Congressional appropriations. Periodic payroll reductions, layoffs, and threats of complete closure created uncertainty about the yard's role in the city's future, fluctuations in the local economy, and a persistent source of grievance for editors and political leaders.

Of even greater significance were the policies of the powerful railroad company. It should have been apparent as early as the fall of 1871 that those policies would be neither consistent nor necessarily conducive to the anticipated boom in Vallejo. For almost as soon as it had fully absorbed the California Pacific Company, the Central Pacific removed the offices of its new subsidiary to the parent company's headquarters in Sacramento. During the following winter, nature added its own warning about exclusive dependence upon railroads when moderately heavy rains flooded the California Pacific line in the Sacramento Valley and drowned Vallejo's dreams of becoming the regional grain depot just as effectively as they inundated the tracks. Simultaneously, persistent rumors—especially of Leland Stanford's alleged intention to rationalize the Central Pacific's circuitous Oakland-Sacramento line by way of a Benicia-

Martinez bridge, thereby isolating Vallejo—caused trepidation in the town and reluctance to move there on the part of prospective new residents. Finally, by early 1873 it had become apparent that railroad officials had been less than candid about their plans; they removed even the California Pacific's minor maintenance yard from Vallejo to Sacramento and announced the impending transfer of all administrative facilities to San Francisco. Thus, the romance of the rails ended for one small city. The Central Pacific's vacillating policies—coupled with the Crédit Mobilier scandal and the nationwide Panic of 1873, both of which reduced the company's options in California—terminated the Vallejo boom almost as suddenly as it had begun.[43]

Many local residents in 1873 began to feel both the pinch of a declining economy and the disappointment of unfulfilled dreams. One of them, Christopher Buckley, found himself either unwilling or unable to pay even $6.75 in delinquent property taxes, left James Nevins with the X-Change Saloon, abandoned his quest for fortune in Vallejo, and with his father returned to San Francisco in the spring.[44]

CHAPTER

From Instant City
to Metropolis

Despite Christopher Buckley's failure to achieve the level of success that he and others anticipated in Vallejo, the two-year interlude there did not culminate entirely without benefit to him. For in the later 1860s, the small city had acquired a reputation as more than a potential railroad boomtown where great fortunes could be quickly made. A combination of conditions, some unique and others common to most American cities of the period, prompted observers to identify Vallejo as "one of the best-known training schools for higher statesmanship" in California.[1] It was a locale where apprentices and even journeyman politicos might learn from accomplished masters implementing the complex techniques involved in the practice of nineteenth-century statecraft.

As an early nexus for railroad operations in the state, for example, Vallejo became a vantage point for the observation and assessment of the Central Pacific's impending role in the affairs of California and its cities, the not infrequent caprices of its policies, and the nuances of the relationship between company officials and local political leaders. Concurrently, Vallejo Republicans utilized the thousands of federal positions at the Mare Island Navy Yard to elevate to a science the complex art of patronage distribution and to demonstrate the critical function of that process in the tenuous business of maintaining a successful partisan organization. Those same statesmen, like their counterparts in other cities, sponsored and courted quasi-official agencies—volunteer fire companies, militia units, ethnic associations, and the like—whose members not only doused flames, donned elaborate regalia to march in parades, and indulged in a boisterous sort of camaraderie but also constituted the disciplined permanent cadres of local party machines. Finally, Vallejo contributed its own innovations to the confused and frequently questionable practices of municipal politics, including the celebrated "tapeworm ticket" introduced there in the election of 1871 and subsequently emulated throughout the state. A novel product of the Solano County Republican Committee's genius, printed on a yard of narrow and marginless paper, the ballot could be altered ("scratched") only with great difficulty, and it virtually assured victory for the party's entire slate of candidates.[2]

This is not to say that such tactics constituted the whole of politics in Vallejo. Nevertheless, a fortuitous coincidence of circumstances—the portentous presence of the railroad, the vigor of local political activities, and the inventiveness of the city's partisan practitioners—made Chris Buckley's brief sojourn on the Carquinez Strait an enlightening phase in his own progress toward mastery of the techniques of "higher statesmanship." The experience provided an opportunity to whet the political acumen acquired during his apprenticeship with Bill Higgins to an even keener edge and to observe the skillful application of many of the partisan practices which would serve him so well during his own career.

Still, metropolitan San Francisco—not bucolic Vallejo—provided the principal and critical influence upon Buckley's grooming during his first two decades in California. Historians and contemporaries alike have narrated the history of that city in the generation following the discovery of gold essentially in terms of its excesses and sensations. These were not, however, the major influences upon either urban development or the molding of a political boss. To be sure, the dramatic and even the melodramatic did remain in proliferation: the violence of the lawless, a residual of the vigilante style in responses to disorder, the frequently phony oppulence of the Bella Union and other Barbary Coast pleasure palaces, the variety and skill of the city's ubiquitous harlots, the inveterate gambling of the forty-niners and the speculators who succeeded them, the exotic mystery of the Chinese districts, and more.[3] But of substantially greater significance for both Buckley and San Francisco were the processes of urbanization which transformed the instant city of the 1860s into the industrial metropolis of the 1870s.[4]

As an abstraction, the term *metropolis* has been neither precisely defined, clearly understood, nor consistently employed, even to identify chronological periods in the schema of urban development. Historians, for example, are by no means unanimous in their application of the concept to the evolution of cities in the United States; some utilize it in a strictly circumscribed manner to describe exclusively twentieth-century regional phenomena, while just as many of the more eclectic among them expand the idea to embrace aspects of the nineteenth-century industrial city as well.[5] It is quite clear, however, that in a more pragmatic sense a metropolis constitutes something other than an abstraction, that it is more than simply an ordinary or traditional city writ large, and that a cluster of specific interacting characteristics define it, distinguish it from other stages of urbanization, and provide the benchmarks by which the historical progress of a city like Buckley's San Francisco may be understood and assessed.

Most apparently, the metropolis obliterated the traditional "walking city," the most prevalent form of urban organization at mid-nineteenth century and in previous eras when a combination of conditions kept settlements small and relationships within communities intimate and personal. Prior to the application of steam and electric power to intra-urban transportation and to other machines formerly dependent upon human and animal muscle, time and distance conspired to limit communities to relatively restricted spaces, usually to the distance which could be conveniently walked in an hour, about a three-mile radius. Geography imposed similar restrictions; only the portion of the terrain which was habitable without major alteration could be included in the city, and settlement was forced to conform to the configurations of the land. Consequently, although the outlines of the walking city varied — an irregular circle in peninsular Boston, a rough amphitheater where

27

hills and a curve of the Ohio River confined Cincinnati, or a linear cluster of pockets among San Francisco's hills, sand lots, and valleys — its basic qualities were nearly universal: a compact and heterogeneous entity based upon intimate contact in social, political, and economic activities. The inhibitions imposed by spatial and temporal restrictions fell equally upon all in the walking city; the employer, for example, required approximately as long, even with a carriage, to arrive at his business as did the employee to get to his work, a condition which forced random residential patterns and discouraged specialization in other forms of land use. Only two elements in the urban population found themselves excluded from the general pattern of settlement: the very poor and manufacturing operations producing offensive smells or noises, which were relegated to the less convenient outskirts of the city. Moreover, the organization of work itself, usually into relatively small commercial or manufacturing units, reinforced the frequency of direct contact among a variety of individuals.

Finally, the characteristics of the walking city had important implications for urban life itself. In the first place, despite substantial differences in wealth and income, members of the community knew one another. They lived and worked in constant interaction, belonged to many of the same churches and social organizations, and involved themselves in the same political associations. Even though the politics of deference and duty most frequently placed eminent merchants and professionals in important municipal offices, members of the working classes not infrequently served on school boards, city councils, and similar bodies.[6] In short, although conflicts did exist, the mid-nineteenth-century walking city was a community based upon familiarity; it was a setting in which, for example, a San Francisco carpenter adding to his savings in the Bank of California might still address bank founder William C. Ralston as "Bill" and be greeted in return as "Mike."

These broadly outlined characteristics of the walking city may, of course, be amplified and elaborated in some of their particulars and modified in others. They do, however, serve to describe general conditions in a now unfamiliar and practically extinct urban setting and to provide a sharp contrast to the radically different milieu of the metropolis. For if nothing else, the metropolis "precisely reversed the social geography of the walking city," not as a consequence of the mechanical workings of

28

impersonal, deterministic forces but rather as the result of "hundreds of thousands of separate decisions" which individuals consciously or unconsciously made.[7] Certainly, technology, immigration, and economic reorganization all contributed to the emergence of an altered urban environment, but in San Francisco as elsewhere, the important consideration involves responses to innovations and the manner in which those responses produced something quite unexpected and unique in the urban experience. Decisions made in order to attain principally individualistic goals fostered conditions which were, paradoxically, at once centripetal and centrifugal and which involved a "sorting-out process . . . [that] created a more intensely specialized system of land use and residential segregation" and a new kind of city.[8]

These two elements, specialization and segregation, provide the major keys to understanding the late-nineteenth-century industrial metropolis, even though size and complexity are its most obvious contrasts with the walking city. Technological innovations in urban transportation, in construction techniques, and in the ability to alter topography and sophisticated forms of economic organization made possible expanded boundaries, taller buildings, greater populations, and enlarged business and working units. But even more significant were the divisions which accompanied physical growth and influenced virtually every aspect of metropolitan life. Recreation, commerce (itself subdivided into wholesaling and retailing), finance, industry, and residence—once interspersed throughout the city or clustered in a few nonspecialized districts—were soon relegated to discrete regions. The resultant separations, especially in residential areas which were set apart not only from business and industrial districts but also from one another according to economic or ethnic standards reflecting increased disparity of wealth and diversity in the population, epitomized novel urban conditions.

Affluent suburbs, middle class neighborhoods (called "zones of emergence"), and congested districts of working-class homes, tenements, and outright slums existed strictly apart from one another, and despite advances in the technology of communication, their residents rarely shared personal encounters. Specialization and separation, moreover, extended beyond geographic realities to involve institutions and individuals as well. Churches, for example, responded to the spiritual needs of specific groups and regions within the urban community. The development of many municipal facilities—museums, libraries, parks—reflected the ideologies of particular segments of urban society, as did the practice of municipal politics itself, which became increasingly the province of the professional. Businessmen, too, became specialists in the metropolis, and so did their establishments and those employed in them. In short, nearly every facet of urban life became "fragmented," to borrow Robert Fogelson's term, and the reality of the metropolis provided a dramatic contrast to conditions in the type of community which it was replacing. Even the idea of community itself underwent drastic revision in the more complex setting; each of the entities—in reality separate social, political, ethnic, economic, or residential communities within the larger community—which composed its pluralistic society tended to define the city with particular reference to the limitations of a specific urban experience.[9]

Although they would culminate in a regional metropolis only after the turn of the century, the processes transforming San Francisco were already in motion when Buckley returned to the city in 1873; indeed, he recorded his own observations of at least the physical manifestations of the changes in progress.[10] Andrew Hallidie's first cable car line approached completion on the Clay Street hill, and despite the persistent scoffing of the skeptics, its anticipated opening in August had already begun to alter attitudes toward land use in the city. Work on a Montgomery Street extension (now Columbus Avenue) pushed the thoroughfare diagonally to the northwest and promised access to a new sector of the city. Toward the south, crews had completed the foundation of a magnificent new city hall on the site of the old Yerba Buena Cemetery, and construction in progress on a dozen other major buildings—including William Ralston's $7,000,000 Palace Hotel—confirmed the shifting center of urban activities already apparent in the 1860s. Across Market Street, even within walking distance of formerly prestigious Rincon Hill, expanded manufacturing and shipping enterprises extended southward toward Hunter's Point. And throughout San Francisco, new street railway systems facilitated the movement of an augmented population among the city's increasingly specialized districts.[11]

Taken together, the physical changes which Buckley observed provided graphic evidence of a city in transition, but the process was not necessarily the sudden development he apparently presumed it to be. Instead, tangible alterations testified to the cumulative impact of responses to various interrelated processes operative in San Francisco since the early 1860s. The consequences of the Civil War, implications of the transcontinental railroad, the discovery of the Nevada silver bonanza, technological innovations in industry, transportation, and agriculture, and a constantly increasing population combined to accelerate the transfiguration—not only of the city's appearance in the 1870s but also of the economic, social, political, and demographic conditions of urban life. For San Francisco, as one contemporary observed, "the decade between 1860 and 1870 was, next to the gold rush, the most important" period in its history.[12]

With the exception of a few episodes, the Civil War itself had little apparent impact upon the political history of the city. Rumors of alleged and actual secessionist plots, fears of filibustering raids upon the mineral wealth stored in local vaults, and agitation for the formation of an independent Pacific Republic composed of western states sporadically disturbed the relative calm. So too did the editorials and oratory of a handful of Confederate sympathizers, including the Reverend William Anderson Scott whose intemperate sermons and prayers for Jefferson Davis earned him a hanging in effigy and an invitation to leave the city. Support for Scott also won the wife of prominent industrialist (and subsequently mayor) Thomas H. Selby a trip to Europe, at her husband's instigation and expense, for the duration. Even though such escapades increased suspicion of many of the other former southerners residing on Rincon Hill and called forth occasional demonstrations of patriotism, for the most part political controversy over the issues of the war occurred at the state level where Douglas and Breckenridge Democrats vied with one another and with the recently formed and increasingly potent Republicans for control of California. In the city itself, neither national party played a major role in the conduct of municipal affairs; instead, the People's Party retained the essential dominance which it had exercised since 1856, San Franciscans remained firm supporters of the Union, and the conflict raging in the East altered political conditions and attitudes but slightly.[13]

In sharp contrast to its limited influence upon political affairs in the city, the Civil War combined with the simultaneous anticipation of a railroad spanning the nation to set in motion developments which would dramatically transform the economic context and demographic fabric of San Francisco and turn the instant city into a thriving industrial metropolis. Although telegraph wires had coupled East and West in 1861, both the city and the state remained remote frontier outposts during the remainder of the decade, and the war only served to intensify the isolation. The consequences of separation, however, were not wholly detrimental; conditions imposed by war propelled formerly dependent California—and especially San Francisco—toward greater economic autonomy in agriculture and manufacturing alike and forced diversification of the city's maritime trade to include direct commercial exchange with Europe and the Orient in addition to its previously established intercourse with the eastern seaboard. During the same years, news of the Central Pacific Company's charter (1861) and passage of the Pacific Railway Act (1862) precipitated immediate and persisting expectations of a prosperous future based upon unobstructed overland access to the nation's markets. Optimism not only prompted higher levels of capital investment in the manufacturing, processing, and overseas commerce necessitated by wartime contingencies but also induced an upsurge in real estate speculation which concentrated upon potential railhead locales and, ultimately, altered the physical configurations of the city.[14] None of these developments, once under way, would terminate with the close of either the Civil War or the 1860s.

Despite the existence of a substantial number and variety of workshops operating in the 1860s, and even in the 1850s, in the North Beach region, along the waterfront, and in the districts south of Market Street, local business observers persistently lamented the detrimental consequences of what they presumed to be the city's historical dearth of factories.[15] Their pessimism and dissatisfaction may have involved a form of myopia conditioned by the absence of major or dominant enterprises such as Pittsburgh's iron industry rather than a valid assessment of economic realities, for in the first decade following the American conquest of California, boot and clothing manufacturers, tanneries, vintners and food processors, chemical refiners, a gas works, and numerous other concerns produced significant quantities of high quality merchandise for both local and export markets. Even the iron and textile industries which provided the basis for the nation's initial strides toward large scale manufacturing were effectively represented in the frontier city. In 1849, for example, Peter Donahue established his Union Iron Works as little more than a blacksmith shop. Within a decade and a half, the firm employed over 100 workers to smelt iron ore and fabricate mining equipment and agricultural implements specifically adapted to California's unique requirements, and several additional enterprises—the Vulcan Iron Works, the Pacific Rolling Mill, the Risdon Iron and Locomotive Works, and the Selby Silver Smelting and Lead Works among them—had entered the field. Simultaneously, major textile plants made their appearance. Concentrating at first upon converting raw wool from the Santa Clara Valley to the south into bulk fabric for export, mills such as the Pioneer, the Pacific, and the Mission rapidly diversified to produce goods ranging from high grade yardage and blankets to fine quality clothing and knitwear; by 1861, in fact, a local editor could boast somewhat chauvinistically of the quantity, variety, and excellence of the textile products made entirely in the city from the state's raw materials.[16] Thus, notwithstanding the perennial gloom of contemporary local observers, early San Francisco was not totally devoid of significant manufacturing activity. Indeed, by the 1860s it provided an important supplement to the city's primary dependence upon commerce, and by reducing the necessity to import innumerable essential commodities, augmented local economic independence.

Through the early 1860s, most of the manufacturing enterprises remained relatively small in scale, but the forces transforming commercial San Francisco into an industrial metropolis, once in progress, proved irreversible and the process of change sharply altered both the physical shape of the city and its economic conditions. During the Civil War years, San Francisco manufacturers interspersed their activities with various other aspects of urban life throughout the community. In the later 1860s, however, new manufacturing enterprises joined with those already established to define the perimeters of specialized industrial districts, especially in the south of Market Street region between Potrero Hill and Hunter's Point where the Dickie Brothers, Matthew Turner, the California Drydock Company and others operated extensive shipyard and maritime services on the bay. Several considerations impelled the relocation of economic activities, among them the persistent mystique of the rails. In 1864, Peter Donahue's locally financed San Francisco and

San Jose Railroad, presumably destined to become the final link in the heralded transcontinental transportation system, entered the city through San Bruno Pass to the south and terminated at a point where the tidelands and marshes along Rincon Point and Mission Bay would—once properly filled—provide the city's sole suitable locale for construction of the major facilities needed to bring quantities of raw material to burgeoning industry. In combination with existing and proposed wharfage for ore and grain carriers, lumber ships, and other freighters, the anticipated railhead would mitigate the isolation of the peninsular city and make the South of Market district—soon to be dubbed "Tar Flat"—an ideal setting for expanding industrialism.[17]

Other regions of the city became less congenial to entrepreneurial needs, making the southern locale even more attractive. Congestion which escalated land values and further impeded the already restricted intraurban movement of people and goods, for example, prompted Thomas Selby to transfer his smelter and shot tower, North Beach landmarks since 1856, to the South of Market in 1864 and another future mayor, William Alvord, to construct the Pacific Rolling Mill at nearby Potrero Point in 1866. Subsequently, a variety of firms—including Hills Brothers and several other food processors, Cornelius Vanderbilt's Pacific Mail Steamship Company, the Consolidated Tobacco Company, and the San Francisco and Pacific Sugar Refining Company—joined Selby and Alvord and scores of other enterprises in the region.[18] By the 1870s, they had helped to transform the area, which Jack London—born there in 1876—called "South of the Slot," into the city's principal industrial district, a section of the metropolis teeming with "factories, slums, laundries, machine shops, boiler works, and the [tenement house] abodes of the working class."[19]

Entrepreneurial responses to the impact of the Civil War, the coming of the railroad, and urban congestion were not, however, the sole factors contributing to a transformed South of Market, industrialization, and metropolitanism in San Francisco. Changes in economic activities external to the city, especially in mining and agriculture, an augmented urban labor pool, increasing levels of capital available for investment in manufacturing and related enterprises, and intensified speculation in city real estate all added their own impetus to the dramatic transition.

From the 1860s onward, gold mining in California and silver mining

34

in Nevada became less and less the pursuit of the individual prospector with his gold pan and cradle and more and more the province of heavily capitalized corporate organizations involved in gouging tons of earth from mountains and rivers in order to retrieve a few ounces of gold or silver. Hydraulic mining and the other extractive processes employed in such large scale mining required pumps, crushers, and a variety of highly specialized heavy equipment. Specific developments in Nevada which, almost from the beginning of the Comstock bonanza, involved shaft mining at extreme depths in virtually impenetrable rock were even more demanding. The unique conditions of the Comstock mines required equally unique equipment: compressors to operate diamond-tipped air drills and to ventilate shafts, elevators to carry miners to work faces far underground, rails and cars to transport ore through the tunnels, and engines and the flat wire cable developed by Andrew Hallidie to haul both men and ore to the surface. All of these, as well as the smelters and crushers necessary to convert raw ore into precious metal, initially imported from the East and frequently requiring major adaptations to make them compatible with local conditions, quickly became the products of San Francisco factories.[20] And the process of providing them not only advanced industrialization in the city but also lessened the Far West's dependence upon external sources to satisfy its needs.

Simultaneously, somewhat less dramatic but ultimately even more significant innovations in California agriculture precipitated similar results. Despite the potential, the soil of the state remained a resource untapped commercially in the early 1860s. By the middle of the decade, however, concurrent experimentation and development in the growth and processing of numerous crops—wine grapes, sugar beets, cotton, hops, deciduous fruits, and even tobacco—all made increased demands upon San Francisco industry for farm implements and processing facilities. Perhaps the upsurge in the production of a new form of California gold—wheat—proved to be most significant in both immediate and long-range terms. Indeed, so lucrative was raising wheat that contemporaries borrowed a metaphor from the mining experience and called the ranches which generated the boom in grain production "bonanza farms." Wheat cultivation in the state expanded when abundant rain succeeded years of drought in the late 1860s, especially in the broad and, before the introduction of irrigation, semi-arid Sacramento and San

Industrial San Francisco in the 1880s.
The South of Market District looking toward Telegraph Hill.

Joaquin Valleys where wheat barons reigned. One of them, Dr. Hugh Glenn, oversaw production on a 55,000-acre domain (named Glenn County in his honor after 1891) along the Sacramento River. Only broker Isaac Friedlander of San Francisco, known as the "Wheat King," outranked Baron Glenn in the hierarchy of the California grain nobility, but in the valleys hundreds of ranchers tilled thousands of acres to produce millions of bushels of wheat. And in the city, operators of wharf facilities, granaries, mills, and tool companies fabricating the combine planters and reapers, adjustable gang plows, tractors, and other specialized implements demanded by large scale agriculture in wheat and other commodities reaped their own harvests of profits.[21]

Many San Franciscans—individuals like sugar refiner Claus Spreckels, silver smelter Thomas Selby, and Union Iron Works owner Peter Donahue—built or augmented their substantial fortunes by capitalizing upon the interaction between the Civil War, the arrival of the railroad, innovations in mining and agriculture, and industrial technology; in the process, they helped to accelerate both industrialization and metropolitanism in the city. For many others, the relationship between themselves and the forces shaping a transformed San Francisco was quite a different one. Through the middle years of the 1860s, labor in the city experienced favorable conditions which also contributed to the relatively

36

slow development of manufacturing. Numerous factors, including the lure of the mines and reduced immigration during the Civil War years, kept labor scarce and wages high and forced San Francisco businessmen to promote organizations intended to attract workers to the city.[22] Never very successful, the immigrant associations did little to alleviate the problem, and conditions favorable to labor and unfavorable for the expanding industry persisted. For skilled workers like Chris Buckley's father, circumstances were particularly advantageous; although his annual earnings were never sufficient (a minimum of $800 until 1864 and $600 after) to require him to pay income tax during the Civil War, by 1870 he had accumulated real property worth $7000 and personal property valued at $1200.[23] Such conditions kept wages at high levels, made workers—especially the skilled or semiskilled—reluctant to accept industrial employment, and discouraged local manufacturers from expanding their operations.

In the later 1860s, several factors began to change the situation appreciably in a manner detrimental to the position of labor and beneficial to the expansion of industry. Despite a decline in the overall growth rate of the state, the city population—and hence the number of workers available for employment in large scale manufacturing—increased substantially, from 56,802 in 1860 to 149,473 in 1870. The augmented population included over 70,000 foreign born, many of whom became part of a growing labor pool, and the influx persisted into the early 1870s when an estimated 100,000 were added in just four years.[24]

Not all of these new San Franciscans made their way directly to the city; substantial numbers had migrated from the eastern United States, from Europe, or from the Orient to work in the mines, to construct the railroad, to farm the land, or, like the Buckleys, to otherwise seek their fortunes. Optimism brought them to California, but expectations were not always fulfilled, ironically as a consequence of many of the same developments which accelerated industrialization in San Francisco. Changing conditions in the mines disillusioned many individual miners and displaced others with machines. As the Central Pacific neared completion, the company dismissed a large proportion of the Irish and Chinese laborers it had imported for the project. In the fields, agrarian depression, drought, mechanization, and the consolidation of land holdings drove both workers and small owners from the farms. And once completed in 1869, the transcontinental rail system began to transport increasing numbers of migrants westward. Many of those who were variously displaced or disappointed, along with newcomers to the state and the seasonally unemployed, drifted to San Francisco to seek work, to further congest the tenements south of Market Street and in other regions, to depress formerly high wages, and to provide the labor pool essential to an urban economy based upon large scale fabrication and processing as well as commerce and finance.[25]

Thus, external developments contributed to circumstances supportive of growing industrialism in the city. More abundant and cheaper available labor combined with the raw material surpluses produced by intensified agriculture and with the demands which resulted from innovations in farming and mining to create a climate favorable to the expansion of manufacturing. But one additional and critical ingredient—capital— originated principally within San Francisco itself. From the city's beginnings, its economy had been a highly speculative one, and so it remained. Residents of all socioeconomic strata risked their savings, great or small, on virtually anything: mining ventures, water rights, real estate, railroad stocks, currency manipulation, or whatever scheme seemed at the moment to promise rapid and substantial rewards.[26] For some, investments produced great levels of wealth, a fact with which San Franciscans seemed perennially preoccupied.[27] And well they might have been, for the fortunes amassed in the city, apparently overnight, were staggering even by twentieth-century standards. Of the wealth of the railroad barons—Leland Stanford, Mark Hopkins, Charles Crocker, and Collis P. Huntington—enough has been written elsewhere. Concerning the silver kings—John W. Mackay, James Flood, James Fair, and William O'Brien—who rivaled the magnates of the rails in the 1870s, a single example will suffice. In 1877, a European newspaper rated Mackay as the richest man in the world; his income, estimated at twenty-five dollars *a minute,* placed him ahead of both Baron Rothschild and Tsar Alexander II of Russia![28] Other examples, although not quite so spectacular, serve to illustrate just how lucrative California enterprise might be; by 1871, for instance, the elder James Phelan's commercial and banking activities had increased his net worth from its 1851 level of $25,000 to $2,500,000, and James Lick, formerly the richest man in San Francisco with assets totaling $750,000, had dropped to sixth place with $3,000,000.[29]

Such immense aggregations of wealth obviously provided the potential for substantial investment in the expansive economies of both the city and the state, but prior to the silver boom of the 1860s two conditions—scarce money and more lucrative alternate opportunities—diverted the flow of capital into channels other than manufacturing. During the initial gold rush years, the limited availability of cash maintained interest rates at prohibitive levels, often as much as ten to fifteen percent a month. Gradually, as mining and commerce produced more abundant money supplies, rates declined to between four and six percent monthly in the mid-1850s and to an average of two and one-half percent in 1860. Even the lower rates (triple those in New York City) remained high, however, and speculative Californians—lenders, borrowers, and savers alike—continued to risk their funds in economic ventures which promised rapid returns and to avoid manufacturing enterprises which were frequently hampered by inadequate labor and raw material supplies and limited demand for their products.[30] Like commerce and mining, schemes in agriculture, irrigation, real estate, and transportation involved fewer apparent risks and a greater possibility for reaping rewards commensurate with the value of the money invested. These ventures often produced nearly instant prosperity, even for a few fortunate members of the working classes, and thereby perpetuated both the impression of an open and democratic society in San Francisco and the speculative nature of the city's economy.[31]

Recent investigations demonstrate the instability of the San Francisco economy in the 1860s and 1870s and confirm the fact that in general local merchants and investors fared less well than did their counterparts in other frontier cities. Still, to contemporaries the potential for wealth seemed almost infinite. A river of riches flowing from Nevada supplied additional voltage to the already electric atmosphere and began to alter matters appreciably. It did not, however, diminish San Franciscans' enthusiasm for speculation. In the first quarter of 1863 alone, 300 new mining companies capitalized at $50,000,000 incorporated and threw their stocks on the market. At the same time, nearly 4000 brokers in the city received orders which came "literally, from the kitchen to the pulpit; from every shade of life, and every nationality [in the city]" and traded $200,000,000 worth of mining company shares for their customers. The mania continued until 1876 when a record half-billion dollars in silver stock changed hands. Not only eager individuals and consor-

tiums of daring entrepreneurs participated in the dynamic silver speculation; even established commercial firms became involved, some risking
accumulated business profits and others gambling to recoup previous
losses.[32]

Success was less than universal, of course. As quickly as they materialized, immense profits evaporated in the frequently erratic and unpredictable milieu, often taking initial investments with them. In just
months in 1867, for example, shares in the Hale and Norcross Mine
plummeted from $3600 a foot to $650, costing investors millions.[33] On
the other hand, silver speculation also produced millions which, in turn,
increased capital accumulation in the city, drove interest rates down, and
precipitated a search for alternate channels for investment. Some
capitalists turned their attention to railroads, others to a search for new
sources of mineral wealth, and still others to manufacturing, especially
as changed economic conditions increased both the availability of raw
materials and labor and the demand for products of local industry and
made it potentially more attractive to foreign and domestic speculators
alike.

Initially, the local capital which reinforced and accelerated the development of manufacturing in San Francisco originated not in the mines
of Nevada but in the activities of the most successful local merchants and
businessmen who diverted profits into manufacturing operations akin to
the enterprises which produced them. Isaac Friedlander, for example,
financed the Eureka Flour Mills with funds derived from his lucrative
wheat brokerage, and Peter Donahue utilized the income of the Union
Iron Works to expand and diversify his works and its output. But ultimately the lion's share of the money which supplemented a significant
influx of foreign capital and stimulated industrialism in the city emanated directly or indirectly from the Comstock Bonanza.[34] Numerous
successful San Franciscans, enriched by their ventures in Nevada silver,
directed accumulated profits into local manufacturing enterprises, and
none better exemplifies altered attitudes toward industry and toward the
city itself than the founder of the Bank of California, William Chapman
Ralston.

Born in Ohio in 1826, a fourth-generation descendant of Irish immigrants, Ralston arrived in California in 1854 after brief but successful
careers clerking on a Mississippi riverboat and acting as a steamship

The Montgomery Block.

company agent in Panama. In San Francisco, he turned to banking and investment, earned a reputation as the financial community's pillar of stability during the crises of the late 1850s, married Elizabeth Fry in 1858, and later settled with his family on Rincon Hill. Ralston quickly adopted the city as his own and simultaneously evolved an image of himself as an energetic leader in the cultural and economic progress of both the city and the state. In keeping with that vision, in 1864 he joined with Darius Ogden Mills and a roster of eminent backers who included a former mayor and a future one (Henry Teschemaker and William Alvord) to found the Bank of California, capitalized with $2,000,000 in gold, principally the returns on bank investors' Comstock Lode speculations.[35]

From its opening, the bank itself proved to be a profitable venture; during the first year of operation its capital stock increased in value by $250,000. It also provided a full range of services for its customers: savings facilities for large and small depositors, available money for speculators in mining and other ventures, financing for railroad projects, and, for the city's increasingly international commercial community, currency exchanges and letters of credit honored anywhere from Paris to Hong Kong. Equally important for local developments, Ralston diverted

41

substantial sums of his own and bank funds—injudiciously in some cases—into the promotion of both cultural development and manufacturing in San Francisco. In addition to financing the Grand and Palace Hotels and the California Theater, he backed a host of industrial ventures including the California Steam Navigation and California Drydock Companies, Buena Vista Winery, Consolidated Tobacco Company, Mission Woolen Mills, San Francisco and Pacific Sugar Refining Company, watch and furniture manufacturers, and a lock works, among others. Some of Ralston's investments were sound, but others quite literally constituted subsidies to marginal operations and may have combined with declining silver production, the exigencies of the nationwide Panic of 1873, and other of his unwise ventures to abet the Bank of California's temporary suspension—and Ralston's own death—in August 1875.[36]

For the city, however, and certainly for its future, the willingness of Ralston and other investors to underwrite industry in the 1860s and early 1870s should not be underestimated. To be sure, external factors such as the Civil War, anticipation of rail connections with the East, increased supplies of labor and raw materials, and expanded local markets all contributed to the industrialization of San Francisco and to industry's appeal as an avenue of speculative investment. But without the capital generated locally and in the Comstock region and its conscious diversion into new channels, changes in the city would have been neither so rapid nor so permanent. By the time Chris Buckley returned in 1873, San Francisco clearly had become an industrial city as well as a commercial and financial center. During the 1860s alone, the value of its manufacturing output quadrupled, the amount of capital invested in industry increased tenfold, the number of industrial workers multiplied eighteen times to include nearly half of a constantly increasing work force, and the transformation of the economy—and the city—would continue and even gain momentum during subsequent decades.[37]

The change did not transpire wholly during Buckley's two-year absence, nor did factories and industrial districts alone comprise the sole physical evidences of metropolitanism which greeted him upon his return. Spatial arrangements, the center of the city's activities, and even the urban terrain itself had undergone obvious alterations, principally at the hands of real estate speculators who, not content with turning profits, proceeded also to "changing mother earth." Investment in property had persistently appealed to the gambling instincts of San Francisco's venturesome populace, frequently with results little short of dramatic. Indeed, the desire to rationalize speculation in urban real estate constituted one of the primary concerns of the first American city council (*ayuntamiento*) when in 1847 it commissioned engineer Jasper O'Farrell to impose a rectilinear gridiron plat upon the irregular and unyielding topography of what was still the virtually uninhabited village of Yerba Buena.[38] From that time onward, numerous projects—filling the bay frontage along Montgomery Street, leveling the dunes of Happy Valley south of Market, opening the disputed outside lands to the west for settlement and development—attested to San Franciscans' avid preoccupation with speculation in land and radically altered the face of their city. Well before Buckley departed for Vallejo, several such projects were in progress. Their accomplishment testified not only to the determination and political acumen of those who prompted them but also to the frequently unanticipated consequences for the city of decisions made in the pursuit of individualistic goals.

In the 1860s, truncated streets which terminated a few blocks south of Market limited access to the growing industrial districts and forced traffic across the steep Second Street grade over Rincon Hill. To its elite residents, the height overlooking the bay represented the epitome of urban gentility, a pastoral retreat from urban bustle and congestion, but to others—among them John Middleton—it stood as an impediment to progress. A gold rush physician who once called San Francisco "a garbage heap . . . [and] the most abhorrent place that man ever lived in," Middleton later altered his attitude toward the city and began to promote it as an active Democrat, a member of the San Francisco Stock and Exchange Board, and an aggressive real estate speculator and developer. In 1867, he secured election to the state Assembly in order to further one of his visions, a major thoroughfare bisecting Rincon Hill and facilitating communication with the manufacturing and transportation centers emerging south of Market Street.[39] Toward the end of his single term in the legislature, Middleton sponsored a bill, quickly passed and signed by Governor Henry Haight, to "authorize the Board of Supervisors of the City and County of San Francisco to modify the grades of certain streets." Despite the vague and seemingly innocuous phrasing of

43

its title, the legislation specifically mandated the notorious (to some) "Second Street Cut," a project which would cost $90,000 in municipal funds and destroy the idyllic charm of Rincon Hill. When protests by hill residents prompted the municipal government to balk at enforcing the law, Middleton appealed to the courts which upheld the legislation and ordered its implementation.[40] And by the end of 1869, some 500 workers had sliced through the hill to a depth of seventy feet, providing the roadbed for an artery linking the central district with the industrial region to the south and setting the stage for the ultimate obliteration of what had been a refuge for affluent San Franciscans.[41]

A few of them, like Thomas Selby who called the cut "an act of vandalism" and Asbury Harpending who termed it a "sordid bit of real estate roguery," denounced what they considered to be confiscation of property if not outright desecration.[42] For the majority of San Franciscans, however—including most of the elite residents of the despoiled hill—the cut represented progress for themselves and their city, and progress toward metropolitanism took precedence over other considerations.[43] Most of those displaced adjusted their domestic lives in favor of urban development, moving to other heights when cable cars provided access to them, establishing residences among the city's luxurious hotels, or—like William Ralston—becoming suburbanites on southern peninsular estates.[44] In the process, they helped to define even more emphatically the increasingly metropolitan character of San Francisco.

Nor was Middleton's the sole real estate scheme intended to link the central city with the South of Market, alter the urban terrain, and substantially enhance property values. Almost simultaneously, the ubiquitous William Ralston involved himself in a project to extend Montgomery Street southward to the bay. Whether Ralston's sponsorship of the proposal involved genuine civic pride, or a speculative interest in business properties along Market Street and in potential residential sites in the Mission and Potrero districts, or a combination of both is not clear. Whatever the case, he did use his status in the community to exert sufficient pressure to secure approval for the project—and the appropriation of municipal funds to complete it—in the spring of 1864. Then, with Asbury Harpending, he began to acquire property along the proposed right of way, only to have the "Montgomery Street Straight" ordinance founder after protracted disputes. When owners who resisted both

Ralston's offers and city condemnation proceedings—383 individuals representing 36,376 frontage feet—protested with sufficient vigor, Mayor Henry P. Coon vetoed the measure in October 1867.[45] Apparently undaunted by the reversal, a persistent Ralston emulated Middleton when he turned to Sacramento for relief from the mayor's decision, but he encountered considerably less success than the champion of the Second Street Cut had experienced. With Harpending and several others, Ralston had formed the Montgomery Street Real Estate Company which continued to purchase property along the proposed extension and Market Street, including one parcel acquired only when the earthquake of 1868 induced a reluctant owner to sell. At the same time, the associates guided bills mandating the Montgomery Street project and the municipal acquisition and leveling of Rincon Hill through the state legislature—at an estimated outlay of $35,000 for the bills' managers and $400 a day to entertain congenial assemblymen—only to meet with renewed frustration. Despite Harpending's suit filed against Governor Haight, vetoes killed both measures late in 1870, leaving "Montgomery Street Straight" nothing but "An Unpleasant Corpse."[46]

Still, neither the expenditure of effort nor the considerable monetary investment were entirely fruitless for Ralston and his associates or without significant consequences for San Francisco. Even before Haight's vetoes, Ralston had secured legislative approval—purportedly costing another $25,000 in political gratuities—for one more civic project and the sanction of the municipal government for another. A state law enacted in March 1870 ordered the northwesterly extension of Montgomery Street (to be called Montgomery Avenue and subsequently renamed Columbus Avenue), and two months later Mayor Thomas Selby signed a city ordinance approving the construction of a new city hall at Yerba Buena Cemetery on Market Street near the southwestern fringe of settlement.[47]

The Montgomery Avenue improvement began squarely on property owned by Tom Maguire and assessed at over $200,000, and its loss may have contributed to his difficulties in 1870. When completed in 1873, the new boulevard passed diagonally through North Beach, between Telegraph and Russian Hills, to North Point and facilitated movement from the tip of the peninsula to Market Street and beyond, opened previously remote sections of the city to commercial and residential development, and substantially increased real estate values in the regions it bisected. The shift of the seat of government from the old central district had an even more profound and immediate impact. It is clear that new municipal facilities were essential; city government had long since outgrown the Jenny Lind building on Portsmouth Square and the adjacent Union and El Dorado buildings acquired in 1864. But it is also apparent that, even though the new city hall would not be dedicated until 1897, approval of the transfer was in itself sufficient to precipitate significant changes. Values of nearby land—much of it in the hands of the Montgomery Street Real Estate Company—skyrocketed as it became apparent that the obscure site, formerly a city-owned cemetery on a street which "began almost nowhere, . . . and ended exactly nowhere," would become the hub of San Francisco's commercial, financial, and political life.[48]

The cumulative effect of these and other real estate schemes in the late 1860s and early 1870s proved to be momentous in both immediate and long-range terms. The episodes testified, of course, to a continuing willingness on the part of promoters, the municipal government, and much of the citizenry to accept the use of public authority and funds to achieve private purposes in the city. Not quite so obviously, manipulations transacted under the guise of civic improvement tended to reinforce the influences of the industrial developments to which they were intimately tied. Together, they set the stage for an increasingly specialized and segregated metropolis. After the completion of the Second Street Cut and the failure of Ralston's leveling project, Rincon Hill languished; the *Real Estate Circular* called it a "city excrescence," a shabby district of marginal working class residences and depressed land values, standing in stark contrast to its former charm.[49]

Elsewhere, changes were equally significant if not so immediately apparent. In the region of the new city hall, along Market Street, in the newly opened districts to the northwest, and on the heights, property values soared and in the process sharply defined the uses to which urban land might be put. On the one hand, only enterprises which promised substantial returns could locate feasibly in the new business districts; on the other, only families with more than moderate resources could settle in the attractive residential areas which promoters had opened. Marginal businesses and less affluent families remained confined to the older and increasingly crowded regions of the city where congestion also tended to escalate property values. At one end of the scale, Charles Crocker and Leland Stanford could ensconce their families in multi-million-dollar palaces atop Nob Hill and sponsor a cable car line to make them accessible while businesses like the San Francisco and Pacific Sugar Refining Company and the Bank of California expended hundreds of thousands for their new facilities. At the other end, throngs of transient workers crowded into the South of Market and other tenement districts along with the pawn shops and saloons which catered to their needs. And somewhere in the middle, families like the Buckleys moved from one working class district to another.[50]

A divided city presaging the conditions and relationships of the modern metropolis was not the intent of real estate promoters like Middleton, Ralston, Harpending, or the others. Nor was it the goal of the entrepreneurs, investors, and speculators who were their contemporaries as city builders. Indeed, all of them—if they contemplated the issue at all—most probably conceived of the urban setting that they were creating, consciously or unconsciously, in quite different terms. Like the boosters of street railways, industry, and civic improvements in cities across the nation, they were quite likely motivated not only by the obvious profit potential but also by a progressive sort of urban vision which involved an enlarged and extended version of the walking city that was so intimate a part of their nineteenth-century experience.[51] As is all too frequently the case in the history of human affairs, however, the cumulative consequences of actions and decisions taken by individual San Franciscans were not entirely those anticipated. Instead of being a community in which technological and economic development overcame the divisive influences of time and space to preserve familiar human relationships as they had traditionally existed, the San Francisco which emerged in the later 1860s, and the urban patterns established for subsequent generations, embodied the characteristics of the segregated, specialized industrial metropolis, and the harmony and civic progress expected turned out to be confusion and even chaos for many citizens.

47

3

The Making
of a Boss:
Journeyman Years,
1873–1881

Individual San Franciscans reacted to the complexity and unfamiliarity of their city in a variety of ways, many of them private, others public, and most fraught with significance for Christopher Buckley's career. The most obvious of their responses involved a habit inherited from their gold rush era predecessors; isolated citizens of an equally isolated community had attempted to establish their own sense of identity and to preserve at least tenuous connections with a familiar but physically remote past by organizing themselves on virtually any pretext, from common nativity (in the United States or abroad) to sharing a hazardous voyage around Cape Horn in the same vessel.[1] In the 1860s and the early 1870s, as the city took on its metropolitan characteristics, the associative proclivity continued and even increased, but with highly suggestive new dimensions implying growing concern not only for reinforcing individual identities in an amorphous and frequently strange setting but also for asserting a modicum of control over specific aspects of a novel and unpredictable urban milieu.[2]

The most apparent differences included a tendency for even traditional forms of association—such as militia units, volunteer fire companies and, after the establishment of a paid department in 1866, the "exempt" fire brigades (exempt from jury duty and certain taxes)—to become even more ethnic in character, socioeconomically stratified within their ranks, and involved in the affairs of the city.[3] Similarly, benevolent associations—always principally nationality-oriented—became even more so in the later 1860s and also responded to specifically urban conditions in their support of charities which included a Home for Aged and Infirm Females, a Home for Inebriates, temperance societies, orphanages, and the like.[4] San Francisco churches doubled in number to eighty-one in the decade following 1863 and included three Chinese missions and five synagogues, as well as French, Italian, German, Scandinavian, and black congregations and a host of societies and sodalities providing both spiritual and secular succor for their members.[5] Cultural associations likewise reflected altered concerns. In 1870, for example, the California Historical Society joined the Society of California Pioneers established in 1850 in the effort to preserve elements of a rapidly vanishing past. Within two more years, members of the San Francisco Art Assocation (1871) and the San Francisco Academy of Sciences (1872) had dedicated themselves to the advancement of their special interests in the maturing city and by 1875 a variety of national, religious, trades, and social organizations sponsored twenty-eight libraries, all of which antedated the public facility founded in 1879.[6]

Contemporary social organizations also responded to a wide spectrum of the populace. At one end of the scale, the Union Social Club, the Occidental Convivial Club (for bachelors), and the San Francisco Olympic Club—all established in the 1860s—were joined by the California Olympic Club (1871) and the Bohemian Club (1872) founded specifically to recreate the pungent atmosphere of the "good old days" when the nation's literati had haunted the city. For individuals at other points on the social scale, scores of clubs and associations made urban life more amenable, and for the thousands otherwise unaffiliated there were the trade unions, ward political clubs, and the "poor man's clubs," the ubiquitous working class saloons.[7]

This remarkable upsurge in both the number and variety of organizations formed in the 1860s and 1870s attested to San Franciscans' concern for an altered urban environment and to their efforts to find their own places in it. It also suggests that associational life had begun to replace or supplement original acquisitive goals,[8] but not entirely. For nothing better exemplifies the relationship between associational activity and metropolitan conditions than the agencies and institutions created precisely to maintain a climate favorable to the continued acquisition of wealth. Gamblers though they were, San Franciscans were not altogether willing to risk all on an unpredictable turn of a roulette wheel, a faro card, or a Nevada silver strike.[9] Those who had been most intimately involved in building the metropolis through their decisions and their utilization of capital retained their essential concern for economic realities and attempted to regulate their often erratic course.[10] As early as the 1850s, businessmen and merchants had organized the San Francisco Chamber of Commerce and the Merchants' Exchange to stabilize economic activity. With business transactions increasing in volume and complexity in the 1860s, rationalization became even more critical, and local entrepreneurs responded with a multitude of new institutions: the San Francisco Stock and Exchange Board, later the San Francisco Mining Exchange (1862), the San Francisco Board of Brokers and the Pacific Board of Brokers (1867), the California Stock Exchange (1872), the Pacific Stock Exchange (1875), and the San Francisco Board of Trade (1877).[11] At the same time, citizens who had not been privy to the decisions which altered the city but who were equally affected by them organized themselves to preserve their own economic positions. Associations such as the Mechanics' League (1861) and the San Francisco Trades' Union (1863) sought the protection of the general status of skilled labor, while the Eight-Hour League and the shortlived Anti-Coolie Association agitated for more specific goals, and a host of trades—among them carpenters, joiners, butchers, cigar makers, millmen, iron molders, tanners, and stonemasons (John Buckley, secretary)—affiliated in order to maintain the prestige and compensations of their respective crafts.[12]

In some respects, success rewarded the efforts of businessmen and craftsmen alike. Bids for seats on the San Francisco Stock and Exchange Board, originally valued at $100, rose to $43,500 by 1875, testifying to the profitability of membership in such institutions. Workingmen managed to maintain wage levels during the 1860s, to restrict the use of convict labor in local industry, to extract promises of reduced employment of cheap Chinese labor, and to secure eight-hour legislation from both city and state governments.[13] But neither group even approached the attainment of their larger goal: elimination of the vagaries and fluctuations of the metropolitan economy. Only a mild recession in 1864 marred the general prosperity—for both business and labor—of that decade. In 1869, however, a more severe setback in commerce, real estate, and mining activity augured a protracted decline in the 1870s.[14] Economic activity—predicated principally upon the deceptive boom in mining speculation—remained brisk but erratic until 1875, which one contemporary described as "the greatest, grandest, most profitable year" in San Francisco's business history.[15] Despite such optimism, the halcyon days were illusory and impermanent, and nothing more graphically illustrates the severity of the reversal of fortunes than the Bank of California's suspension of its operations on August 26.

San Franciscans had regarded William Ralston's bank as an exemplar of fiscal reliability during previous crises, a fact which rendered the institution's temporary collapse in 1875 all the more dramatic and turned many citizens against the man who had been regarded as something of a local hero. And Ralston must be assigned a substantial share of the responsibility, for he had permitted the use of bank funds in a number of highly questionable ventures. His investment in marginal industries, many of which retrenched or collapsed entirely in the face of eastern competition after 1869, has already been noted. He also allowed bank deposits to be diverted to several abortive transbay bridge and railway schemes and to a dubious effort to corner the stock of the Spring Valley Water Company (of which Ralston was the major shareholder) in order to sell the utility to the city at a profit of some $8,000,000. At the same time, the bank involved itself actively in a stock war over control of the Nevada silver mines which precipitated radical fluctuations in silver share prices, prompted many depositors to withdraw cash in order to buy stock or cover losses, and further depleted the bank's resources.

But there were also conditions which neither the bank nor Ralston could control and which affected the city as well as the institution. In the early 1870s, numerous countries throughout the world, including the United States, demonetized silver, a move which was especially detrimental to an urban economy highly dependent upon the production of the metal. Almost simultaneously, the delayed impact of the national

Panic of 1873 hit California, adding rigor to the local business decline which followed completion of the transcontinental railroad and accelerating business failures—and unemployment—in the city. Cumulatively —and in conjunction with other factors—Ralston's indiscretions and general economic adversity resulted in "a collapse [which] was most terrible."[16]

Although the Bank of California reopened on October 5, 1875, and not all financial institutions in the city suffered severely, the event had significant implications. It precipitated Ralston's death—probably from a cerebral hemorrhage—while indulging in his habitual daily swim in the bay on August 27, 1875.[17] Placed in the broader historical perspective, the bank failure assumes an even larger importance, for it revealed fundamental flaws in the urban economy which ultimately would affect not only the major elements of the San Francisco business community and the city's smaller scale entrepreneurs but also the vast majority of workingmen as well.

Nothing so dramatic or precipitous as the collapse of the Bank of California delineates the reversal of workers' fortunes in the city. During the 1860s, as has been observed, a persistent shortage of labor and a generally high level of prosperity maintained wages and even permitted some progress toward improved conditions and other goals. In the closing years of the decade, however, a combination of conditions contributed to the erosion of labor's position. Local business stagnation, the completion of the transcontinental railroad, altered economic realities in the interior of California, and increasing immigration from outside the state resulted in an augmented urban labor pool, declining wages, high unemployment, and even the loss of some previous gains, including the eight-hour day.[18] By early 1870, economic exigencies which labor could not control, despite the vigorous efforts of its various trade associations, had all but eradicated its previously advantageous position. Estimates placed the state unemployment rate at twenty percent (higher in the cities) and the number out of work in San Francisco itself at 7000.[19] Coupled with sharply reduced wages for what little work was available, unemployment precipitated occasionally violent responses. Indeed, some of the jobless vented their hostility on one another, as they did when over 1000 applicants appeared to claim 115 city jobs clearing Yerba Buena Park and a near riot resulted. Others aimed their frustrated outbursts at California labor's perennial target, the Chinese, or at vaguely defined conspiracies involving the "octopus" railroad or the "capitalists." A few of the more youthful—male and female alike—supported themselves as urban vagabonds or "hoodlums," all of whom, one nativist editor erroneously insisted, had "Irish Roman Catholic name[s]."[20] Most, despite continually deteriorating conditions, relied upon their trade associations, futile and sometimes ugly strikes, local benevolent associations, and political agitation until 1877, when more than 15,000 were jobless in San Francisco alone and the majority turned for relief to the principal associative effort of the period, the Workingmen's Party of California (WPC).[21]

With the possible exception of the WPC, the associations which workers formed to discipline an unruly urban economy succeeded no better than did those established by contemporary members of the business community. Nor were social, cultural, or ethnic organizations significantly more capable of exercising control over any but the most limited and specialized urban conditions which affected the lives of their members. Indeed, chaos and confusion prevailed as the most universal characteristics of life in industrial San Francisco during the "terrible 'seventies,"[22] and they were but little abated by official agencies in the city. A municipal government and partisan political practices which owed more to the traditions of the village than to the realities of the metropolis not only provided few remedies but also virtually demanded the strong hand of a boss. Within a very few years, it would be the hand of Christopher Augustine Buckley.

When Buckley returned from Vallejo, he wasted little time before expanding his familiarity with the governmental system of San Francisco, and he found that, even in 1873, the metropolis continued to struggle with the inadequacies of an archaic charter designed nearly two decades earlier for a town of a few thousand residents. Settlers who had come to California initially to seek wealth, not to build cities, quickly discovered that social and political organization was essential to the achievement of their principal goal; instant citizens of an instant city required at least the rudiments of an equally instant government.[23] As early as 1846, in fact, they had resorted to an expedient synthesis of Hispanic and Anglo-American forms of municipal government, even retaining the titles of *alcalde* (mayor, but with judicial as well as executive authority) and *ayuntamiento* (legislative and advisory council) and appointed Lt. Washington A. Bartlett (USN) the town's first Yankee alcalde.[24] Subsequent developments—a state constitution, admission to the Union, and explosive population growth—demanded the hybrid system's replacement with one more in keeping with American traditions, and on April 15, 1850, San Francisco was chartered as the ninth city in California.[25] The City Charter of 1850 eliminated the *alcalde* and *ayuntamiento* in favor of a more familiar mayor and bicameral city council, but the new organic law neither resolved residual problems remaining from the Mexican period and emerging from the Treaty of Guadalupe-Hidalgo nor provided adequate government for a burgeoning and changing city. Nor would two subsequent charters (1851 and 1855) enacted prior to the Consolidation Act of 1856 prove substantially more effective.[26]

The state legislature approved the Consolidation Act (also known as the Hawes Act for its principal sponsor, Know-Nothing Assemblyman Horace Hawes) on April 19, 1856; it took effect on the following July 1 and would remain the basic framework for municipal government until 1898.[27] In some ways, it was a unique document. At a time when most American cities were attempting to aggrandize their territory, San Francisco actually denied itself the possibility of expansion. San Francisco County had stretched southward along the peninsula for many miles, but in the name of economy and efficiency, the Consolidation Act reduced the size of the county by about two-thirds to less than fifty square miles, made its boundaries coterminus with those of the city, and placed both city and county under the jurisdiction of a common set of agencies and officials.[28] Both positive and negative consequences attended the maneuver. On the one hand, although some county officials remained, eliminating substantial duplication did reduce the cost of government materially, at least for the time being. The Consolidation Act also created a kind of municipal reservation—small enough to be governed, large enough to provide for the needs of current growth, and protected from the potential encroachment of suburban municipalities which might otherwise have been incorporated in county territory along the city's fringes. On the other hand, the new charter also sentenced the city to confinement on the tip of the peninsula and to permanent crowding and congestion when subsequent growth changed the potential for expansion from a liability to an asset.[29]

Despite the Consolidation Act's innovative solution to the problems of territorial limits and competing jurisdictions, in most other respects it outlined a system of municipal government quite representative of the political thought and practice of its time. The act established basic standards and procedures for municipal elections, defined and restricted fiscal policies, and eliminated previously overlapping authorities. It vested legislative power and responsibility in a board of supervisors, each of its members to be elected biennially by the voters of one of the city's twelve wards (originally called "districts"). Twelve school directors, similarly elected, would govern the educational system. The principal executive officer, called the "president of the board of supervisors" until 1862 when the title mayor was reinstated, would be popularly elected every two years and exercise only strictly limited authority. Beyond this, the Consolidation Act listed the traditional roster of elective and appointive city and county officers, prescribed their duties, terms, and salaries, specified twelve standing committees of the board of supervisors, and— reflecting its Know-Nothing authorship—eliminated public support for parochial schools. Finally, still in keeping with current standards of municipal government, San Francisco carried self-denial beyond questions of boundaries and executive power and deferred much of its civic authority to the state.[30]

During the 1860s, the Consolidation Act served the city reasonably well and permitted the establishment of many essential services and even some of the amenities of urban life. An expanded school system provided basic education for some 15,000 children, although not entirely without conflict among its teachers, administrators, and political officials. By the middle of the decade, the city had doubled the size of its police force to more than 200 officers, instituted a paid fire department to replace the traditional volunteer companies, and installed one of the first electric fire and police alarm systems in the nation.[31] In emulation of eastern and European practices, the board of supervisors had reserved land and made plans for municipal parks (including Golden Gate Park) to supplement Woodward's Gardens and other private resorts and had authorized a grand boulevard (the Great Highway) skirting the Pacific shoreline.[32] City streets, a persistent source of grief during rainy seasons, had begun to show improvement as permanent materials such as macadam replaced wooden blocks and other makeshift surfaces. Through federal intervention, the nagging dispute over the "outside lands"—regions included in

55

neither the original pueblo nor the terms of the 1848 treaty with Mexico and subsequently contested by city, state, and a host of squatters—approached amicable settlement.[33] Simultaneously, both taxes and municipal spending—notwithstanding recurrent complaints to the contrary—remained at reasonable levels.[34] Despite these and other substantial accomplishments, however, there were also problems, many of which emanated from weaknesses inherent in the Consolidation Act itself.

One of the most serious difficulties involved the office of the mayor. With the exception of a few truly dynamic individuals, a succession of municipal executives found themselves unable to exercise the sort of leadership which would make government responsive to the requirements of a rapidly growing and changing city. Hampered by the restrictions which the Consolidation Act imposed, most early mayors became principally caretaker administrators and advisers to the board of supervisors, when they were not in conflict with it. The vested interests of the supervisors—especially those of the "solid nine" who would override mayors' rarely exercised vetoes—became the real authority in municipal government, with the result that personal and partisan issues frequently took precedence over matters critical to the city.[35] A second problem involved the original act's apparent simplicity, a quality which in practice became inflexibility. Virtually every novel situation required a charter amendment—frequently involving state action—before the municipality could respond, and the document quickly became an almost incomprehensible and often contradictory legal maze. Indeed, as early as 1861 Mayor Henry F. Teschemaker and the board of supervisors found it necessary to order a codification of the Consolidation Act, its amendments, and the city's municipal code; a decade later, Mayor Thomas Selby, almost in desperation, recommended an entirely new and responsive charter.[36]

Portions of Selby's arguments in favor of a new organic law spoke specifically to a third major flaw in the Consolidation Act, one which may have constituted its major impediment to effective municipal government. Too much authority over city affairs had been relegated to officials in Sacramento. The state had not usurped these prerogatives; San Franciscans had abrogated them when they wrote their charter in 1856 and forced the state government to devote inordinate attention to the affairs of the city. Between 1866 and 1876, for example, each biennial session of the legislature enacted an average of 123 laws (and considered many more) pertaining specifically to San Francisco. The statutes included measures to order street improvements such as those which Middleton and Ralston instigated, to authorize new city boards and commissions, to alter election dates, to grant utility franchises and set rates, and even to settle private claims against the city.[37] Some of the actions were absolutely essential to the welfare of the city. Others involved petty issues which should have been settled locally, and some—like the infamous Parson's Bulkhead Bill episode which culminated in state control of the San Francisco waterfront from 1863 until 1968 and a variety of real estate schemes—were thinly disguised efforts to secure private gain at public expense.[38] Whatever the case, dependence upon state action and authority required and encouraged the intervention of an increasingly antiurban government at Sacramento in San Francisco affairs. In combination with the impotence of the mayor and the inadequacy of the city charter itself, the interference rendered municipal government confusing, chaotic, and frequently ineffective and made it for decades the target of San Franciscans' vigorous complaints.[39]

Other conditions produced equally persistent dissatisfaction, including an outmoded legal framework for partisan activities which, like the charter itself, had been devised on the basis of conditions prevailing in the walking city of a previous generation rather than for those of the modern metropolis. With the exception of the Consolidation Act's enumeration of elective officials and their terms of office, its designation of a date—frequently changed by state intervention—for holding local elections, and the specification of an election commissioner to oversee partisan contests and voter qualifications, few regulations of any sort governed municipal political activities in nineteenth-century San Francisco. As Chris Buckley himself observed, the "vice of the old political system . . . was the lack of recognition and regulation by law," a circumstance which made city politics "purely a go-as-you-please affair."[40] Indeed, for much of the later nineteenth century, there was not even a great register of voters kept, and when it did exist, it provided something less than a reliable means of control. In Buckley's case, for example, his name remained on the San Francisco record while he was also registered in Vallejo, and when he returned and reregistered in 1873, his name appeared *twice* on the same page of the official roster of voters (see

4210	15675	Buckley, Andrew	42 Ireland	Laborer	127 Shipley	10	Nov. 7, 1864, Sonora, Cal, 5th Dist	Nov. 4, 1872
4211	14183	• Buckley, Christopher Aug.	21 New York	Bookkeeper	136 Pacific	2		June 3, 1867
4212	b14355	Buckley, Cornelius	21 Ireland	Machinist	108 Beale	9		July 25, 1868
4213	b14355	Buckley, Charles P	28 New York	Carpenter	5 Calhoun			Aug. 11, 1868
4214	7628	Buckley, David	42 Ireland	Clerk	569 Mission	1	Mar. 26, 1856, New York, Com. Pleas	June 27, 1866
4215	2878	Buckley, Daniel	42 Ireland	Miner	56 Minna	7	Sept. 15, 1860, Jackson, Cal. 16th Dist	June 18, "
4216	16514	Buckley, Edmund	43 Canada	Mason	Virginia	4		June 29, 1867
4217	b16433	Buckley, Edward Minturn	31 New York	Minstrel	Clay above Kearny	6		June 29, "
4218	44247	Buckley, Edward Joseph	24 Australia	Actor	917 Stockton	6		Aug. 7, 1871
4219	b24252	Buckley, Edward Robert	38 Louisiana	Miner	What Cheer	3		Aug. 3, 1868
4220	39597	Buckley, Edward Patrick	40 Ireland	License	Col. 2006 Powell	3	June 13, 1866, San Francisco, U.S.D.	Sept. 5, 1870
4221	2153	Buckley, Francis	49 Ireland	Builder	Devisadero n. Turk	12	June 9, 1865, San Francisco, 4th Dist	June 14, 1866
4222	1840	Buckley, Jr., Francis	21 Chili	Builder	Turk & Devisadero	12		June 12, "
4223	b35401	Buckley, James	38 Mass	Brickmaker	cor. Polk & Green	12		Aug. 14, 1869
4224	18059	Buckley, Joseph Aloysius	21 California	Student	Devisadero,b.Turk & Edy	12		July 29, 1867
4225	45812	Buckley, James Alexander	34 Dist. Col'a	Mason	Pacific	4		Aug. 29, 1871
4226	10629	Buckley, Jeremiah	33 New York	Carpenter	Outside Lands	12		July 11, 1866
4227	1145	Buckley, Jeremiah Joseph	32 Mass	Porter	cor. Bryant & First	9		June 7, "
4228	6777	Buckley, John	45 England	Laborer	cor. Bay & Midway	2	July 23, 1866, San Francisco, U.S.Dis	June 23, "
4229	12285	Buckley, Jeremiah	24 New York	Blacksmith	365 Minna	10		Oct. 30, 1868
4230	34109	Buckley, Jeremiah	46 Ireland	Blacksmith	318 Stevenson	10	Jan. 29, 1868, New York, Com. Pleas	Oct. 19, 1869
4231	37496	Buckley, Jeremiah	25 New York	Blacksmith	51 Third	10		Mar. 9, 1870
4232	37624	Buckley, Jeremiah	27 Australia	Bookkeeper	731 Vallejo			June 24, 1869
4233	b35007	Buckley, John Lawrence	35 Ireland	Cooper	925 Broadway	4	May 12, 1857, New Orleans, U. S. Cir	Aug. 9, 1871
4234	43973	Buckley, John Henry	24 Missouri	Boilermaker	407 Natoma	10		Sept. 2, "
4235	46461	Buckley, John Arthur	31 Ireland	Blacksmith	182 Stevenson	10	Oct. 27, 1859, New York, Com. Pleas	Sept. 14, 1868
4236	26091	Buckley, Michael	26 Ireland	Expressman	38 Natoma	7	Aug. 21, 1867, San Francisco, 4th Dis	Aug. 21, "
4237	21703	Buckley, Michael	34 Ireland	Laborer	26 Fourth	10	March 6, 1862, Nevada, Cal., 14th Dis	Aug. 2, "
4238	10146	Buckley, Patrick	47 Ireland	Laborer	Broadway, n.Mason	4	June 8, 1866, San Francisco, 4th Dist	July 11, 1873
4239	1393	Buckley, Patrick	28 Ireland	Saloon	320 Kearny	5		Sept. 25, 1868
4240	dd52552	• Buckley, Christopher	35 Indiana	Inspec'r Cus	630 Sacramento			Oct. 1, "
4241	28635	Buckley, Thomas	35 Indiana	Inspec'r Cus	Stockton, n. B'dw'y	4	Oct. 25, 1865, New York, Com. Pleas	Aug. 6, 1864
4242	31225	Buckley, Timothy	27 Ireland	Hostler	Polk, n. Green	12		Aug. 15, 1870
4243	14616	Buckley, William	40 Mass	Brickmaker	What Cheer	3		Oct. 15, 1868
4244	y49512	Bucklin, Edward Pearce	41 Rhode Isl'd	Hotel Keeper	311 Stockton	8		Aug. 16, 1871
4245	33541	Bucklin, John Willington	50 New York	Broker	515 Bryant	9	Aug. 5, 1871, California, 12th Dist	June 22, 1866
4246	45145	Buckling, John	34 Prussia	Grocer	515 Bryant			

Great Register of the City and County of San Francisco, 1873, page 49.
Buckley is registered twice, lines 4212 and 4240.
The *dd* designates a transfer from Solano County.

illustration).[41] Obviously, such slovenly execution of even the most basic controls could do little to prevent the practice of city bosses' traditional admonition to their constituents: vote early and vote often. Neither death nor lack of citizenship was sufficient to preclude the exercise of the franchise in nineteenth-century San Francisco. On election day, graves miraculously gave up their occupants, whiskers sprouted and disappeared as repeaters made their rounds, and even the crews of foreign men-of-war lying at anchor in the bay came ashore to cast their votes— often in false-bottom ballot boxes.[42]

But voting irregularities comprised only a minor portion of the system's peculiarities, as attested by the published memoirs of three of the most adept practitioners of the art and science of municipal politics: Buckley, his Republican contemporary Martin Kelly, and the younger Abraham Ruef.[43] The paucity of laws regulating partisan affairs—even primary and general elections—left party organizations, especially county committees, free to make their own rules, and control of the county committee "virtually meant control of the entire [party and] election machinery."[44] Organization began in numerous clubs established in each ward or district and headquartered in their own halls or neighborhood saloons. Part of the individual motivation for membership involved camaraderie and sociability; clubs frequently provided alternatives to the saloon and sponsored family outings, picnics, dances, and similar functions not otherwise available to the working classes. Affiliation also involved pragmatic considerations related to urban conditions. Partisan clubs controlled the distribution of patronage jobs promised by potential candidates eager for the organization's nomination and support, and they acted as employment and welfare agencies when few other such institutions existed in the city. On these bases, the neighborhood units, replete with a hierarchy of officers sufficient to give recognition to faithful ward heelers and precinct captains, kept large numbers of voters loyal, registered, and mobilized to participate in primary and general election campaigns under the guidance of their leaders.[45]

In actuality, however, county committees exercised real control, especially through their power to call primary elections. Since places and times designated for primaries were often sufficiently remote to discourage all but the hardiest voters, the selection of a club's county committee representatives, election officers, and delegates to municipal nominating conventions—all chosen at the primary election—frequently fell to a small nucleus of dedicated partisans. Consequently, although internecine strife among rival factions regularly disturbed their deliberations, the conventions actually represented the agency through which county committees effectively regulated voters' options in the municipal general elections.[46]

Nor did committee authority end there. The central organization printed tickets—often unique in design and counterfeiting the opposition's ballot—for general elections, nominated officials to monitor polling places and tabulate results, chose local representatives to statewide party councils, and conducted the general campaign.[47] Not all political activities fell under the aegis of the county committee, however; fire companies and militia units became powerful political agencies in their own right and granted their services and support to the party most responsive to their particular needs for patronage jobs, favors, or more tangible rewards.[48]

Other groups capitalized upon the lack of partisan regulation to form "piece clubs" such as the Independent Democratic Liberal Republican Anti-Coolie Labor Reform Party which made its appearance during the late 1870s.

[A]ny group of cheap skates could assemble in a back room, create a sham party with a high-sounding name, and claim to have four or five thousand voters. . . . With this for an asset, the head manipulators could sally forth and mace candidates of the regular parties out of large sums of money for nominations or endorsements.[49]

An even less cohesive group of political foot soldiers called the "push" stood ready to cast its lot with either party as convention packers, poll watchers, and vigorous campaign organizers. Buckley described the push as

the boys of the bejasus order, with the spring-bottom pants, who rivaled Orpheus on the concertina, who chanted that most moving of all songs, "Big Horse, I Love You," in one breath and unlimbered their awful battlecry in the next.[50]

On each election day, this contingent of shoulder-strikers and rock-rollers poured out of the saloons—especially those south of Market Street—to persuade voters, to stuff (or steal) ballot boxes, and frequently to precipitate sufficient violence and disorder at polling places to intimidate substantial numbers and dissuade them from casting ballots at all.[51]

Quite obviously, in nineteenth-century San Francisco the "game of politics [was] not a branch of the Sunday school business."[52] A strangely mutated system had emerged there in the urban chaos of the 1860s and 1870s, as it did in many other American cities. With apparent sarcasm, Buckley attributed the phenomenon to "our [national] genius for organization [which] created a government—a system without any warrant of law."[53] Many other contemporaries—latter-day Jeffersonian agrarians, perhaps—assumed that the problem lay with the inherent evil of cities and the ignorance and venality of their disproportionately foreign populations.[54]

But there was much more involved in the system's emergence and persistence for many generations, not the least of which was an apathetic public more concerned with the pursuit of material gain than with the political life of the city. Municipal government under an antiquated charter also contributed to the political climate. It obviously failed to regulate partisan activity, but even more importantly, rigidity and complexity joined with outside interference from the state to render local government incapable of response to changing urban conditions. The weakness all but demanded an alternative source of authority, one which partisan organizations and the masters who managed them willingly supplied. Finally, the unfamiliarity of a novel urban setting, a condition which precipitated an upsurge of associational activity in other spheres in the 1860s and 1870s, had a similar influence upon political organizations and alignments. Successful citizens involved themselves—often surreptitiously—in the hybrid system in order to protect or extend their varied interests, while the less successful

balanced their failures with membership in political groups that worked to adapt democratic process originally designed for the face-to-face contact of rural settings [or walking cities] to the anonymity of urban politics.[55]

Bosses and machines did not create the confusion in municipal affairs or corrupt the political system, but they did capitalize upon existing flaws and weaknesses in both.

Thus, in the decade between Chris Buckley's first arrival in 1862 and his return in 1873—not wholly during his absence—the city had changed profoundly. Entrepreneurial activity and technological progress had transformed commercial San Francisco into an industrial metropolis in little more than an historical instant. A substantially increased population, more diverse and dispersed over a larger area, had become increasingly specialized, stratified, and segregated. Disparities of wealth had become greater, more apparent, and seemingly more permanent. The city had become more cosmopolitan and sophisticated, supporting the professionals, intellectuals, libraries, theaters, museums, and learned societies which constituted the hallmarks of nineteenth-century urban culture. Buildings were taller, streets more congested, and communications more efficient (but not necessarily more effective). Even the face of mother earth had been altered.

In other respects, however, the city remained essentially as it had been. Municipal government had failed to keep pace with the demands created by urban change; it was still the same in basic form and function as it had been when a comparative handful of San Franciscans inhabited the peninsula. Similarly, partisan practices were unadapted to new metropolitan realities, at least in any official sense. Nevertheless, given the obsolescence of the governmental structure itself, the flexibility of an unregulated political system perhaps provided the sole sufficiently responsive mechanism for accomplishing either private or public goals. The tension between the dynamism and inertia inherent in the process of urbanization in San Francisco furnished the principal basis for the advancement of Buckley's career. And, to borrow a phrase from one of his New York City counterparts, he "seen [his] opportunities and [he] took 'em."[56]

Opportunities presented themselves almost immediately. After his sojourn in Vallejo, Buckley renewed acquaintances in the city and affiliated himself with the Democratic party, allegedly because his old mentor Bill Higgins refused him a position in the hierarchy of the Republican organization. Whatever the motivation, his shift in allegiance illuminates an important facet of municipal politics in the Gilded Age. During the period, the major parties hammered out fairly definitive organizational positions on the tariff question, currency reform, industrial regulation, foreign affairs, and other similar issues.[57] And in most national and state matters, Buckley's partisan behavior generally conformed to Democratic policies after 1873. In municipal concerns, however, not party ideology but personal leadership and immediate responses to the equally immediate needs of the urban populace were the critical considerations. Thus, a shift in partisan affiliation had little intrinsic significance in the career of the would-be city boss. Nor did merely changing parties assure immediate access to the political heights, even though Buckley's memoirs reduce the story of his rise to just four brief episodes, imply a sudden and dramatic accession to power, and overlook a decade of careful preparation.

According to his version of the events which made him a boss, early in 1882 a committee of prominent citizens summoned him home from a holiday and placed the responsibility for reorganizing a defunct local Democracy squarely and almost exclusively upon his shoulders. By that time, defections had left the party with "scarce a grease spot . . . to mark its place," Denis Kearney's Workingmen's Party of California and the Republicans dominated municipal affairs, the state and national elections of 1880 had culminated in ignominious defeat for California Democrats, and the municipal contest of 1881 had ended similarly. Therefore, Buckley departed from the city, unwilling to "lead a party that couldn't win" and "determined to let politics and politicians take care of themselves thereafter." His absence proved to be somewhat briefer than intended, for the year 1882 promised to be "something epochal in the history of California politics," and the council of San Francisco Democratic luminaries, anticipating momentous victories in the fall elections, urgently petitioned Buckley to return to the city. He responded to the request, devised a unique club plan of organization to rebuild the shattered party, and engineered a sweeping success at the polls in November. In recognition of his accomplishments, a reluctant Buckley then "was made a sort of uncrowned king by the deliberate act of perhaps the ablest and best intending men ever gathered in the history of California."[58]

Such is the substance of an essentially accurate narrative of the developments which first gave Buckley virtually unchallenged supremacy over San Francisco Democratic politics and initiated a hegemony which would endure until 1891. His abbreviated version of the episode, however, with its implied immediacy and spontaneity, omits far more than it reveals, even if only political realities in the 1870s or Buckley's role in molding his own career are considered. Confused and less than auspicious circumstances confronted local Democrats throughout the decade, providing numerous opportunities for a budding politico well before the WPC episode. Moreover, from 1873 onward Buckley actively—perhaps even consciously—pursued a course which would culminate quite logically in the events of 1882. His partisan role was consistently far from passive, and his emergence as the Blind Boss constitutes something other than a fortuitous or unanticipated sequence of events for either himself or his party.

As Buckley accurately observed, the Workingmen's party did decimate the local Democracy in the late 1870s. Depression in the city and state, seemingly constricted opportunities for the working classes, the failure of traditional parties to check the monopolistic practices of the railroad and other interests, dislocated urban conditions, and the perennially presumed threat of the Chinese combined to add substance to the harangues of the dynamic sandlot orator Denis Kearney who promised radical social, political, and economic change. Although Kearney appealed principally to the masses, members of all social strata—professionals, leaders of the city's nascent labor organizations, and adherents of both major parties—flocked to the WPC banner, if only temporarily. But the Democratic party, with its heavily working class and immigrant composition, suffered most severely. The precise extent of the loss is difficult to assess, but Buckley's estimate of over eighty percent is probably accurate. By 1880, less than 3000 disorganized, discouraged, and leaderless Democrats remained on party rosters which once contained some 25,000 names.[59]

Despite the gravity of the debacle, its implications for the career of a budding Democratic chieftain, or his subsequent reputation as an unmitigated opportunist, Buckley himself did not defect.[60] Once he became a Democrat in 1873, he remained a supporter of the party until his death, consistently loyal in national affairs but just as consistently the pragmatist in local matters where partisan orthodoxy mattered little. Indeed, he commenced his activities as a Democrat shortly after his second arrival in the city. He opened a saloon at the corner of Bush and Kearny Streets in the new commercial and entertainment district and operated the venture with a succession of partners—including Con Mooney, long an activist in San Francisco Fire Department politics. Simultaneously, he formed several additional important associations: a friendship with Matt Fallon who operated a rival groggery in the same neighborhood and who, from 1879 until 1885, would be Buckley's partner in the Alhambra Saloon at 323 Bush Street, and political affiliations with Al Fritz and Sam Rainey.[61]

Alliance with this triumvirate would prove highly fortuitous for his political career. Fallon, several years Buckley's senior and an old and seasoned party wheelhorse, had participated in state and local politics from the chaos of the 1850s through the dislocations of the 1870s. As a result of his experience, Fallon could impart to his younger colleague the political lore and wisdom of a generation, effectively completing the apprenticeship commenced under Higgins a decade earlier.[62] Fritz, Buckley's chronological contemporary, was the proprietor of a South of Market saloon and an amusement park and captain of the Gatling Battery, a state militia unit (Company A of the Second Artillery Battalion) which devoted substantially more attention to politics than to its intended martial functions. By the 1870s, Fritz had earned a reputation as a leader in both state and local politics, holding important party offices at both levels, exercising substantial influence in the Democratic organization, and able to deliver a dependable block of votes to his party's tickets. It was Fritz who first recognized in Buckley a capacity for leadership which equaled his own.[63] Finally, the bluff and blustery Rainey controlled the fire department in an era when "every firehouse was the bivouac of some political contingent." With intelligence, persuasiveness, and liberally distributed patronage—as well as with his hammerlike fists—he maintained a reliable coterie of loyal supporters active and at the disposal of the party, ready to act as voters, campaigners, or shoulder strikers as the occasion demanded.[64]

In concert with this trio of indomitable Tenth District warriors— Fallon the greybearded strategist, Fritz the young tactician, and Rainey the aggressive field general—and joined by the political veteran John C. Murphy who "ran things with a high old hand" in the Ninth District, in 1873 Buckley engaged in what he termed his "first casual experience in San Francisco politics." In reality, the experience was no more casual than it was his first. During the 1860s, after all, he had earned a reputation during Bill Higgins' Republican campaigns. Moreover, the 1873 contest represented a concerted challenge to the established party control of bosses Jack Mannix (Buckley's former partner) and Owen Brady, leaders of the so-called "Chivalry" faction of the Democracy and previously masters of the politically potent Gatling Gun Battery. Despite its vigor, however, the confrontation resulted in inglorious defeat for Buckley and his cohorts and another victory for the People's Party. Still, the partnership persisted, and in the municipal primaries and general elections of 1875 it made serious inroads into the Mannix-Brady dominance when, on a reform platform, it elected Andrew Jackson Bryant mayor and captured all remaining city offices and most of San Francisco's legislative delegation.[65]

Aid in the enterprise appeared from a totally unexpected source and exemplifies the many fortuitous occurrences which punctuated Buckley's career. Buckley was sitting alone in party headquarters—probably the back room of the Alhambra—contemplating the forthcoming campaign and the dismal state of the organization's exchequer. Someone entered the room and addressed him by name. Because he did not recognize the voice, Buckley initially felt some trepidation, but his mood quickly shifted from fear to disbelief to exultation when the stranger introduced himself as "J. D. Craig, late of Yolo County." He was a Democrat intent upon securing the nomination for the state senate from San Francisco's Tenth District and willing to contribute substantially to the party war chest: $2500 on the spot and a matching sum once the nomination was secure. Needless to say, Buckley and Fritz granted Craig's wish.[66] The unanticipated windfall sustained a more energetic campaign and undoubtedly influenced its outcome. Local Democrats vanquished their opposition, Craig won his seat in the senate, and Buckley, Fritz, Fallon, and Rainey established themselves in firm control of the local organization.

Buckley and his cohorts repeated their victory in 1877, but just as permanent success seemed imminent, fortune reversed itself for both Buckley and his party. Depressed conditions intensified by drought and declining mining activities brought economic distress to California and especially to San Francisco which became a refuge for displaced farmers and miners. Unemployment, dismal commercial prospects, and increased agitation of the Chinese question combined to provide a fertile soil for the germination of seeds sown by Denis Kearney's appeals. And by 1879, defections left no real residual of hope for the new Democratic coalition. Even earlier, probably beginning in 1873, Buckley himself suffered a personal tragedy; he went blind.

Critical accounts attributed the loss of sight to youthful dissipation and the quality of merchandise dispensed in his various saloons. The boss insisted that it resulted from defects on the optic nerves. It may have involved both. But whatever the case, such a disaster might have terminated the political career of most men, but not that of Chris Buckley. He consciously and conscientiously cultivated remarkably acute faculties of hearing and memory to compensate for his loss and to amaze even his most consistent enemies. It was said, for example, that he could recite the Consolidation Act and its amendments, even though they only had been read to him. He allegedly could identify individuals by voice, handclasp, or even footfall. One story, perhaps apocryphal, is illustrative. At a state convention Buckley purportedly met a "hay-seed" delegate with whom he discussed agrarian questions; at the subsequent meeting—two years later—he not only identified the individual by his voice but also resumed the conversation. Such tales may have exaggerated. Nevertheless, they underscore the compensatory faculties which permitted Buckley to remain active in Democratic affairs throughout the dark days—for his party as well as for himself—of 1879 and 1880.[67]

And they were dark days indeed. The WPC gathered strength and elected Isaac Kalloch, a Baptist minister known as the "Sorrel Stallion" for his amorous exploits in Kansas, to the mayoralty in an 1879 campaign punctuated by violence which included even members of San Fran-

Isaac Kalloch, Workingmen's
Party mayor of San Francisco.

Denis Kearney, leader of the
Workingmen's Party of California.

cisco's elite. In response to insults, Charles De Young, who published the *Morning Call* with his brother Michel, shot and wounded Kalloch shortly before the election; six months later, Charles De Young died at the hands of Kalloch's son.[68] But even in such an atmosphere Buckley managed to keep his career alive. In fact, the Democratic debacle and Buckley's fidelity to the party quite probably hastened his rise to prominent positions on the County and State Central Committees by 1879, just six months after his initial affiliation with the Democracy.

Buckley's political acumen may have dictated the very course which resulted in his rapid progress. Clearly, remaining within the organization while both its numerical ranks and its leadership declined provided opportunities—"certainties," as Buckley put it—for the promotion of a budding career. Quite possibly, also, persistent reports of discord within the WPC suggested an early demise for that party and advantageous prospects for both Buckley and his organization. Whether conscious design or mere chance prompted his actions will probably never be known. But when the momentum of the Kearney movement began to subside late in 1879, no politically naive or reluctant Buckley—despite his protests to the contrary—participated in the reconstruction of his own party. It was, rather, a seasoned campaigner, the product of apprenticeships served under political masters in both parties, and a journeyman Democrat who had advanced his career by remaining loyal during a dismal and critical period. Not yet the boss in his own right, he was an experienced leader, prepared to participate vigorously in the impending combat with both opposition parties and contending elements within his own.

Neither contest was long in coming. Well before 1882, the traditionally accepted year of Buckley's ascendancy, new political opportunities began to present themselves, again occasionally from unforeseeable directions. Throughout 1879 and 1880, Buckley held office in both county and state Democratic organizations,[69] and he persistently capitalized upon fortuitous circumstances to enhance his status in the party. In May 1879, for example, when adoption of a new California constitution caused consternation over its implications for local politics and precipitated demands for special elections and a new city charter to comply with its still vaguely defined provisions,[70] Buckley turned the confusion to his own advantage.

On the basis of inside information—probably from among the very magistrates who would ultimately decide the question—he knew that no elections for state or local officials would be held in California in 1880, and intuitive judgment convinced him that the proposed city charter would fail at the polls in September. Therefore, he engineered a remarkably shrewd and politically profitable arrangement with Denis Kearney. In return for promised Democratic support for the Workingmen's state and municipal tickets, Kearney agreed to throw the weight of his organization behind Democratic presidential electors and congressional candidates. Although it subsequently became apparent that only federal elections would be held and that the city charter was doomed—as Buckley had anticipated in both cases—Kearney kept his bargain, thereby placing California's electoral vote in the Democratic column. Simultaneously, he maintained his activity on both county and state committees and in the Young Men's Democratic Club formed to support the County Committee in its jurisdictional dispute with currently organizing district clubs in the city. And as a member of the State Central Committee, Buckley assisted in the resolution of that controversy which centered upon methods of selecting San Francisco representatives to the state convention. Thus, even though the contest of 1880 meant little in terms of the party's fortunes, it had a special significance for Buckley and his career. As he later commented upon the events of the period:

> I am afraid I slipped one over on Dennis [*sic*] during the process of the negotiations. . . . Through the large Democratic majority in San Francisco the Hancock electors carried the state by a small margin, but without affecting the main result. . . . In one way or another, I was given credit for the compromise with Kearney, thus healing the deep wounds of the Democratic party. I was high in the councils of the reorganized Democracy. I was consulted on every particular of importance.[71]

Although many wounds remained yet unhealed, by the end of the year numerous Democratic defectors to the WPC were returning to the original fold, partially as a result of improving economic conditions and partially as a consequence of genuine disgust at the failures and excesses of the Kearney movement.[72] The reconversion of these prodigals, coupled with the anticipation of municipal elections to be held under the old law in 1881, raised the hopes and prospects of San Francisco Democratic leaders, including Buckley, and early in the spring optimistic and intensive preparation and reorganization began.

Despite its inability—or lack of opportunity—to score decisive victories in previous years, by late 1880 the Fritz-Buckley faction of the local party had successfully wrested control from the Mannix-Brady element and had gained both representation and recognition in the State Central Committee of the party. Persistence and Buckley's personal coup over Kearney undoubtedly constituted major elements in their success. Al Fritz had been elected chairman of the County Committee, his followers dominated that body, and he, Buckley, Fallon, Rainey, and their allies in the party hierarchy were confidently styling themselves the Yosemite Club. Like other Democrats, the Yosemites recognized the need to solidify their organization at its grassroots in order to win elections, and to that end they solicited proposals through George Hearst's *Daily Examiner* early in 1881.[73]

Of the numerous and varied responses, two submissions received the greatest attention and consideration. One of these suggested a return to the traditional organizational format involving a single Democratic club in each of the city's five state senatorial districts, each club with eight delegates to the County Committee. Opponents of this scheme argued that it smacked of elitism and that its limited scope would discourage many potentially active party workers, thereby perpetuating the problems of the organization. Numerous smaller clubs in each of San Francisco's voting precincts—resulting in a County Committee of 154 members—would, they argued, ultimately prove more effective and secure the desired purpose: a loyal and victorious Democratic majority. Sources of the two proposals remain obscure but opposition to the precinct plan surfaced immediately, and in the County Committee it emanated principally from Buckley and other representatives of his Tenth Senatorial District on the grounds that numerous clubs would prove unamenable to discipline and that a large County Committee would be unwieldy. To these arguments, Buckley's opponents responded that the real motivation for opposition involved the fact that the Tenth District would lose representation in the reapportionment that the precinct plan would necessitate. Whatever the merits of the arguments, on April 21, 1881 the County Committee voted in favor of the district proposal, and that formula became the basis for Democratic reorganization in the city.[74]

Although intraparty factionalism persisted during the spring, Democrats expeditiously implemented their newly-adopted organizational scheme and prepared for municipal elections in September, despite continuing doubts that the contest would be held at all. In each senatorial district, organizational meetings attracted substantial numbers of members and party rosters fattened, at least in comparison to their emaciated condition only a few months earlier. Encouraged by reports of growing support—as many as 300 members registered at the initial meetings of some clubs—the County Committee exercised its authority and set May 7 as the date for primary elections to select club representatives to a new Democratic governing body for San Francisco. Although the committee acted within its legitimate jurisdiction, in this case calling for primary elections may have been both precipitous and premature, despite the subsequent nomination and election of a majority of Yosemite adherents, Chris Buckley among them, to a reconstituted County Committee.[75]

Success proved to be a rather mixed blessing. To be sure, even Michel De Young's *Morning Chronicle* acknowledged the outcome of the May 7 "battle of the bosses" as a clear and final victory for the forces of Buckley and Fritz over those of Mannix and Brady.[76] Nevertheless, the primary contest precipitated open and active resistance in what had been a latent opposition. Indeed, less than one week after the County Committee accepted the district plan of party reorganization and on the very day that it announced the coming primary election, the Golden State Democratic Club—allegedly the remnant of the Mannix-Brady-Chivalry faction— appeared on the scene and proclaimed its opposition to the "present corrupt County Committee." The club lasted only until mid-June, but it predicted impending unfavorable developments.[77] For during the campaign of early May, every district—with the notable exception of Buckley's Tenth—nominated a slate of "anti-ring" County Committee candidates, and in many districts the contests proved sufficiently close and acrimonious to reveal serious disharmony within the ranks of a supposedly united Democracy.[78] Moreover, despite the Yosemite's sweep of the May 7 primary and Buckley's personal victory, hostility to their rule persisted within the party and would resurface not only during subsequent primary elections and at the municipal conventions but also throughout the general election campaign.

For Chris Buckley, however, the controversy constituted simply another experience of a journeyman preparing for mastery of his chosen profession in his adopted city.

4

The Making of a Boss: Mastery, 1881-1882

By 1881, Buckley had armed himself with the weapons essential to participation in the partisan strife on which he seemed to thrive and, when the occasion arose, to turn it to his advantage. Indeed, he was well on his way to fulfilling the particulars of a characterization of him set down by one of his most outspoken enemies nearly a decade later when Buckley was forty-four years old and at the peak of his power:

[A]ided by a sound and logical brain, he is no mean lawyer and can discuss decisions and quote authorities with the best of them. He rarely uses profane language and has acquired a suave and polished address, such as properly belongs to one of much travel and refinement. Always carefully dressed in the very extreme of fashion, with a lithe, erect person, he looks one full in the face with his large sightless orbs below his smooth and serene forehead, and seems to be all innocence and candor. He wears no beard, and his dark mustache covers a firm mouth, and [he has] a face beaming with intelligence. . . . He speaks with a perfectly distinct and pleasant intonation and in a low tone. . . . He is quite youthful in appearance, and looks in fact, as he goes along the street, arm in arm with his companion, like a quiet, gentlemanly swell of about thirty-five.[1]

Although the description was part of a scathing attack, it captures qualities which Buckley exhibited in both earlier and later years. To be sure, the dark mustache would turn to white and the lithe figure would become somewhat portly, yet the basic traits which he had acquired in his maturity would persist—and serve him well—throughout his life.

Perhaps as a result of submission to a physical regimen imposed by his companion Alex Greggains, Buckley always retained his erect posture and—despite several severe illnesses—his youthful appearance, and he also kept the qualities of character which rendered him a congenial companion. His enemies would be legion, but his friends outnumbered them and included social luminaries and prelates of the Roman Catholic Church to which he was always faithful, as well as the unfortunates who were the recipients of his open-handed charity. He remained devoted to his family: to his mother and father while they lived and to his wife and only child Christopher, Jr., born in 1893. Equally important, Buckley constantly cultivated his intellect, perhaps as an extension of habits acquired during his early years. As a youth, he had been entranced by the literary and theatrical personalities whom he encountered in San Francisco, and as a blind budding politico he had employed readers to keep him abreast of developments important to his career. In later years, he combined elements of the two experiences when he added history, literature, and the classics to his lectors' repertoires and even committed to memory long passages from the Bible, Homer, Shakespeare, Thucydides, and Gibbon. And despite his own inability to see, he was an enthusiastic traveler who took his family on excursions abroad so that his son could experience the world.[2]

Obviously, Chris Buckley did not conform to the stereotype of the crude, unlettered city boss which Thomas Nast and other nineteenth-century cartoonists portrayed for patrons of the yellow press, if such an archetypical specimen ever existed at all.[3] Still, in both background and personal characteristics he did resemble many of the municipal statesmen who were his contemporary counterparts in cities across the nation.[4] By the early 1880s, the experience of a decade and more had prepared him in every aspect of his chosen profession—and to Buckley and others like him, politics *was* a profession. He was ready to exercise his leadership

FAST IN THE FILTH OF THE PAST.

JURY BRIBING
SALES OF NOMINATIONS
POLITICAL FILTH
CORRUPTION OF PUBLIC OFFICIALS
R. Edgren.

This Unconvicted Felon Struggling to Escape From the Quagmire of His Own Crimes.

Journalistic portrayal of the Blind Boss.

not by means of reasoned political philosophy or rhetoric but by virtue of broad experience and the force of personality. Despite his reputation for cultivated and articulate speech, Buckley never addressed a political conclave larger than his own club or a county or state committee; instead, his leadership would be an intensely personal affair, based upon response to specific problems and situations and a reputation for commitment to his word rather than upon the exposition of metaphysical theories of government. Moreover, his intimacy with the city—acquired since the period when he guided an omnibus through its streets—permitted him to exercise that unique quality of the city boss which Robert Merton has called "a keen sociological intuition" and apply it to the needs of the masses and classes alike in order to organize the "scattered fragments of power" which typified metropolitan life and politics.[5]

Consequently, when yet another unforeseen event promoted Buckley several more ranks in the party hierarchy, he was equal to the occasion. On May 26, 1881, Al Fritz died in circumstances which bordered upon the bizarre. Despite his justified reputation as an affable raconteur, Fritz was the victim of a vice which he himself understood only too well. He enjoyed his bottle, a proclivity hardly unique among the saloon-based city politicos of his era. But when in his cups, he lost control of his usually congenial and even temperament and became uncontrollably violent and destructive. Because he recognized the implications of his malady—and because he was a physically powerful man capable of doing substantial damage—Fritz formed the habit of requiring his wife to shackle him hand and foot when he was drinking, using a restraint called an "Oregon Boot." On the evening of May 26, she performed her duty for an intoxicated Fritz and left the house. On her return, she discovered her husband dead in bed, strangled by one of his chains. After great public uproar—including rumors that Buckley might be involved in the affair—and a sensational inquest, a coroner's jury ruled Fritz's demise either accidental death or suicide.[6]

No evidence ever emerged to connect Buckley with the episode, and there is no reason to presume that he was involved. Nevertheless, he did profit from the death of his friend. With Fritz gone, the Yosemite faction and the Democratic party itself urgently required a leader. The aging Fallon and Murphy both lacked the essential vigor, Mannix and Brady had lost their following, and Rainey, although vigorous enough in his own way, possessed neither the diplomatic talent nor the organizational skill required. Therefore, the mantle of the deceased captain fell upon Buckley, to the satisfaction of some but the intense consternation of others.

Notwithstanding the hostile voices raised against him, Buckley apparently accepted his position willingly. Indeed, during the two weeks preceding Fritz's death, he had been increasingly active in both the old and the new Democratic County Committees, almost as if he anticipated his future status. Early in May, the committee appointed him as an emissary to urge the state supreme court to arrive at an expeditious decision on the question of municipal elections in San Francisco in 1881. Late in

1880, in an effort to achieve consistency with the Constitution of 1879, the state legislature had passed the Hartson Act. In effect, this statute amended San Francisco's charter once again by altering the terms of elected city officials and changing the dates of municipal elections. In May 1881, San Franciscans—including many city officials, private citizens, politicians, and "leading lawyers"—petitioned the high court to consider the law and to declare it unconstitutional, thereby paving the way for municipal elections in September according to provisions of the charter. Because it recognized Buckley's intimacy with the judges, the local party selected him to work for a swift and favorable decision. The actual extent of his influence is not known, but early in June the desired decision came forth; municipal elections would be held in September 1881 in San Francisco—but nowhere else in the state.[7]

The appeal to the court constituted Buckley's final act as an official of the old Democratic County Committee. In the meantime, he participated in the organization and launching of the new committee and in its preparations for the fall elections, despite allegations that he opposed the contest because it might displace numerous of the party faithful who held patronage positions in the city and county government.[8] The rumor is hardly credible, since few real Democrats held jobs under what was a preponderantly WPC municipal administration. Nor do Buckley's activities as a member of the new County Committee suggest that he was anything but eager for the election to occur. At the initial meeting of the committee, he secured the unanimous election of his nominee and Tenth District associate George Marye to the body's chairmanship, and he himself won a seat on the powerful Committee on Constitution, By-Laws, and Rules. At the next meeting, ironically on the very night that Al Fritz died, Buckley became the Tenth District delegate on the Executive Committee, the real decision-making agency of the county organization, and urged that body to make immediate and vigorous preparations for the impending campaign.[9] Thus, although he had been elected to an impoverished organization (a treasury balance of only $290 remained after the May primaries), Buckley apparently intended to make the new County Committee a vital agency for the advancement of the party's fortunes and his own.

When the state supreme court handed down its final decision on the fall election question on June 16, the Democracy seemed prepared and united for vigorous participation in the contest. Upon Chris Buckley's motion, the County Committee immediately voted to call yet another primary election, this one on June 30 for the purpose of selecting club delegates to a municipal nominating convention scheduled for July.[10]

Confidence of victory increased when, almost simultaneously, Yosemite Democrats joyfully marked the collapse of the sole apparent source of intraparty opposition. The Golden State Club—irreverently dubbed the "Tar Flat Club" in reference to the oozy swampland near a gas works south of Market Street—adjourned itself *sine die.* Jubilation died just as quickly, however, for within days organized dissent appeared from another direction. As it had in May, the call for a primary election seemed to stimulate resistance to the leadership of Buckley's faction of the party. Indeed, even before the primary announcement, rumors suggested intrigues to create an organized rivalry to supplant the obviously moribund Golden State Club. Less than a week later, rumor became reality when the Manhattan Club, formed by what the *Chronicle* called the "high-toned elements of the party," appeared in the field. Organizers and adherents included Dr. J. Campbell Shorb, financier James Phelan, mining magnate George Hearst, Judge Frank W. Lawler, attorney Joseph Rothschild, several former supporters of the Mannix-Brady contingent, a sprinkling of Chivalry Democrats, and elements of the Hancock Democrats of 1880. The announced purpose of the club involved a direct challenge to the "Yosemite-Fire Department faction," a clear reference to Buckley and Rainey. Originally constituted by dissidents in the Thirteenth District, the Manhattan Club quickly gathered momentum throughout the city and nominated convention delegates in every district, including Buckley's own Tenth where selections included Shorb, Rothschild, and William McCann, an anti-Buckley rival for leadership of the Young Men's Democratic Club of 1880 and an aspirant to the office of sheriff.[11]

No definitive policy or philosophy explains Manhattan unity, with the sole exceptions of opposition to the Yosemite faction—especially Buckley—and a desire to control the party. Nor is the assertion that it consisted solely of "high-toned" Democrats entirely valid. To be sure, the club did include elite members of the professional and commercial classes, but many of its adherents also had ties to the rough and tumble elements of the South-of-Market push. There were also independent idealists like Shorb and political opportunists like McCann and perhaps Hearst. In addition, several Manhattanites—including Rothschild and Hearst—would subsequently ally themselves with Buckley, while others like Phelan would not only remain persistent in their opposition to him but also bequeath their hostility to a subsequent generation.[12] Nevertheless, their apparent diversity did not prevent the Manhattan faction from nominating convention delegates throughout the city and maintaining sufficient cohesion to make the primary contest an interesting affair, particularly with the discovery of counterfeit Manhattan tickets complete with the club's emblem—a portrait of General Winfield S. Hancock— and a full slate of Yosemite candidates.[13]

It is possible that Buckley had something to do with the bogus ballots; he candidly admitted his willingness to employ such tactics when the occasion demanded.[14] In this case, however, the ploy was probably superfluous, for the Manhattan Club had attracted few supporters outside party officialdom, and even then it remained a minority faction. When the dust from the disorderly June 30 contest had settled and its outcome had been assessed, it became clear that the Yosemite Club had retained control of the party organization. Buckley candidates, "Regular" Democrats, had won overwhelming victories in every district, including the Manhattan stronghold in the Thirteenth. Indeed, so decisive was the triumph that for the first time a local newspaper, De Young's *Chronicle,* somewhat prematurely proclaimed Chris Buckley the unqualified boss of the San Francisco Democracy.[15]

Still, the contest was not over, and the party's most severe trials remained in the future. Immediately after the primary results were known, Rothschild, Shorb, and other Manhattan leaders met to formulate official protests against the election and resolved to hold a separate municipal convention if necessary. Their objections, formally presented to both the County Committee and the State Central Committee, revolved around two major points: the authority of the Yosemite faction to call a primary election in the first place and the conduct of the election itself. Both, according to the protest, involved fraud. It is hardly surprising that, on Buckley's motion, the County Committee rejected the Manhattan demurrer and resolved to proceed with the organization of a municipal convention. Compromise proposals attempted to resolve the dispute, but the dissident leaders refused to settle for anything less than equal representation in the convention, despite the verdict of the polls.[16] Thus, confusion and contention continued to rend the party, a multitude of candidates whose names filled two full columns of a local journal vied for the sanction of each side, and two separate Democratic municipal conventions—auguring a divided and probably defeated party in the September election—met in San Francisco in 1881. And even though a new boss had emerged, at least in the opinion of one editor, the local Democracy remained splintered and in dubious condition for political combat.

When Democrats gathered in mid-July—the Yosemite regulars in Mercantile Library Hall and the Manhattan insurgents in Platt's Hall a few blocks away—each group proceeded with the business of organization, writing platforms, and nominating candidates as if the other assemblage did not exist. Neither Buckley nor his cohorts made any apparent effort to heal the breach, confidently rejecting an eleventh-hour Manhattan appeal for equal representation in a single convention and on the forthcoming Democratic ticket. Indeed, the Yosemites afforded a more cordial reception to a proposal from the Workingmen's Party, concurrently holding its own convention in a last-ditch effort to retain something of its former influence in the city, and agreed to nominate common Democratic-WPC candidates for auditor, sheriff, tax collector, treasurer, two members of the board of supervisors, and two school directors. This bargain, to which the Yosemite convention agreed, ultimately would present a major impediment to party unity. But in the meantime, two Democratic conventions continued to conduct their business independently and in an atmosphere of hostility, each disparaging the efforts of the other and both providing substantial fodder for the wits and wags writing for San Francisco's Republican journals.[17]

By the end of the month, when no settlement evolved, the Democratic State Central Committee began to find the spectacle in San Francisco something less than amusing. A rift in party ranks in the city, which contributed forty percent of the state's legislative delegation and an even greater proportion of its Democratic voters, portended serious future problems. Therefore, the secretary of the state organization, William D. English of Alameda County, dispatched a letter to both conventions suggesting a conference and threatening direct intervention should the dispute remain unresolved. In response, the Yosemite meeting immediately appointed a conference delegation—which included

Buckley—to meet with representatives of the state party and the County Committee—which also included Buckley. At Platt's Hall, however, the reaction differed sharply. On Joseph Rothschild's motion, the Manhattan convention voted to table the state committee's communique without action, and when the proposed conference met at the end of July, compromise proved impossible. No representatives of the dissident faction appeared and the meeting dissolved. To this development, the state committee responded with a threat to dismiss both conventions, invalidate their nominations, and appoint an entirely new assembly to replace them. This caveat—along with growing realization that neither official recognition nor victory at the polls was likely under existing circumstances—apparently had sufficient impact upon Shorb, Rothschild, and other Manhattan leaders to prompt the selection of a conference committee and an agreement to meet with representatives of the Yosemite convention and the state and county committees.[18]

It was principally the state party hierarchy—not Buckley—which initiated moves toward tentative rapprochement in the summer of 1881. Indeed, the Blind Boss had been something of an obstructionist in the matter, suggesting that he may have overestimated his authority and that the *Chronicle's* assessment of his status was premature. Subsequent developments tend to reinforce that analysis. When a joint conference finally met on August 2, all parties confronted each other: Yosemites, Manhattans, and delegates from the state and county committees. As a representative for his faction, Buckley proposed the creation of a joint convention with proportional representation based upon the results of the June 30 primaries, a scheme which would give the Yosemites 125 delegates and the Manhattans 75. Although state and county committee members, perhaps reflecting Buckley's growing influence, favored this solution, Rothschild countered with a proposal for equal representation and when it was unfavorably received, the Manhattan delegation angrily departed from the meeting. Once again the situation remained unresolved, and the Manhattans' behavior triggered immediate reactions in the city, including charges that Republican "sack" motivated their intransigence and suggestions that an independent Democratic movement be organized to hold yet a third convention.[19]

Simultaneously, fresh warnings emanated from the State Central Committee, this time in the form of threatened disciplinary action against the uncooperative elements, clearly implying the Manhattan Club and precipitating dissent within that faction. As it became increasingly apparent that state officials favored the Yosemite position, Manhattanites began to waver in their commitment. Nevertheless, as both conventions continued with the business of nominating candidates, leaders of the dissident group remained insistent upon equal representation in a compromise convention and increased their demands to include twenty-five additional delegates to be appointed by the state committee and total abrogation of the Yosemite agreement with the WPC. Continued intransigence precipitated a joint ultimatum from the state and county committees; failing the immediate assembly of a compromise convention, both the Yosemite and Manhattan meetings would be dissolved and new primary elections would be called. Apparently, this final threat struck responsive nerves in leaders of both factions, for at an August 12 conference with all parties in attendance, a settlement finally emerged. The Yosemites conceded equal Manhattan representation in the convention, the Manhattans relinquished their demands for additional delegates and the negation of the commitment to the WPC, and the first meeting of the new conclave was set for the following night.[20]

Precisely what had encouraged the obviously self-defeating intractability of both sides of the issues never came to light, and when the joint convention assembled in Mercantile Library Hall on August 13 and during the following week proceeded with the business of formulating a platform and nominating candidates, conflicts of the previous months seemed resolved.[21] Despite Buckley's apparently obstructionist posture that summer, his influence in unraveling the tangle may have been more substantial than is immediately obvious. Several state and county representatives on the various peacemaking committees—including William D. English and John H. Wise—were or soon would be his political affiliates. Moreover, Buckley was a political realist, and he must have known that continued intraparty strife would result in certain disaster in the general elections. Still, the episode made it plain that in 1881 he had not yet achieved the status that would ultimately be his. Although Buckley exercised substantial influence in the party, it was not sufficient to permit him to whip dissidents into line, overcome discord, or weld a unified Democracy in San Francisco.

Still, there were significant lessons to be learned from the conflict, for both Buckley and his party. Factionalist delays retarded the nomination process until just weeks before the September 7 elections with the result that many qualified individuals declined to run as eleventh-hour candidates, mediocre nominees won the majority of places on the ticket, and the platform devised under the pressures of time and expediency consisted of a patchwork of compromises paying lip-service to traditional formulas: Chinese exclusion, lower taxes, better schools and municipal services, and party regularity. And the subsequent canvass, an apathetic affair which interested less than half of the city's voters, culminated as Buckley unquestionably anticipated it would, despite his expressions of optimism as he and other party leaders awaited the outcome in the Alhambra Saloon. He would later summarize the whole affair accurately and succinctly: "the [municipal] convention degenerated into an ignoble scramble, named a shaky ticket, and was harshly and properly criticized for its work. It was disastrously defeated at the polls."[22]

The Blind Boss, of course, must bear a substantial portion of the responsibility for the persistent factionalism which prevented all but four Democrats—two of them joint WPC nominees—from winning office. But the Republican *Chronicle* termed the result a conquest over bossism in all parties and "a triumph of law, order, and decency." The Democratic *Examiner,* on the other hand, called it a victory for the Spring Valley Water Company and other similar interests. In reality, as Buckley probably knew, the local Democracy had precipitated its own disaster during the summer of 1881, a fact which prompted his departure for southern California and his temporary renunciation of both politics and its practitioners.[23]

City and state party leaders, however, elected a different course. While Buckley spent his vacation "rusticating in the southland," San Francisco Democrats ruminated on the lessons of 1881 and previous years and commenced an intensive effort to discover means to prevent recurrent debacles. Within weeks of the September election, the County Committee, still chaired and dominated by Buckley's associates, once again began consideration of several schemes to reorganize, revitalize, and unify the party in anticipation of yet another potential municipal election in November 1882. The contemplated arrangement included one, submitted in response to the committee's published solicitations, which owed a significant debt not only to the rejected precinct plan of the previous April but also to the organizational principles of Denis Kearney's Workingmen's Party in the city. According to the anonymous proposal, the city should be partitioned into numerous neighborhood units even smaller than precincts with a partisan club established in each. Moreover, social functions should be grafted onto the primarily political purposes of the clubs in order to broaden the base of appeal to the urban working classes and encourage their participation, much as the WPC had done only a few years earlier.[24]

Although the concept elicited substantial favorable response in the County Committee, agreement remained elusive during November and December. Therefore, the local organization, in concert with the State Central Committee, opted for the creation of an independent body charged with responsibility for examining the status of the San Francisco party, reviewing various means to reestablish its strength, and recommending an organizational system which would avert a repetition of the events of 1877 through 1881. Obviously, California Democrats had reason for concern about the condition of their party, but many also believed that they had substantial reason for optimism about its future in the state. The Chinese question, for example, had long been agitated by Californians and by their representatives in Washington. By the 1880s, the issue had generated extensive local resentment toward federal interference with state laws regulating the activities of Orientals and presumed Republican recalcitrance toward a national restriction law which a Democratic majority passed late in 1881, only to have it nullified early in 1882 by President Chester A. Arthur. In the state, response to both events was entirely predictable: jubilation at congressional action and outrage at the Republican president's veto. Simultaneously, growing antagonism toward the monopolistic status and seemingly arbitrary policies of the "octopus"—the Central Pacific Railroad and its subsidiaries—and dissatisfaction with ineffective efforts to regulate its activities furnished a second aggravated issue upon which California Democrats could attack their enemies. In addition, the hydraulic mining question, growing municipal debt, enforcement of the state's Sunday-closing law, and suspected corruption in the management of city affairs raised the level of discontent. And rightly or wrongly, many residents of the city and the state placed responsibility for failure to resolve such nagging questions squarely upon Republican shoulders.[25]

Thus, conditions in California created a sense of urgency among Democrats, especially to revitalize the party in San Francisco, its traditional source of strength, and to accomplish the task prior to the fall elections. Political realities and the necessity for expedient action undoubtedly dictated the course which the party followed. In December 1881, local and state leaders agreed to create an independent Committee of Fifty on Reorganization with twenty-five of its members to be appointed by the County Committee and twenty-five by the State Central Committee. In order to ensure objectivity, no one affiliated with either appointing body would be allowed to serve, and once the Committee of Fifty had completed its work the current county leadership would be required to resign, thereby obviating the potential for another fiasco such as those which previous power struggles had produced. With remarkable dispatch, probably motivated equally by memories of previous defeats and anticipation of impending victories, San Francisco Democrats agreed to the proposal and by the end of the year the assemblage of the "ablest and best intended men" which played such an important role in Chris Buckley's career became a functioning reality.[26]

If the Blind Boss participated directly in the formulation of the reorganization scheme, the record does not show it. Moreover, when he described the committee in his memoirs in 1918, time and perhaps a failing memory apparently impaired his recollection of specifics. Instead of fifty, Buckley recalled forty members appointed equally by state and local leaders. In addition, his chronicle refers to Frank McCoppin, mayor of San Francisco from 1867 to 1869, as chairman of the body and the individual who solicited his participation in devising and implementing the reorganization plan. Actually, McCoppin served as a vice-president of the main committee and as a member of the Subcommittee on Plans. Attorney Thomas B. Bishop presided over the Committee of Fifty, and journalist William P. Frost headed the thirteen-member subcommittee, a body which Buckley recalled as consisting of just four.[27]

Despite such discrepancies of detail, however, the boss's description of the committee, its composition, and its purpose is essentially accurate.

The assertion that it consisted of the ablest men in California is, of course, open to serious challenge. But a survey of individual members tends to validate Buckley's suggestion that the group represented something of an elite; of the forty-four committee members who can be identified positively, no fewer that thirty-three were directly involved in San Francisco's business and professional community. Of these, eleven attorneys contributed the most substantial single block of representation; they were joined by a physician, a journalist, and twenty businessmen of various pursuits. The remainder of the committee included four minor public officials (all holders of patronage positions), three private policemen or watchmen, and one skilled and three semiskilled workmen. All districts of the city received recognition on the committee, but—as might be expected—working class neighborhoods such as those south of Market Street contributed disproportionately few members. The political experience or philosophy of individual participants is somewhat more difficult to discover or summarize. The group included political veterans, men with substantial careers yet ahead of them, and others who would disappear from the public arena once the charge to the Committee of Fifty had been fulfilled. Adherents of Buckley's Yosemite Club faction outnumbered Manhattanites by a small margin, but representatives also came from other elements of the party: Chivalry Democrats and former Unionists, traditional regulars, returnees from WPC defections, and independents whose previous partisan activity had been limited or even nonexistent.[28]

On January 9, 1882, when the mixed lot that comprised the Committee of Fifty convened in party headquarters at 632 Commercial Street and commenced its deliberations, it constituted a reasonably representative body, at least of party leadership although not necessarily of the population of the city itself. During the first month of its existence, the committee added a democratic dimension to its proceedings by soliciting proposals from the populace at large and found itself inundated by a variety of schemes including a recommendation to return to traditional district organization, an anonymous proposal to array the party in quasi-military companies, and numerous others suggesting the creation of from 5 to 154 Democratic clubs in the city. In response to this flood, the committee created its Subcommittee on Plans—composed of a cross-section of the party—to review all proposals and submit its recommendation to the parent body, in effect making the smaller group responsible for reorganizing the local Democracy.[29]

Contemporary San Franciscans apparently understood the nature of the party's dilemma and the Committee of Fifty's purpose quite clearly; indeed, reorganization efforts even inspired at least one advertisement, a suggestion to Democrats that smoking Duke of Durham pipe tobacco would soothe tensions and ease deliberations.[30] But little additional evidence remains to record the committee's activities from early February until mid-March of 1882 or to substantiate Buckley's claim that he acted as its chief adviser.[31] It is entirely possible that he did, for no fewer than six of the thirteen members of the Subcommittee on Plans, including chairman William P. Frost, had prior ties to the Blind Boss in the Young Men's Democratic Club of 1880 or the Yosemite Club of 1881. Through these individuals Buckley well may have exercised considerable influence, and circumstances strongly suggest that possibility. When the subcommittee submitted its report on March 23, Frost introduced, defended, and received credit for authorship of the majority proposal, a reorganization scheme based on 47 clubs and the very system that Buckley subsequently claimed as his own.[32] Substantially identical except for its provision for 27 clubs, the minority report had no apparent connection to the Blind Boss. Moreover, following a brief debate on the merits of the two proposals and on methods for verifying potential club members' residence, Buckley's old crony John C. Murphy—present at the Committee of Fifty meeting as another member's proxy—moved the adoption of the majority plan. Although the committee disallowed Murphy's proxy and all others and adjourned without specific action, less than one week later the 47-club plan received the committee's official endorsement.[33]

Even that eventuality, however, does little to clarify Buckley's precise involvement in the procedure. On March 28, when the Committee of Fifty assembled to cast its final vote, it found itself confronted by yet another proposal, one advocating 154 clubs as more "democratic" and impervious to control by bosses. Since this third suggestion elicited little positive response and the 27-club system seemed inequitable to many districts, the Committee of Fifty accepted the majority report by a vote of twenty-two to eleven and recommended its adoption by the County

Committee, an action which clouds rather than clarifies Buckley's role. At least four adherents of his Yosemite faction opposed the committee's final decision, leaving the strength of his actual part in Democratic reorganization in 1882 somewhat enigmatic.[34] To be sure, circumstances tend to support the assertions of authorship made in his memoirs which are substantially candid and accurate in other respects and no one, either at the time or subsequently, challenged his claim. Nevertheless, opposition from within his own faction of the party suggests a hand in the matter somewhat less firm than he later recalled.

Whatever the case, Buckley described the reorganizational scheme, which the County Committee did approve on his motion on April 3, as simplicity itself. It would "portion off the city into forty-seven districts and organize Democratic clubs in each. Every Democrat in the district [would be] eligible to membership and each club entitled to elect a pro rata number of delegates to both state and municipal conventions."[35] In reality, the scheme involved much more and required twenty-eight pages of elaboration in the party's official pamphlet.

The authors of the organizational system—whether Buckley, the Subcommittee on Plans, or a combination of both—left little to chance and exercised care to preclude the jealousies and intraparty strife which had undermined cohesiveness in previous years. Careful designation of boundaries of the forty-seven precincts—based upon the city's eighteen Assembly Districts rather than its five Senatorial Districts—ensured an approximately equal potential membership of between five and seven hundred.[36] Similarly, detailed requirements made gaining membership substantially more difficult than Buckley's brief summary suggested. To be eligible, a voter had to inscribe his name on a club roster in open meeting, provide evidence of registration and residence in the appropriate district, and renounce membership in all other political associations.[37] A temporary examining committee in each club (appointed by the county organization until clubs elected their own) undertook responsibility for verifying the eligibility of prospective members and posting rosters of those accepted in order to facilitate the hearing of grievances and appeals against committee decisions.[38] After a ten-day period to permit enrollment and authentication of applicants' qualifications, each club was to meet on the specified day (May 5, 1882) to conduct the business of organization and to elect its permanent officers: president,

PLAN

FOR THE

Reorganization ⚡ of the ⚡ Democracy

— of —

THE CITY AND COUNTY OF SAN FRANCISCO

ADOPTED BY

THE COMMITTEE OF FIFTY

AND APPROVED BY THE

Democratic State Central and County Committees,

April 6, 1882.

Donovan & Shahan, Printers. 521 Clay St S F

Title page of the 1882 Democratic Party Reorganization Plan attributed to Buckley.

vice-president, secretary, treasurer, two sergeants-at-arms, and an examining committee.[39]

The plan also specified policies for primary elections—still called by the County Committee—and the various delegates and officials to be chosen, principally County Committee members, representatives to municipal, state, and legislative nominating conventions, and election officers for each club's precincts.[40] Finally, the organizational plan outlined general procedures, specified biweekly meetings, proscribed individuals from belonging to more than one club or attending more than one convention in any year, and left the drawing of by-laws and the initiation of local activities to the individual units.[41]

After the plan was accepted in early April, local Democrats directed their efforts toward launching their new system of organization. On Buckley's motion, the County Committee named two delegates from each Senatorial District—including the Blind Boss from the Tenth—to consult with the Committee of Fifty and expedite implementation of the club plan. Appointment of temporary club presidents, reservation of halls, setting times for organizational meetings, and publicizing boundaries and other information followed in rapid succession. By mid-month, the party had completed its preparations and scheduled initial club meetings for April 20. Simultaneously, the Yosemite and Manhattan Clubs disbanded with appropriate mutual compliments and praise for renewed party harmony.[42] Democrats' energy and dispatch reaped rich rewards almost immediately, for the first meetings of the neighborhood clubs added over 5000 names to party rosters, and the total continued to grow. Buckley himself took an active part in the proceedings as a member of the County Committee, as a temporary official of his own Club Number Nine, and in other aspects of "the preliminary work, which was like marshalling an army, involving the employment of trained assistants, engaging halls, bonfires and brass bands, [and which] required much time and some money." By the end of April, the County Committee expressed its satisfaction and pronounced the San Francisco Democracy ready for permanent organizational meetings. And with that event early in May, state party leadership granted its imprimatur to the revitalized local party and the *Examiner's* editor enthused that "victory is assured in the coming election."[43]

More than successful reorganization contributed to Democratic optimism in the spring of 1882. President Arthur's veto of the Chinese exclusion bill prompted anti-Republican protests ranging from denunciations in the local press to mass gatherings of thousands of San Franciscans. Enforcement of state Sunday-closing laws resulted in police sweeps which gathered in numerous substantial citizens, including historian-publisher Hubert Howe Bancroft, and inspired vigorous and vociferous negative response. Anti-railroad elements agitated the monopoly issue by persistent waving of California's version of the bloody shirt, the "Mussel Slough Tragedy" of 1880, and hints of scandal, extravagance, and corruption heightened dissatisfaction with the current city administration. Thus, when news arrived in San Francisco—on the same day as word of Arthur's veto—that a majority of the state high court had agreed that local elections would be held in California in 1882, lines for the impending contest had already been sharply drawn.[44]

The subsequent series of campaigns—which the San Francisco Democracy conducted through its newly-created clubs—involved precisely these issues. In May, organizational and recruiting activities accelerated in preparation for the state convention scheduled for June 20 in San Jose, and even though Club Number Nine did not place Buckley among its delegates in the June 2 primary, he nevertheless exercised significant influence in the convention's deliberations and decisions and further established himself as a leader in the state party organization.[45] Within the city, the club system continued to function so efficiently that by mid-June local Republicans determined to emulate it in order to resolve their own intraparty difficulties. Since early in the year, a "listless harmony" had disguised rampant factionalism in Republican ranks, originating in the Eighth Ward Club and spreading throughout the city. To combat the schism, the party's county committee moved toward reorganization with a program resembling the Democrats' but with significantly less success. So limited, indeed, was the positive effect that the Republican primary election in August inspired only 7211 voters to register a choice for municipal convention delegates, and in September two Republican conventions—dubbed the "bluffers" and the "duffers" by the local press—precipitated a spectacle reminiscent of their opponents' fiasco of the previous year.[46]

Meanwhile, the Democratic organization continued to flourish, gathering strength in numbers, unity, and efficiency and adding new dimensions to the clubs' functions. Buckley's contribution to the process included organizing and campaigning behind the scenes and publicly heading the County Committee's Naturalization Bureau which assisted immigrants with the problems of acquiring citizenship and guided new voters into appropriate neighborhood Democratic clubs. With its budget of between four and five thousand dollars—a far cry from the $290 pittance which constituted the party's entire treasury in 1881—the bureau unquestionably added substantial numbers to club rosters. And when September brought primary elections to select delegates to the coming municipal convention, despite a residual of factionalism apparently related principally to the gubernatorial campaign, the San Francisco Democracy had evolved into a highly organized and potent force recalling something of its stature in the days before the WPC.[47] Moreover, although Buckley maintained a low public profile during the summer of 1882—and throughout most of his subsequent career—he managed to build upon the influence which he had already acquired and to enhance his status in the party. Indeed, even before the primary elections two additional journals, perhaps more realistically at this point, proclaimed him the boss of the local organization.[48]

Thus, when the municipal convention assembled early in October, it provided a sharp contrast to the anarchy of 1881 for both Buckley and his party. Conflict existed, to be sure, and the Blind Boss found himself embroiled in a dispute over his very presence. Since his club had not chosen him a delegate, he attended the convention on a proxy. He had been involved in a similar fashion at the San Jose state convention in June, and thus he and several others were in violation of the Committee of Fifty's rule against participation in more than one party convention in a given year. Buckley, however, resolved the problem adroitly; he volunteered to relinquish his vote while retaining his seat—and therefore his influence—in the convention. This maneuver, in conjuction with the election of Buckleyite Edward B. Stonehill to the convention chairmanship and Buckley's own reelection to the County Committee, inspired De Young's *Chronicle* to once again assert that "Buckley Is Boss."[49]

Subsequent developments at the convention not only substantiate De Young's proclamation but also further demonstrate Buckley's shrewd ability to compromise and conciliate when the necessity arose and the opportunity demanded. If he did control the local party—and at this point there is little to suggest that he did not—he managed it with remarkable discretion and tact. When, for example, he guided Stonehill, a former Confederate officer, to the powerful position of convention chairman, he not only enhanced his own influence but also mollified remnants of the old Chivalry faction who supported the mayoral aspirations of John H. Wise. Washington Bartlett—variously described as an inveterate Buckley "lamb" and as the ticket's concession to respectability—received the nomination, but Wise had already garnered recognition of another sort, elevation to the chairmanship of the State Central Committee. Buckley also carefully balanced the roster of convention officials with his own followers and former opponents and with representatives of the wide variety of nationality and interest groups in San Francisco. The composition of the municipal ticket itself likewise reflected the Blind Boss's determination to concede and pacify in order to weld the party together for its own future benefit and, of course, his own. It included a former Manhattanite and antagonist from the Young Men's Democratic Club, William McCann, as candidate for sheriff, representatives of virtually all factions of the party as nominees for other offices, and even one Republican infiltrator supplied by Bill Higgins. Similarly, although the 1882 platform did not consist solely of concessions to expediency, it did reflect a shrewd assessment of precisely those issues most likely to attract a majority of San Francisco voters: clear opposition to continuing Chinese immigration and to the Sunday-closing law, demands for regulation of municipal transportation and utility interests and for material reductions in their rates, and promises of improved municipal services, reduced taxes, and the application of the "dollar limit" to local property levies.[50]

Results of the ensuing brief, vigorous, and occasionally disorderly canvass testify not only to Buckley's sense of politics and the city and to the effectiveness of his party's reorganization, but also to the futility of journalistic appeals to "good" Democrats to reject the "saloon-keeper's ticket." More of the city's voters (38,756 out of 42,072 registered) cast ballots than at any time since 1877, and they gave the Democracy a sweep not only of every municipal office, the first for either party since 1867, but also of virtually the entire San Francisco delegation to the state legislature. Rather ironically, the sole exceptions—a state senator and an assemblyman—occurred in Buckley's home district. Still, it is clear that by the culmination of the 1882 elections, the Blind Boss had "erected his own political machine on the ruins of the city [Democratic] party."[51]

By the fall of 1882, Chris Buckley had attained the status that would be his for at least the remainder of the decade; he was clearly the boss of the San Francisco Democracy and an increasingly important factor in the councils of the state party. Quite obviously, however, neither the victory of that year nor the club plan assured his rise to preeminence and power or the perpetuation of his position. Both, to be sure, played major roles; the successful sweep of the November elections and the preceding primaries testified to his political judgment and to the skill of his leadership, and the club system—whatever Buckley's part in its formulation —made the success possible. But during the 1882 struggles, the Blind Boss also established policies which would serve him well throughout the remainder of the decade. Despite disparagement by journalists, the slates presented by the Buckley organization were not composed of party hacks and incompetents but rather of members of the middle echelons of the business community, individuals of sufficient talent and respectability to appeal to voters throughout the city. Tickets also were persistently cosmopolitan, including nominees whose surnames identified them with politically potent Irish, German, French, Jewish, and Italian communities. The machine regularly accrued its most substantial pluralities in regions of the city populated disproportionately by the working classes, immigrants, and single males, confirming the effectiveness of the neighborhood clubs. But it also won with substantial consistency in wards and districts which provided homes for the affluent, attesting to the skill with which Buckley constructed tickets and platforms which appealed to the broadest possible cross-section of San Franciscans.[52]

Thus, no individual contest or organizational scheme guaranteed either the emergence or sustained hegemony of a boss. Nor could changes in the city, an obsolescent and confused city charter, or even the the unregulated practice of partisan politics. Critical considerations also involved Buckley himself and the cumulative experience of two decades which prepared him to capitalize upon circumstances and convert opportunities into certainties. In politics, the apprenticeship with Higgins, the journeyman years with Fallon and Fritz, and even the Vallejo experience all contributed to the mastery of his chosen profession and to a steady climb through the ranks of the party hierarchy following his return to the city in 1873.[53] Whether a calculated tactic or not, Buckley's decision to remain within the party fold during the debacle of the late 1870s—when defection to the WPC well may have seemed the more advantageous course—served to enhance his reputation among his peers and also placed him in a favorable position when opportunities for advancement arose. He had acquired the requisite skills and experience to capitalize upon such fortuities as the unexpected windfall from Craig, the death of Fritz, the compromise with Kearney, the collapse of the WPC, and intraparty factionalism in order to further his own career and the cause of his party. Indeed, as Buckley clearly recognized, the Democracy's future and his own were inextricably intertwined after 1873, and despite his handicap he worked energetically and assiduously for both, not just in 1882 and after but also throughout the previous decade.

In similar fashion, Buckley's experiences of twenty years in the city provided a foundation for the successful fusion of politics with the realities of urban life, especially through the medium of the clubs. Traditional issues such as taxation, utility regulation, and civic improvement—especially important to the urban elite, including those who had made Buckley an "uncrowned king"—remained integral features of the party program throughout the decade. But the Blind Boss also understood the more pragmatic day-to-day concerns of the masses of voters: lower streetcar fares, housing, employment, Chinese competition, and especially the increasing anonymity of life in the industrial metropolis. Therefore, he steered the clubs on a course which the Committee of Fifty had not charted and probably had not intended. Taking a page from the book of Denis Kearney and the WPC and responding to conditions which precipitated numerous other forms of associational activity, Buckley made the Democratic clubs responsive to considerations beyond pure partisanship. They became social institutions through which members and their families could participate in outings, "clam bakes, bull-head breakfasts and the like, [which] followed each other in perpetual succession." They provided recognition and status with offices so numerous that "it was an unlucky member who could not boast that he held down some kind of official station." Each unit also functioned as

94

"an employment agency on the most wholesale scale possible," supplying patronage jobs on the city payroll or positions in the firms of congenial supporters of the party. Thus, by providing these and other services unavailable through alternate agencies in the city, the clubs made political participation more than a mere abstraction or philosophical expression; it became a real and intimate facet of existence in urban society.[54]

This is not to say, of course, that the principal purpose of the clubs—or of Buckley himself, for that matter—remained anything but partisan. Nevertheless, the extrapolitical functions of the neighborhood associations—underwritten in various forms by more affluent party contributors—provided the cement which bound the city organization together, especially where those who provided the bulk of the party's votes were concerned. This aspect of the clubs' activity explains the regularity with which Democrats cast their votes in both primary and general elections in the early 1880s, and it may also elaborate Republican failures when they emulated only the mechanics of the club scheme in 1882 and subsequent years. But more than anything else, the expansion of the clubs' role in the city underscores Buckley's intuition and his ability to respond to the "dynamite of [San Francisco which] was composed of one part vigor and one part unsatisfied passion."[55] On the basis of consummate skill, personality, experience, and above all familiarity with the city, the Blind Boss overcame his own handicap and built a power base which would sustain him for a decade, or at least until the city changed again, perhaps in ways which Buckley did not thoroughly understand.

CHAPTER

5

Continuity
and Change in
the 1880s

The economic, demographic, so-
cial, and cultural patterns which characterized San Francisco urban development and influenced political life—including Chris Buckley's
career—in the 1880s remained essentially extensions and reinforcements
of those defined during the previous decade. After the economic disaster
of the middle and later 1870s, brisk recovery charted a sporadic but
generally upward course. Manufacturing activity continued to gain
momentum, with iron and brass foundries, machine shops, toolmakers,
breweries, and tobacco processors adding both quantity and variety to
the city's industrial output. Producers responding to the demands of new
technology, especially as it was applied to transportation and utilities,
showed the most substantial overall growth, but other activities—like
the shipbuilding firm which in 1888 launched the cruiser *Charleston,* the
first heavy warship built on the Pacific Coast—registered impressive
gains throughout the decade, as San Francisco advanced to rank ninth
among the nation's cities in both population and industrial output.

Simultaneously, despite a radical decline in the volume of precious metals flowing through the city and an erratic pattern of expansion and contraction, commercial activity also enjoyed a vigorous and prosperous resurgence. Barley joined wheat and other commodities to replace the almost vanished mining stocks on the boards of the city's brokerages and exchanges and stimulated new processing and shipping ventures. Along the waterfront and in the railroad yards, the volume of goods transported increased with each successive year, and banks and other financial institutions recorded annual increases in loans, deposits, credit exchanges, mortgages, and transactions of all sorts. The banks' best customers included real estate developers and builders who, responding to a reviving economy and a growing population, suffered through occasional dull years to reap substantial profits throughout the 1880s.[1]

Commensurate with a revitalized economic climate, labor enjoyed more favorable conditions than in the previous decade. Employers continued their stolid resistance to the principle of organization and ignored demands for remedies to hazardous working conditions, and the labor shortages of the 1860s disappeared as the population of the city increased. Still, wages in California—and especially in the city—surpassed those in the East by twenty-five to fifty percent, and local leaders raised the number of trade unions in the city from eighteen in 1878 to forty-five by 1883.[2] Under the guidance of Burnett Haskell, Sigmund Danielwicz, Charles W. Pope, and others hostile to the stridence of Denis Kearney and the Workingmen's party, representatives of local trades in 1878 formed the San Francisco Federated Trades Assembly (later the San Francisco Federated Trades Council and currently the San Francisco Labor Council) which during the presidency of Frank Roney in the 1880s influenced the creation of the state Bureau of Labor Statistics, supported strikes for higher wages and the right to organize and against continued employment of convict labor and the Chinese.[3] Labor's perennial anti-Oriental agitation did not disappear in the 1880s, despite enactment of the Exclusion Act of 1882; it simply took different forms and became more closely attuned to the ebb and flow of the general economy. Between 1880 and 1882, nearly 60,000 Chinese entered the state, and in just ninety days before federal restrictions took effect, 15,769 sojourners arrived. To combat the new wave of potential competitors, early in 1882 Roney organized the League of Deliverance which

North on Powell Street toward the Golden Gate.
Panoramic view from Nob Hill in the 1860s
(this and next four illustrations).
Later development brought slightly more order but no less congestion to
San Francisco.

adopted boycotts of Chinese-made goods and firms which employed the
Chinese or sold their products and campaigns for the use of white-labor
labels, especially in the cigar industry, as its principal weapons. Although such activities did reduce Chinese employment substantially, the
League began to disintegrate with the enforcement of the Exclusion Act
and with the growing recognition that those whom boycotts most ad-
versely affected were not merchants and employers but rather working-
class families forced by their own poverty to utilize Chinese services and
goods in the name of economy.[4]

Even without the League of Deliverance, however, anti-Oriental agitation continued throughout the 1880s, especially among unskilled and
previously unorganized workers. It remained an issue which permeated
local politics and it would be one of the shoals upon which efforts to
unite San Francisco labor would ultimately founder. Not content with

Powell and Sacramento Streets with Telegraph Hill in the background.

simple exclusion, Roney and other trade unionists demanded Chinese expulsion by force if necessary, a position which brought them into conflict with more radical and politically-oriented laborites like cooperationist Haskell and socialist Danielwicz and shattered the ideological harmony which had prevailed for the first half of the decade. The clash of policies resulted in the formation in 1885 of the San Francisco Federated Trades Council (Frank Roney, president), an organization dedicated to the pure and simple trade unionism of Samuel Gompers and the nascent American Federation of Labor.[5] In addition to differences concerning the Chinese, several less tangible factors undermined labor unity in the city in the 1880s and 1890s, especially employers' vigorous opposition to organization, the erratic nature of economic cycles, competition with the political activism and "one big union" philosophy of the Knights of Labor and similar organizations, diminished public sympathy following the Haymarket bombing in Chicago in 1886, and perhaps most significantly, the exclusion from the labor movement of the masses of unskilled workers who flooded the city, contributed to its steady growth, and taxed the capacity of its institutions.

Looking due east with Old Saint Mary's Church (center) and Grace Cathedral (right) visible on California Street.

Although the rate of population increase diminished during the 1880s, San Francisco continued to expand. U.S. Bureau of the Census tabulations enumerated just under 150,000 residents in 1870, nearly 234,000 in 1880, and almost 300,000 in 1890, and the augmented citizenry made novel, persistent, and frequently urgent demands upon municipal services. The basic composition and origins of the enlarged population remained generally consistent with established traditions, as they would for the balance of the century. Like other transitional urban societies, San Francisco provided a home for a disproportionate number of males, many of them transient and unmarried members of a growing unskilled labor pool. At two men for every woman during the 1880s and seven to five in the 1890s, the ratio more closely approximated the norm than did the eleven to one of the 1850s and 1860s, but it remained a significant factor which contributed to the persistent rawness of life in the city and perhaps to the uninhibited style of its politics. Sources of

Southeast corner of Powell and California Streets.

the throngs of single men shifted somewhat during the later decades of the century; they came less frequently from the mining districts and more often from the fields of California and other states. But the origins of the general migration to the city remained principally what they had been. With the exceptions of an increase in Italian immigrants, a slightly enlarged black community, and the brief upsurge in arrivals from China early in 1882, new foreign-born San Franciscans in the 1880s arrived from European countries which traditionally had contributed to the population and rendered it highly cosmopolitan. Throughout the decade, the proportion of residents born in other countries hovered at approximately forty percent, and of those born in the United States, one third counted at least one immigrant parent.[6]

The variety of the city's populace undoubtedly contributed to the uniqueness of its cultural life, but already perceptible changes occurring both outside San Francisco and within its boundaries also had significant implications for both physical developments and political affairs. Rail-

South on Powell Street toward Union Square (center).

road rate wars—especially after completion of the Atchison, Topeka and Santa Fe line to California in 1885—dramatically lowered fares from St. Louis and Kansas City and precipitated an influx of thousands of midwestern "Pullman immigrants." These newcomers, frequently Republicans who settled in the southern counties of the states, began to challenge established political traditions. In the 1880s, twenty-five percent of all Californians still lived in usually Democratic San Francisco, and with skillful gerrymandering and astute log-rolling, the city on occasion could control up to forty percent of the state legislature. By the middle of the decade, however, even though Lord James Bryce could still assert that "California . . . is a country by itself, and San Francisco a capital," changing immigration patterns had already begun to undermine the hegemony of both the city and the Democracy, and the transition would have important implications for both Chris Buckley and his career.[7]

Of even greater and more immediate significance for both the man and his city were internal developments resulting from the increasing population. More and more people pressed into a physically restricted space, escalating land values in older urban districts and forcing residents to seek shelter beyond the exceedingly congested original regions of settlement. Debauched Rincon Hill, formerly the haven of the city's elite, languished as a crowded and unsavory tenement and factory district where little other than Kate Wiggin's free kindergarten, the Sailors' Home (formerly the Marine Hospital), and St. Mary's Hospital relieved pervasive drabness and desperation. Despite repeated campaigns to level the mound and relocate its residents in 1906, 1913, and 1921, the area would remain essentially unchanged until the completion of the Bay Bridge in 1937 finished what John Middleton's cut had begun seventy years before. In the meantime, the surrounding region south of Market Street, described by Rudyard Kipling in 1889 as a "hopeless maze of small wooden houses, dust, street refuse, and children who play with empty kerosene tins," became increasingly congested, inhospitable, and, for many, uninhabitable.[8]

From such districts, those who were able fled, leaving former residences to be divided and subdivided as apartments or razed and replaced by additional tenements and factories. The first departees included the wealthy who migrated to more congenial neighborhoods, first along Stockton Street near the center city, then westward to Van Ness Avenue, and then to the Western Addition where Chris Buckley would join them in 1883. Following the establishment of the first cable car line, the truly rich began to occupy the heights of the city, and after the opening of Leland Stanford's California Street line in 1878, they ascended to the very pinnacle of Nob Hill where the silver kings and railroad barons and those who moved in their rarefied circles built their splendid mansions. Other members of the urban aristocracy sequestered themselves in the Palace, the Baldwin, the Occidental, and similar luxury hotels or in the suburbs. Meanwhile, the increasing congestion south of Market Street and adjacent to Telegraph Hill forced upwardly mobile members of the working classes to desert those regions and move farther south and west, frequently into the recently vacated homes of the city's middle classes. And for those middle classes, newer homes in areas even farther to the west beckoned as developers opened regions near the Pacific shore and surrounding Golden Gate Park to residential settlement.[9]

The city's inhabited area thus doubled during the 1880s, and once under way the process of dispersal would continue until San Franciscans occupied every acre of ground within the confines of the metropolis. Kipling had commented that "one-fourth of [San Francisco] is ground recovered from the sea. . . . The remainder is ragged, unthrifty sand hills, pegged down by houses," but land speculators had quickly and profitably converted even the unthrifty portions to uses ranging from residences and parks to factories and a variety of commercial establishments.[10] In the process, they helped to spread the population to every corner of the city and to situate urbanites of all classes in locales increasingly remote from the economic and social centers of their lives. A reciprocity between technology and necessity not only made the dispersal possible and isolated San Franciscans from one another but also precipitated a clamor for public transportation which would become one of the major themes of municipal politics in the decade. Transit capitalists and their political agents responded to the cry with alacrity and keen foresight. Boss Martin Kelly observed that in order to circumvent stringent restrictions embodied in the new state constitution of 1879, every street railway firm operating in San Francisco petitioned the board of supervisors for a new fifty-year franchise. All were granted, along with permits to open new routes on previously unoccupied streets. In that single year, the city issued twenty-six new permits and extensions to astute businessmen, among them Leland Stanford and his associates whose 1879 licenses would provide the basis for the Market Street Railway system and, ultimately, for the United Railroads of San Francisco. Even though public opposition to the hazards of overhead electric trolley wires would exclude that mode of transportation from downtown regions until 1891, in its New Year's Day edition of 1884, the *Chronicle* could boast that no resident of the city lived more than three blocks from one of the street railway lines which carried over 40,000 passengers daily.[11]

Street railways—not to mention other urban amenities such as water supplies, sanitation, and lighting—not only altered the character of the city but also became highly significant adjuncts of the lives of all San Franciscans in the 1880s and, consequently, major issues in municipal politics. Various elements of the working classes—especially after former mayor Frank McCoppin steered five-cent fare legislation through the state legislature in 1878—relied upon the cars for essential transportation between homes and work and for occasional excursions to Woodward's Gardens in the Mission District, Golden Gate Park on the city's western fringe, and other amusement centers.[12] To the more affluent San Franciscan, they were equally necessary for movement about the metropolis, since even the carriages of the very wealthy could negotiate many of the city's hills only under optimum conditions. At the same time, however, the transit systems had the paradoxical consequence of reinforcing even more rigidly the metropolitan separatism already evident in the 1870s. Because street railways obviated the necessity for residence in proximity to all centers of urban activity, patterns of land use developed along lines even more specialized than those established earlier, neighborhoods became more closely identified with the socioeconomic level of their inhabitants, and traditional contacts among various elements of urban society became less frequent or essential. The streetcars themselves, places of work, and a few equally transitory associations remained, but the frequent intimate contacts characteristic of life in the walking city diminished. In San Francisco, mechanized transportation did not produce the demographer's classic pattern of an impoverished core surrounded by rings of increasing affluence; instead, it resulted in pockets of specialized land use dispersed across hills and valleys and distinct neighborhoods which included the churches and other institutions serving their limited groups of residents. In that setting, intimate exchanges less often crossed the informal but rigid boundaries which separated citizens, and the boss, the partisan system, and the precinct clubs replaced more traditional institutions as avenues of political communication. As a result, also, the varied elements in urban society tended to develop independently of one another in late nineteenth-century San Francisco.

For more aristocratic residents of the city in the 1880s, the process involved an obvious and self-conscious emulation of European and Atlantic seaboard society, and their eagerness to imitate, to the delight and amusement of disparaging eastern critics, periodically resulted in the acceptance and adulation of bogus nobility.[13] Indeed, wealthy San Franciscans seemed entranced by titles and other concomitants of status; they married their daughters to barons, earls, and the sons of eastern tycoons, built mansions which rivaled the splendor of Park Avenue and the Côte d'Azur, and organized balls and cotillions supervised by imported dancing masters. At regular soirees at the Palace, Baldwin, and Oriental Hotels and adjoining theaters and Nob Hill ballrooms, the cream of society coquetted and cavorted in splendid isolation from the remainder of the city. Young ladies of fashion adopted the Parisian decolletage—much to the consternation of local editors and clergymen and the delight of their escorts and observers—and their beaux arrayed themselves in the kid gloves, Oxonian haberdashery, and flowing cravats popularized by Oscar Wilde and the international set.[14] During nightly promenades along Market and Kearny Streets, which had replaced Montgomery as *the* place to be seen, and in carriages in Golden Gate Park, *the* Sunday drive in the 1880s, the city's fashionable hummed and whistled airs from Gilbert and Sullivan instead of the popular "One Fish-Ball" of a previous generation and led Kipling to conclude that "San Francisco is a mad city—inhabited for the most part by perfectly insane people whose women are of a remarkable beauty."[15]

The extravagances which inspired Kipling's commentary did not confine themselves solely to the rarefied strata of the Nob Hill aristocracy. When, for example, Judge William T. Wallace, described as one of the "Apollo [Hall] beaux" of the 1850s, married his daughter to the son of industrialist Peter Donahue in 1884, no fewer than 700 "elegantly attired ladies and gentlemen" attended the ceremony at St. Mary's Cathedral and a reception in the judge's Van Ness Avenue home.[16] Nor was display the sole characteristic of San Francisco's society. While some of the city's elite disported themselves in a lavish manner, many of their peers expressed a concern for different aspects of urban life. Some involved themselves in spiritual matters, flocking to revival meetings conducted by visiting evangelists Dwight L. Moody and Ira D. Sankey and to the sessions of resident mediums, spiritualists, phrenologists, and other assorted fakirs. Society women formed associations such as the Laurel Hall Club which challenged the exclusionism of the city's all-male social associations, inspired a host of similar women's groups, and collaborated with them to support Donaldina Cameron's Chinatown mission and numerous social betterment enterprises. In a more secular effort, San Franciscans concerned with health and the fact that nearly half of the city's practitioners had never attended medical school had, by the 1880s, sponsored two training facilities for doctors: Cooper Medical College and the Toland School of Medicine, later respectively affiliated with Stanford University and the University of California. The community, moreover, had produced in the person of Richard Beverly "King" Cole (former Vigilance Committee doctor and president of the Toland School) a physician of sufficient stature to become president of the American Medical Association.[17]

During the same period, although the city was no longer the Bohemian haven it had been in the 1860s, the cultural level of San Francisco attained sufficient stature to attract numerous dignitaries and representatives of the arts to visit or to perform before large and consistently appreciative audiences. Lord James Bryce, Rudyard Kipling, and Oscar Wilde—whom San Franciscans initially adored but quickly dismissed as a dandified and insufferably boring fop—came principally as observers, while Julia Ward Howe arrived as both a tourist and an advocate of the feminist cause.[18] Bryce, Kipling, Wilde, and other luminaries including Edwin Booth, Charles Dickens, Jr., Anthony Trollope, James Anthony Froude, and the returning prodigal Mark Twain were feted lavishly at the exclusively male Bohemian Club and with their female counterparts including Howe, Sarah Bernhardt, Adelina Patti, Lily Langtry, and members of the Booth and Barrymore families, in the homes of the city's elite. They also lectured and performed for audiences who, like many in the audience at Patti's 1884 performance in *Traviata,* willingly paid inflated scalpers' prices for their tickets.[19] In addition to performing artists, the city also regularly hosted royalty ranging from Queen Victoria's liberated daughter Princess Louise to the family of Hawaiian King Kalakaua who died in the Palace Hotel during his final visit in 1891, and it produced at least one literary luminary and periodically served as a second home to another. Poet Robert Frost was born in San Francisco in 1874, the son of Harvard-educated William Prescott Frost, editor of the *Evening Bulletin,* collaborator with Henry George on the *Post,* and before his death of tuberculosis in 1885, member of the Democratic Committee of Fifty and political ally of Christopher Buckley. Robert Louis Stevenson in 1880 lived at a Bush Street address in the neighborhood of Buckley's saloon, married an Oakland widow and moved to Calistoga, and returned to the city in 1888 to establish temporary residence in the Occidental Hotel. Later, with his stepson San Francisco printer Samuel Lloyd Osbourne, he coauthored the novel which gave the Blind Boss a place in popular fiction.[20]

Demographic, economic, social, and cultural developments, however, provide only a partial profile of life in the city during the 1880s. Although Rudyard Kipling believed that the nightly Market Street promenades involved a cross-section of the urban populace and that the splendid regalia worn leveled "all distinctions of rank as impartially as the grave," San Francisco society was never as democratic as he assumed. To be sure, the working classes of the California city were more favorably endowed with opportunities for pleasure and sociability than were their counterparts elsewhere, but many among them, especially the unskilled about whom the promenading elite knew little and whose contacts with many of the positive aspects of urban life were minimal, remained virtually invisible and voiceless in the affairs of the community, struggled to preserve marginal existences, and frequently turned to their partisan organizations for redress. An isolated black community of a few thousand, under the guidance of editor Phillip Alexander Bell and other leaders, expended substantial energy to retain a semblance of dignity and cohesiveness through their churches and benevolent associations. At the very lowest level of the socioeconomic scale, the secluded Chinese, constantly harassed by restrictive laws, hostile workingmen, and youthful hoodlums, depended upon the inconsistently effective influence of their Six Companies and their own traditions to maintain their limited status.[21] And beneath the city's veneer of gentility—substantial at some points but easily penetrable at others—remained a residual core of frontier violence, aggressiveness, and lack of inhibition which permeated all levels of society.

Almost daily, detailed scenarios of assault, mayhem, and murder—not only along the waterfront and in Chinatown and the Barbary Coast but also in more respectable sectors of the city—competed for headlines and the attention of avid readers with the revelations of the Hill-Sharon and Colton-Huntington trials.[22] In the seamier districts, crimps routinely abducted and robbed seamen and unsuspecting visitors, toughs molested unwary passersby, and vicious brawls punctuated by the thud of the slung shot erupted upon the most innocuous provocation or none at all. Even more dignified citizens settled differences with weapons, but not necessarily according to provisions of the gentlemanly *duello*. In 1884, for example, Adolph Spreckels avenged slurs against his shipping and sugar magnate father by storming into Michel De Young's Chronicle Building offices and, in a scene reminiscent of the 1880 shooting of Charles De Young, pumping two bullets into the publisher's plump body. De Young would recover and Spreckels would be acquitted after a spirited defense by society lawyer Hall McAllister, but the episode did little to alter an atmosphere of violence in which San Franciscans— including politicians—were frequent targets.[23]

Martin Kelly recalled that during the 1888 primaries, a disgruntled partisan named Billy Harrington (in Buckley's employ, according to Republican leaders) entered party headquarters in quest of Boss Higgins. Not finding his intended target, he fired at those present, killed two men, and wounded Kelly:

He bored me through before you could say Jack Robinson. . . . At the first perforation I had enough and started to run. Harrington took careful aim and I would have been his meat had not a man . . . knocked down his pistol. Even then he scored a singular hit. As I raised my foot in running, the ball struck the thick sole of my shoe and lodged on the under side of my big toe.[24]

Chris Buckley himself somewhat laconically recorded a similarly dramatic but substantially less painful experience in his own saloon:

Once a party for whom I had been unable to find a job snapped a pistol in my face as I was sitting in a chair. I might have taken more interest in the affair at the moment had I been aware of what was going on. All I knew [then] was that someone was dragged, without much ceremony, from the room.

Obviously, neither local politics nor San Francisco life in general in the 1880s were branches of the "Sunday School business."[25]

Nor were many forms of urban entertainment which recalled the climate of the not too distant frontier era. During the period, San Franciscans of all social classes could find their pleasure in an increasing number of respectable resorts, including theaters, opera houses, libraries, and the expanding Golden Gate Park. But they also habituated the some 2000 saloons (one for every 117 residents) and the scores of dance halls and bawdy houses which dotted the city. The working classes patronized establishments where drinks were cheap and of dubious quality and the atmosphere less than decorous, while more affluent citizens resorted to more elegant and expensive—but not necessarily more respectable— establishments, including French restaurants like Maison Riche, Marchand's, the Poodle Dog, and the Pup, which dispensed the finest foods and wines. And like other pleasures of the flesh, prostitution penetrated all strata of society. From the cribs of Chinatown and the cowyards and dives of the Barbary Coast, which served the city's unattached and transient males, to the more luxurious and discreet upper floors of the French restaurants and parlor houses of the downtown Tenderloin, both of which catered to businessmen, politicians, and even the scions of the Nob Hill aristocracy, the world's oldest profession flourished by the Golden Gate in the 1880s.[26]

Thus, during Buckley's first real decade of power, San Francisco remained a transitional city characterized by contrasts, at once united and divided and moving toward sophistication and modern metropolitanism while retaining many of the raw edges inherent in its origins. And like the city itself, the Democratic machine which dominated the municipal campaign of 1882 also embodied a host of contradictions. It represented an amalgam of old and new, a mixture of political tools and techniques inherited from the Mannix-Brady-Fritz era and the Workingmen's Party fused with responses, devised by Buckley and the Committee of Fifty, to the currently prevailing conditions which affected every sector of society. The machine's emergence also constituted a uniquely local phenomenon which typified a multitude of similar developments occurring in cities across the United States. To explain this nationwide coincidence of events and the seemingly alien political forms and practices which evolved from them, contemporary observers and subsequent scholars have posited a plethora of hypotheses: the presumed avarice and ignorance of increasingly foreign (especially Irish) city populations, the rapacity and amorality of politicos and their supporters, the political apathy of the urban public and its preoccupation with material gain, the inherent evil of cities and their residents, the need for the kinds of services which only the machines could deliver, the rigidity and obsolescence of municipal governments, and the absence of adequate means of communication and interaction in the industrial metropolis, to name but a few.[27] All of these analyses—including even the polemics of nativist, quasi-Spencerian, and neoagrarianist theoreticians—have significance for comprehending the political realignments taking place not only in San Francisco but also throughout the country. No single factor, however, suffices to answer the complex question: Why did bosses like Buckley and their machines thrive in late nineteenth-century American cities? And no explanation is complete without reference to the relationship between municipal politics and the process of urbanization itself.

As already observed, San Francisco and other centers changed profoundly in the decades between 1850 and 1890. Remaining vestiges of the familiar walking city vanished, and their disappearance prompted Stanford University sociologist Edward A. Ross to complain that "the *community,* undermined by the stream of change, has caved in, carrying with it part of the foundations of order" which included the system of face-to-face contacts upon which the polity of the city had been premised, the similarly intimate underpinnings of the economic life of the community, and the relative simplicity and homogeneity of urban society.[28] By 1880—sooner in some settings and later in others—cities like San Francisco were composed of increasingly diverse, isolated, often antagonistic, and frequently overlapping communities within the larger community, each defining the metropolis in terms of its own special interests and competing for recognition in the municipality. A more rigidly stratified and heterogenous society had emerged, more intricate patterns of social and economic organization had evolved, technological innovation had transformed the urban landscape, and many of the qualities which would identify the twentieth-century city already had appeared.

Municipal governments, however, changed little and persisted in the attempt to resolve the most urgent and unprecedented problems of urban life on the basis of the thought and practice of previous generations, despite the dramatic transformation of cities. This is not to say that governments endured wholly unaltered; they did become larger and more complex. Novel conditions laminated layer upon layer of jurisdiction upon existing structures, obviating the assignment of responsibility and adding to the confusion of city management. Philosophies and functions remained essentially what they historically had been, and that circumstance precipitated a "search for order" which included a quest for means to resolve the frequent conflicts and contradictions inherent in day-to-day metropolitan existence.[29] Bosses and their machines—and indeed the progressive reformers who supplanted them—were an integral part of the search; each provided transitional political structures devised to span the chasm between old and new urban realities.[30] To perform that task, political organizations—whether the bosses' or the reformers'—required power, especially over the potent municipal legislative agencies which relegated city executives to virtual figurehead status. For the machines, access to power emanated partially from the largely immigrant working classes who provided the all-important votes and partially from members of the cities' business communities who contributed the equally essential dollars.

Immigrant residents—majorities of the populations of many major cities—did cast their ballots for the bosses' candidates, but not as a consequence of innate perversity and ignorance as many contemporary observers contended. Working-class immigrants as well as their native-born counterparts acted upon their own version of the concept of "enlightened self-interest" propounded by William Graham Sumner (he would not have appreciated the analogy) when they supported machines in exchange for essential services otherwise unavailable in cities which isolated them physically and politically. Benevolent societies, church associations, and other private charitable organizations did exist in San Francisco and elsewhere, along with public workhouses, orphanages, county hospitals, and occasional work-relief programs.[31] Never adequate and traditionally premised upon preurban assumptions of individual or family self-sufficiency, they were quickly overwhelmed and relegated to atavistic futility by the process of growth and change, and the bosses and their machines stepped into the breach—not altogether altruistically— to establish rudimentary relief programs for many members of the marginal urban working classes.

Affiliation with the political machine might entail, as had joining the Workingmen's Party and agencies such as volunteer fire companies, little more than an opportunity for the sociability and camaraderie involved in membership in a recognized association. But it could also secure more fundamental services which neither reluctant municipalities nor overburdened private organizations could provide: temporary housing for a burned out family, rent money when eviction threatened, cash for medical expenses, food and fuel to tide families over hard times, a neighborhood bath house to alleviate at least a portion of the dinginess of tenement life, and even a few scholarships for promising youngsters. The organization also acted as an employment agency, securing jobs for the scores of citizens perennially unemployed or underemployed. Most were patronage positions on the municipal payroll, made available by elected officials—superintendents of schools and streets, supervisors, sheriffs, tax collectors, county clerks, and the like—in exchange for machine support for their nominations and candidacies, but others were positions in the establishments of local businessmen, furnished in return for the bosses' services to them. In addition, representatives of the partisan organization guided immigrants through the labyrinth which led to citizenship, acted as personal ombudsmen when the exigencies of unfamiliar laws threatened, provided an intermediary with authorities in requests for business permits or other concessions, and generally maintained lines of communication with municipal government. Perhaps of greatest significance to many intensely religious and proud immigrant families, the machines could finance a church wedding for a daughter or ensure a decent burial in sanctified ground for a deceased parent, without injuring the dignity of recipients of their largesse.[32]

Although bosses themselves made occasional and not wholly symbolic appearances at christenings, weddings, and wakes, they were unable to respond personally to every plea for assistance. Instead, corps of trusted subalterns in each precinct of each ward not only kept their neighborhoods organized and got out the vote on election days but also helped their constituents to circumvent frequently impossible, usually demeaning, and always protracted appeals to private charities or city hall. In Buckley's organization, officers of the forty-seven clubs and a contingent of hand-picked representatives—"mostly active young men prominent in the ward or district where they were probably born," not disinterested bureaucrats or amateur social workers bent on identifying the deserving poor—responded to a variety of appeals.[33] In the process of performing their duties in the neighborhoods, lieutenants secured for the organization and for the Blind Boss himself a substantial body of loyal followers who premised their political behavior upon their interests, not their ignorance. At the same time, the bosses' agents acquired for themselves a modicum of status among their peers, the potential for promotion within the ranks of the party hierarchy, and perhaps even appointment to a city position or nomination for elective office. There were, of course, prices to be exacted for the machines' beneficences to members of the urban working classes, but they were nominal and quite willingly rendered: consistent support and a vote (or votes) at primary and general elections and assessments upon the salaries of those holding patronage positions or municipal office.

For other beneficiaries of the organization, costs were somewhat higher and more tangible, but still not excessive in view of possible compensations. Neither Buckley nor any other city boss could long survive on loyalty alone; their operations required substantial sums of money to provide the jobs and other services which ensured the fealty of their followers, to reward the arduous effort and not inconsequential investment of time which establishing and maintaining political control required, and especially to finance the partisan structure and election campaigns which ultimately determined the success or failure of the machine. In Buckley's San Francisco, success involved nominating and electing a host of city officials. A bare minimum "Solid Seven" on the twelve-member board of supervisors could introduce and enact desired ordinances and franchises and a cooperative mayor could sign them into law, but a "Solid Nine" supervisors was mandatory insurance against the vetoes of recalcitrant municipal executives. In addition, majorities of the school directors and of the numerous city and county departmental officials were essential adjuncts to the control of municipal government. Finally, only a substantial number of the city's state legislative contingent could protect municipal (and partisan) interests in Sacramento.[34] Successfully placing such an extensive roster of candidates in office required a substantial monetary investment, and members of the urban business community provided the necessary financial backing in the form of fees for services rendered or anticipated.

A broad range of business opportunities proliferated in the expansive atmosphere of San Francisco and other nineteenth-century American cities and involved a profit potential which made political contributions a sound proposition. Utility and transportation companies, building contractors, suppliers of goods and services essential to the conduct of municipal affairs, real estate speculators, saloon and hotel keepers, and merchants in general could anticipate significant rewards based upon responses to the growing needs of expanding urban populations. But they also required an economic climate more stable and predictable than the chaotic and highly individualistic conditions characteristic of most cities and, in many cases, favorable treatment at the hands of municipal authorities. In an earlier period, personal appeals to civic officials—such as William Ralston's effort to promote public support for his private ventures—had been possible. As governments became bloated and more complex and simultaneously fell under the exclusive dominance of powerful political organizations, new conditions rendered direct approaches less feasible and made the boss's function as a broker virtually essential,

especially in cities like San Francisco where increasingly complex municipal jurisdictions and contradictory provisions of the Consolidation Act
rendered mandatory annual renegotiations of utility rates and privileges
highly unpredictable affairs.[35] Moreover, with new and potentially competitive enterprises—especially water, lighting, and transportation
schemes—appearing in rapid succession, the boss's intervention became
an indispensable antidote to possibly ruinous rivalries.[36]

For other firms aspiring to a portion of the municipality's trade, the
boss also had services to offer; he could expedite the award of contracts
for the construction and repair of schools and other public buildings, for
the opening and improvement of streets, for books and official stationery, for printing and publishing, and for the multitude of services and
supplies essential to the functioning of the city. And for large and small
entrepreneurs of all sorts, the organization and its representatives could
perform critical functions: reducing property assessments, deferring taxes
and other debts to the city, influencing action (or inaction) on applica-
tions for business licenses, assuring tolerant treatment in cases of litigation, and many more.[37]

Throughout most of the 1880s, Buckley managed to maintain control
of city government and relations with the city's business sector in a
tenuous balance, and for his part in organizing the political economy of
San Francisco he demanded and received substantial compensations, a
fact which he never denied. Indeed, in his memoirs he commented with
candor and apparent pride, "I placed a stiff value on my services and
always rated myself as a high-priced man."[38] Just how high his price
might rise is illustrated by the allegation that on one occasion a consortium of Spring Valley Water Company and California Electric Company
executives paid Buckley $25,000 for himself in addition to between
$7000 and $10,000 for each supervisor who voted in favor of their
franchise renewal requests for a single year.[39] If even approximately
accurate—and holdings in the Blind Boss's estate suggest that the sum
is at least plausible—the amount involved infers several things, most
obviously that both municipal utilities and the profession of politics
were lucrative propositions in nineteenth-century San Francisco, despite
Buckley's lament that "the entire race of bosses died poor."[40] It implies,
in addition, the absence of satisfactory alternative means for entrepreneurs
to attain their ends, just or otherwise, under the aegis of confused and

archaic systems of municipal government and illustrates the bosses' real value to the economic life of their cities. It also reveals that, despite contemporary economists' panegyrics to the virtues of laissez faire policies, urban businessmen themselves opted, albeit reluctantly, to pay dearly for the privilege of operating in a regulated and noncompetitive environment.

The scale of the utility interests' contributions in particular prompted Martin Kelly to comment that the bosses "milked the corporations to some extent" and to muse, "Would that I had them by the windpipe again."[41] No hard evidence, however, indicates that Kelly, Buckley, or any other San Francisco politico conducted his affairs on a scale even remotely comparable to the depredations of William Marcy Tweed's infamous New York City ring; not even investigations related to the conviction of Boss Abraham Ruef early in the twentieth century revealed anything approaching the scope of the Tammany chieftain's courthouse swindle.[42] Nor could Buckley or the city officials with whom he shared fees enrich themselves by retaining more than a fraction of their compensations. Indeed, like others in his position, Buckley quite probably diverted profits from private business to provide the lubricant which kept the cogs of the machine revolving smoothly.

Whether the Blind Boss in the 1880s had any source of personal income other than the Alhambra Saloon is not a matter of record. It is nevertheless logical to assume that, like his counterparts in other cities, he frequently acted upon inside information to make shrewd investments in land along future street railway routes and adjacent to proposed municipal building sites and engaged in other ventures of the sort which George Washington Plunkitt of Tammany Hall defined as "honest graft" and Buckley himself termed "certainties."[43] It is likely, moreover, that a portion of his profits was reinvested in the Democratic organization as subsidies for the machine's services to the working classes and in the maintenance of his own image as a boss which required that, on occasion, he

swagger into a saloon, slap down twenty dollars, call up the house, and tell the barkeeper to freeze onto the change. He must call a hack when he would rather walk. He must submit to the tonsorial art twice a [week]. He must lose a hundred dollars in a faro bank now and then. He must dispense the cold bottle and hot bird in higher social intercourse. He must never forget his lowly retainers, for whom he must find jobs, kiss their babies and send them Christmas presents. In other words, it was his duty to be in close touch with all strata of the social system.

Most of all, as a figure constantly in the public eye, the boss was forced, even at considerable expense, to "not only be great but seem great."[44]

Consistent success required that the city boss perform a Bismarckian juggling act, maintaining a set of interacting and not infrequently contradictory considerations—the demands of the working classes and the business community, the necessity to win elections, and his own and the party's fiscal needs—simultaneously aloft and in motion. For Buckley, therefore, victories at the polls during the 1880s represented not culminations which assured a comfortable, relaxed, and secure career in San Francisco politics but rather only a sequence of beginnings. The duration of his hegemony would remain highly speculative and dependent upon his continuing ability to retain a consistently reliable partisan organization at the popular level, to provide essential services to a variety of elements in the urban population, and to respond appropriately to the increasing complexities of a constantly changing city. It would depend also upon the reliability of the candidates whom he selected and supported for municipal office, a consideration which, in his first victory in 1882, especially involved Washington Bartlett, a fifty-eight-year-old bachelor and the Buckley ticket's alleged concession to respectability.

When Bartlett assumed office on January 8, 1883, both he and the organization which had engineered his victory had reason to anticipate a highly successful administration, despite a nearly bankrupt city treasury and the ominous snows and gales which ushered in the San Francisco New Year. In the tumultuous canvass of the previous November, voters had given him their approval by a nearly 2000-vote margin over his opponent, Republican incumbent Maurice C. Blake. Even more significantly, perhaps, twice the number of participants in the 1881 election had cast ballots, carried a full slate of Democrats into office, and provided the first sweep for any party in more than fifteen years.[45] Although Bartlett had been charged with weakness, inexperience, and even senility during the campaign—perhaps as a consequence of his innate shyness, limited oratorical ability, and inherently Whiggish political principles—he was neither reluctant to accept the challenge of public office nor unfamiliar with the social, economic, or political development of the city.

Washington Bartlett, mayor of San Francisco (1883–1887) and governor of California (1887).

Born in Georgia in 1824, Bartlett arrived in San Francisco in 1849, after an apprenticeship in journalism served under his father. He established three daily newspapers in the city—each destroyed by fire during the 1850s—and affiliated himself for a time with the *Daily Alta California*. He also published what may have been the first book in English printed in the state, Felix Wierzbicki's *California as It Is and as It Might Be*. During the 1860s, however, Bartlett abandoned the press, participated in the founding of an early savings and loan association, studied and gained admission to the bar, and practiced law with his brother Columbus in San Francisco and Oakland. In the following decade, he also involved himself in a variety of business ventures, including real estate speculation on both sides of the bay, and remained active in civic life. By the time he ascended to the office of mayor, Bartlett had been president of the Society of Pioneers, a member of the Vigilance Committee of 1856, a successful People's Party candidate for county clerk in three separate elections, a state harbor commissioner in 1871, a state senator from 1873 to 1877, and a member of the Board of Freeholders selected in 1880 to draft a revised city charter. And after two terms as mayor, he would in 1886 become governor of California.[46]

Still, in 1883 Bartlett remained something of a political enigma, as did many—if not most—of the supervisors and other city officials elected with him. Despite assessments by De Young's always hostile *Chronicle* and those of some historians,[47] the Democratic nominees did not comprise a mere collection of political hacks, mediocrities, or perennial office seekers who required Bartlett's presence on the ticket to establish respectability. Indeed, even the solidly Republican and staunchly conservative Frederick Marriott, publisher of the *San Francisco News Letter and California Advertiser,* found the slate commendable and, for the most part, worthy of voters' support.[48] To be sure, as the *Chronicle* and other opposition organs frequently and vociferously observed, a disproportionate number of Gaelic surnames—about thirty percent in contrast to a roughly twenty percent representation in the population at large—occupied positions on the Democratic ballot. But their presence did not constitute evidence of an Irish-dominated "Tammany Hall West" which did not in fact exist; no national group in the city enjoyed sufficient cohesiveness to control the fortunes of either local party. Nor were the candidates a collection of ignorant saloonkeepers, roustabouts, or ruffians from the south of Market Street push, as contemporary journalists contended. Instead, the Buckley nominations of 1882 and after—like the Committee of Fifty with which several of the candidates had been affiliated—consisted primarily of members of the middle echelons of the local business and professional communities, few of whom had previously sought or held public office, and they comprised an essentially balanced slate which confirmed the acuity of Buckley's personal and political judgment.[49]

The new board of supervisors included three self-styled capitalists, three real estate agents, three businessmen, a boat builder, the proprietor of a saloon on Market Street near the new city hall, and—somewhat incongruously for a municipal official—a livestock breeder. Similar backgrounds characterized the twelve individuals chosen to guide the fortunes of the city educational system: four attorneys, three physicians, three businessmen, a journalist, and a salesman.[50] All of the judicial officers elected during the 1882 campaign were practicing attorneys, some affiliated with major law firms in the city and some with already established reputations on the bench. The remainder of the list of victorious candidates entailed a somewhat less illustrious cross-section of San Francisco society but still consisted of something other than the cohort of opportunists so frequently associated with the tickets of municipal machines. The roster included two attorneys and a student of the law, a stockbroker and several businessmen, a physician, a contractor, and a furniture finisher who was the sole working-class representative on the entire slate.[51] In fact, during the 1882 municipal campaign, with the exception of the perennial anti-Chinese plank in both platforms, neither Democrats nor Republicans made any substantial appeal to the labor vote in terms of either candidates or programs. That oversight would cost Buckley's party dearly in 1884.[52]

In 1882 and most subsequent elections during the decade, however, the Democratic tickets were sufficiently representative of the substantial elements of the San Francisco community and respectable enough in their own right—even without the inclusion of Bartlett and others like him—to win decisive victories at the polls, and the successes typified the local political tradition in several ways. San Francisco voters rarely returned incumbent supervisors to office, rejecting them not on the basis of reasoned Jacksonian principles such as rotation in office, but simply because they mistrusted them and preferred new blood. Regarding the office of mayor, on the other hand, San Franciscans reflected a persistent respect for achievement and clung tenaciously to the politics of deference. With the pointed exception of the Workingmen's Isaac Kalloch in 1879, they elevated a succession of accomplished businessmen to the city's principal office, and the elections of neither Bartlett nor his nineteenth-century successors—Edward B. Pond, George H. Sanderson, Levi R. Ellert, Adolph Sutro, and James Duval Phelan—shattered the tradition. Somewhat less consistently but nevertheless with considerable regularity, San Francisco bosses, reformers, and even the Workingmen's party nominated candidates for supervisor, school director, and other municipal offices not from among the laboring classes but from the business and professional elements of the urban community.[53] In this respect, with the exception of Chris Buckley's presence, a formidable factor indeed, the election of 1882 represented continuity rather than change in the San Francisco political tradition, and tickets nominated during succeeding contests in the 1880s would maintain the patterns essentially intact.

Precisely why the city's successful respectabilities and on occasion even fashionables should commit themselves so zealously, often at the risk of incurring the recrimination of their peers, to the periodically hazardous tumult of nineteenth-century municipal politics—including Buckley's constantly condemned machine—remains a matter of substantial conjecture. For marginal members of the working classes, motivations are considerably more obvious; they involved themselves out of pressing need for the jobs and services the machine provided and for the sociability and recognition emanating from affiliation with the organization, positions in city agencies, or advancement in the party hierarchy. The forces impelling more secure citizens are not so apparent. For a few—like Raphael Weill, proprietor of one of the city's major drygoods emporiums and perennial candidate for office—a sense of duty may have been a factor. For a few more, the potential prestige of higher office beyond the city may have been a consideration; San Francisco mayors regularly sought the California governorship. William T. Wallace, Jeremiah Lynch, and George Hearst aspired to a seat in the U.S. Senate but only Hearst achieved the goal, and George T. Marye, Jr. coveted a place in Congress which he never won.[54] More, however, probably felt the influence of pragmatic concerns such as the advancement of their own economic interests or sharing in the largesse of corporations seeking favors from the city. But participation in politics also may have involved a less tangible consideration closely related to the process of urban change: the opportunity for recognition and advancement of status in a milieu characterized by increasing rigidity, anonymity, and separatism.

The late Richard Hofstadter has argued, not altogether persuasively, that substantial numbers of elite citizens who committed themselves to progressive reform politics in the early twentieth century did so in an effort to recapture social positions lost as a consequence of profound changes in the nation.[55] It is also possible that many who participated in machine politics responded, in a kind of inversion of the process Hofstadter describes, to similar motivations by seeking the acquisition or enhancement of status through politics, one of the important avenues of upward mobility in the metropolis.[56] In the San Francisco society of the 1880s, still dominated by a persistent and frequently exclusionist mystique surrounding the gold and silver eras and their participants, the quest for status through politics could involve not only members of the working classes but also the middling and upper echelons of urban society. Moderately successful merchants and professionals often found themselves moving on the fringes of but rarely admitted to inner circles still dominated extensively by remnants of the old South Park crowd, ensconced in Nob Hill and its environs, and in many cases they turned to activity as municipal officials, as members of state and county committees and bodies such as the Commitee of Fifty, and as leaders of precinct clubs and other partisan agencies as alternate means to gain recognition in an exceedingly status conscious community. Indeed, even *déclassés,* individuals who had enjoyed a modicum of acceptance in earlier decades, in the 1880s became deeply involved, perhaps in an effort to hurdle the barriers which kept them on the margins of the real San Francisco aristocracy, as candidates on Buckley's tickets, as avid activists in his organization, and occasionally as his lifelong friends and associates.[57]

For those relegated to the lower rungs of the ladder, the same impulses toward social and material advancement prevailed, perhaps even more insistently, and for them political activism often assumed a critical dimension in even the minimal mobility which might well involve generations. A worker submerged in the urban labor pool, for example, could affiliate himself with a machine such as Buckley's in order to augment his income, status, or security through a patronage appointment to a semiskilled position in one of the city's departments. His bright son or daughter might escape blue collar status entirely as a teacher or municipal clerk and, in the absence of civil service systems or qualifying examinations, enlist the political organization's support in the venture.[58] Working within the organization itself also could provide significant opportunities. A successful and dedicated career as a party functionary virtually guaranteed freedom from the drudgery of earning a living or, as the Blind Boss put it, allowed "a good fellow [to] pick up a few simoleons without overtaxing his strength."[59] But for the ambitious and talented few, the profession of politics could provide the key to substantial social advancement (but not necessarily social acceptance) and a significantly more congenial lifestyle. Nothing confirms the reality or scope of the potential in San Francisco in the 1880s quite as emphatically as Chris Buckley's own personal career.

Unlike many of the immigrants who were their contemporaries, the Buckley family, in San Francisco at least, never found itself obliged to reside in the most dismal tenement quarters of the city. Nor would Christopher himself, even during the struggles of his young adulthood. In the years following his return from Vallejo, Buckley made his home in the Fifth Ward, a congested triangle of land bounded by Market, California, and Kearny Streets and teeming with businesses, commercial establishments, boarding houses, and family residences in which boarders routinely helped to pay the rent. Those who lived in the region—the most crowded in the city with the exceptions of areas south of Market Street, in Chinatown, and along the waterfront—consisted principally of representatives of the working classes: married and single of both sexes, every age and ethnic group, and every skilled and semiskilled trade in San Francisco. The final year of the 1870s found Buckley somewhat more prosperous than the majority of his neighbors. With a partner he operated a saloon at the corner of Bush and Kearny Streets, and with his Maryland-born wife Sallie he maintained an adjacent rooming house where eighteen tenants—including nephew John Parrotte, now a twenty-six-year-old carpenter—constituted a veritable cross-section of the ward's populace.[60]

Just one year later, although the future boss remained a resident of the same neighborhood, he had come to enjoy considerably more comfortable and auspicious circumstances. Buckley had shed his own financially marginal groggery and the boarding house, lost his first spouse, and embarked upon his ultimately profitable decade-long association with Matt Fallon in the more substantial and eminently more successful Alhambra Saloon.[61] By late 1883, remunerations from the Alhambra— and probably fees earned as a political broker—permitted yet another move upward to a home purchased at 2440 Post Street in the new and fashionably suburban Western Addition where he would subsequently own substantial real estate. No Nob Hill, the area was nevertheless a highly respectable and desirable upper-middle-class section of the city populated by prominent professionals and businessmen, and it represented a decisive upward step from the teeming Fifth Ward.[62] From his new address and from St. Patrick's Catholic Church on Mission Street, Buckley buried his father in January 1884. John Buckley, perhaps his son's closest friend and companion over the years, died a relatively poor man who, according to the Blind Boss, "left me nothing but the state of California to make a living in."[63]

South of Market in the 1880s.
A working-class neighborhood in transition.

Obviously, however, the son was not dependent upon a patrimony in 1884; he had already made effective use of his father's more lucrative bequest. And within months, Buckley mitigated his personal loss and alleviated the solitude which he could not abide by remarrying, this time taking as his bride not the daughter of an obscure Argonaut but instead Elizabeth Hurley, the daughter of prominent Bostonians.[64] Perhaps in celebration of the nuptials and in recognition of his new wife's status, in the spring of 1885 Buckley purchased some seventy-five acres in the Livermore Valley, built a home there, and called his estate Ravenswood after an amusement park recalled as one of his most appealing childhood memories. In subsequent years, he constructed a more sumptuous dwelling on his land, entertained his friends there in the manner of a country squire, and became a vintner of some repute.[65]

Despite the obvious pleasure which Buckley derived from the ability to divide his time between the calm of Ravenswood and the bustle of San Francisco, he well understood that it was the city itself which permitted him to enjoy his bucolic retreat and to become a respected member of the rural Livermore community.[66] In an almost meteoric rise, he emerged from comparative obscurity to a position of prominence and power, augmented his wealth impressively, and established dominance over the local and state Democracy.

Several factors contributed to the success, most apparently his extensive preparations. The experience of nearly two decades of careful obser-

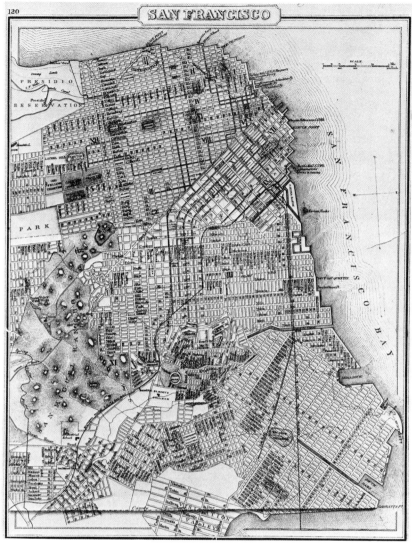

Map of San Francisco in the 1880s.
Roman numerals indicate wards.

vation and energetic activity had schooled him as a thorough master of
his profession. Numerous others, however, had undergone the same experience but failed to capitalize upon it. What seems to distinguish
Buckley from the rest is not only ambition and temperament but also a
remarkable sensitivity to the relationship between urban change and the
politics of the metropolis and .the ability to structure his organization

and direct his own career according to the realities he observed. He also recognized that retaining his position precluded a retreat to a life of rural simplicity, even after his initial overwhelming victory. A sustained hegemony demanded that the boss remain closely attuned to continuing changes in the city and to the issues and problems which agitated its citizens. If he lost contact with the true sources of his power, he certainly would be displaced by the determined, hostile, and vociferous opposition which emerged, even within his own party, almost as soon as the votes were tabulated in the fall of 1882.

The Machine in Power

Chris Buckley reveled in the amenities permitted by life in the suburbs, including the status involved, the ability to entertain friends in sumptuous surroundings, and the opportunity to keep a pair of the fast trotting horses which he so much admired. He would become equally fond of the leisured style of an impeccably tailored country gentleman, vintner, and distiller of fine brandies and of the capacity to retreat from the bustle of the city, regale associates and family in a pastoral setting, and relax as friends read to him from works in the library of rare volumes which he assiduously assembled. Despite their obvious pleasures, however, both suburban and rural lifestyles involved hazards and challenges for the boss, especially the potential for detachment from the urban affairs which provided the basis for both his political preeminence and the rewards of his newly acquired status. Removal from the centers of activity in San Francisco, his principal haunts for two decades past, could diminish intimacy with the voters who constituted the sinews of the machine's strength and with the issues which were its *raison d'être*. Indeed, a lapse of attention—perhaps the consequence of recent property acquisitions and remarriage—to the details which had ensured success in 1882 may explain a temporary but serious reversal of fortunes between 1884 and 1886.

Be that as it may, unlike the majority of his neighbors in the Western Addition and residents of other suburban regions—many of whom would become involved in a variety of anti-boss factions as the decade progressed—Buckley attempted to retain his contacts with his lower ward constituencies and the city at large in several important ways. When at home in San Francisco, he was visible almost daily in his carriage, with a team of spirited trotters in the traces and a companion—Sam Shear or Josh Cochrane in early years and later Alex Greggains—at the reins, dashing along Montgomery and Market Streets and other avenues and byways, attending to the affairs of his profession. When in residence at Ravenswood, Buckley embarked upon biweekly circuitous journeys by Western Pacific rails from Livermore to Oakland and then by ferry to the city where, until he sold the establishment in 1885, he held court in his own Alhambra Saloon. Subsequently, he habituated other watering holes, established himself at the revived Manhattan Club and at party headquarters on Bush Street, frequented the financial and commercial districts of the city, remained constantly active in his own precinct club and in county partisan associations, and attuned himself to the nuances of urban life and polity which constituted the foundations of his economic and political success.[1]

In contrast, the Blind Boss's principal antagonists—especially those who regarded themselves as representatives of the city's better classes and conservators of its political integrity—for the most part eschewed the populistic role of the municipal politico and frequently insulated themselves from many aspects of urban life. They restricted their contacts in the city to their own strata of San Francisco society and focused their attentions upon business and professions, exclusive clubs, and homes in the suburbs or posh hotels while rejecting as beneath them the boss's complex communication network designed to maintain intimate contact with the city, its people, and its affairs. Reformers also tended to dismiss as mere opportunists, ruffians, shoulder strikers, or worse the army of ward heelers and district captains who visited Buckley in his headquarters and apprised him of the conditions and opportunities in the city. The respectabilities likewise defined as sheer fraud, demagoguery, economic waste, and outright corruption the patronage system which compensated many of the machine's foot soldiers.[2] Bosses, on the other hand, understood and acknowledged the function of their cadres of junior officers as vital links in the political chain of command and the underpinnings of the organization's resiliency. Neighborhood leaders made it possible to recover and rebound from defeats like that of 1884 and to win decisively in subsequent partisan battles, but neither ideology nor loyalty provided sufficient motivation for their essential services. Instead, the potential for tangible improvement of their lot in the city impelled them to perform with diligence and devotion the tasks which enhanced the Blind Boss's power.

Just how completely Buckley and other San Francisco politicos acknowledged the significance of the party's workers became apparent early in 1883 when candidates on the victorious 1882 ticket—like their successors for the remainder of the decade—made the payment of political debts virtually their first item of municipal business. No records remain to document the distribution of patronage to the rank and file of the party faithful, but if published reports provide an even approximate assessment, the new city officials embarked upon the traditional distribution of spoils with gratitude, generosity, and—in some cases—uninhibited abandon, neglecting not even the most menial positions on the municipal payroll. In its initial official act, the board of supervisors dismissed without comment outgoing Mayor Maurice C. Blake's Republican janitor and replaced him with loyal Democratic clubman Alex Fisher, and within a month it had sanctioned a host of changes in the city's administrative departments. With the board's approval, for example, Superintendent of Streets Timothy Lowney made his son a chief deputy and appointed John Buckley as his principal office deputy. Nor were these the sole instances of nepotism. John Parotte (Buckley's nephew and formerly an employee in the Alhambra Saloon) found a place on the police force; the nephew of a police court judge became a county jailer; the nephew of the new county recorder emerged as superintendent of the county hospital; and the county treasurer found a place for his son as his own chief deputy. Simultaneously, political allies received their due. Among them, ward leaders James C. Nealon and William Gavigan ascended to positions as court clerk and deputy tax collector, and in what may have been the most blatantly partisan appointments, the supervisors made Sam Shear, Buckley's bodyguard and Al Fritz's former partner, superintendent of the House of Correction and assigned Sam Deal, former Yosemite stalwart and member of the Committee of Fifty, to the post of Shear's principal assistant.[3]

Nowhere, however, did the dispensation of municipal positions to friends, family, and constituents evolve into a more audaciously contrived system than among members of the school board, and nowhere were the negative political consequences ultimately so apparent. At their final meeting, defeated Republican school directors had appointed a host of newly licensed teachers to positions in the city's classrooms, despite the expiration of half of the annual school term. In swift and certain retaliation, the new Democratic directors dismissed the system's entire clerical and maintenance staffs and replaced them with loyal partisans, including Democratic club leader Frederick Raabe as head of the carpenter shop and Buckley's cousin by marriage, Charles Johnstone, as Raabe's chief assistant. The action, according to De Young's *Chronicle,* "brought sorrow to a score of Republican hearts" and sufficient outrage to the soul of Director Raphael Weill to prompt his temporary resignation.[4] Weill's shortlived indignation—apparently only substantial enough to absent him from a single board meeting—had little impact upon his fellow directors' determination to use the public payroll to reward their constituents; nor were they willing to permit an established policy of retaining teachers on the basis of their performance to impede the process. Within weeks of their installation, the school directors created a unique administrative official, the Inspecting Teacher, whose negative evaluation alone could justify teacher transfers or dismissals and, not incidentally, create vacancies to be filled with favorites. Almost immediately, the potential became apparent when Laura T. Fowler, principal of the Mission Grammar School and the niece of a prominent Democrat, received her appointment to the new office. To replace Miss Fowler at the Mission School, directors selected Nettie Craven, former vice-principal, purported paramour of Director Isadore Danielwitz, and subsequent "companion" to silver king James Fair. In her place, they installed Grace Cahalin, a teacher with only two years' experience but coincidentally the daughter of a school director, and subsequently gave

Miss Cahalin's classroom to the alleged mistress of School Director James M. Eaton, M.D.[5]

The directors' brazen maneuvers precipitated protests, but no immediate resignations. Nor did an equally outrageous partisan use of school patronage result in more than mild reactions among school directors or the general public. With little or no explanation, the school board abolished the principalship of the Night School, created the office of Night School Inspector, and appointed party stalwart Joseph O'Connor—already a deputy school superintendent—to the new position and to its additional seventy-five dollar monthly salary.[6] Although the move did produce dissent from among opponents of the machine, even that was effectively squelched when City Attorney William Craig decided—on the basis of a fine distinction between an "administrator" and an "inspector"—that O'Connor's dual salaries conformed to the letter of the law. And the precedents set by the first Buckley school board's patronage policies, especially those involving the Inspecting Teacher, would keep the San Francisco system in turmoil for the remainder of the decade.[7]

The Blind Boss's precise role in the distribution of patronage in 1883 and in subsequent years is impossible to ascertain. Obviously, the inclusion of members of his family and intimate supporters in the municipal largesse implies something more than a passing interest. On the other hand, the school board's lack of discretion and overt defiance of public opinion suggest that, even though Buckley probably acceded to their actions, he was not so fully in control of matters as might be assumed. Attuned both personally and politically to public sensitivity in educational matters, he asserted in his memoirs that he sincerely wished the conduct of the public schools to remain divorced from politics and that when he discovered misguided henchmen—"friends of education," he called them—exacting fees of up to $200 for teaching appointments, he immediately halted the practice and disciplined those involved.[8] The price Buckley quotes surely involves substantial exaggeration (few San Francisco teachers earned even $100 a month in the 1880s), as do charges that none but whores and hoodlums became teachers during his regimes, and the disclaimers in his reminiscences may reflect attempts at self-justification. Nevertheless, given the political acuity which he otherwise demonstrated, the Blind Boss must have recognized that the school directors' conduct could have dire consequences which would cost him dearly. If he did not, he miscalculated seriously, and he would be forced to learn from bitter experience. The Inspecting Teacher scheme—for which the *Chronicle* gave him exclusive credit—would be the source of persistent problems, the school board's interference with strictly academic affairs would result in a protracted dispute with Principal John Swett of the Girls' High School, and Raabe's mismanagement of the school carpenter shop would precipitate accusations of graft and the use of school department supplies in Democratic headquarters, in the construction of a barn on the boss's Post Street property, and in the refurbishing of an Eddy Street house of ill repute called The Basket.[9]

True or not, the allegations had their eventual effect. No Buckley candidate for school director would emerge victorious from the election of 1884, not only eliminating a major source of the machine's patronage but also making it clear that such heavy-handed tactics were no longer feasible in a generally tolerant but increasingly sophisticated city, especially in view of a concurrent nationwide agitation for the application of civil service principles to all positions of public office.[10]

It is possible that school directors—and other municipal officials to a lesser degree—engaged in a form of private enterprise in their distribution of favors and that circumstances forced Buckley, however unwillingly, to sanction or tolerate their actions. Still, the Inspecting Teacher stratagem was a stroke worthy of his genius, and the nearly 1400 positions on the city payroll—half of them in the school department— did provide a promising reservoir which the machine could tap to reward the faithful and to fulfill its obligations as an employment agency. No boss could afford to ignore such facts; patronage was simply too important to be neglected or left to chance. The distribution of positions on the city payroll involved substantially more than nepotism, jobs for deserving but impoverished supporters, favors to constituents, or payments of debts incurred during political campaigns. It also constituted an integral feature of the machine's function in the nineteenth-century city, one which contributed in a major way to the perpetuation or termination of the authority of both the boss and his organization. Thus, Buckley well may have had a hand in the Democracy's patronage policies in 1883 and after. He even may have instigated the Inspecting Teacher scheme but, through a temporary lapse of attention or the inability to exercise the kind of control historically attributed to him, permitted it and the school board to overreach themselves, at substantial subsequent cost to himself and his party.

The first Buckley regime's record on another major issue which required the careful attention of the Blind Boss, specifically municipal finances, is substantially clearer and essentially more positive. During the campaign of 1882—and in each subsequent contest during the decade—civic spending and taxation constituted principal political issues among Democrats and Republicans, machines and reformers alike. Washington Bartlett and his fellow candidates, as well as the party platform itself, promised strict fiscal accountability, rigid compliance with the One-Twelfth Act of 1878, and adherence to a dollar-limit on municipal taxation. The One-Twelfth Act, introduced in the state senate by former San Francisco mayor Frank McCoppin, restricted monthly municipal expenditures to one-twelfth of the total budget, but before 1883 the law had been totally ignored by city administrations. The dollar-limit idea, in contrast, was first broached in the editorial pages of the San Francisco *Bulletin,* which argued that property taxes should not exceed one dollar for each hundred dollars of assessed valuation. Despite Republican Mayor Blake's vigorous and persistent denunciation of the program as excessively stringent, it became an important plank in the platforms of both his party and the Democracy, but the incumbent's stance combined with his administration's weak fiscal record (just how weak only became apparent in the early months of 1883) to make the dollar-limit issue a particularly potent weapon in the hands of his challengers. Indeed, along with other features of the Democrats' economic program, it may explain the decisive margin of victory provided by a disgruntled citizenry angered at extravagant spending while civic facilities remained in a decrepit state, distressed by rumors of fraud and malfeasance, and eager for a change in city hall.[11]

Capturing the municipal government proved to be a more readily achieved goal than unraveling the city's financial snarl, despite the tempered optimism of the inaugural address which Mayor Bartlett delivered on the apparently auspicious occasion of the anniversary of Andrew Jackson's birth. The new municipal executive touched upon the major issues of the campaign—water rates, the Chinese, and the deplorable condition of streets, sidewalks, wharves, and other municipal properties—but he emphasized the disastrous fiscal plight of San Francisco and added a note of caution aimed at the new Democratic government: "We are not as fully masters of the 'situation' as could be desired."[12] The actual severity of the economic tangle which Bartlett inherited from the previous administration did not become entirely clear until a citizens' committee which the mayor had appointed to analyze fiscal problems reported back to him in February; careful study revealed a municipal debt in excess of one-quarter of a million dollars and a treasury on the precipice of bankruptcy. Although the investigative committee did not identify the precise sources of the deficit, it was generally assumed that misfeasance within the Blake administration was involved, and the almost immediate arrests of several former deputy street superintendents on charges of forging municipal warrants tended to confirm suspicions and, by comparison, to enhance Bartlett's standing with the San Francisco public.[13] But popular denunciation of the previous mayor did nothing to resolve the city's immediate fiscal problem; that would require energetic action by both the mayor and the board of supervisors.

Once aware of the scope of the difficulties confronting them, the supervisors' Finance and Auditing Committee cast about for means to reduce the deficit and stave off disaster. Their first response was also the most simple and direct: reduce municipal expenditures in every way possible. In a move which most certainly brought sorrow to more than a score of Democratic hearts, especially to those only recently appointed to positions on the city payroll, the supervisors sharply reduced the salaries of numerous employees—including the police, janitors, gardeners, watchmen, and maintenance personnel—and even abolished some positions. Simultaneously, they abrogated several existing contracts for municipal services such as street cleaning and, in their most stringent move, suspended the lighting of the city streets for a period of four months. Not surprisingly, such economy measures precipitated a storm of protest not only from individuals and firms whose incomes would be reduced but also, ironically, from among the same journalists who had previously excoriated the city government for its overextensions and from dissident supervisors who argued that salary cuts were neither fair nor sufficient to alter the desperate fiscal situation.[14] The latter position clearly had merit, and both Bartlett and the supervisors sought additional expedients to save San Francisco from financial disaster, among them an idea which emanated from the supervisors but which the mayor emphatically rejected.

Early in March 1883, the board took the extraordinary steps of enacting an ordinance authorizing a municipal bond issue of $500,000 to cover the deficit and simultaneously lobbying in Sacramento for enabling legislation to permit the necessary special election in the city. Almost immediately, De Young's *Chronicle* linked the maneuver to Buckley and identified it as an effort to create a treasury surplus ($250,000 more than needed to retire the municipal debt) to be looted by unscrupulous politicos. The validity of neither accusation is substantiated by the record; the supervisors who voted in favor of the measure were not consistently those most closely affiliated with the Blind Boss. In any case, in less than a month Mayor Bartlett closed the matter when he vetoed the ordinance as "unreasonable and unfair" in view of the continuing fiscal crisis, and the supervisors failed to muster the requisite nine votes for an override.[15] If the bond issue scheme was intended to provide a reservoir of funds to be tapped for illicit purposes and if it was of Buckley's instigation, the finale of the episode suggests that the "solid nine" supervisors identified as tools of the boss were more myth than reality, and fluctuating alignments on various subsequent issues tend to confirm that judgment.

Somewhat paradoxically, in fact, the program which did finally resolve the city's fiscal dilemma—at least temporarily—originated neither with Bartlett nor with individuals in the city government purportedly most inimical to boss rule. Instead, it emanated from Fleet F. Strother, one of the supervisors allegedly submissive to Buckley's dictates. Strother had lodged vehement protests against the board's policy of cutting salaries and services in order to reduce the debt. His denunciations, in fact, had been sufficiently vocal and persistent to prompt one local editor to accuse him of making "an indecent exposure of his mind" at every supervisorial meeting. Nevertheless, the Buckleyite's suggestions were eminently sound: either tap the municipal sinking fund to pay the debts or, preferably, collect municipal taxes owed by several utility companies for three years or more.[16] For his part, Bartlett shrewdly adopted the latter course and took preliminary steps to institute legal proceedings against the delinquents, focusing especially upon the major debtors, Spring Valley Water Company and San Francisco Gaslight Company. Although protracted negotiations ensued, the threat of litigation proved sufficient to obviate the need for actual court action. Following extended exchanges of proposals and counterproposals between the companies' attorney and city officials, the utilities settled their debts early in the summer; Spring Valley paid $225,000 into the city exchequer and San Francisco Gaslight contributed an additional $272,000, sufficient between them to place the municipality on a sound financial footing for the first time in nearly a generation.[17]

Thus, neither the One-Twelfth Act nor the dollar-limit led to San Francisco's solvency; instead, balancing the city's ledgers resulted from a proposal initiated by an alleged functionary of a political machine which was purportedly waiting to pounce upon the city treasury. Adherence to the One-Twelfth Act and the dollar-limit, however, did facilitate the generally sound fiscal record compiled by Bartlett's two administrations and those which followed. Prior to the Democratic victory in 1882, recent city tax rates had hovered around $1.50 per hundred dollars of assessed value and inflated property valuations usually totaled approximately $400,000,000. By 1884, both the rate and the assessments had declined substantially to $1.20 on $221,000,000, and they fell to $1.05 on $200,000,000 by 1886, drastically reducing the tax burdens of individual San Franciscans. With payments of bonded indebtedness excluded, the tax rate actually dropped below the magical and much heralded dollar-limit and remained at essentially that level throughout the remainder of the decade. Paradoxically, with the victories of antiboss reformers in the 1890s, levels of taxation and spending would climb once again.[18] In the meantime, Bartlett's fiscal record permitted him—but not most of the supervisors who probably deserved equal credit for financial stability, lowered taxes, and efforts to identify sources of waste in the Blake administration—to establish sufficient support in the city to secure renomination and election in 1884. The much maligned Strother, who actually wanted to be mayor, would also be among the few victorious Democrats of that year; San Francisco voters elected him city auditor in every election from 1884 to 1890.[19]

Efforts to restore and maintain the fiscal integrity of San Francisco certainly raised the prestige of Chris Buckley's Democratic organization, but they also raise several important questions about the Blind Boss himself and about bossism in general. In the first place, if Buckley exercised the dictatorial control over the board of supervisors which has been attributed to him, why did voting alignments shift constantly, not only in 1883 but also throughout the decade? And why did even reputedly anti-boss officials like Edward B. Pond (who would receive the nomination for mayor in 1886) frequently vote with the "lambs"? It would seem that, in reality, the boss's control was tenuous at best and demanded carefully programmed, balanced exchanges of reciprocal favors based upon the realities of a changing city to secure desired results on individual issues and measures. Answers to other questions are even more speculative, but the questions themselves are significant enough to be raised. What, for example, explains the boss's use of such fiscal programs as the One-Twelfth Act and the dollar-limit in his various campaigns; were they mere shams, or were they actually efforts to gain popular support by giving the urban public what it both wanted and needed? And finally, what did Buckley intend concerning municipal funds; did he plan—in emulation of New York City's Tweed Ring in the previous decade—to loot the city treasury? Or was it his purpose to use it in relatively minor ways—to provide income for constituents on the patronage rolls, for example—and to seek major sources of personal and partisan wealth elsewhere?

These questions probably cannot be answered definitively; only Buckley himself held the key to his motivations and calculations. But in the case of intended sources of income for himself and his party, developments during and after the fiscal crisis of 1883 indicate that he identified agencies external to city government as the most lucrative and reliable financial fountainheads. In the 1880s, continuing urbanization and expansion produced incessant demands for extended municipal services, and not only a larger population dispersed across the peninsula but also real estate promoters and others desirous of responding to citizens' needs made persistent appeals to partisan leaders and civic authorities. In Buckley's words:

For a variety of reasons, sometimes substantial and evident, sometimes remote and unintelligible, . . . it was surprising to see how universal was the desire among men of substance, firms and corporations, to get on the right side of politics.[20]

Many of those to whom the boss referred, especially entrepreneurs aspiring to operate cable cars and trolleys on city streets, made neither remote nor unintelligible their willingness to pay handsomely for privileges. In

San Francisco and other cities during the 1880s and 1890s, municipally owned transportation systems were rare indeed, and according to Martin Kelly:

A deep bass voice called for more railway franchises. . . . It was a most happy coincidence. The people wanted better transportation facilities for the rapidly expanding city. The capitalists were falling over each other to get into the game. And we [the politicians] were masters of the game.[21]

Bosses like Buckley and Kelly were more than willing to capitalize upon their mastery for both power and profit.

Andrew S. Hallidie's first successful cable car trial in 1873 actually initiated the rush for post-horsecar-era street railway franchises in San Francisco, but as the city expanded physically and the clamor increased, two events in the late 1870s provided additional impetus. In the spring of 1878, the state enacted five-cent fare legislation applicable to cities (there was only one) of over 100,000 population. The law made transportation by street railway especially appealing to members of the urban working classes and, despite early fulminations by traction company executives, ultimately provided a significant stimulus to their business.[22] Simultaneously, a convention of Californians labored on a new state constitution which, among other provisions, would place new and stringent restrictions upon corporations of all types, including those operating under municipal franchises. To circumvent limitations embodied in the new organic law, approved by voters on May 7, 1879 and effective on the first day of 1880, transportation entrepreneurs bombarded the San Francisco board of supervisors with appeals. Martin Kelly recalled that,

in 1879, . . . every existing street railroad company in San Francisco applied for a new franchise for fifty years, all of which were granted, besides franchises for railroads on hitherto unused [and in some cases nonexistent] streets.[23]

The supervisors and Mayor Andrew Jackson Bryant approved a total of twenty-six new permits in 1879 alone, including several for the chieftains of the Central Pacific Railroad Company whose grants ultimately formed the nucleus for the Market Street Railway Company's virtual monopoly of public transportation in the city,[24] and subsequent administrations would prove equally generous.

Like their counterparts on the school board, the outgoing supervisors

RE PUBLICANS !... *Will You Let This Brute Rule San Francisco?*

Martin Kelly, Buckley's Republican counterpart.

of 1881–82 conducted business up to the eleventh hour of their terms, including the grant of a fifty-year franchise to the Sutter Street Railway Company on January 5, 1883 in the final week of their incumbency.[25] Shortly thereafter, the onslaught on the new Buckley board commenced in earnest, as traction magnates with cash in hand paid their visits to

"Buckley's City Hall," the back room in the Alhambra Saloon. Although Mayor Bartlett ultimately vetoed numerous requests—principally on grounds that fifty-year grants were too long or that the promoters sought only to monopolize routes, not provide services—more than a dozen franchises became law in 1883 and 1884, most of them with the municipal executive's signature. Indeed, only a single permit—the Market Street Company's proposed extension and expansion through Golden Gate Park in June 1883—passed over the mayor's objection during his first term, despite the purported subservience of Buckley's "solid nine" supervisors.[26] Controversial permits to the Park and Ocean Railroad Company and the California Street Cable Company, also owned by Charles F. Crocker and the proprietors of the Market Street system, became law with Bartlett's approval and presumably with considerable compensation to the Blind Boss, if not to the supervisors.[27]

Although the composition of the board changed considerably during Bartlett's second term and Buckley had little influence over its eleven Republican members, the flood of franchise requests and grants continued unabated, suggesting that rival bosses Bill Higgins and Martin Kelly also recognized the sources of a new bonanza in San Francisco. Once again, only a single veto was overridden in two years. In that case, eleven dutiful Republican supervisors (only the lone Democrat Edward B. Pond voted to sustain) and Boss Kelly received $5000 apiece from grateful traction capitalists. Despite frequent outcries from an urban public determined to have its transportation network, the mayor did obstruct numerous requests approved by the supervisors during 1885 and 1886, but many more became law with his approval—more, in fact, than during the prior Buckley regime—and little changed during Pond's two subsequent administrations. By the late 1880s, the rights of way of more than a score of separate traction companies traversed every district of San Francisco.[28] And in the post-Buckley 1890s, following state legislation—for which Martin Kelly claimed credit—overturning a city ordinance prohibiting overhead trolley lines, a new form of opportunity presented itself and dozens of additional franchises, especially in the regions south of Market Street, emerged from congenial boards of supervisors.[29]

How many of the cable and trolley grants ultimately resulted in functioning transportation services is not clear; nor is it clear how many of them were actually intended for completion. Some were "corkscrew routes," zigzagging across the city and monopolizing access to given streets. Others were simply holding actions; the Market Street Company, for example, never built on the route granted in 1883, despite extensive (and expensive) successful efforts to subvert Bartlett's veto. But the line was held secure and it would become an important adjunct of the Southern Pacific-owned Market Street Railway Company's consolidation in 1893. Promoters also sought franchises in hopes of either selling them to competitors at a handsome profit or dumping stock on still eagerly speculative San Franciscans. Martin Kelly argued that, with the exception of those backed by the Southern Pacific or other major interests,

> not a single railway company organized after 1880 had any more capital behind it than barely enough to pay the Supervisors the usual fee for granting a franchise and to buy a stock certificate book, blank bonds, and a little stationery. . . . The dear people did the rest.[30]

The "dear people" often suffered substantial losses in such schemes, and they were also treated to shams such as the battle pitting trolley poles against underground conduits which Kelly insisted was principally a diversion to facilitate the Market Street Company's monopolistic ventures.[31]

Precisely what bosses and subservient municipal officials garnered from the race for traction franchises is unknown, despite allegations by journalists, critics, and reformers; secrecy, after all, was essential to the success of the transactions. But both Buckley and Kelly—and their successor Abraham Ruef—admitted receiving substantial recompenses for their services, and they considered their fees well earned:

> Often these [street railway] franchises yielded millions to the beneficiaries. We, the bosses, were the distributors of these good things. When men of wealth came to us for gifts which meant golden fortunes for themselves, does any fool suppose we didn't ask for a modest "cut"? Of course we did. Was it not equitable and just?[32]

Both the modesty of the bosses' cuts and the equitability and justice of the means employed to earn them may, of course, be debated.

It is certain, however, that their compensations fattened their own bank accounts and those of cooperative elected officials, swelled the war chests of partisan organizations, and permitted Buckley in particular to invest in various business ventures and in real estate and to enjoy the graces of suburban and rural life. Indeed, in this respect the boss's astute comprehension and ability to capitalize upon the interrelationship between the city, its needs, its political climate, and his own economic activities becomes exceedingly apparent. For Buckley's speculative ventures included such items as Sutter Street Railway Company bonds valued at $100,000, and he was able to use his influence upon municipal government not only to acquire additional franchises for the company but also to protect his investment by gaining for the firm reduced valuations at the hands of congenial assessors and favorable decisions from submissive coroners and city attorneys when litigation involving death or damage threatened.[33] Ultimately, even though funds which paid the boss's fees and provided his business profits did not come directly from the municipal treasury, San Franciscans would pay for them in the form of higher fares, poor services, and shabby and even dangerous facilities, and they would come to begrudge their contributions to the Blind Boss's wealth.

For most of the decade, however, the majority of the city's residents, eager to secure adequate services for their expanding metropolis, remained essentially immune to the implications of the process or at least tolerant of conditions which contributed to similar ends for both bosses and the public. The quest for water provides a significant case in point. Dwellers on the arid San Francisco peninsula endured a plight not unlike that confronting Coleridge's ancient mariner. Surrounded on two sides by the Pacific Ocean and on a third by a majestic bay, they were forced to search diligently for sufficient water to slake their thirsts, to fight their recurrent fires, and to produce their food. Until the completion of the municipally owned and controversial Hetch Hetchy water system in 1928, they depended for the precious commodity—as they did for transportation and other utilities—upon private suppliers, especially the Spring Valley Water Company founded in 1860.[34] Moreover, according to data provided by the Spring Valley Company itself, in the late nineteenth century San Francisco's need for water increased faster than did its population. In 1865, each of the city's 110,000 residents consumed approximately twenty-one gallons of water daily, in 1870 the rate of consumption had risen to forty gallons each for 150,000 people, and by 1880 it stood at seventy-three gallons for each of 233,000, simultaneously challenging the capacity of water suppliers and increasing the potential for profits. In 1883, moreover, an investigation by the local Board of Insurance Underwriters revealed that the fire department would be unable to control a major conflagration with water from Spring Valley's antiquated mains and pumping systems. In an indignant response, the company attributed the fault to the supervisors who allegedly had failed to provide sufficient fire hydrants and water distribution arrangements, both of which the firm would gladly furnish—along with water for drinking, irrigation, and other purposes—for an appropriate price.[35]

Despite charges of inadequate supplies, defective equipment, and extortionate rates, circumstances forced the municipality to deal with Spring Valley Water Company; from the time of William C. Ralston— one of the firm's major stockholders and principal promoters—the company had virtually monopolized San Francisco water supplies. As a consequence, Spring Valley grew increasingly arrogant, even challenging in court the city's right to regulate its rates and blatantly keeping both politicians and municipal officials on its payroll. Legal restrictions tended to worsen the situation and make it even more susceptible to manipulation. According to provisions of the Consolidation Act, utility companies did not receive long-term franchises from the city. Instead, the organic law mandated annual renegotiations of the terms of their contracts, a fact which kept the water issue in the forefront of local politics, under constant debate, and subject to corruption. In the 1882 campaign, Democrats made water rate reduction and control of Spring Valley major issues, and shortly after taking office in 1883 they had the opportunity to act upon their promises.

To some degree, the courts facilitated the new administration's task by declaring invalid the water company's action challenging the legality of municipal rate fixing.[36] Earlier, the supervisors' Committee on Water and Water Supplies had held hearings which culminated in a condemnation of the company's methods of calculating its profits as "fictitious" and its rates as "extortionate" and with a recommendation that water rates be reduced by thirty-seven percent. The threat implicit in the committee's report prompted the company to seek the injunction which the court overturned, but there was little of substance to fear. For the ordinance which the board subsequently produced and passed on March 15—although it purportedly reduced Spring Valley's gross income by one million dollars—did not involve anything resembling the threatened rate decrease and ultimately may have increased the company's profits. In any case, a reluctant Mayor Bartlett signed the measure, with the following comment:

Owing to the diversity of opinion existing in the Board, I am satisfied that no amendments can be secured which would justify me re-opening the whole question, or compensate for the uncertainty and anxiety which would follow until a new order could be passed.

The mayor compromised in the name of expediency and to secure the order he so much desired for his city—not to mention the precious water—and the Democrats failed to fulfill their campaign promise of a "material reduction" in water rates, although they did enact an ordinance requiring water suppliers to submit detailed reports of their capitalization, resources, income, and profits before applying for franchises for the following year.[37]

The latter action—and those which preceded it—may have been, in fact, elements in a charade which Chris Buckley and compliant supervisors concocted in order to grant the water company's requests without incurring the wrath of a disgruntled public and, incidentally, to earn their retainers. When Spring Valley applied for water-rate increases in 1884, Fleet Strother's investigation revealed the company's income to be more than $200,000 in excess of the amount permitted by the previous year's franchise, confirming Bartlett's suspicion that the 1883 legislation did not provide for a material reduction.[38] Nevertheless, despite evidence that the company had violated its agreement with the city, supervisors took no punitive action; instead they devised and approved a law maintaining rates as they stood. An angry mayor vetoed the measure, but it became law when only two supervisors (Pond and Ames; Strother was absent) voted to sustain him.[39] The evidence, to be sure, is entirely circumstantial, but it is difficult to avoid the conclusion that the water rate question in 1884 was carefully orchestrated from the beginning—including the company's request for increased rates—and that Chris Buckley occupied the prompter's box, if not the podium, during the final performance in the supervisors' chambers. Whatever the case, the Democracy once again reneged on its campaign promise, and the action (or lack of it) almost certainly contributed to the party's defeat in the election of 1884 when only Bartlett, Pond, and a few additional city officials "swam ashore from the Democratic wreck."[40]

"WOW! I OWN THE TOWN."

San Francisco version of New York's Tammany Tiger.

Little changed during the Republican interlude of 1885–86, when according to Martin Kelly the survivors drew retainers from Spring Valley and other utilities to the cumulative tune of between $12,000 and $15,000 a year.[41] The board persisted in its demands for detailed reports of the water company's finances and public denunciations of its policies, only to pass ordinances essentially in keeping with its requests, and Bartlett continued to veto the measures, only to be over-ridden.[42] Indeed, the fiasco of 1885 proved to be the greatest debacle of the decade when, on the grounds that Spring Valley earned profits three times greater per capita of population than any city in the United States, the mayor negated three successive rate laws and no water ordinance emerged until June.[43] Nor would conditions change substantially after 1886 when the Buckley machine recaptured the municipal government and placed Edward Pond in the mayor's office from 1887 to 1890. In fact, only in 1891—with Republican George H. Sanderson at the head of municipal government—did a water ordinance become law without a veto, and that measure did not bring the desired material reduction.[44] With Bartlett, most other city officials and civic leaders,

145

the general public, and the bosses for various reasons reluctant to move toward municipal ownership of utilities, the pattern would persist in one form or another for a generation, as Buckley himself observed: "Such controversies raged for more than thirty years, at the cost of many scandals, great sums of money spent on both sides and the general discomfiture of the city in endless litigation."[45]

Many of the scandals would involve the Blind Boss and a substantial portion of the money spent would find its way into his pockets, as the $25,000 in Spring Valley Water Company first mortage bonds (he had little faith in stocks) in his portfolio attest.[46] Equally extensive holdings in the bonds of other utility firms suggest that he also profited from protracted transactions involving gas and electricity suppliers and the municipality.[47] Gas for lighting streets and buildings had been available in the city since the late 1850s, principally from the San Francisco Gas Light Company which had, by the 1870s, absorbed most of its competitors. In the 1880s, however, electric arc lighting came into its own and precipitated recurrent battles for contracts involving the old gas company, the newer Standard Gas Company, the California Electric Light Company, the Electric Generator Company, and the city.[48] Although competitive bidding tended to control rates and made the character of the lighting issue substantially different from the water debate, results of the controversy remained essentially the same. Each year the companies made their appeals to the board of supervisors in the form of sealed bids for contracts for lighting specific streets, buildings, or sections of the city, and each year during the 1880s, the supervisors divided the municipal largesse between them, despite heated debates over the comparative merits of their products and usually without substantial mayoral objections.[49]

The nature of the competition also altered the role of the bosses— Democratic and Republican alike—in the quest for municipal lighting contracts. Both the gas and electric companies were corporations chartered by the state and franchised to operate in the city, and their annual appeals to the board of supervisors involved not only the question of rates but also contracts to provide specific services to the municipality itself. And the presence of two firms offering similar services and competing on a relatively equal basis confronted politicos like Buckley and Kelly with an interesting choice. They could either divert all municipal business to one and undermine the other, or they could act as brokers, dividing the city's lighting contracts between the two and collecting fees from both. Apparently the latter course proved to be more profitable, for the record shows a relatively equal distribution of favors throughout the 1880s. In addition to serving as brokers, the bosses also aided the existing companies by minimizing the competition from other firms attempting to enter the field; potential rivals could be denied a share of the city's business or their appeals for franchises could be refused entirely. Martin Kelly, who received a $300 monthly retainer and a $26,000 annual expense account from the California Electric Light Company for just such services, found himself in a unique position when a potentially competitive firm offered him and his supervisors $75,000 to betray their original client.[50]

Despite the appeal of the offer—and the laments of greedy underlings—he refused, for to renege on a commitment once given would terminate his credibility with both current and prospective patrons. Buckley records no such experiences; nor is he as specific as Kelly about fees received from gas or electric companies. But given his political and economic acuity, his ability to identify "certainties"—in the form of both fees and investments in transportation and utility enterprises—when they came his way, his influence with the municipal government, and his intimacy with the affairs of the city, it is doubtful that he would have allowed the opportunity to pass.

According to contemporary journalists, he did not; the local press bombarded San Franciscans with specifics of Buckley's services to utility companies and details of his emoluments, in some cases grossly exaggerated but in others carefully gleaned from municipal tax records and other official sources. In 1880, the Blind Boss had owned almost nothing, but by mid-decade he paid taxes on several choice residential and business properties in the city, in addition to his estate at Livermore. In subsequent years, he increased his holdings in San Francisco and added more in Los Angeles and San Diego, simultaneously augmenting his investments in transportation and utility companies and accumulating an estimated $200,000 in United States government bonds. With political cronies Max Popper and Michael J. Kelly, he also formed several profitable firms whose business with the municipality included contracts for cleaning city streets and plastering a major portion of the new city hall building, and by 1890, estimates placed his net worth at over $600,000. Some segments of the population reacted sharply to revelations about Buckley's wealth, questioned the possible legitimacy of such a phenomenal aggregation—especially since after 1885 he had engaged in no apparent business, not even that of saloonkeeper—and banded together to oppose him even within his own party.[51] But most citizens, for the time being at least, tended to tolerate his activities and those of his counterparts as normal facts of political and economic life in the nineteenth-century American city.[52]

Concerning some aspects of the boss's activities, however, a substantial cross-section of the urban public displayed considerably greater sensitivity. From the time of Horace Mann's reforms in the Jacksonian era, public education had been considered an integral facet of the American ideology, hailed as the conservator of culture and a facilitator of mobility.[53] Citizens of all social strata and national origins regarded public education with a kind of reverence which made its involvement in partisan politics particularly intolerable and hazardous for a boss. At least during the 1883–84 period, Buckley either did not comprehend this fact or failed to allot sufficient attention to it. For despite their apparently respectable character, several of the school directors elected in 1882 proved to be severe disappointments to San Franciscans as well as liabilities to the Blind Boss, kept the educational system in constant discord throughout their tenures in office, and provided abundant ammunition for the salvos fired by hostile journalists and rival politicos.

Dissatisfaction began almost with the inauguration of the new board, and especially concerned its distribution of patronage and implementation of the Inspecting Teacher scheme. But it did not end there. Although they were by no means novelties in the history of San Francisco public education, personal scandals aroused popular indignation directed particularly toward alleged assignations involving Directors James Eaton and Isadore Danielwitz and female members of the teaching staff.[54] Revelations that the school board was manipulating the school system in ways which affected the city's children proved to be even more distressing to the public and damaging to Buckley's machine. Like other major cities in the United States, San Francisco experienced a disproportionate increase in the number of school age children in its population, a development which demanded additional schools and teachers in order to respond to increasing public concern for adequate education.[55] Instead of reacting positively to the situation, the 1883–84 school board dismissed teachers, reduced salaries, and closed schools in the name of economy, thereby increasing congestion in already overcrowded schools, eliminating even the possibility of enrollment for hundreds of children, and reducing the potential for decent schooling for those able to attend. The fault did not lie entirely with the Democratic school board; their predecessors had left them with a deficit of more than $15,000.[56] Nevertheless, they bore the brunt of public indignation, especially when other aspects of their spending policies came to light.

In a period of grave financial stringency, waste and inconsistency characterized the school directors' actions. While closing schools, dismissing teachers, and cutting salaries—which were restored only after emergency funding by the board of supervisors—in the name of economy, they hired favorites and paid a dual salary to at least one of them and permitted graft and corruption in other areas. The operation of the school carpentry shop and the activities of its head came under particularly close scrutiny and heavy criticism. Not only were materials and equipment being diverted to unauthorized purposes and a score of individuals labeled "Buck's Bums" padding the payroll, but it was also discovered that the chief carpenter was employed at another full-time job while supposedly performing his duties for the school department and had, in fact, purchased a closed school building for a pittance. His second employer, moreover, was the major supplier of lumber and coal for the city schools, and inspection of the shop's books revealed that purchases of both of those commodities far outstripped the quantities actually used for school purposes. An investigation of the shop—conducted by the school directors—not too surprisingly proved inconclusive, but the adverse publicity which the affair generated irreparably damaged the school directors' political futures.[57]

Nor were their problems, or Buckley's, alleviated when the public learned that publishers had bribed the board to discard all currently used textbooks and purchase new ones for over $187,000.[58] Public pressure halted the transaction, but the conduct of their colleagues prompted several directors to protest vigorously and one of them, Dr. Lee O. Rodgers, to resign. Unlike Weill before him, Rodgers never returned, and he left behind a board so badly factionalized that not even 308 ballots were sufficient to elect a new president for 1884. Yet many of the school directors were sufficiently brazen about their activities or immune to public outrage to run—with Buckley's blessing—for reelection in 1884, only to be soundly defeated along with all other Democratic candidates for the school board.[59] Their ouster, however, would do little to alter conditions in San Francisco public school politics during the Republican interlude of 1885–86 or even during the post-Buckley 1890s.[60]

Whether the Blind Boss sanctioned the blatant malfeasance of members of his first school board or simply permitted them to evade his close surveillance and control is not certain, but it is clear that the episode inflicted severe political damage upon his organization. Not only in 1884 but also in every subsequent campaign in which he was involved, the school issue became a powerful weapon against him, more devastating perhaps than charges of impropriety in awarding franchises and contracts, distributing patronage, or dispensing other favors through the municipal government.[61] Possibly, the relatively minor monetary considerations involved in school department manipulations, when compared to utility and traction graft and other potential sources of income, deluded Buckley into an underestimation of the importance of school politics and into allowing the school directors to act essentially as free agents, pursuing their own goals. If such were the case, he overlooked two critical considerations: public sensitivity to matters which concerned their children and the fact that the funds involved, no matter how relatively insignificant, came principally from the municipal treasury. He would pay a heavy price for his oversight, but he would also learn from it. For after the Blind Boss reasserted his control over the municipal government, his school directors would, with the possible exception of the well-publicized conflict with Girls' High School Principal John Swett, maintain a significantly lower public profile than they had in 1883 and 1884.[62]

Learning additional lessons and mastering additional political challenges as the decade progressed would preclude lapses of the sort which allowed the school board's lack of discretion to undermine the machine, required even greater adaptability than Buckley had displayed earlier in his career, and demanded that he focus his attentions and his energies almost exclusively upon the city, its people, and its affairs and not upon his suburban and rural retreats. The dynamism of San Francisco in the

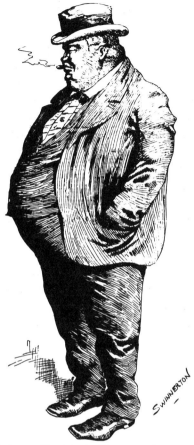

Sam Rainey, Buckley's Democratic partner.

1880s, although different in character from previous decades, continued
to produce transformations in social, economic, and political realities,
and altered conditions influenced the practice of the Blind Boss's profession fundamentally and made persistent and intimate contact with the
city even more imperative, not only to cope with political hazards but
also to meet novel economic challenges. Growth and innovation in a
more complex metropolis also forced Buckley to rely more heavily upon
his associates for essential information, and after 1884 trusted lieutenants like Sam Rainey provided a liaison with the fire and police departments, militia units, and elements of similar political importance in the
city, as well as with the organization's army of representatives in Sacramento. Simultaneously, the boss turned to entrepreneurs like George

Hearst and professionals like attorneys Delphin M. Delmas and Garrett McEnerney for equally critical insights into the attitudes and affairs of the strata of urban society which they represented. But Buckley's greatest asset remained his own close association with the partisan clubs and county and state committees whose communications networks tapped every segment of the San Francisco and California communities.

In the end, however, success or failure would hinge upon the Blind Boss himself, his ability to assimilate the information he gathered, and his capacity to adapt his political and financial practices to persistent changes which would involve not only the economic interests which were his principal clients but also the altered expectations among the increasingly sophisticated urban citizenry which furnished his constituency. To maintain his authority, Buckley would be forced to respond to persistent adverse publicity, to react to challenges from within his own party, to maintain constant attention to state political affairs, to supervise what amounted to a biennial reconstruction of his organization, and to translate his understandings of the city into positive partisan action.

Combat with
the Soreheads,
1884–1887

Throughout his career—including
the years following his retirement from active political life—Chris
Buckley acted as a lodestone for controversy, perennially attracting both
partisan and personal attack. Journalists seeking sensations to increase
readership found him a convenient topic, genuine reformers and those
who simply coveted his power assailed him in county and state committees and at the polls, business competitors and some associates hailed
him into court in a variety of causes, and neighbors and even family
members instituted litigation in pursuit of a portion of the boss's growing wealth. On the rare occasions when he discussed his antagonists
publicly, Buckley habitually dismissed them as a collection of "soreheads" envious of his authority or affluence and disgruntled at their own
failures. Although the comment was essentially accurate in most instances, its implicit indifference does not convey an entirely true impression of his responses to attacks. He felt personally and deeply those
attacks on his reputation or character or those which involved individ-

uals close to him, and he attempted to resolve such issues without publicity or controversy. To attacks which threatened his position as a political leader, however, he gave his close attention and responded energetically with every means at his disposal.

Formal challenges to Buckley's control of the San Francisco Democracy commenced almost as soon as the inaugurations of 1883 confirmed his leadership in the victorious elections of the previous November. By spring, intraparty opposition had surfaced in several precincts in the form of A.B.C. associations (officially Anti-Boss Clubs but, as contemporaries understood, actually Anti-Buckley Clubs) which contested the legitimacy of the organizations established under the aegis of the Committee of Fifty and dominated by the Blind Boss. In addition, aggregations of dissidents also evolved around a variety of displaced Democratic leaders, especially remnants of the once dominant Chivalry faction of the party and ideological conservatives earnestly preparing to contest their party's anticipated anti-railroad stance at its state convention in 1884. Among the challengers to Buckley's authority and that of the Democratic County Committee itself were the Democratic True Blues (formerly the Stoneman True Blues), the Soborn and De Voto Clubs (named after their founders), the San Francisco Municipal League (in which young James Duval Phelan was involved), and one contingent sporting a name probably longer than its membership roster: the Anti-Boss, Anti-Monopoly Lone Mountain Democratic Club of San Francisco. Such collections of dissatisfied Democrats, considered not soreheads but the "better elements of the party" by De Young's *Chronicle,* initially constituted no great threat to either Buckley or established party leadership in the city.[1] Early in 1884, however, developments rendered their challenges substantially more formidable.

Dissidents' opportunities to attack Buckley's position or at least to act as spoilers actually involved two separate but closely related events. During 1883, in response to growing and shifting populations in both the city and the state, the California legislature enacted laws which required redistricting prior to the elections of 1884, and in its 1882 plan, the Committee of Fifty had mandated periodic party reorganization in San Francisco to conform with changes in apportionment.[2] In March 1884, when the State Central Committee ordered the local Democracy to realign itself in compliance with the law and its own constitution, dissatisfied partisans recognized their opportunity, especially since disputes concerning the form which reorganization might take already had precipitated factionalism within the ranks of the local leadership. County Committee Chairman James T. Fogarty, a politico only moderately committed to Buckley, and a substantial number of committee members advocated the absolute dissolution of the clubs established in 1882 and a complete restructuring of the party in conformity with the new election precincts—approximately 150 in number—laid down by state legislation, a proposal which Buckley vigorously opposed.[3] Apparently assuming that Fogarty and Chairman John H. Wise and other San Francisco delegates to the State Central Committee would support them in their opposition to the Blind Boss and the club plan, anti-Buckley forces pressed for a precinct plan of organization.[4]

Just as apparently, they seriously underestimated the influence which their nemesis already had established at both state and local levels. For when the state committee made its will known to the local organization, its resolutions called not for a radically altered local Democracy but simply for at least three additional clubs to compensate for population growth, revisions in club boundaries to conform with the state law, and a third division of the local convention in the form of a separate judicial and educational conclave in addition to the traditional municipal and legislative nominating bodies. Although Buckley objected to the third division of the convention, he compromised on that point and used his influence with the state committee in order to secure victory on the principal issue. The precise nature of that influence remains enigmatic, but it probably involved a *quid pro quo* in the form of future cooperation in municipal affairs and support for antimonopolist Democrats at the impending and potentially explosive state party convention in Stockton. Whatever the case, the boss's opponents found themselves vanquished—at least temporarily—and by early spring the local Democracy had completed its reorganization along the lines prescribed by the state committee. Indeed, in the same primary elections which revitalized the club system, voters selected a new County Committee which included Buckley as chairman of its executive council and a substantial majority of his supporters on its roster.[5]

Through rapid response based upon his political judgment, the Blind Boss confronted and diverted an early challenge to his position in the party, and in the process he convinced many of his former critics to drop their opposition and return to the fold as dedicated lambs. Others, however, refused to recant, persisted in their hostility, threatened to defect to Republican ranks, and ultimately united to place the Citizens' Independent ticket (derisively termed the "amalgamated sideshow") in the field at the November municipal election, at substantial cost to the regular party.[6] Many of the dissidents—especially those who rejected their party's increasingly rigid anti-railroad stance—also carried their opposition to the state party convention in Stockton in June. Indeed, the anticipation of a major confrontation at that meeting may explain the vigor and persistence of many anti-Buckleyites' efforts to control the local organization in order to elect their own majority of city representatives to the statewide gathering of Democrats.

Like his critics, Buckley clearly understood the significance of state politics to himself and to his career. In the first place—as his recent victory in local organizational strife attested—influence with the California Democracy could provide a source of strength at home. It also constituted a source of tangible rewards, as one exuberant Democrat observed in 1882:

When the Lord created the universe, He looked around, and said it was good enough for ordinary mortals, but there must be a new and better piece of handiwork for the Democracy, and He created California.[7]

The tone of the comment predicted Buckley's own allusion to his father's legacy, but more than the sheer wealth of the state made it imperative that a municipal statesman involve himself in its partisan affairs and maintain a reliable Sacramento connection.

In California, as in most states during the late nineteenth century, city charters reserved substantial authority over local affairs to the state legislature which, at each session, acted upon scores of measures critical to Buckley: amendments to the Consolidation Act, enabling laws for the collection of taxes, approvals of many appropriation measures, laws to permit issuance of municipal bonds or the creation of new agencies, permission to alter or open streets, revised procedures for the granting of franchises, and many more. The governor also retained the power to appoint numerous civic officials—commissioners of the police and fire departments, the new city hall, Golden Gate Park, the waterfront, local elections—and each had substantial patronage at his disposal. In 1883,

Buckley attempted to alter the situation by having an assemblyman introduce a bill to permit local authorities to name fire and police commissioners, but even though similar measures would be hailed as home rule when sponsored by charter reformers, the boss's effort met denunciation and defeat, principally at the hands of legislators involved in the country-city conflict (San Francisco versus the rest of the state) which plagued California politics and constituted yet another reason for involvement at the state level. In addition, a kind of reciprocity existed among partisan leaders; Buckley and the emerging leader of the party's country and antimonopoly wings, Stephen Mallory White of Los Angeles, for example, persistently appealed to one another for aid in placing favorites in patronage positions and for other services. Finally, there was the railroad. Southern Pacific interests in San Francisco included street railways, depot locations, access to a waterfront under state control since 1863, and numerous other matters potentially requiring state action. Therefore, if the Blind Boss hoped to act as the corporation's agent, a firm hand in Sacramento was an indispensable asset.[8]

In recognition of these realities, Buckley exerted a determined effort, from his first experience at a state convention in 1882, to make his presence felt in the California Democracy, and he successfully retained sufficient authority to influence those state governmental and political affairs which directly involved San Francisco.[9] In 1884, however, a single issue dominated the biennial assemblage of Democrats which met at Stockton: the question of railroad regulation and taxation. At the previous convention in Los Angeles, George Hearst's gubernatorial ambitions had been squelched, despite the efforts of Buckley's city delegation. Nevertheless, another and perhaps more sincere advocate of regulation and opponent of monopoly, George B. Stoneman, had been nominated. With encouragement from Buckley and other prominent Democrats, Governor Stoneman subsequently called the legislature into special session specifically to deal with the question of controlling the railroads, a task ineffectively performed by the Railroad Commission authorized under the California Constitution of 1879. Much to the disappointment and chagrin of antimonopolists, the rancorous legislative session terminated in May 1883 without appreciable result; conservative Democrats joined with the Republican minority in the state senate to defeat regulatory legislation introduced by San Francisco Assemblymen William T.

Wallace and Thomas F. Barry. The action—or lack of it—precipitated a major controversy within the party, prompted the San Francisco Democracy to appoint a Committee of Seventeen with Buckley at its head to appeal to recalcitrant legislators and ultimately to censure them, and left a residue of partisan conflict which simmered until it boiled over at the Stockton convention in 1884.[10]

There, divisions became even more readily apparent and intractable, but despite the controversy Buckley managed to emerge from the meeting with augmented strength in the state party. As the convention opened, he hammered out an alliance with country and antimonopoly Democrats by aligning himself behind their spokesman, Stephen Mallory White. With the support of George Hearst and his San Francisco *Examiner* the boss threw his weight and that of his city delegation behind White's candidacy for the chairmanship of the convention and behind resolutions which not only supported the principle of railroad regulation and read its opponents out of the party but also denounced the presidential ambitions of conservative Justice Stephen J. Field in favor of those of Grover Cleveland. Buckley himself had sincere doubts concerning the wisdom of the latter actions, but he nevertheless supported them and by doing so simultaneously managed to engineer the selection of a State Central Committee composed principally of his allies and chaired by William D. English of Alameda. Thus, even though his party had undergone a severe test which at times threatened to become less than decorous and even violent, the Blind Boss departed from Stockton as a major factor in state Democratic politics. He had the support of a majority of the party's governing body, he had negotiated a tentative truce with the country wing of the party, and he had established himself in the state hierarchy as the undisputed leader of the still-dominant city wing of the California Democracy.[11] Apparently the boss also had assessed his options and chosen the certainties of partisan leadership rather than the unpredictable potential of railroad politics.

Most antimonopolists left the convention with high hopes for the coming campaign, but Buckley, who realized that his own political battle would be fought not in terms of economic ideology but on the basis of issues which agitated the wards and precincts of the city, was substantially less sanguine than many of his copartisans about the ultimate outcome of the contest. For one thing, while Grover Cleveland remained a virtual unknown in the state, the Republican presidential standard bearer, "Plumed Knight" James G. Blaine, had accumulated immense popularity in both California and San Francisco on the basis of his stand on the Chinese question. Consequently, the Blind Boss considered the city and the state "lost on national issues" and feared that a victorious Republican national ticket would sweep local candidates into office in its wake.[12]

State affairs also gave cause for trepidation. Obviously, the Stockton affray had split the party badly, and sincere reformers, conservative opponents of the antimonopoly plank, advocates of Field's presidential aspirations, and those who directed their animosity toward Buckley personally could be expected to render only token support for municipal and state tickets and, in some cases, to work against them. Some important Democrats, indeed, harbored mixed feelings toward their party's program for all of these reasons, among them the ideologically conservative and eloquent editor of the San Francisco *Daily Alta California,* John P. Irish. Buckley, after all, had thwarted Irish's hopes for the chairmanship of the state convention, and the editor also regarded the antimonopoly stance as radicalism if not sheer socialism. Many Californians who recalled the Kearneyite episodes five years earlier shared his views, and even though partisan loyalty prevented Irish from attacking the Democratic ticket overtly in his columns, his support remained less than enthusiastic throughout the campaign. Other Californians, including Buckley, retained a nagging suspicion—probably misplaced—that Democratic legislators had sold out for railroad coin during the extra session; it is more probable that sincere conservatives allied with Republicans and voted their consciences, but the damage done was the same. Finally, the Stockton resolutions had antagonized railroad officials, cemented their ties to the Republican party even more securely, and ensured that the Southern Pacific's political manager, W. W. Stow would pour the company's funds—always a critical factor in nineteenth-century California politics—into the war chests of the boss's opponents.[13]

In the city itself, Bill Higgins and younger leaders like Martin Kelly and Phil Crimmins worked energetically to rebuild their own Republican organization, with substantial railroad support, in preparation for a concerted assault upon recently erected Democratic bastions. And despite the Bartlett administration's commendable record on fiscal matters, there remained numerous vulnerable chinks in the Buckley party's armor. To be sure, the mayor and the board of supervisors had given San Franciscans, for the first time in nearly a decade, a balanced budget, a solvent treasury, and reduced taxes and assessments. On the other hand, they also had failed to meet their constituents' expectations in several major areas; among other things, essentially unaltered water and utility rates, streets and sewers in their usual decrepit and unsanitary state, and municipal facilities and services unfinished and in disrepair remained persistent focal points for criticism. In addition, both Buckley and his organizaton came under sharp attack for the peccadillos and major failures of Democratic municipal officials. Outrageous patronage grabs and the perfidy of the school directors remained fresh in voters' minds, a well-publicized grand jury report on the eve of the municipal campaign confirmed suspicions of misfeasance in several municipal agencies, a jury tampering scandal involving several lambs surfaced in the coroner's office, Buckley's cohort Sam Shear came under sufficient fire as the superintendent of the House of Correction to prompt his dismissal, and a basically hostile press took undisguised delight in linking each new revelation to the Blind Boss and his machine.[14]

Clearly, circumstances in the city did not augur well for success in the municipal campaign of 1884, and premonitions of impending defeat—and perhaps, as previously suggested, changes in his personal life—seem to have discouraged Buckley from participating in the campaign with the ebullience and vigor which characterized his involvement in previous and subsequent contests.[15] While Democratic partisans occupied the months between Stockton in June and the municipal conventions in October with energetic preparations, organization, and primary elections in the clubs, the Blind Boss carried out his duties as chairman of the county committee's executive council and a member of its finance committee in an almost perfunctory manner. He remained, to be sure, the frequent target of attack by both the opposition press and rival Democrats who accused him of assuming his antimonopolist stance only to advance George Hearst's senatorial ambitions, of striking bargains with Stow and the railroads on the regulation issue, and of surreptitiously conferring with Stephen J. Field and New York City boss Honest John Kelly during a journey to the East.[16]

In other matters, however, Buckley's name was curiously absent from the pages of contemporary journals which devoted substantially more space to rival organizations than to his partisan activities. Democratic schismatics twice attempted to unite with independents, nonpartisans, and anti-Higgins Republicans, first as the Independent Taxpayers' party and then as the Citizens' Independent party, to place a municipal ticket on the November ballot, but they experienced substantial difficulty in persuading their nominees to accept places on their slate.[17] Nevertheless, the scorned amalgams did field candidates for most principal offices and gained recognition by the election commission, and their presence in the race undoubtedly drew sufficient votes from regular Democrats to have a telling effect upon the final result of the contest.

While dissident splinter parties and coalitions prepared their attacks, regular Democrats held primary elections to select representatives to their own municipal conventions, and when the results were known — despite the Blind Boss's apparent lack of interest or activity — the fifty clubs had chosen delegates "wholly and absolutely under the control of Boss Buckley." Of the 164 votes at the convention, lambs would cast 154, and when the conclave assembled in B'nai B'rith Hall, they proceeded to nominate a municipal ticket composed principally of the boss's adherents.[18] Unlike their Republican rivals who met simultaneously in Metropolitan Hall just a few blocks away and composed a mixed slate with wealthy commission merchant William F. Merry at its head and several representatives of the trade union movement as candidates for supervisor and other offices, the Democrats nominated a straight business and professional ticket reminiscent of 1882.[19] Only in the contest for the mayoral nomination did even perfunctory competition emerge among Washington Bartlett, Edward B. Pond, and Fleet F. Strother, but in the end Bartlett received the nomination he deserved, Pond was renominated for supervisor (and probably promised the top of the ticket in 1886), and the candidacy for auditor consoled Strother. With few exceptions, the remainder of the Democrats' candidates remained the same as they had been two years previously, including several discredited school directors and other municipal officials whose selection suggests that Buckley had insufficient interest or confidence in the campaign even to insist upon an electable slate of nominees.[20]

A lackluster convention which produced a ticket dominated by mediocre candidates and a platform which did little more than give lip-service to traditional issues—the dollar-limit and economy in government, the Chinese, rate regulation, better schools, and improved city facilities—predicted an equally desultory Democratic campaign. Republicans translated national and state issues, such as their party's stance on the protective tariff and railroad regulation, into direct local appeals to workingmen who still smarted under the prolonged impact of the depression of 1883 and struggled to maintain the viability of their organizations. Simultaneously, they hammered away at the failures and misconduct of the previous government and at Buckley himself. Democrats remained content to mount a primarily passive campaign, relying upon bonfire rallies and mass meetings like the one which met in Metropolitan Hall with James D. Phelan acting as chairman and delivering his maiden speech in San Francisco politics, an abstract defense of the principles of railroad regulation. For the rest, Democrats appealed to their record—none too sound, in many cases—in municipal government, Chinese exclusion, and antimonopoly efforts, and depended upon bland responses to their opponents' spirited and frequently well documented attacks. Despite admissions that several incumbents had performed well and that, on the surface at least, the Blind Boss's ticket conveyed an air of respectability, San Francisco journalists maintained an incessant barrage of criticism aimed at the machine which supported them, apparently with substantial effect. Indeed, with Irish holding his *Alta* aloof from the contest, Hearst's *Examiner* constituted the sole Democratic organ in the city, and when the dust of the November 4 election cleared and the votes were tallied, the state and local Democracy found itself contemplating a near disaster.[21]

A Democratic year for most of the nation, 1884 in California and in San Francisco brought Buckley's party a resounding defeat at nearly every turn. Blaine won the state's presidential electors and five of its six congressmen were Republicans. George Stoneman's reelection to the office of governor provided one of the few bright spots, but it hardly compensated for a state legislature in which Republicans dominated the assembly and shared the senate evenly. In the city, the ballot count revealed equally dismal results. Bartlett retained the mayoralty by 2000 votes out of 46,000 cast, Pond returned to the board of supervisors by the same margin, and Democrats captured the offices of sheriff, auditor, and county clerk by slim pluralities provided, according to Martin Kelly, by Buckley's election officials who concealed pencil leads under their fingernails to scratch Republican ballots. If the Blind Boss did employ such tactics, it was in a losing cause, for Republicans swept all remaining municipal offices and the patronage potential that went with them.[22]

Reasons for the few Democratic victories are not difficult to ascertain; Stoneman, Pond, and Strother all had compiled commendable records during their incumbencies, and the victorious candidate for sheriff had been a respected police officer. Explanations for their losses are equally apparent but somewhat more complex. Buckley had beaten back the local soreheads in the contest for control of the party, only to confront other obstacles which weighed heavily against success. In the first place, James G. Blaine enjoyed a strong following in the state, sufficient even to offset scandals connected with him during the campaign, and his popularity carried numerous California Republicans into office. More importantly, perhaps, San Francisco Democrats presented a far from united or cohesive front; the Stockton controversies has severely damaged the party, even at the municipal level, and the various A.B.C. organizations—despite their defeat on the larger issue of party control—had eroded the Democratic vote sufficiently in some close races to give offices to Republicans. Buckley himself, the source of many dissidents' hostility, also played a detrimental role. Revelations and allegations concerning his conduct and that of his municipal officials seriously undermined partisan support, and the boss's apparent lack of attention to details during the campaign also cost his party votes. This was particularly true of the Democracy's failure to nominate electable candidates or to appeal to an increasingly important labor movement which represented an estimated twenty-five percent of the city's vote in 1884. Finally, the aftermath of Stockton had important consequences for the San Francisco campaign: the funds furnished by railroad officials dissatisfied with the Democrats' action at their state convention permitted Republicans to wage an energetic and broadly based canvass, not only on state and national issues but also on those which concerned the municipality. And in combination with other factors—including the disaffection of many important party leaders—railroad financing virtually assured a Democratic defeat in both the city and the state.[23]

When Washington Bartlett led the new administration into office in January 1885, he somewhat unrealistically appealed for "cooperation and harmony" in a municipal government comprised of a single supervisor and a handful of other officials from his own party.[24] Chris Buckley, however, did not share in the mayor's apparent optimism, despite the patronage potential involved in the few offices which Democrats had won. Indeed, judging by the boss's subsequent actions, the defeat of 1884 and the grim prospects which it predicted may have triggered one of his numerous periodic decisions to retire from politics.[25] In January 1885, he did participate in an antimonopoly Democratic conference on federal patronage in California, and he served as a member of a state delegation sent to Washington early in the spring to discuss the question with President Cleveland. With a variety of federal offices—Superintendent of the Mint, the Postmastership, Collector of U.S. Customs, Naval Officer of the Port, and Surveyor of the Port among them—the issue was especially critical in view of the local party's recent defeat. Each federal official would have at his disposal numerous minor positions to distribute, an important substitute for the potential lost at the state and city levels. The sojourn to the national capital proved fruitless, however, despite the efforts of more than forty "California pilgrims," and the president paid little heed to their pleas, including those of Buckley who gained but a ten-minute audience with the chief executive. Cleveland did grant one place to a lamb; he made William J. Bryant postmaster. But he appointed many more anti-Buckley Democrats—including Stuart M. Taylor who became Naval Officer of the Port—to federal positions in the city, and for the most part he avoided controversy by distributing plums to partisans like Wiley J. Tinnin of Trinity County, the new Surveyor of the Port, who remained untainted by the factionalism of the Stockton convention.[26]

A disappointed and pessimistic Chris Buckley returned to San Francisco in the spring of 1885. His party had suffered defeat at home, his hopes for at least a modicum of federal patronage upon which to sustain his machine had been dashed, and he could anticipate little in the way of rewards or opportunities from the state or municipal governments in power. Therefore, although he retained his membership on the county committee and its executive council, he willingly abrogated the major responsibility for guiding the party's fortunes to the new county chairman, contractor Maximillian Popper, and turned his attention to other concerns.[27] Although he involved himself in occasional political matters, including an effort in 1885 to secure increased state appropriations for Golden Gate Park, the Blind Boss's major concern during the year following the Democratic defeat seemed to involve more personal matters.[28] In fact, the year constituted a period of transition for him.

As already observed, in the months prior to the 1884 campaign several changes occurred in his life; he married a Boston socialite, his father died, and he moved from the congested Fifth Ward to the suburban Western Addition. Prior to his departure on his mission to the nation's capital, Buckley also had negotiated the purchase of his acreage in the Livermore Valley; upon his return, he consummated the acquisition and began to devote substantial attention to the development of his rural estate and, with leading valley vintners Concannon and Wente, to the promotion of the local wine industry.[29] In the subsequent fall, he made another important change when he transferred his interest in his old political headquarters, the Alhambra Saloon on Bush Street, to Ben Cotton, a black entertainer. Claiming that the transaction represented his irrevocable retirement from the tavern business—which, in fact, it did—Buckley turned his attentions to other matters.[30] During this hiatus from politics he began to learn "for the first time what making money really was," as he put it, and to invest in lucrative ventures such as contracting partnerships with Max Popper and Michael J. Kelly, in traction and utility enterprises, and in real estate in San Francisco and elsewhere. He also embarked upon the first of many overseas journeys, a trip to Hawaii where he enjoyed the hospitality of King Kalakaua.[31]

The boss did not, however, divorce himself entirely from the political life of San Francisco, nor did his decreased involvement in partisan affairs exempt him from continuing attacks at the hands of rival politicos, hostile journalists, or others envious of his success. In fact, Buckley's increasingly apparent affluence may have partially precipitated an attack by another sort of sorehead, an event which forced him to appear before the state supreme court to defend himself against charges of contempt. The complex episode had its origins in the period before Buckley had begun to assert real political authority in the city and involved the Bonnet brothers, contractors who had in 1881 undertaken certain Montgomery Street improvements for the municipality. Even though the city accepted their work, it refused to pay some $12,000 due to the brothers and their partner, and they brought suit against the civic authorities and won their case. Subsequently, the city appealed to the state's highest court, but again the Bonnets' claim was upheld. In the interim, however, the brothers fell upon hard times and sold their interests, including the potential receipts from their claim against the San Francisco government, to yet another contractor, Joseph W. Taylor. When a later dispute erupted between the Bonnets and Taylor, it resulted in yet another court case and, indirectly at first, involved Chris Buckley.[32]

During the course of the action against Taylor, one of the Bonnet brothers, in an effort to recover at least a portion of his investment, testified that in May 1884, at Taylor's instigation, he had paid Buckley $500 to expedite a favorable state supreme court decision in his pending case against the city. Consequently, a committee of the San Francisco Bar Association initiated an investigation and, in October 1885, had the boss arrested and charged with receiving money under false pretenses (acting as an attorney).[33] Although Sam Rainey immediately furnished bail for his friend and the court subsequently dismissed the case, the affair did not terminate there. Before the end of the month, Buckley was summoned again, this time to appear before the supreme court to defend himself against charges of contempt of that tribunal. Before both the high court and the Bar Association's investigators, Buckley admitted accepting the money, but he consistently and adamantly insisted that his promised services involved not the court—over which he had no influence—but the San Francisco board of supervisors—which in 1884 was under his control. The justices did not condone his actions but they did accept his testimony and that of other defense witnesses, and in February 1886 they handed down an acquittal.[34] The Bonnets and those who had pressed their case were less fortunate; proceedings before the court effectively destroyed the already less than savory reputation of the younger Bonnet by revealing, among other things, an incestuous affair with his half-sister and also resulted in the disbarment of the brothers' counsel and the city attorney involved in their original litigation against the city.[35]

Although the court exonerated Buckley, the prolonged episode which generated 264 pages of testimony and scores of newspaper columns from Sacramento to Los Angeles occupied a substantial portion of his time in

1885, damaged his reputation, and distracted his attention from other interests. But the Bonnet affair also may have precipitated quite unanticipated results; for soon after the court rendered its final verdict, the boss once again threw himself into the partisan arena in preparation for the 1886 campaign which he later recalled as a "battle royal."[36]

Several other considerations, however, also inspired Buckley's political reinvolvement, especially those which—if properly exploited—held out substantial promise for his party's success. By 1886, San Franciscans were disenchanted with their municipal government, and even though Mayor Bartlett was severely criticized, Republican supervisors and other city officials bore the brunt of public wrath. At the same time, the Republican party itself experienced serious internal divisions as factions displaced in 1884 attempted to regain power and younger politicos vied for their share of authority in the organization. In addition, a new political contingent, the American Party, became first a promise and then a reality, and its nativist programs posed a greater threat to Republicans than to Democrats. Finally, despite the remaining presence of soreheads within Buckley's own party, the regular organization under Popper's leadership appeared substantially more harmonious and cohesive than before the 1884 campaign. Together, these conditions prompted the Blind Boss to conclude that "1886 opened with flattering prospects for the Democracy" and probably inspired his resumption of an active political life.[37]

Buckley's principal consideration involved the failures of the municipal government since 1883. Throughout Bartlett's second administration, the Republican press—especially De Young's *Chronicle*—attacked the mayor, but usually in an abstract manner which denounced his failure to expose the "crying roguery" permeating San Francisco's civic affairs.[38] Specific charges of misfeasance fell most heavily upon Republican supervisors and other officials, and when a grand jury published its assessment of municipal government in May 1886, it found little to praise except the performance of the few Democratic officeholders: the mayor, the auditor, the sheriff, and one lone supervisor. "Dummies" occupied numerous positions on city payrolls, a high percentage of the municipal contracts granted by the supervisors involved fraud, the street department was blatantly corrupt, and perhaps worst of all, the $180,000 surplus which had existed in 1884 had dwindled to $41,000.[39]

San Franciscans also had additional areas of complaint about the conduct of their municipal government and the condition of their city. Promised reductions in water rates failed to materialize, despite the efforts of Bartlett, Pond, and Strother. In fact, rates had actually increased and the board of supervisors for some quite unfathomable reason had granted a substantial portion of Beach Street to the Spring Valley Water Company. Moreover, even though the rate question diminished in urgency in the city, another matter concerning water quickly replaced it; a series of disastrous fires—some exceeding $1,000,000 in resultant damages—swept portions of the city and in virtually every case critics who included the local board of insurance underwriters laid a substantial portion of the blame upon supervisors' tolerance of inadequate water company facilities.[40] To compound grievances, the board of supervisors, at the behest of both traction and real estate interests, continued to grant street railway franchises without adequate provisions for regulation or safety, archaic sewers dumped effluent onto poorly surfaced and frequently impassable streets and sidewalks, extravagant expenditures left the new city hall incomplete, the city's school facilities and policies were in shambles, persistent squabbles over the relative merits of gas and electricity precluded both adequate lighting and the undergrounding of utility lines, and a scandal involving the House of Correction made Sam Shear's previous derelictions seem mild by comparison.[41]

For these and a host of accumulated shortcomings, San Franciscans— justly or not—held their Republican municipal officials culpable, and the Republican party itself simultaneously added to the Democracy's flattering prospects. Even in 1884, intraparty factionalism—principally involving minor anti-boss elements—had been apparent, but two years later disagreements changed in character and erupted into a full scale internal feud. In the previous contest, in concert with Martin Kelly and Phil Crimmins, Bill Higgins had employed his organizational skills and his ability to attract railroad financial support to capture virtually complete control of the Republican party machinery from his rivals Dick Chute and Mike Conroy. Early in 1886, Chute and Conroy—displaced for two years from the centers of power and sources of patronage in the party—allied themselves with Jim McCord, the powerful superintendent of the Sutter Street Railway Company, and girded for a challenge to the Higgins-Kelly-Crimmins supremacy, a maneuver which resulted in "severe internal troubles" for local Republicans.[42]

The troubles were severe indeed, and as the rivalry persisted and control vacillated between one faction and the other, violence punctuated primary elections called to select club officers and delegates to the county committee. During those primaries, a new figure appeared upon the San Francisco political scene in the person of Abraham Ruef—twenty-three years old and fresh from the University of California's Hastings College of Law—who underwent his initiation into the rites of partisan conflict. He would later recall that during his introductory contest, "Organized gangs of roughs went to and from meeting places on both sides and broke up meetings, destroyed furniture and fixtures and threw voters into the street." Those same contests, Martin Kelly commented, would be "remembered as a battle of the Marne by the survivors of that day." Some, in fact, did not survive.[43]

As the contention persisted into the summer and Republicans attempted to discover the sources of their difficulties, rumors suggested that Chris Buckley surreptitiously backed either his old mentor Higgins or the insurgent Chute-Conroy-McCord faction, an allegation which the boss denied with the comment that, despite his regard for Higgins and affiliation with McCord in the Sutter Street Company, in politics "each played entirely off his own bat." The Blind Boss himself believed that the Southern Pacific acted as a financial angel to the insurgents, but Martin Kelly—probably more accurately—recalled that Stow and the corporation "held aloof" from the controversy, waiting for the outcome to determine the recipient of its support. In the end, neither Republican faction reaped the reward. Despite the appointment of a Committee of Ten—the "Harmony Committee"—combat continued throughout the primaries and into the Republican municipal convention itself. Although the Higgins contingent controlled delegates from thirteen of twenty districts, the gathering degenerated into an unharmonious scene punctuated by heated rhetoric, vilification, and even brawls. It constituted the final performance in a year of rancorous controversy which cost the Republicans not only the railroad's confidence in either faction but also, in the final analysis, the election itself.[44]

Nor were internal divisions and public dissatisfaction the sole conditions which diminished the Republicans' potential and enhanced that of Buckley's party. While the combatants inflicted critical if not mortal wounds upon one another in San Francisco, some one hundred and fifty miles away in Fresno nativist Californians organized the American party which was destined to garner most of its adherents from Republican ranks. A minority party which ultimately would attract a small national following, the new organization presented yet another manifestation of the urban-rural dichotomy in the state and responded to heightened resentment of immigrants stimulated by the Haymarket bombing and other labor disturbances and to the apparently increasing foreign dominance of cities and their politics. In the Golden State, antipathies focused upon San Francisco where a disproportionate number of foreign-born residents—the highest percentage of any city in the nation in the 1880s—seemed to control the government, where occasionally violent labor disturbances of suspicious origins had been frequent in 1884 and 1885 and both Burnett Haskell's radical Workingmen's Association and Frank Roney's more conservative Federated Trades Council were deemed alien, and where the ten percent of the population of Irish origins apparently dominated political life. There, under the leadership of the volatile and erratic Frank M. Pixley, editor and publisher of the weekly *Argonaut,* the party accrued its greatest numerical strength.[45]

Responding to what they believed to be evidences of subversion of traditional values in the city, the state, and the nation, San Franciscans comprised a majority of the several hundred Californians who assembled in May 1886 to organize their party and hammer out a platform which called for immigration restriction, repeal of the naturalization laws, prohibition of alien land ownership, limitations on suffrage and government employment, and elimination of teaching in languages other than English in the public schools.[46] Although Buckley identified the party as being especially hostile to the "Pope's Irish" like himself, most Americans scrupulously avoided the sensitive religious issue and concentrated upon the more universal issue of nationality, made few distinctions between "old" and "new" immigrant groups, remained silent on the Chinese controversy, and denounced both major political parties as subservient to alien influences. But neither in San Francisco nor elsewhere did the party convert many Democrats; instead, its appeal remained principally to dissatisfied Republicans, disgruntled independents, and a handful of perennial "crackpots" (soreheads?), and by the election of 1886 it had attracted some 7000 adherents in the state, nearly two-thirds of them in the city. Buoyed by the apparent success of their appeal, the Americans optimistically held municipal and state nominating

Frank M. Pixley, nativist editor of the San Francisco *Argonaut*.

conventions and placed a full slate of candidates in the field, only to meet nearly total defeat in November. Nevertheless, the party did have a particular significance for both Buckley and his opponents; the few thousand votes which each of its candidates drew from Republicans were sufficient to alter results in several closely contested municipal races.[47]

Although Buckley could not anticipate that precise result, his keen political insight certainly enabled him to recognize the combined potential for Democrats inherent in the American party's appeal and the Republicans' own failures and factionalism. As for his own party, a residue of the 1884 controversies remained, and it was represented by a single contingent of challengers rather than a multitude of minor groups of soreheads vying for the sanction of local and state partisan officials. The circumstance which provided opportunity for dissidents to assert their authority and to challenge the boss's control, however, was essentially what it had previously been: the biennial necessity to reorganize the party in preparation for the impending campaign. Early in the spring of 1886, with an increasingly active Blind Boss clearly in evidence, the Democratic County Committee commenced its arrangements. In his capacity as executive council chairman, Buckley recommended a reconstitution of the rank and file of the party in accordance with the *Plan of the Committee of Fifty* and recent changes in districting, a proposal which passed with but two negative votes and debate limited to the number of new clubs to be formed. Still, the partisan harmony proved to be more apparent than real; within a week of the county committee's approval of the boss's recommendation, a rival organization—the Precinct and County Democracy headed by perennial reformers Stuart M. Taylor and Dr. J. Campbell Shorb and several lambs including Thomas O'Connor—made its appearance and began to issue denunciations of Buckley and the county committee as his tool and demands for the abolition of the clubs—allegedly too large to provide adequate representation—and the total reorganization of the party on the basis of smaller and more numerous (164) election precincts.[48]

The regular county committee, ignoring the plaints and accusations of the soreheads, spent the month of May revitalizing the clubs—now augmented to fifty-one on the boss's recommendation—along their traditional lines. In the process, including the primary elections which placed his followers in the overwhelming majority of club offices, a ubiquitous Buckley played an active role, guiding the affairs of his own club, participating in the business of the county committee, and even finding time to lobby successfully before the State Central Committee in favor of San Francisco as the site for the state party convention and against the country wing's pleas for Los Angeles.[49]

By the first week in June, in a series of lively but essentially orderly primaries, Democrats had chosen numerous substantial citizens—among them Judge William T. Wallace who defended the club system as the most equitable for all—to head neighborhood organizations, and apparently the party had been successfully reconstituted. The results, however, satisfied Precinct and County Democrats neither in the form which reorganization had taken nor in their confirmation of Buckley's preeminence in the local party. Taylor, Shorb, and other dissident leaders continued to meet with increasing numbers of followers, denounced the

Blind Boss's leadership which allegedly cost the party 20,000 votes in 1882, questioned the sources of his growing wealth, and threatened to elect their own delegation to challenge the regular Democrats for recognition at the state convention scheduled to meet on August 31 in Odd Fellow's Hall in San Francisco. Most importantly, the Precinct and County Democracy persistently and vigorously petitioned the state committee for a complete reorganization of the local party.[50]

By mid-July—with the state convention in the offing, memories of 1882 still clearly in mind, and potential disaster threatening a badly divided San Francisco Republican party—the California Democratic leadership, perhaps at Buckley's instigation, responded to the continuing Precinct and County clamor. The dissidents' argument, in fact, had considerable merit, given the city's increasing size and complexity and the growing unwieldiness of many of the larger existing clubs. The source and nature of the ultimate solution to local party difficulties, however, astonished members of both factions and provides insight into the Blind Boss's unique political perception. The state committee, still chaired by William D. English and dominated by Buckley's delegates, initiated matters with a call for an open meeting of all city Democrats to air differences and resolve controversies. While some Precinct and County leaders resisted what they deemed a potentially immoral compromise with Buckley and just as many regulars regarded the conference call as an unwarranted intervention in local affairs, the Blind Boss himself assumed the role of peacemaker, urging supporters and opponents alike to comply with the state committee's resolution. Following the July 17 harmony conference, attended by few Precinct and County representatives, state party leaders unveiled their proposal which, for all practical purposes, involved a capitulation to the demands of the San Francisco dissidents and the dissolution of the clubs established by the Committee of Fifty in 1882. After abrogating the results of the May primaries, the local party would be required to reorganize itself entirely upon the basis of voting precincts, and it would do so under the scrutiny of a representative Board of Supervision and Arbitration approved by all local factions and the state leadership. Even more startling than the nature of the new plan, given Buckley's undisputed influence with the state committee, was the specific source of the proposal: George T. Marye, one of the boss's oldest and most intimate political associates.[51]

Neither party to the local dispute found the plan entirely to its liking. Precinct and County leaders feared—perhaps with some justification, considering its origins—that the proposal would favor entrenched regulars and that, even though it was a concession to their position, the Blind Boss's presence lurked somewhere in the background. Buckley himself expressed initial reservations concerning the proposal's impact upon the authority of the San Francisco County Committee, concern that Democrats would not enroll in the unfamiliar precinct clubs, and apprehension that the supervisory process would be too complex to be effective. Very likely, however, the boss dissembled for the benefit of the public, the press, and his partisan opponents, for in his official capacity his reticence evaporated and he urged compliance with the proposal in the interest of party harmony, advised all Democrats to enroll in the clubs and participate in primary elections, and exuded confidence in the regulars' ability to maintain their position in the party, even under an organizational system involving apparently total submission to the opposition.[52]

It is highly probable, in fact, that the new plan originated with the Blind Boss who realized that his own and his party's success depended less upon the structural form of the partisan machinery than upon continued appropriate responses to the varied needs and concerns of his urban constituency. It is improbable, moreover, that a trusted associate like Marye would propose or an essentially submissive state committee would sanction any system of organization which had not received the San Francisco potentate's imprimatur or which was inimical to his interests. Whatever the case, Buckley underscored his approval of the change by strenuous efforts during subsequent enrollment, registration, and organization activities, and the results amply rewarded his devotion and that of his copartisans and emphatically confirmed his political judgment and confidence. By the end of August, over 12,000 Democrats had enrolled in the 164 precinct clubs, the boss's supporters had captured an unprecedented majority of the party's leadership positions at both the neighborhood and county levels, and Buckley himself could rejoice not only in his own selection as a county committeeman from the Tenth Precinct Club of the Forth-Second District but also in the defeat of yet another contingent of soreheads.[53]

Buckley's political mastery and diplomatic skill had defused the attack

174

upon his position and simultaneously lured scores of wayward lambs back into his fold, and when the new county committee assembled on the eve of the Democratic State Convention, a spirit of harmony and confidence pervaded the gathering. To add to the sense of solidarity and optimism, following his selection to the powerful Committee on Constitution and By-Laws and to the equally important executive council, the Blind Boss announced his intention to provide a new and more commodious Democratic headquarters in his building at 313 Bush Street, across from his old groggery.[54] Simultaneously, committeemen learned that a solidly regular convention delegation could be expected not only from San Francisco but also from the remainder of the state. Not even the news that on the very same evening a rump minority of the Precinct and County Democracy had rescinded its agreement to abide by the results of reorganization and intended to persist in its opposition could dampen the euphoria appreciably.[55] For the moment, at least, Buckley's San Francisco Democrats had larger and more critical concerns involving the state convention meeting in their city.

Despite William D. English's assertion that Chris Buckley's sole interests in the Democratic State Convention of 1886 involved its potential implications for the success or failure of his municipal ticket and for the senatorial ambitions of George Hearst, the gathering had substantial additional significance for both the boss's career and the future of his party.[56] Democrats had learned in the aftermath of the Stockton convention that partisan factionalism—even in an admirable cause—could have disastrous consequences, and with the exception of a few intractables like Barclay Henley who would retire from politics following the 1886 meeting and some members of the pro-Field Democratic League of California, they would also admit that the antimonopoly issue did not have the anticipated popular appeal. Indeed, by the end of 1885 when Hearst dismissed the antimonopolist editor of his *Examiner* and increasing numbers of country Democrats had begun to urge more conciliatory postures, it was clear to most that the issue constituted an impediment to unity and victory and that a greater spirit of accommodation would prevail in the 1886 convention and campaign.[57]

There were conflicts at the gathering, to be sure, especially concerning the convention chairmanship and the gubernatorial nomination, but even those potentially explosive selections found amicable solutions,

175

both of which involved Chris Buckley. As he did in 1884, the Blind
Boss threw his own influence and the votes of the San Francisco delegation behind the ambitions of Stephen Mallory White for the convention
chairmanship and a state senate nomination. Simultaneously, even
though he preferred a different aspirant, he backed Washington Bartlett,
an anti-Stocktonite whose candidacy for governor constituted, as John P.
Irish wrote in the *Alta,* "an appeal and a concession" to the more conservative elements of the party. Despite the misgivings of many partisans,
the convention also endorsed the quest of George Hearst, whom Governor Stoneman had appointed to a vacancy in the U.S. Senate earlier in
the year, for a full term in Washington, and it adopted a platform which
retained carefully tempered vestiges of the old antimonopoly position,
reiterated the party's stance on the Chinese and on election and school
reform, supported a bimetallic monetary system, advocated tariff revisions and an enlarged navy, called for new water and irrigation legislation, and affirmed the state party's commitment to the candidates and
platform of the national party.[58]

When the Democratic assemblage adjourned, Buckley emerged a
winner in several important respects. He retained the simultaneous support of the mutually antagonistic Hearst and White, he augmented his
strength in the councils of the State Central Committee, and assurances
of a harmonious state party enhanced his chances for a victorious municipal campaign in San Francisco. Therefore, it was with substantially
greater confidence than had been apparent two years earlier that he
turned his attention to the local contest.[59] Remnants of the Precinct and
County Democracy remained active in their opposition, and as they had
done in 1884, they would make determined but futile efforts to consolidate their strength with several of the reform and special interest parties
which attempted to field slates of municipal candidates. Indeed, by
November 1886 no fewer than twenty-six distinct partisan conventions—including that of the United Labor party which Buckley purportedly attempted to infiltrate—had named full or partial tickets
which drew support principally from among Democratic voters.[60]

In the final analysis, however, intraparty resistance degenerated into
factionalism which prevented unity among dissident groups and precluded major inroads into the bastions of the regular Democrats who,
with Buckley in the forefront, girded for the municipal campaign with

greater harmony and optimism than they had experienced since 1882. In preparation for municipal convention primary elections, the county committee's Naturalization Bureau and other agencies assisted the foreign-born—perhaps with greater expediency than the law allowed—to obtain citizenship and register as voters, supported the establishment of Democratic clubs in the city's numerous national communities, appealed directly to a growing number of urban craft associations, and swelled the ranks of the party's adherents in every district of the municipality. When partisans recorded their choices for delegates to municipal nominating conventions, the rewards of the Buckley organization's efforts became apparent; each of the 164 precinct clubs designated a slate of representatives solidly loyal to the Blind Boss.[61]

In emulation of the state convention held in the city just one month earlier—and in sharp contrast to the strife-ridden and protracted Republican municipal convention which met simultaneously—the Democratic assemblage which convened on October 2 reflected a new-found party harmony, beginning with the selection of old-line conservative Isadore Gutte as chairman and permeating the entire proceedings. To head their ticket, Buckley Democrats selected fifty-two-year-old Edward B. Pond, prominent businessman and highly respected two-term supervisor from the Sixth Ward. Behind him, the Buckleyites ranged their traditional business and professional slate of candidates—with the important exception of a substantial labor representation, especially in legislative nominations. In their platform, the Democrats also recognized the augmented significance of a growing labor vote by including support for workingmen's goals alongside the traditional planks advocating reduced utility rates, Chinese exclusion, improved schools, the dollar-limit, completion of the new city hall, and a revised city charter.[62]

Buckley's party obviously had learned from its 1883 experience, for the campaign which followed the conventions and a ratification meeting of "thousands of Democrats" in the California Theater persistently recognized labor objectives, denounced the extravagances and malfeasances of incumbent Republican city officials, and made overtures to increasingly important organizations of women who, although they could not vote, exerted substantial influence upon those who could. The usual disruptions marred the canvass, persistent denunciations of Buckley emanated from opposition factions, and escalating Republican internecine

Edward B. Pond, mayor of San Francisco (1887–1891).

warfare prompted Police Chief Patrick Crowley to prepare his minions for a particularly difficult day at the polls, even for San Francisco. The election of 1886, like the campaign which preceded it, however, passed in relative decorum, despite the *Chronicle's* eleventh-hour charges that Buckley himself moved among scores of polling places, paying up to three dollars apiece for votes.[63]

When the final results were in—after nearly three weeks of counting and recounting and persistent accusations of fraud, ballot-stuffing, and repeating hurled from all sides—the only real surprise involved the narrowness of several Democratic victories. In the state elections, Bartlett defeated John Swift by a bare 654 votes out of nearly 200,000 cast, probably as a consequence of the former mayor's outspoken attacks upon the principles of the American party and revelations that he employed Chinese workers in his laundry business in San Francisco and on his ranch in Santa Clara County. On the other hand, the Republican candi-

Chris Buckley in Fire Company uniform.

date for lieutenant-governor, Robert Waterman, courted nativist support and defeated his Irish-born opponent by almost 2500 votes. Although lavish dispensations of "railroad sack slaughtered" four congressional candidates, Democrats dominated state offices and the legislature where Stephen Mallory White won his seat in the senate. In the city, 46,000 voters went to the polls and elected Buckley's candidates to nearly all municipal offices. Pond captured the mayoralty by over 5000 votes, although many contests finished substantially closer, and a few Republicans who had remained aloof from their party's conflicts or ran against weak Democrats—candidates for county clerk and superintendent of schools, one school director, and supervisors from the Eighth, Ninth, and Twelfth Wards—won their races by narrow margins.[64] The sweep was not so complete as that of 1882, but Democrats—including businessmen who had backed Pond—were jubilant, and for Chris Buckley the results of the election constituted a personal triumph.

Triumph was not without serious negative implications, although they were hidden by the momentary flush of victory. Concessions to the Manhattan Club types represented in the County and Precinct Democracy began almost immediately to alter the character of the partisan organization which had served the boss so well and provided his principal base of popular support. The opposition would soon recognize that fact and capitalize upon it in their efforts to capture control of the party and the city. For the time, however, Buckley's position seemed eminently secure.

At the
Zenith of Power,
1887-1889

Several important conditions—including public dissatisfaction with the performance of municipal government during the previous two years, factionalism which weakened the Republican organization, the impact of the American party upon closely contested races, and Chris Buckley's skillful management of a potentially divisive situation in his own party—combined to ensure a Democratic success in San Francisco in 1886. The party hierarchy acknowledged the significance of all these factors, but on the evening of November 17, well before ballot recounts made election results official, they clearly demonstrated their assessment of the most critical ingredient in the victory. Chairman Max Popper conducted a delegation of county committee officers to the Blind Boss's Post Street home to present him with a sumptuous 130-piece sterling silver dinner service, a "token of their esteem and appreciation" for his leadership. A few days later, accompanied by his wife and a retinue of retainers, Buckley departed for Europe to relax and recover his strength after a strenuous canvass, to

Chris Buckley at the zenith of power.

consult with specialists in the hope of regaining at least a portion of his sight, and to investigate municipal conditions across the Atlantic. After nearly seven months, one hundred still appreciative followers assembled once again on Post Street, on this occasion to serenade the boss and his wife, to express their "friendly regard . . . [and] to congratulate [Buckley] on his safe return" to San Francisco.[1]

182

Democratic leaders had reason to be grateful in the aftermath of the 1886 contest, and the Blind Boss, satisfied with his accomplishments and certain that his hiatus from the tumult of partisan strife was both well earned and eminently safe, candidly commented that "I was then at the zenith of my power."[2] The party had maintained its control over the mayor's office, it had elected a solid majority to the board of supervisors and to the school board, and it had won nearly all remaining municipal offices and the control of their patronage. In Sacramento, even though Bartlett had not been Buckley's first choice for the position, a former Democratic mayor of San Francisco sat in the governor's chair, and copartisans exercised sufficient control in the legislature to grant George Hearst the honor he had sought since 1882: a full term in the United States Senate. When the state senate convened in 1887, moreover, the pro tem presidency was voted to Stephen Mallory White, who owed a substantial debt to the boss and his city machine. And in the party itself, harmony on the antimonopoly question and other issues had returned many of the dissidents of 1884—including even intransigents like John P. Irish of the *Alta*—to the fold, if not as lambs at least as loyal partisans. The boss's supporters held most of the important positions in local and state committees, and Buckley once again chaired the county organization's powerful executive council. Finally, even though Mayor Edward B. Pond's inaugural address emphasized continuing problems in the city—persistent fiscal distress, unsatisfactory streets and civic facilities, the inability to control utility and transportation rates, the disastrous state of the House of Correction and the school system, and the pressing need for funds to complete Golden Gate Park and the new city hall—in California and in San Francisco Buckley and the Democracy could contemplate the future with substantial optimism.[3]

Still, even though the fact did not become immediately apparent, not all consequences of the election of 1886—not even some of the seeming successes—ultimately proved beneficial to the boss or his organization. Hearst's senatorial triumph, for example, was an event fraught with potential conflict. His previous appointment to fill a vacant seat had antagonized numerous influential figures, including the increasingly powerful White, but Hearst's ambition had produced an even earlier controversy. Following the election of 1884, when Democratic legislators could not hope to elevate one of their own to the U.S. Senate, a minority caucus dominated by Buckley's San Francisco delegation nevertheless endorsed a senatorial candidate, Hearst, in anticipation of the potential vacancy. The action produced outrage among other aspirants, including Barclay Henley of Sonoma County who was the state's only victorious congressional candidate in 1884. Henley presumed himself to be the frontrunner for the caucus endorsement, ascribed his rejection to Buckley's influence, and never forgave the boss for the presumed affront. Hearst's appointment to the vacancy and subsequent election to a full term in the senate only confirmed Henley in his antagonism, and despite his announced retirement from politics following the convention of 1886, he soon moved to San Francisco to establish a law practice and join with a growing number of city Democrats bent upon deposing the Blind Boss.[4]

Hearst's ambition precipitated other unanticipated consequences as well. On the day that he departed for Washington and on the eve of his son's twenty-fourth birthday, the new senator turned his *Examiner* over to William Randolph Hearst whose subsequent efforts to make the journal the "Monarch of the Dailies" in the city soon involved rabid attacks upon Buckley and political alignments with the boss's enemies, despite the harm which such tactics might inflict upon the the senior Hearst's career. The damage to both the senator and the boss ultimately proved substantial, for the situation in San Francisco was unlike that in New York City when Thomas Nast's cartoons prompted William Marcy Tweed to complain, "I don't care a straw for your newspaper articles, my constituents can't read, but they can't help seeing them damned pictures." Buckley's constituents could read, and the younger Hearst soon gave them the vitriolic Ambrose Bierce and, before long, pictures too.[5]

Nor was the editor the sole representative of a new generation entering San Francisco politics in 1886; James Duval Phelan had involved himself with the San Francisco Municipal League in 1883, cofounded the Young Men's Democratic League in 1884, made his first speech to a mass political audience in 1886, and would become increasingly active in the ranks of reformist Democratic factions in subsequent contests. Still other new leaders—including Max Popper, currently county committee chairman and loyal to the boss but soon to aspire to the chair of the state committee and to gravitate toward anti-Buckley elements in the party, and young professionals like attorneys Alex Vogelsang and

George Hearst.   William Randolph Hearst.

Eugene Deuprey—began to seek their places. And White, himself a representative of the new leadership, had his authority unexpectedly increased. Governor Bartlett died less than a year after his inauguration, Republican Robert Waterman ascended to his place, and the pro tem senate president became, for all practical purposes, lieutenant governor of the state and decreasingly dependent upon Buckley and the San Francisco organization.[6]

In addition to the challenge implicit in the emergence of young and ambitious political leaders, continuing urban development provided evidence of simmering change which could threaten both Buckley's position and his methods. In his remarks upon turning the mayor's office over to his successor, Washington Bartlett emphasized the city's desperate need for a revised frame of government adapted to urban realities radically transformed since the adoption of the Consolidation Act in 1856. It was not Bartlett's first expression of such concerns; in 1879 he had served on a fifteen-member Board of Freeholders appointed by the mayor under provisions of the new California constitution to draft an appropriate charter for the city. Nor was that document, rejected in March 1880 by nearly 13,000 votes out of the 20,000 cast, the initial effort to provide

185

San Francisco with a more functional organic law.[7] As early as 1873, Mayor William Alvord attempted to persuade citizens to revise the Consolidation Act which he condemned as a patchwork of amendments proscribing civic progress, precluding such critical advances as the acquisition of a municipal water supply, and necessitating excessive state involvement in local affairs. Later in the same decade, the state legislature, to no avail, twice attempted to amend the Consolidation Act in response to altered urban conditions, and critics subsequently echoed Alvord's complaints, adding to them denunciations of the limited authority of the mayor, decentralization which precluded accountability in civic departments and agencies, and the confusion and opportunity for corruption created by an organic law "amended almost out of shape."[8]

Chris Buckley recorded his own belief that the city required no new charter, that the Consolidation Act "served San Francisco well for almost half a century," and that corruption was, in any case, inherent in municipal government, regardless of its form.[9] There were, however, many citizens who disagreed with his conclusions, including younger members of the business and professional communities in the city and emerging political leaders like Phelan who persisted in the effort to secure a modified charter. Although each proposed organic law differed in specifics from its predecessors and successors, all embodied a set of essentially common principles. Proponents of charter reform universally deemed increased authority in the office of the mayor absolutely essential. Specifically, they included in their documents provisions permitting—and in some cases mandating—the mayor to function as a true municipal executive by initiating action on civic matters and assuming powers, especially those involving personnel policies and appointments, traditionally within the purview of the board of supervisors. Under the proposed new concept of city government, the mayor would exercise direct control over municipal agencies and departments, and their heads—more frequently appointed than elected—would be directly and solely responsible to him. Conversely, proposed charters sharply reduced the independence of boards of supervisors and school boards, made elected and appointed administrators coequal with the boards, and in the case of the supervisors eliminated the familiar ward representation in favor of at-large nominations and elections.[10]

Additionally, projected revisions in the organic law attacked the much-denounced patronage system, the backbone of machine power, by instituting the rudiments of civil service programs. They also attempted, somewhat unrealistically, to eliminate the worst political abuses by increasing the number of appointive offices at the disposal of the mayor and establishing, particularly in the school system and similar agencies, the principle of nonpartisanship in elections. Obviously, a powerful mayor could appoint as many scoundrels to office as voters could elect and a nonpartisan candidate could be as unethical or incompetent as a member of a regular organization, but a recognition of these facts did not temper reformers' faith in their principles. Nor were they any more timid about other charter changes which were universally proposed in the 1870s and 1880s: expanding the city's authority over its own affairs (home rule), providing for municipal ownership and regulation of utilities, and codifying contract and franchise procedures to bring them under stringent control. Proponents of charter revision in San Francisco sought a more efficient, businesslike, and responsible municipal government which would at least reduce partisan involvement, and in their attitudes and goals they closely resembled "good government" advocates concurrently promoting similar reform programs in cities across the nation.[11]

Advocated changes struck directly at several of the conditions which permitted Buckley and his counterparts to function in the nineteenth-century city, especially the patronage system, franchise policies, inherent confusion in government, and the principle of ward representation which not only provided the basis for the machine's organizational effectiveness but also, in fact, served urban dwellers well for generations. Charter reformers made two additional attempts to impose their version of a sound municipal government which would preclude bossism in San Francisco during the 1880s, but without success. In March 1883, they very nearly succeeded when their proposed organic law suffered defeat by a scant thirty-two votes, but in April 1887 a third Board of Freeholders witnessed the inundation of their handiwork by more than 4000 ballots.[12] In both special charter elections, and in the one which preceded them in 1880, less than one-half of the city's eligible voters participated. Indeed, the fraction probably was closer to one-third, making it apparent that, despite the enthusiasm of members of the local business and professional communities, most San Franciscans had little vital interest in the question of charter reform. Although the defeats most frequently have been explained in terms of opposition by Buckley, Higgins, and other politicos, there is no evidence of vigorous activity by the Blind Boss in the campaigns of 1880, 1883, or 1887, and it is far more likely that failures resulted principally from apathy on the part of the urban public.[13]

Many San Franciscans, in fact, harbored considerable reservations about the entire matter. Since the 1850s, residents of the city habitually had abdicated the responsibility for municipal government to representatives of the Vigilance Committee's political successor, the People's party, and even after the demise of that organization the habits and practices remained unchanged. Equally important, the 1870s and 1880s were turbulent decades for the young metropolis—involving the chaos of the WPC-Kalloch interlude, severe and recurrent economic depression, rapid urbanization, and the persistent Chinese controversy—and citizens had little desire for additional changes which might compound the confusion. There were those, too, who regarded charter provisions calling for municipal ownership and enhanced regulatory powers, innocuous as they may seem from a twentieth-century perspective, as a socialistic sort of radicalism. Finally, although most San Franciscans conceded the imperfections of their municipal government and acknowledged the abuses which resulted from them, they also suspected the remedies which Boards of Freeholders and other reformers advocated, particularly provisions which might "give the Mayor power to suspend the whole City Government" and become a "great municipal mogul."[14] For all of these reasons—apathy, fear of change, and a latter-day Jacksonian suspicion of centralized authority and potential privilege—no charter reform movement succeeded during Buckley's tenure. Following the 1887 effort, there would be no further attempt until 1896, and only in 1898 would a new organic law garner voters' approval. Nevertheless, the growing pressure for change which charter movements represented in the mid-1880s clearly implied a threat to the Blind Boss and demonstrated an altered attitude toward the city among many emerging San Francisco leaders.

Other developments also evidenced changes in attitudes and expectations. By 1886, the urban population had reached approximately 275,000 (some enthusiasts placed it as high as 325,000) and it continued to spread inexorably across the peninsula. To accomodate a larger and more widely dispersed citizenry, steam-driven cable cars, electric trolley systems, and remnants of the old horsecar lines crisscrossed the city with their nearly 100 miles of track. A half-dozen gas and electric firms provided light for streets, public buildings, and a growing number of private homes in most districts of San Francisco, and the telephone was becoming a popular convenience, despite condemnations of the unsightly maze of poles and wires which it produced in congested areas. Business, commercial, financial, and manufacturing enterprises had grown in both number and size, and most enjoyed brisk activity in the recovery which followed the depression of 1883.[15] Despite the apparent prosperity and obvious progress toward modern metropolitanism, however, residents continued to articulate their traditional dissatisfactions with their city and its government: taxes and assessments increased inordinately, municipal facilities were inadequate and in disrepair, streets and sidewalks and sewers failed to serve their intended purposes, utility rates remained exorbitant and apparently uncontrolled, water supplies often fell short of needs, and the fire and police departments were both corrupt and incompetent.

During the later 1880s, public criticism of municipal deficiencies persisted, but it assumed a discernibly different tone, especially as it emanated from more influential and articulate elements in the population. With unemployment decreasing during relatively prosperous times, labor officials affiliated with the Federated Trades Council urged their followers to seek, in addition to jobs and the expulsion of the Chinese, more advanced concessions including shorter hours and higher wages, improved conditions, and especially the right to organize, an effort which was punctuated by recurrent strikes and occasional violence.[16] In other quarters, San Franciscans who were no longer satisfied with the mere existence of facilities and services began to demand quality, efficiency, and safety. The altered tenor of their complaints focused upon numerous civic problems: the street railway companies' disregard for the safety of both passengers and pedestrians, archaic equipment and poorly trained personnel in both the fire and police departments, the persistent use of obsolete or substandard materials in street paving and other construction, and the general inadequacy of the municipal government.[17] The barrage of criticism also revealed a new sense of civic pride when it scored the obvious ugliness and shabby workmanship involved in civic structures, especially the new city hall facility, still unfinished after a decade of work and millions of dollars expended. And it attacked a public school system which not only hired incompetents to teach and performed educational functions poorly but also housed the city's children in unsanitary and unsafe facilities and excluded an estimated 10,000 of them due to deficient accommodations. Even the exalted dollar-limit suffered denunciation; economy in government, it seems, had become a less appealing prospect if its tangible results did not comply with the heightened civic consciousness of many influential San Franciscans.[18]

Nothing more emphatically elaborates the ramifications of altered attitudes toward the city than concern for sanitation and public health during the 1880s, especially responses to the smallpox epidemic which plagued San Francisco from the spring of 1887 until the early months of 1888. During the episode, residents recognized the inadequacy of the municipal health facilities upon which they depended, encountered conflicts between local, state, and federal agencies, subordinated their concern for physical well-being to economically-oriented concerns for the city's public image, and revealed a sharp awareness of the socioeconomic distinctions separating urban residents and districts from one another. The epidemic originated on May 3, 1887 when the S.S. *City of Sydney* out of Hong Kong arrived in San Francisco and several passengers made their way ashore. Although local residents assumed the carriers to be Chinese, the disease respected neither race nor status; within months of the *City of Sydney*'s arrival, over 300 cases of smallpox were reported throughout the city, and the nearly 100 who perished included members of the more affluent classes, among them the son of railroad czar Mark Hopkins. Before the scourge passed, over 1000 cases had been identified and treated, and approximately one-fifth of them died.[19]

Initially, local officials and journalists—with the exception, perhaps, of Irish of the *Alta*—tended to minimize the presence of disease, hoping to avoid the "pesthole" reputation which would divert critical commercial traffic from the waterfront. With the coming of the new year and the realization that smallpox cases had appeared among more substantial citizens as well as among the Chinese and poorer working classes, citizens vociferously demanded that their municipal government take action. In response, city health officers erected a temporary canvas "pesthouse" (quarantine hospital) on Portsmouth Plaza, initiated innoculation drives among school children, closed numerous public buildings including eventually the jail, undertook inspection and fumigation operations in lodging houses in Chinatown and south of Market Street, and moved to quarantine ships arriving from the Orient.[20] Each of these measures reflected a growing recognition that a crisis confronted the city, but each also revealed problems and conflicts within the metropolis.

The construction of the pesthouse, for example, precipitated immediate outcry, especially from among "better" citizens who regarded its presence as an eyesore, a public nuisance, and an all too graphic reminder of the contagion abroad in the city. The quarantine hospital controversy, indeed, provided the smallpox episode's sole instance of comic relief when, with exaggerated indignation, former county coroner Dr. C. C. O'Donnell (in reality a veterinarian with prior ties to the WPC movement) swore out a warrant against Mayor Pond and had him arrested for permitting the building on a public square. Other citizens, however, took a more serious approach to the problem and besieged municipal authorities with demands that the pesthouse be relocated at some less obvious site, preferably to the south of Market Street, at Hunter's Point, or entirely out of the city on a hospital ship anchored off Goat Island in the middle of the bay.[21] The question of innoculation revealed equally serious conflicts in the city. Vaccination programs which on occasion reached 400 persons a day and included more than 50,000 in the first five months of 1888 quickly exhausted local serum stocks, and although appeals to federal agencies ultimately replenished supplies, clashes remained rampant and illuminated divisions in the municipality and confusion in its government. When school directors authorized the innoculation of children in schools, the superintendent of schools attempted to overrule them, precipitating a bitter debate and causing a major delay. Within weeks, the board of supervisors' entry into the dispute added to the turmoil, and a protracted confrontation among public health physicians arguing about the benefits and hazards of innoculation exacerbated the problem. Finally, external agencies entered the fray; officials of the state health department and the United States Customs Service each asserted their own claim to jurisdiction over aspects of the innoculation program, further delaying and diluting its effect.[22]

Activities such as the isolation of residents of Chinatown and the city

jail or the fumigation of tenements and lodging houses did not specifically involve affluent or influential San Franciscans and therefore caused
little controversy. Quarantine measures directed at the waterfront, on
the other hand, underscored the conflicts involved in the innoculation
and pesthouse issues. Merchants whose businesses would suffer objected
strenuously to regulations preventing vessels from landing their cargos
and passengers, and editors joined them in denouncing the policy as an
admission of the epidemic's seriousness which, if pursued, would result
in vacant wharves. Even those who supported quarantine proposals could
not agree upon implementation; some favored a zone estabished conveniently offshore, but those sensitive to the prospect of ships potentially
bearing the insidious disease at anchor within sight of the city argued for
a more remote locale discreetly shielded from view. Simultaneously,
three distinct jurisdictions vied for the authority to devise and supervise
any quarantine policy: the municipal health department, the state-
appointed Board of Harbor Commissioners, and federal customs officials.[23] And the conflicts resulted in contradictory regulations or none
at all, countermanded directives, and perhaps additional cases of smallpox in the city.

The epidemic in San Francisco did not reach the magnitude of out-
breaks of the same disease in New Orleans and other American cities
during the nineteenth century. Nor did it touch Chris Buckley personally; during the critical months, he spent his time in Livermore and
journeyed to the city only when imperative political concerns made his
presence mandatory. Nevertheless, the episode did reveal altered political conditions and urban attitudes with which the boss would be forced
to contend. Typical of events during the entire episode, officials and
citizens could not even agree when the epidemic ended. The board of
health declared the danger over in mid-March 1888, but sceptical residents and journalists continued to report numerous cases of smallpox—
including individuals found dead of the affliction in Golden Gate Park
and other public places—until late October. Despite their obvious resentment of outside interference during the crisis, moreover, when it
subsided San Franciscans expressed their dissatisfaction with municipal
government by appealing for increased federal authority over the port in
the event of a recurrence.[24] More importantly, responses to the epidemic
manifested serious conflicts within the city government and between the

city and other jurisdictions, and many who regarded the disputes as merely symptomatic of larger problems increased their clamor for more efficient municipal services, charter reform, and home rule. Finally, reactions to the crisis reflected transformed attitudes toward the urban community and increasingly individualist views (Sam Bass Warner, Jr. has called it "privatism") which effectively delineated the demise of the traditional walking city.[25]

On the basis of threats to their economic interests, businessmen denounced quarantine regulations and joined with editors and other spokesmen to minimize the seriousness of the crisis. Other affluent citizens resisted the establishment of an adequate smallpox hospital in their own residential or business locales or where it would detract from the esthetics of the city and insisted that the facility—and the equally essential quarantine zone—be located in regions populated by people other than themselves. In short, many influential San Franciscans confronted their city's crisis in terms of their own interests and views of the metropolis and, even at substantial hazard to their own health and that of their fellow citizens, they tailored the expectations of municipal government accordingly. They also made it clear that they would willingly use their substantial influence to impose their ideas upon the city and, if necessary, carry their demands into the political arena.

Chris Buckley's continued success in his profession would depend upon how effectively he responded to all of these changes and also to altered policies and expectations among his major clients. In San Francisco, as elsewhere during the late nineteenth century, a trend toward business reorganization had already begun to manifest itself in the form of larger, more highly integrated economic entities. By the middle of the 1880s, for example, an informal street railway trust, coordinated by Jim McCord of the Sutter Street Company and represented by attorney Evan S. Pillsbury, existed in the city. Consisting principally of McCord's firm and the Southern Pacific's local interests, the Market Street cable system, the consortium aimed at eliminating competition and influencing such political matters as the regulation of fares and services. Total control of the street railways would be approached only with the consolidation of the Market Street Company's practical monopoly in 1893, but the presence of the earlier cartel posed immediate problems for the Blind Boss and other politicos. And the existence of similar associations among the Spring Valley Company and other utilities (also among Pillsbury's clients), active business organizations which included the Chamber of Commerce, the Board of Trade and Phelan's Young Men's Commercial League, as well as an increasing number of major corporate entities reinforced the threat.[26]

No longer so able to play one interest against another, Buckley would have to be sufficiently flexible to adapt to dealing with businessmen who opted for cooperation over competition and thereby undermined the boss's position as a broker of privilege. Such formal and informal associations could, if sufficiently stable and cohesive, bring direct pressure to bear upon civic authorities, as William C. Ralston had done a decade earlier, in order to influence desired political results in the city and the state without the boss's mediation.

Several changes in the policies of the Blind Boss's city governments suggest that he clearly understood the implications of the transformations occurring in San Francisco and that he attempted to respond to them. The board of supervisors, for example, scrutinized both the dollar-limit policy and the One-Twelfth Act in order to ascertain means for the appropriation of more funds for civic improvements, and they sought the advice of experts on the question of the sewers and employed a new architect to develop final plans for the city hall complex. Simultaneously, authorities pressed for the completion of Golden Gate Park and other projects, passed ordinances mandating rudimentary safety devices at street railway crossings, recommended—but did not enact—laws requiring that utility lines be placed underground and water and traction companies be more stringently regulated, and brought the school and penal systems under close investigation.[27] Although such programs had little immediate impact (the new city hall, for example, remained incomplete and public complaints about street railway safety persisted for a decade) and they may have involved motivations other than civic altruism, they did illustrate an awareness of altered public attitudes.

As the guiding force in his party, Buckley also made tangible efforts to increase the Democracy's responsiveness to changing conditions, with substantial and surprisingly rapid results. After the reorganization of 1886—and to some degree after the defeat of 1884—the neighborhood clubs lost many of the characteristics which made them particularly effective and important to their members. The 1882 *Plan of Reorganization,* moreover, had discouraged the establishment of partisan associations external to the club system. With the 1886 precinct modifications, the clubs became almost strictly administrative entities concerned with the naturalization and registration of voters, the conduct of primary elections, and the maintenance of party records. The change did not diminish Democratic enrollments appreciably, but the precinct associations no longer fulfilled many of the social functions which had maintained partisan activity and loyalty. To counter this development, shortly after Buckley's return from his European sojourn, the Democratic County Committee began to encourage the formation of alternate partisan organizations which would appeal to the special interests of a variety of voters. In that policy, the Blind Boss participated actively as a cofounder and sachem of the Tammany Society which was composed of local party leaders, city and state elected officials like Judge William T. Wallace, holders of patronage appointments under the national government (known as the "Federal Brigade"), and a contingent of local Democratic businessmen which included James Duval Phelan and William Randolph Hearst.[28]

Unlike its New York City namesake, the San Francisco Tammany Society, which evolved into a new Manhattan Club in 1890, did not constitute the official central organization of the local Democracy. Instead, it functioned, except during campaigns, principally as a social club based upon the common interests of the upper echelons of the party. It was, in fact, the city counterpart to the statewide Iroquois Club of which Max Popper was San Francisco "wigwam" president and the State Democratic Club which included Phelan among its vice presidents.[29] Buckley also participated in the formation of other associations appealing to the varied special interests of city Democrats. He involved himself, for example, in the Businessmen's Democratic Club—later to merge with the Manhattan Club and become the Occidental Club in 1893—and with the Western Addition Democratic Club which included many of the boss's suburban neighbors. Nor were Buckley's party affiliations limited to those involving affluent members of San Francisco society. He joined, for example, the newly-established partisan organization in his old midtown neighborhood and chaired its headquarters search committee, and he encouraged the formation of similar associa-

James Duval Phelan, reform mayor of San Francisco (1897–1901) and sponsor of the Charter of 1898.

tions which included the Mission District Democrats, the Folsom Street Democrats, the Eighth Ward Cleveland and Thurman Fire Brigade, the North Beach Democrats, and the "Old Ninth" Democratic Club.[30] Groups based upon voters' origins also emerged early in 1888: the Bandana Buckeyes (from Ohio), German-American Democrats, Colored Democrats, French-Born Democrats (Raphael Weill, president), Irish Democrats, Portuguese Democrats, and many more.[31]

Also included in the host of new associations were those organized around a particular political interest, philosophy, or personality. The Pond Democratic Club espoused Jeffersonian principles and promoted the career of its favorite, the Hickory Club adhered to Jacksonian tenets, and the Young Democrats and the Anti-Coolie Democratic Club came together to advance their particular interests. Some organizations had no apparent reason for existence other than party solidarity, sociability, or affiliation with a group with a readily identifiable name; these included such clubs as the Americus (to which Chris Buckley also belonged), the Eureka, the Monumental, the Buffalo, and more. Whether founded for a single purpose or simply for the sake of unity and camaraderie, the new clubs provided urban Democrats with numerous activities in addition to their partisan functions. Some sponsored elaborately uniformed drill and shooting teams and marched in gala parades, while others engaged in banquets, picnics, family outings, and a variety of amateur theatricals.[32] All of them drew Democrats into the party organization on the basis of their views of the city and provided members of the business community, civic associations, neighborhood and ethnic groups, and the like with opportunities to express their concerns through Democratic party channels. They also allowed Buckley, personally or through associates, to remain in contact with various elements in the rapidly changing city. Simultaneously, however, they tended to undermine cohesiveness, the source of the organization's strength.

By the spring of 1888, the Democratic County Committee had sanctioned a multiplicity of such associations, many of them with overlapping memberships, but party officers could not rely upon such extramural clubs to perform the functions of a thoroughly disciplined machine. Early in the year, therefore, Chairman Popper, Buckley, and other leaders initiated efforts to prepare the party for yet another biennial contest. In January they collaborated with the State Central Committee in a campaign to bring their party's national convention to San Francisco, an effort supported even by Republican journals like Michel De Young's *Chronicle*. The drive failed, but until St. Louis received the national committee's sanction in April, the California city remained in contention.[33] That fact enhanced the confidence of local partisans and provided impetus for their own activities. During the first months of the year, far in advance of traditional practice, the county committee accepted and implemented Buckley's recommendation that the 1886 precinct organization plan be retained intact, and by the end of March the party had established a club in each of the city's 176 precincts.[34]

With soreheads nowhere in evidence, the preliminary campaign of 1888 certainly constituted the most uneventful in the Blind Boss's career. The Democracy enrolled several thousand new members, registered them to vote, and proceeded with its primary elections. In mid-April members selected permanent officers for the precinct clubs, a week later they chose their new county committee, and early in May over 14,000 Democrats selected their delegates to the state convention scheduled to meet in Los Angeles. Each step represented a victory for Buckley; his followers again won a majority of the offices in the precinct clubs and on the county committee and the boss once again headed the executive council. Furthermore, even though the delegation selected to represent San Francisco at the Los Angeles convention did not include the boss, it was composed of party regulars eager to do his bidding.[35]

When the county committee assembled in its spacious new quarters in Buckley's building at 729 Market Street, it could anticipate the coming contest with substantial confidence. For the Blind Boss, however, one incident of an apparently personal but probably partisan nature marred the otherwise propitious events of early 1888. On the eve of the state convention, the boss was once again in the hands of the law, arrested in San Francisco on a Los Angeles grand jury warrant and charged with conducting a gambling operation. The device involved was a "clock game" in a disreputable "bucket shop" called the Turf, Grain and Produce Exchange located in a seedy section of Los Angeles. Apparently based upon a clock mechanism connected to a switching system on a tally board, the game involved wagers upon the rise and fall (rigged by the operators) of stock and commodity prices. Those who managed the device vigorously denied that Buckley had anything to do with either the game itself or the property it occupied; nevertheless, Los Angeles authorities demanded his appearance to answer the charges against him. The boss, in turn, appealed for aid to Stephen Mallory White who not only arranged bail but also obtained a trial date coincident with the state convention and agreed to represent Buckley in the litigation. During the subsequent course of events, White settled at least a portion of his debt to the Blind Boss; for the senator's skill as an attorney and influence with Los Angeles authorities secured both the desired speedy and separate trials and a dismissal of all charges.[36] Buckley was vindicated, but the incident, coinciding as it did with the state convention, proved to be a political liability, albeit a minor one. Indeed, as the boss himself believed, the episode probably was no coincidence at all but rather another instance of soreheads' efforts to discredit him.[37]

Whatever the case, with the exception of considerable inconvenience and probable embarrassment, the accusation and subsequent trial inflicted little real harm. In fact, when Buckley departed from San Francisco, as always carrying his battered old valise, to attend the Los Angeles convention, he manifested little evidence that a felony indictment hung over his head. Nor did he exhibit any evidence of concern for two other issues which troubled California Democrats in 1888: the census returns and Grover Cleveland. Concerning the first problem, little could be done. No doubt any longer existed that migration to California from other regions of the United States had increased Republican strength dramatically in the state, especially in southern counties where it constituted a majority by 1888. This reality confronted Democrats with the absolute necessity of maintaining the always shaky alliance between city and country and waging an energetic campaign to win newcomers— "tenderfeet," they were called—to the Democratic fold.[38] Both were monumental, if not impossible, assignments.

Nor was the problem of Grover Cleveland any more amenable to simple solution. California Democratic leaders sanctioned his renomination and planned no major bolt from support of the national ticket, but since 1885 many of them—including Buckley and White—had grown increasingly disenchanted with the president, specifically with his patronage and antisilver policies and his apparent inconsistency on the tariff issue. In December 1887, Cleveland did redeem himself to some degree with an aggressive speech outlining the evils of protection and announcing his attention to make tariff reform a priority issue during the following year.[39] He also made an eleventh-hour appeal for California votes on the eve of the 1888 election when he took decisive and probably politically inspired action on the still troublesome Chinese question. Since the passage of the Exclusion Act of 1882, nearly 40,000 Chinese had entered the country, most of them previous migrants returning from visits to their homeland. In March 1888, the Cleveland administration concluded a treaty aimed at halting the flow of returnees for twenty years, but delay and amendment in the senate and vacillation by the Chinese government prevented its ratification. In September, the president risked a major diplomatic blunder and took matters into his own hands. Through Representative William L. Scott of Pennsylvania, he introduced legislation permanently prohibiting reentry of the Chinese, and despite attempted delays in congress the bill became law when the president affixed his signature to it on October 1, thereby recovering some of his appeal to Californians.[40]

Still, Cleveland remained a potential liability and a possible source of controversy when Democrats gathered in Los Angeles, led there, according to Harrison Gray Otis's rabidly Republican Los Angeles *Times,* by "general manager Buckley . . . [of the] Unwashed."[41] Although he was not an official delegate, the Blind Boss—still under indictment in the clock game affair—arrived a day early to entertain party leaders in his hotel suite and to lay plans for the impending meeting. Somewhat surprisingly, the convention passed without major incident. Buckley collaborated with White and the country forces to select former antimonopolist state senator Reginaldo F. Del Valle of Los Angeles to the temporary chairmanship, making it clear that the city-country alliance held reasonably firm. The assemblage evaded the possibility of controversy over Cleveland by drafting a positive but plainly unenthusiastic resolution endorsing the president's renomination and praising his "earnest and intelligent efforts in the interests of the people."[42] In the platform concurrently adopted, California Democrats affirmed their stands in favor of silver coinage, Chinese exclusion, homestead law reform, direct election of senators, and tariff reform, memorialized Washington Bartlett, and included only an innocuous reference to the old antimonopoly issue, now vaguely related to the protection question.[43]

The party apparently had relegated the controversy over railroad regulation to the dust heap of the past, for when it selected slates of presidential electors and delegates to the national convention in St. Louis, they included representatives of both Stockton factions and of the city and country wings of the Democracy.[44] Indeed, White—himself one of the St. Louis delegates—perhaps best illustrates the demise of the antimonopoly issue and possibly its inherent shallowness. Despite his vehement antimonopoly stance, he only relinquished his $10,000 annual retainer as Southern Pacific legal counsel late in 1889, and the apparent conflict of interest raised but few questions among his partisan associates or constituents.[45]

As for Buckley, he departed from the Los Angeles convention as the "cock of the walk" in city and state politics.[46] He employed the 104 votes of the San Francisco delegation not only to turn aside White's alleged efforts to construct a competitive country machine within the party, but also to secure a substantial favorable representation on the State Central Committee. Simultaneously, he managed to reinforce the critical urban-rural alliance through his support for White, Del Valle, and other country leaders, and he solidified that relationship by sanctioning White's candidacy for reelection to the pro tem presidency of the state senate.[47]

There were, however, several consequences of the convention which did not bode well for the boss's political future, and one of them involved White. With Buckley's support, he was chosen a delegate to St. Louis where he became temporary chairman of the national Democratic convention, and recognition by the national party apparently altered his sense of dependence upon the Blind Boss. Within months, indeed, White made his altered attitude only too apparent when he wrote to state party chairman William D. English that "I don't care a cent what Buckley does" with reference to the impending pro tem presidency campaign in the senate.[48] The boss antagonized more partisans when he went "after [Judge Jeremiah F.] Sullivan's scalp" at the convention. Sullivan had pursued the state supreme court chief justiceship since the campaign of 1886, which he lost, the judge believed, because Buckley worked against him. In Los Angeles in 1888, he sought the nomination for the same post, but he was denied by the votes of the San Francisco delegation.[49] What prompted the boss's hostility toward Sullivan is not clear, but it is apparent that he made enemies of both the judge and many of his influential friends in the party.

Events at the convention produced an even more vindictive foe in Jeremiah Lynch, whom Buckley accurately described as " an ambitious young man of wealth."[50] Born in Massachusetts in 1849, Lynch migrated to California as a child, and as a young man he made a considerable fortune through Comstock silver speculation and as an officer of the San Francisco Stock and Exchange Board. He would reap a second bonanza in the Yukon gold rush later in the century. Lynch was also something of a dilettante who described himself as a "capitalist" and fancied himself an authority on many subjects. He traveled the world and returned to his rooms in the Palace or Baldwin hotels to write on Egyptology and his adventures in Alaska and to produce a laudatory biography of his hero, Senator David C. Broderick.[51] He also had political aspirations, and with Buckley's support in 1882 he sought and secured a seat in the state senate where he became a staunch backer of antimonopoly legislation during the extra session of 1883. By 1888, however, Lynch had loftier goals, specifically the Democratic nomination for congressman from the

Fifth District in San Francisco. He was denied, for, as Buckley wrote, "The organization had been pledged to another applicant [Thomas J. Clunie]."[52] Lynch refused to accept the explanation, and the Blind Boss made yet another enemy who would not only attack him in a pamphlet written in 1889—probably with William Randolph Hearst's backing —and affiliate with Sullivan, Barclay Henley, and others in the Reform Democracy of 1890, but also sit in judgment of the boss as a member of the grand jury which indicted him in 1891.[53]

Attacks by Lynch, Sullivan, and their supporters were neither the first nor the last evidences of increasing hostility toward Buckley during the 1888 campaign and its preliminaries. Indeed, every instance of misconduct in the city seemed somehow to be related to him. In 1887, antagonists resurrected the Inspecting Teacher issue, carried it to the courts, and reminded voters of the Blind Boss's suspected role in the creation of the maligned office. Later, flaws discovered in the construction of the new city hall and Buckley's affiliation with one of the contractors, Michael J. Kelly, brought him into that controversy. Soon afterward, when attorney Alfred "Nobby" Clarke was found to be involved in graft related to the fire and police warning system and Max Popper's street cleaning contracts came to light, these too became campaign issues directed against the boss, as did the questionable patronge policies of county assessor James C. Nealon. And when a grand jury report criticized the general conduct of the municipal government in San Francisco, the press and the political opposition attributed the fault to Buckley, who accepted the attacks as an adjunct of his profession and remarked that "In the boss business you have to let it go."[54] Frequent references in his memoirs, however, suggest that he did not let it go entirely and felt personally aggrieved that "every transgression of law, human and divine, was traced back to me by some ingenious process of reasoning."[55]

Buckley also recognized that the attacks had professional as well as personal implications, and he therefore threw himself vigorously into preparations for the coming campaign. Well before the Los Angeles convention, he had been active in both the county committee and the various Democratic clubs to which he belonged, on occasion appearing and speaking at more than one gathering in a single evening.[56] Following his return from the state meeting to the city, he indulged in a bit of personal fence-mending by supporting Jeremiah Sullivan's candidacy for superior court justice. Simultaneously, he persisted in his club activities and involved himself in the county committee's preparations for a massive parade to honor the San Francisco delegation to St. Louis, where California Democrats had influenced the national platform plank on tariff reform.[57] When that parade assembled, it gave evidence of the thoroughness of the local organization's efforts and predicted the character of the campaign in the city. An estimated 5000 jubilant Democrats representing the newly formed clubs, ethnic associations, and trades' organizations interspersed themselves with bands and drill teams and marched by torchlight to hail their returning heroes.[58] Although the campaign did not commence officially for several weeks, the enthusiasm which the procession generated, even for Grover Cleveland, made it seem an auspicious beginning.

Capitalizing upon the apparent zeal of their followers—or perhaps stimulated by it—Democratic county and state leaders, with Chris Buckley in the forefront of the activity, launched their usual preparations with more than usual energy. Naturalization bureaus helped aliens to become voters, and registration committees guided the new citizens to clubs where they affixed their names to rosters and swelled Democratic ranks. In cooperation with the State Central Committee, the San Francisco Iroquois Club launched a drive to coordinate the efforts of all party organizations, not only in the city but also throughout the state. Other official and semiofficial groups planned mass meetings and bonfire rallies, watched over the tactics of a suspect registrar of voters, and generally maintained a high level of enthusiasm. The county committee itself attempted to rectify past miscalculations by taking pains to recognize the objectives of the striking typographers' union and other trade associations in a reasonably successful effort to lure the labor vote to the Democratic cause.[59] Thus, when a massive bonfire rally at Metropolitan Hall officially opened the campaign on August 25, Buckley and the San Francisco Democracy had generated substantial momentum which they would strive to maintain—not always with complete success—throughout the subsequent two months.[60]

As it had two years earlier, Buckley's party received aid in its efforts from outside sources, including the major opposition. Early in the spring of 1888, factionalism became evident in Republican ranks when

Higgins' followers and their rivals vied for control, and by April, when only 6000 voters participated in the state convention primary, it was clear that apathy and disorganization plagued the party. San Francisco Republicans made no apparent effort to emulate the Democrats' successful complex of multi-purpose clubs; nor did the state organization's effort to intervene and pacify local antagonists encounter any more success than it had in 1886.[61] The impasse remained and it culminated in an extraordinarily disorderly municipal primary epitomized by the shooting of Martin Kelly (for which Buckley was blamed) and a badly fragmented party.[62] Higgins, who suffered a heart attack in the midst of the campaign and died in less than a year, managed to retain his position, and the factionalism had little impact upon state or national contests in 1888. But it seriously undermined Republican opportunities in the municipal election and motivated several party leaders (including county committeeman Alex Greggains) to desert to the Democratic ranks.[63] The Blind Boss's organization received additional assistance from an American party even less cohesive than it had been in 1886 and frankly admitting that its presence in the municipal campaign could only aid Buckley and his machine. Despite the apparent insight and the vigorous warnings which Frank Pixley published in his *Argonaut,* the Americans persisted in their efforts, with precisely the results predicted.[64]

Obvious discord in the ranks of the opposition and confidence in the strength of his own machine permitted Buckley to leave the city at the height of the campaign and spend a vacation in San Diego where he reportedly found Democratic prospects "excellent."[65] He could not, however, afford the permanent luxury of relegating responsibility to subordinates, particularly in view of threatened independent Democratic movements—with which James D. Phelan was initially involved—and the possibility that such forces ultimately might fuse with other parties to mount a serious threat in the municipal campaign.[66] Therefore, despite the declining health which motivated his impromptu journey to Southern California, he threw himself into preparations for municipal convention primary elections scheduled for late September. The effort paid enormous dividends; when the municipal conventions met early in October, Buckley's control was sufficiently complete to make the gatherings bland by comparison with previous Democratic conclaves, and absolutely benign in contrast to the concurrent Republican meeting.[67] The

Blind Boss's delegates fulfilled their obligations with great dispatch and little debate. They renominated Mayor Pond and most other incumbents, fleshed out the slate with the traditional business-professional contingent and an unusually strong labor representation. With little more ado, the conventions adopted a platform which reiterated support for state and national party programs, affirmed traditional positions on local issues, and added planks supporting labor's right to organize and civil service reform in city government. With their functions thus complete, the conventions adjourned *sine die* and San Francisco Democrats turned their attentions to the more critical business of the campaign.[68]

Like the conventions and the activities which preceded and accompanied them, the Buckley party's San Francisco canvass of 1888 provided something less than the traditional level of excitement. Crowds thronged to partisan clubs and groggeries and to unusually frequent bonfire rallies, mass meetings, and torchlight parades, but the apparent enthusiasm seemed to mask a declining optimism concerning Democratic prospects for victory in state and national contests. After the exuberance which greeted St. Louis delegates and opened the campaign in August, the effect of Cleveland's tariff message and his anti-Chinese bill waned rapidly and the threat of the tenderfoot vote grew daily more apparent. In San Francisco, the party staged an election eve parade involving an estimated 18,000 marchers, the balloting passed without the usual "general brawl" (but not without the equally usual "general drunk"), and police were required to perform little more than their ordinary duties, despite unprecedented numbers of voters. But when votes were counted, many of the Democratic leaders' worst fears seemed to be confirmed; the result prompted White to complain that "we are whipped" and Buckley to observe that

San Francisco gave Cleveland a plurality over [Benjamin] Harrison of over 3500 votes. The President [crossed] over the Tehachapi [Pass] with a handsome lead, only to be submerged in the Republican high tide in the Southland.

Still, he continued, in the city "the Cleveland majority swept in practically the entire Democratic ticket, headed by Mayor Pond." The loss of federal patronage, however, was a critical blow to a San Francisco Democracy which "was becoming almost daily more and more divided against itself."[69]

The Blind Boss hardly could have been more perceptive in his assessment of the situation. Although Cleveland improved upon his 1884 performance in San Francisco, in the remainder of the state immigrant Republicans overwhelmed the president and delivered California's electoral vote to Harrison. Democrats managed to salvage a scant majority in the state legislature, but the congressional vote sent only two members of the party—Marion Biggs of Sacramento and Lynch's rival Thomas Clunie—to Washington, and party leaders concerned principally with the state and national scenes were disconsolate. While votes were being tallied, White telegraphed Buckley for his estimate of the outcome, and disappointing replies prompted his lament:"I believe we have elected a Constable in a remote, rural precinct which has as yet been undefiled by the tread of the tenderfoot," but not much else. San Francisco, however, was hardly a remote, rural precinct, and there the boss's disciplined organization virtually duplicated its performance of 1886; Democrats lost the sheriff, county clerk, tax collector, two supervisors, and three school directors and swept the remainder of the municipal offices.[70]

The Democratic performance in the city was more than respectable, but Buckley and other party leaders realized that even there not all of the implications of 1888 were positive. Most obviously, California no longer remained the Democratic bastion it had traditionally been. The election returns clearly confirmed what census watchers had suspected; immigration to Los Angeles, to the southern counties, and to other rural districts had been principally Republican, and it sharply altered the political complexion of the state. That fact alone threatened the integrity of the San Francisco Democracy by destroying the near majority status of the urban population and undermining the integrity of the vital city-country alliance. But there was more. The divisions which Buckley observed in the local organization were only too real, despite its recent victory and its apparent strength. A few of the old soreheads remained to fulminate against the boss and his methods, but a more ominous threat emanated from among bitter adversaries like Hearst, Sullivan, Lynch, and Henley and a growing number of new-generation Democrats in association with James Duval Phelan.[71]

The appearance of new leadership in the changing city, perhaps more than anything else, convinced Chris Buckley that conditions conducive to the continued practice of his style of politics no longer prevailed in

San Francisco and that he should step down. In his memoirs, he recalled that

Right there [following the election of 1888] it was my earnest desire to make my parting bow and bid adieu to politics forever. . . . A boss can only have his day and a short day at that, and I had already outlived the period that marks the common tenure of power. . . . The local organization was intact, in most ways was never in better shape. [But] . . . it needed new blood at the top.

The boss communicated both his convictions and his determination to retire to his associates in the Democracy but, perhaps succumbing to a sense of pride or hubris, he permitted his colleagues to undermine his resolve.[72] As subsequent events unfolded, submitting to their flattering entreaties proved to be the most critical error of Buckley's entire political career.

9

Decline and Fall,
1889-1891

*T*he essential accuracy of Chris Buckley's personal evaluation of his position ("at the zenith of my power") in the Democratic organizations of San Francisco and California in the late 1880s can hardly be questioned. He had emerged from the defeat of 1884 to score resounding individual and partisan triumphs in two subsequent contests, and he had established himself as the most formidable individual in the politics of both the city and the state. Simultaneously, however, it also became emphatically apparent— perhaps even to the boss—that his power, coupled with changes in the city and in his own attitudes and habits, increased his vulnerability to the recriminations of a growing contingent of outspoken enemies and critics. In the years which followed the victory of 1888, the Blind Boss came under especially heavy fire from numerous quarters which included even his followers. One lamb (unnamed but possibly Sam Rainey) complained in 1890, for example, that

For the last year [the boss] has not paid as close attention to the minor details of politics as he should have. You hear a great deal of grumbling . . . that [he] does not pay as much attention to his old friends as he used to. The ward workers say they can't go and talk to him now.

In former days, the dissatisfied Democrat continued, Buckley could be found readily available in his tiny, cluttered office at the rear of the Alhambra Saloon on Bush Street. But now he passed his time with more sophisticated cronies at the more elegant and exclusive Manhattan Club in a cornerless lower Nob Hill mansion which he had purchased earlier in the year from the estate of an eccentric widow.[1]

The partisan's reproaches, however mild, had substantial validity and significant implications for Buckley's career. Responding to enhanced status and affluence, in the late years of the 1880s the boss began to move in a rarefied urban milieu which insulated him from contacts with lower echelon lieutenants and constituents and to devote significantly more time and energy to his nonpolitical concerns. In addition, perhaps as a consequence of declining health, he began to absent himself from the city on frequent sojourns to Ravenswood or excursions abroad, thereby further reducing his accessibility to old cohorts and his intimacy with the city. Indeed, in the closing years of the decade the boss's physical condition constituted an important topic of speculative concern not only for Buckley and his intimates but also for an inquisitive San Francisco press and public.[2] And it came as no surprise when, in an interview granted during the summer of 1890, the Blind Boss declared that although he retained an avid interest in Democratic affairs he intended to refrain in the future from vigorous political involvement: "I will never again . . . take the active part I have in the past. My health will not permit of it." Numerous party leaders—including Stephen Mallory White who wrote, "I see that Mr. Buckley has retired!!!!!"—both accepted the declaration and welcomed it.[3] But not all party officials shared White's optimism or credulity; while some feared for the party's survival without the boss's leadership, just as many considered him a liability and doubted the sincerity of his intentions.

Buckley's determination to quit the political arena certainly was open to serious question. Only months before he issued his apparently adamant statement (by no means his first) he had guided the establishment of the Manhattan Club and provided its sumptuous Nob Hill headquarters, and during the weeks following his announcement he plunged into preliminary preparations for the 1890 campaign. Nor were doubts concerning his continuing value to the party entirely without foundation. Neither poor health nor self-proclaimed abdication immunized him from a growing barrage of criticism which commenced well in advance of the contest, and well-publicized denunciations in the local press had a telling effect upon the Democracy. William Randolph Hearst would become one of the boss's most vociferous assailants among San Francisco journalists, but he did not unleash an overt assault until early in 1891. It is not unlikely, however, that in association with Jeremiah Lynch the young editor initiated an earlier covert attack during the spring of 1889. No printer's hallmark appears in Lynch's *Buckleyism: The Government of a State,* but its typographic style closely resembles that of other *Examiner* publications. To announce the work's appearance, moreover, Hearst's journal spread a four-column summary across the front page of its April 11, 1889 edition. In the complete version, Lynch's attack consisted of a thirty-three-page mixture of fact (revealing Buckley's affiliation with Max Popper's street-cleaning enterprises and the machine's patronage policies), innuendo (implying an unsubstantiated link between the boss and a San Francisco gambling operation raised during the campaign of 1888), and half-truth (mentioning accusations emanating from the 1885 Bonnet case but not Buckley's 1886 acquittal). And it proved sufficiently effective and convincing to be adopted in edited form as the principal campaign tract of the anti-Buckley Reform Democracy during the 1890 contest.[4]

Whatever the merits or shortcomings of Lynch's pamphlet and the extent of Hearst's connection with it, the diatribe acted as a signal which precipitated a spate of journalistic assaults. The *Examiner* commenced an oblique attack by printing articles implying associations between the Blind Boss and blackmailers and other criminals in San Francisco and reprinting a New York *World* article tying the boss to the eastern underworld.[5] In an effort to compete for circulation with the "Monarch of the Dailies," editors and publishers engaged in a frontal offensive, increasing the frequency of their criticisms and altering their tone by making them more personal and direct. The formerly cautious and conservative San Francisco *Bulletin,* for example, shortly after the appearance of Lynch's denunciation asserted that

A blind bar-keeper turned Boss has his hand in the pocket of every man and woman in the State and is helping himself with great liberality. There are still some impediments to the free and unrestricted enjoyment on his part of all that the people possess, such as the limitation on taxation in this city, and that [restriction] his newspaper organs are trying to break down.[6]

No journal achieved the level of Buckley-baiting attained by the *Examiner* after 1891 or by the San Francisco *Call* following John D. Spreckels' assumption of control later in the decade, but nearly all local newspapers increased the intensity and personalized the tone of their condemnations of Buckley, even criticizing events related to his wedding journey to the East.[7] The boss's second wife, Elizabeth Hurley Buckley, died in December 1889, and during the subsequent spring he journeyed to Boston where he married Elizabeth's cousin, Annie Marie Hurley, in June 1890.[8] As the newlyweds returned to San Francisco by way of New York City, Chicago, St. Louis, New Orleans, Denver, and Seattle, local journalists followed their progress and published frequent original and reprinted articles implying that in each city Buckley consorted with disreputable criminal or political elements and concocted schemes designed to expand his power base in anticipation of his imminent demise in San Francisco affairs.[9]

The Blind Boss indeed may have recognized increasing attacks upon him as symptoms of transformations in his own city which predicted the end of his political career, and that understanding—coupled with his remarriage and declining health—may have stiffened his resolve, at least temporarily, to step down gracefully. If such were the case, he should have followed the instincts which served him so well in the past. For the accelerated frequency and altered tone of the criticism confirmed at least one inescapable fact: Buckley had paid the inevitable price of power; he had made enemies. They were not, to be sure, as numerous as his friends, but they were both influential and articulate. Editors whom he had offended—in Hearst's case by denying the Examiner Company municipal printing contracts—or who responded to genuine civic indignation at the boss's tactics persisted in their barrage, laying nearly every fault discovered in the city squarely at his doorstep. When an inspection

Annie Marie Buckley.

revealed that the northwest wall of the new city hall building was nothing but a hollow shell filled with rubble and debris, the names of contractor Michael J. Kelly and Boss Chris Buckley were raised in the investigation which followed. And even though another builder was found culpable, adverse publicity did additional damage to the boss.[10]

Allegations that the county coroner used his office to shield the Sutter Street Railway Company, in which Buckley owned stock, from prosecution for negligence and that the superintendent of streets collaborated with the supervisors to promise street repairs in districts which supported Buckley's organization in primary elections had similar effects.[11] Traditional complaints about unsafe cable cars, inadequate water supplies and fire protection, decrepit wharves, dead animals and garbage in the streets, and many more all seemed somehow traceable either directly to the Blind Boss or indirectly to him through his municipal officials.[12] Even the celebrated dollar-limit which had been a point of pride for San Franciscans now came under fire; some critics denounced Buckley for his role in maintaining a too stringent system of municipal finance while others scored him for attempting to modify it.[13]

But the roster of Buckley's enemies was not limited to hostile journalists or members of the opposition party. It also bore the names of an increasing number of disgruntled Democrats—including Jeremiah Lynch, Barclay Henley, and Jeremiah Sullivan—to whom his position had forced him to say "no" or otherwise offend, and a substantial contingent of civic-minded reformers like James Duval Phelan. The campaign of 1890 would add to both categories. Despite the ominous signs, however, Buckley's determination to retire from politics wavered. His reconsideration may have been influenced, as the boss asserted, by colleagues convinced of the absolute necessity of his active leadership, or it may have involved a personal compulsion which recurrently impelled him back into the partisan arena which had been his principal milieu for more than two decades. Whatever the case, shortly after his return from the East in the summer of 1890, he was once again deeply embroiled in yet another partisan contest. During his absence, in fact, the local Democracy completed the reorganization of its precinct clubs and held primaries which resulted in the Blind Boss's election to the vice presidency of his club, to a county committee enlarged from 60 to 100 members, and to the local organization's executive council.[14] The newly-organized Manhattan Club also had hosted the State Central Committee during its May meeting in San Francisco, and despite Buckley's absence from the gathering and his professed determination to retire, he rated one of the five pictures included in the *Examiner*'s coverage of the Democratic "love feast."[15]

These and other events during the spring of 1890 imply that the boss's assertions following the 1888 campaign and his subsequent reaffirmations totally convinced neither local partisans nor journalists of his impending retirement, and later developments reinforce the conclusion that Buckley's determination was less firm than he professed or perhaps even believed. At their meeting in San Francisco, California Democratic leaders announced that the party's 1890 state convention would be held in San Jose beginning on August 19, and the approach of that conclave set in motion intensive preparations, many of which involved Chris Buckley. The boss, in fact, had exerted an even earlier effort to reinforce his position in the state party when he telegraphed Stephen Mallory White to arrange an April meeting at San Diego's Coronado Hotel while both politicos were visiting the southern California city.[16] No record remains of their consultations, if they actually occurred, but it is likely that the two leaders met to assess Democratic prospects in California in the impending campaign. And there were some encouraging omens, especially the feud between Leland Stanford and Collis P. Huntington. Huntington resented his partner's involvement in politics, especially since Stanford's 1885 United States senatorial victory over one of Huntington's favorites. Early in 1890, the two railroad magnates had reached a private agreement; Stanford would step down as president of the Southern Pacific in favor of Huntington, and Huntington would refrain from public statements detrimental to Stanford's aspirations for reelection to the senate. In April, however, Huntington pounced on Stanford at a directors' meeting, accusing him of neglecting business responsibilities and using company funds to advance his political fortunes.[17] Stanford, for his part, denied all accusations and made it clear that he intended to utilize his own considerable resources and popularity in a vigorous campaign, but as White observed, it was "mighty poor politics to fight Huntington."[18]

The furor raised Democratic hopes for a divided Republican party in the state and the possibility that Huntington might contribute financially to defeat Stanford, and there were additional indications of Republican discord, especially dissatisfaction with the performance of Governor Robert W. Waterman and Michel De Young's apparent determination to attack him in the pages of the *Chronicle*.[19] But Democrats had few additional reasons for optimism in 1890. For one thing, preliminary results of the decennial census confirmed party leaders' awareness that continuing immigration had reinforced the Republican majority which had contributed to the defeat of state candidates in 1888. Furthermore, neither serious divisions in Republican ranks nor support from Huntington ever materialized, and as the August convention approached, disunity became evident within the Democracy. Part of the problem involved the old city-country rivalry, revived by White's announced candidacy for the United States Senate. Despite numerous appeals from fellow Democrats, White declined the opportunity to seek the governorship and instead supported the candidacy of Mayor Edward B. Pond. But he was determined to pursue the party's endorsement for the senate, regardless of opposition from the Hearsts, the *Examiner*, the city organization, and probably Buckley and minimal support in the state committee. Suspicious of White's motives, many party members believed—probably with justification—that he sought official endorsement in 1890, a decidedly inauspicious year for any Democratic hopeful, only to attempt to unseat the elder Hearst in 1892.[20] At the convention itself, under considerable pressure from party leaders, White withdrew his candidacy by supporting a San Francisco delegate's motion that the meeting make no senatorial endorsement at all.[21] Even so, the episode exacerbated the traditional animosity felt by much of the party toward the San Francisco machine, and it probably increased White's own personal hostility toward Buckley.

Revived rural-urban antagonism was not the only potential for factionalism confronting California Democrats when they gathered in San Jose. The closing years of the 1880s had been economically lean ones for both rural and urban areas of the state, and they had been punctuated by strikes and other evidences of discontent, a revival of anticorporation and antimonopoly attitudes, and the formation of associations which threatened to tap the strength of both major parties. Particularly menacing to the Democratic organization were the predecessors of the People's (Populist) party—Bellamyite Nationalist Clubs and Farmers' Alliances—which at least temporarily attracted substantial numbers of the party's rank and file and many of its leaders, including the mercurial Thomas Vincent Cator.[22]

For Buckley, however, problems encountered at the convention would have even more immediate and serious consequences than either the city-country feud, estrangement from White, or the threat of third-party movements. Although he was not a delegate, the Blind Boss journeyed to San Jose, established headquarters in the Letitia Hotel, met with state party leaders, and directed the activities of the San Francisco delegation. The convention chairmanship which went to Byron Waters of San Bernardino by acclamation caused Buckley no specific problems. Nor did the platform which denounced the Republican national administration and the McKinley tariff bill, advocated continued and more stringent Chinese exclusion and the free coinage of silver, supported the direct election of senators and the adoption of the Australian ballot in California, and endorsed the eight-hour day and the regulation of corporations.[23] But nominations, especially for governor and chief justice of the state supreme court, were another story.

Early in the year, state party chairman William D. English had declared himself a contender for the gubernatorial nomination, despite his knowledge that both Buckley and White favored Edward B. Pond.[24] When the convention decided upon its choice, the boss withheld portions of the San Francisco delegation's vote from Pond, creating the impression that the city delegation opposed the mayor and causing numerous country delegates to shift their votes to him. But on the fourth ballot, Buckley directed all 144 San Francisco votes to Pond, thereby ensuring his nomination. The maneuver infuriated English (who also lost his position on the State Central Committee) and prompted his brother Warren English to call Buckley a "son of a bitch" and exchange blows with the boss's cousin on the steps of the convention hall. But more importantly, it made an implacable foe of English, formerly a powerful ally.[25] Similar consequences resulted from the contest for the nomination for chief justice of the state supreme court. William T. Wallace had been associated with Buckley politically since the mid-1880s. With the boss's support he had been appointed to a vacancy in the state legislature and elected superior court judge in San Francisco, and he had served in various offices in the Democratic organization.[26] At the San Jose convention, Wallace expected to secure the nomination for chief justice, but Buckley had committed himself and the San Francisco delegation to John A. Stanley. Consequently, Wallace received only twenty-two votes from city representatives, lost by a count of 339 to 282, and became the Blind Boss's "unrelenting enemy, never for a moment forgetting the real or fancied wrong."[27]

Thus, when the Democratic convention adjourned, Buckley departed with mixed accomplishments. He retained firm control of the San Francisco delegation and substantial representation on the state committee, but he also contributed to rekindling the smoldering city-country rivalry in the party, antagonized White, and added two more names to what he called his "ever-lengthening catalogue of enemies."[28] When he returned to San Francisco, he encountered an analogous situation; his dominance of the local organization remained reasonably secure, but there were increasingly apparent signs of strengthening opposition from elements within the party. Even before the San Jose convention, indeed, a rival organization styling itself the Reform Democracy had emerged and begun to provide a platform for a new figure on the local political horizon, Gavin McNab. Born in Scotland in 1863, McNab arrived in California in 1865 and lived on a ranch near Ukiah until 1889 when he migrated to San Francisco and became chief clerk or manager of the Occidental Hotel, one of the city's centers of political activity and intrigue. Although he achieved considerable fame as an attorney and eventually numbered Charlie Chaplin and Jack Dempsey among his clients, McNab never attended law school and only gained admission to the California bar in 1901. But he involved himself in San Francisco politics almost from his arrival in the city and became recognized in his own right as the "Scotch Boss" of the local Democracy in 1893 after Buckley's ouster from power.[29]

Initially, however, McNab attempted to keep one foot in each of the Democratic camps, associating with both the Blind Boss's regular organization and the Reform Democracy formed early in July 1890 under the leadership of attorney Eugene Deuprey. John P. Irish's *Alta* ridiculed the reformers as the "purity nine," the "thirteen patriots," and the "shorn lambs," and Buckley probably considered them soreheads, but the faction quickly expanded its membership to include not only Deuprey, McNab, Jeremiah Lynch, Jeremiah Sullivan, Barclay Henley, Stuart M. Taylor, and other intractable Buckley opponents, but also important party leaders such as Thomas V. Cator and James G. Maguire.[30] Unlike the Precinct and County Democrats of 1886, the new faction made no effort to capture the established city organization. Instead, its leaders attempted—without significant success in 1890—to establish a competitive party, principally on the basis of opposition to the boss. During the month preceding the state Democratic convention, Deuprey, McNab, and the reformers organized their party, held primary elections, and called mass meetings to denounce Buckley and his county committee.[31] In the following months, they organized a municipal convention—with delegates selected by officers of the Reform Democracy rather than at primary elections—and met in Irving Hall to name candidates for city, legislative, and judicial offices and to adopt a platform essentially identical, with the exception of its anti-boss plank, to that later devised by Buckley's regular Democrats.[32]

The reform party's subsequent campaign, like its principal reason for existence, was an essentially negative affair based upon reiteration of the charges in Lynch's pamphlet, denunciations of the Blind Boss as a "branded but unconvicted traitor" and worse, and allegations of beatings and other abuse at the hands of "Buckley thugs," but little more.[33] Consequently, the Reform Democracy won neither numerous adherents nor the sanction of the party's state committee. Nor did any of its candidates—even those who did not resign their nominations before the

November elections—capture the offices they sought. During the canvass, the Republican *Chronicle* praised the reformers' opposition to the Blind Boss while the Democratic *Alta* and *Examiner* denigrated them as "Deuprey's Sideshow," a contingent of losers from the San Jose convention, and a piece club devised solely to aid the Republican cause.[34] Whether by design or not, the Reform Democracy probably did assist the opposition by taking votes from regular Democrats in a few close races. But their propaganda influence unquestionably had an even more substantial immediate impact upon the election and long-range effect upon Buckley's career. Although the Democratic journals of John P. Irish and William Randolph Hearst attempted to ridicule the reformers and minimize their significance, Republican dailies such as the *Chronicle,* the *Bulletin,* and the *Call*—as well as numerous weekly and monthly periodicals—gave enthusiastic and thorough coverage to the reformers' efforts and accusations, and Hearst would reiterate their charges in his own subsequent attacks on Buckley.

Neither the boss nor members of his regular Democratic organization could anticipate the specific consequences of the journalists' or reformers' animosity; nor did they fully comprehend their implications. Like the concurrent freshet of newspaper censure, the Reform Democracy reflected transformations in the city and discontent with the consequences of adherence to the political status quo. Buckley, to be sure, constituted the principal target of both reformist and journalistic volleys, and he was more than an imaginary issue. But opposition to the boss also involved more than jealousy of his power, moral outrage at his tactics, or desires to exact vengeance for favors denied. Hostility toward Buckley called the reform party into being, his enemies dominated its leadership, and fear of his power inspired policies such as appointing convention delegates rather than risking infiltration in open primaries. Still, the organization also received both tacit and active support from individuals whose motives involved not personal animosity toward the Blind Boss but rather the conclusion that traditional politics, regardless of party or personality, impeded civic progress in San Francisco and their desire to make the city a modern, efficient metropolis beginning with its system of municipal government and political procedures.

The subtle implications of various critics' campaigns are probably only apparent in retrospect, but the Buckley organization did not ignore their potential threat or that of a local Republican party grown substantially more cohesive after the death of Bill Higgins in 1889 and financed by Stanford's capital.[35] The Democracy opened its municipal campaign with the traditional preliminaries: bonfire rallies, mass meetings, club organization, and registration drives. They also challenged procedures in the office of county clerk William A. Davies—one of the few municipal departments lost in 1888—where appointees extorted fees for filing naturalization papers (especially those of potential Democrats) and deposited charges for copies of legal records in their pockets rather than in the city treasury.[36] In addition, the regulars responded to divisions in Democratic ranks in several ways. During the primary campaign, they invited Gavin McNab, James D. Phelan, and attorney Garrett McEnerney to address a variety of partisan meetings. At the municipal conventions, the regulars named the usual slate of incumbents, party stalwarts, and labor representatives, but there too they made pragmatic concessions. The Democracy nominated McNab for Fifth Ward supervisor, Thomas F. Barry for school director, and several members of the new political generation, in some cases sons of former party leaders and officeholders, as candidates for municipal or judicial positions.[37]

The party platform likewise acknowledged growing sentiments for change by including, along with traditional planks, statements in support of a nonpartisan school board, the Australian ballot, and the eight-hour day. But few Democratic strategies, expedient at best, proved to be effective, and some backfired almost immediately. By acclamation, the convention nominated Frank McCoppin to run for his old office, but the former mayor declined and forced the party to choose another standard bearer. Although Second Ward supervisor James M. McDonald considered himself to be the leading contender for the honor, Buckley engineered the selection of a relative unknown, William F. Goad, and in the process made an enemy of McDonald who joined the ranks of the Reform Democracy and became its mayoral candidate.[38] Within weeks, several more candidates declined their nominations, among them McNab who foreswore his efforts to affiliate with both Democratic factions and committed himself to the reformers. Simultaneously, the regular Democracy's attempt to placate labor lost much of its impact when employees in the furniture factory of tax collector candidate William Krelling denounced him for his opposition to the eight-hour day and went out on strike and the *Chronicle* revealed that Mayor Pond employed Chinese in his Safety Nitro Powder Company in Contra Costa county across the bay and in his Alaskan fishing enterprises.[39]

These and other disappointments made Democrats aware that their prospects for victory in San Francisco in 1890 were less propitious than they had anticipated. Consequently, the campaign which they waged as the election approached seemed desultory and perfunctory in contrast to the vigorous optimism of the two previous contests. Despite the loss in his bid for the party's senatorial endorsement, White flooded California with letters and stumped the state in support of Democratic legislative candidates, still hoping for the elusive senate seat. But the odds—and the *Examiner*—were against him. The State Central Committee offered no significant support and financial assistance from Huntington failed to materialize.[40] In the city, Democrats conducted their traditional mass meetings, rallies, and other activities in an almost routine manner, and the various clubs, usually the vital epicenters of party campaign activity, seemed virtually moribund. Chris Buckley himself—perhaps motivated by pessimism or ill health or both—remained curiously absent from journalistic treatments of the canvass, except for the *Chronicle's* perennial charges that a vote for any Democrat constituted a vote for the Blind Boss, that he plundered the city treasury to amass a fortune at taxpayers' expense, that he falsified voter registrations, and that he conspired with the Southern Pacific to run weak candidates for various offices.[41]

The persistent charges—and the lack of energetic counterattacks by Democratic journals—apparently had their effects. Additional candidates removed their names from the regular Democratic ticket and joined the reformers, many of those who remained on the ballot failed to appear at poorly attended campaign rallies, on one occasion the county committee could not conduct business for lack of a quorum, and an Australian ballot rally drew a larger and more enthusiastic crowd than any of the Buckley party's efforts.[42] The apathy characteristic of the Democratic campaign—and of the boss himself—did not pervade the entire city, however. On election day 53,000 citizens cast their votes, but even though continuing economic depression helped to make 1890 a Democratic year throughout most of the nation, it was not to be in California or in San Francisco. When ballots were counted in the state—a process which required nearly two weeks—the tally confirmed a defeat even worse than the debacle of 1884. California Democrats sent only two representatives to congress, neither of them from the city, and captured no state offices. Pond lost the contest for governor, even in San Francisco, and a state legislature dominated by an eighty-eight to thirty-one Republican majority assured Stanford's return to Washington in 1891. In the municipal election, equally grim results confronted the party. It won only the minor offices of county surveyor and public administrator and three places on the school board. The office of the mayor, the board of supervisors, nine school directors, and all of the important patronage positions went to the opposition. As Buckley summarized, for his party, "The disaster was complete."[43]

While jubilant California and San Francisco Republicans held victory celebrations, Democrats licked their wounds and sought explanations for their ignominious rout. When interviewed concerning the nearly total failure of his party's candidates, Buckley quipped, "I don't know, but I think they didn't get enough votes."[44] Like other Democrats, however, he believed that the principal cause for the disaster involved what Max Popper termed "Stanford's wad," the lavish distribution of funds to Republican candidates throughout the state.[45] In addition, a novel method of counting ballots in the city, approved shortly before the election, allegedly contributed to the defeat by making the vote more amenable to manipulation by election officials, "stuffers," and "heelers."[46] But few Democrats blamed public dissatisfaction with the previous legislature and municipal government or acknowledged factors which they had recognized prior to the election: obvious disunity in local and state organizations, the impact of third parties, and the fact that California was no longer a Democratic stronghold. And partisans increasingly fell back upon a single explanation for their humiliation: the Blind Boss, who had become, in Popper's words, "too heavy a load to carry" as a consequence of adverse publicity.[47]

Sensing his party's growing dissatisfaction with his leadership, disillusioned by the outcome of the election, and fatigued by his exertions, Buckley once again tendered his resignation from all party offices and late in November departed for London and Heidelberg in quest of repose and specialists to treat his affliction.[48] During his absence from San Francisco—and indeed even during the campaign itself—suspicions surfaced that the boss's responsibility for the defeat of 1890 involved something more tangible than a tainted reputation, failures of leadership, or inattention to political detail. Pond specifically blamed Buckley for his defeat in his own race and wrote to White that he believed that the boss had sold out the San Francisco party "lock, stock, and bbl. [barrel]." For his part, White considered the minimal efforts on the part of the state committee and the *Examiner*'s failure to support the state ticket major elements in the defeat, but he too laid part of the blame on Buckley's shoulders. He did not, however, wholeheartedly subscribe to the existence of what has been called the "senatorial compact of 1890."[49]

The compact involved an alleged agreement between Chris Buckley and Leland Stanford. Partisans believed that the Blind Boss sold his party "for coin" in order to provide a Republican legislature which would return Stanford to the senate in 1891. In return, Stanford purportedly promised to work for a Democratic legislature in 1892 to ensure George Hearst's reelection.[50] It is not clear precisely how the suspected exchange of favors would operate in terms of garnering votes for Republican legislators in rural districts where Buckley exercised little influence or how Stanford proposed to guarantee his part of the bargain in 1892. In fact, it is likely that Stanford needed the Blind Boss's assistance only in San Francisco in 1890, if there. The verdict of the census already apparent in 1888 was sufficient to return him to the senate, third parties diverted substantial blocks of votes from the Democrats, and dissatisfaction with Democratic performance at both city and state levels virtually assured a Republican majority in the state legislature, even before the election. White recognized these conditions and therefore he did not entirely concur in the nearly paranoiac conclusions of the many Democratic leaders who informed him of the suspected compact; nor did he emulate the epithets which they habitually hurled at Buckley. But he did agree that the boss had become a liability, "useless timber," to the party and that the San Francisco Democracy required both new leadership and rigorous reorganization.[51]

White's political instincts—as acute as Buckley's—prompted him toward accurate conclusions, but for reasons more valid than those of many of his contemporaries. The existence of a senatorial compact or any such agreement remained entirely problematical for several reasons, in addition to the absence of proof. In the first place, given political conditions in the state in 1890, it is doubtful that Buckley could have influenced sufficient votes to make such a bargain worthwhile to Stanford. Secondly, the Blind Boss was too shrewd and too fond of his own power to enter into tenuous arrangements; he did not speculate but dealt in certainties in both economics and politics. Finally, it is doubtful that Stanford needed the boss; Republican strength in the state was all too obvious. White also dealt in pragmatic considerations, and he recognized that, although the party's defeat involved numerous other factors, Buckley did deserve a substantial share of the blame, especially in the city. The boss had made enemies, and his presence divided the Democracy, probably irreparably until his elimination from positions of authority. He also had failed—as a consequence of his declining health, remarriage, or altered habits and attitudes—to provide the sort of leadership which had won victories and entitled him to his status. In addition, the press campaign had tainted Buckley's reputation irretrievably, making him an impediment not only to the party's ability to win public support but also to its potential for attracting the new political leadership emerging in both the city and the state.

For all of these reasons, despite his suspicions of the motives of many of the affiliates of the Reform Democracy and his reluctance to relegate the San Francisco party to their leadership, White supported efforts to reorient partisan affairs in the city. And when Buckley returned from Europe in the spring of 1891, he confronted a formidable contingent of Democratic leaders representing a variety of interests in the city and determined to provide the organization with fresh leadership acceptable to a broad spectrum of municipal voters. This anti-Buckley Committee of One Hundred consisted of an odd array of partisans: former lambs Max Popper and Sam Braunhart; representatives of the new generation of political leadership James D. Phelan and Gavin McNab; leaders of the still-active Reform Democracy Eugene Deuprey and Thomas V. Cator; members of the "Federal Brigade" of national officeholders John L. Wise and Edward McGettigan; personal enemies Stuart M. Taylor, Jeremiah Lynch, Jeremiah Sullivan, and Barclay Henley; new antagonists like Edward B. Pond; older partisans like Vigilance Committee leader William T. Coleman; and many more. Local reorganizers also received moral support and encouragement from state party leaders who included English, still smarting from the loss of the gubernatorial nomination and state party chairmanship, and White, no longer convinced of Buckley's value to the party. In short, representatives of nearly all elements of the California Democracy had decided, for a variety of reasons, that the Blind Boss must go. Following Buckley's return from Europe, he momentarily considered contesting the Committee of One Hundred to recover his position in the party. But recognizing the inevitable, with a simple statement to the press—"You can say that I have retired from all active interest in politics"—he resigned all of his official positions in the party and in the summer of 1891 moved to his home at Ravenswood.[52]

Not all of Buckley's enemies, however, considered his enforced retirement or his self-imposed exile from the city sufficient retribution, for they still feared his potential power, and his frequent appearances in San Francisco increased their trepidation. One journal, for example, observed that during the summer of 1891,

Every day or so [Buckley] visits the city and passes a few hours at the Manhattan Club. From twenty to seventy-five gentlemen call on him there, mostly for the purpose of borrowing money.

But the boss's enemies were not concerned with his social calls or liberal loans. They feared that he was, in fact, laying the foundations for a renewed campaign to resume his authority in the party, and they would have preferred to see him ensconced somewhere other than the Livermore Valley, preferably in San Quentin.[53]

The opportunity for the reformers to exact their own version of justice arrived by a circuitous route which originated not in San Francisco but in Sacramento. Still uncertain of victory when the new legislature convened in 1891, Leland Stanford distributed generous gifts to Republican assemblymen and senators in order to ensure his return to Washington. Almost simultaneously, on February 28 George Hearst died in the nation's capital, and his demise precipitated a scramble which contributed to the peculations of the "Legislature of a Thousand Scandals," produced the "Wastepaper Basket Affair," sent Charles Felton to the United States Senate, and left Morris M. ("Much Mentioned") Estee to lick his wounds.[54]

Hard on the heels of revelations of Stanford's largesse and of the improprieties involved with sending Felton to the senate came the Faylor scandal. George Faylor, with Buckley's support, had been appointed sergeant-at-arms of the state senate in 1886, and he had utilized the position to act as an intermediary between solons of both parties and those who wished to purchase their favors. Early in 1891, the sergeant-at-arms concluded that each of a score of senators was $400 in arrears in their obligations to him, and in July he audaciously brought suit against them in the court of Judge William T. Wallace. The subsequent litigation revealed scandal after scandal, ruined numerous reputations, and aroused public indignation against their legislators. But for some obscure reason — probably involving tangible persuasion from individuals who feared for their own reputations — Faylor's counsel halted the proceedings when his client seemed to be winning his case.[55] It well may be that the outcome was precisely what Faylor intended and that his decision to attack the senators in open court was shrewd rather than foolhardy, as it appears on the surface. Whatever the case, the episode — which did not involve Buckley directly — created a public attitude conducive to the continued pursuit of political scandals.

In response to that atmosphere, in August 1891 Judge Wallace impaneled a grand jury, ostensibly to investigate the conduct of San Francisco's delegation in Sacramento, including allegations that Assemblyman Elwood Bruner had sold positions on the city police force. Both the judge's methods and the eventual composition of the jury, however, suggest other motives. Buckley always insisted that Wallace and the boss's enemies constituted the jury with the specific intention of indicting him for a crime punishable by imprisonment, and facts surrounding the episode tend to confirm his contentions.[56] According to the Consolidation Act of 1856 and the California Constitution of 1879, Wallace should have selected the nineteen-member panel from a sealed box containing 144 names submitted in January by the city's twelve superior court justices.[57]

On August 17, 1891, the judge began to follow the legal and traditional process by drawing twenty-three names, but he halted the procedure on grounds that thirteen of the slips were in some way mutilated. After being copied on fresh paper, the names in question were returned to the container and Wallace extracted another twenty-five names. He called and questioned nineteen of those drawn and dismissed several of them — including publisher Henry S. Crocker, Fred W. Eaton, and Godfrey Fisher who had been affiliated with Buckley in business or politics. Wallace then accepted ten of the potential jurors drawn and ignored the rest. At this point, the judge should have removed additional names,

Judge William T. Wallace.   Jeremiah Lynch.
Former adherents of Buckley, Wallace and Lynch
led the crusade against him from 1889 to 1891.

examined those selected, and either approved or rejected them for grand jury service. Instead, he took the unprecedented step of terminating procedures entirely, alleging that someone had tampered with most of the slips in the box. The law provided that under such circumstances, a judge must order the sheriff to assemble a new roster of potential jurors or, if that official might be involved in the panel's investigation, assign the duty to the county coroner. But Wallace ignored those legally required steps and skipped to a third; on August 18 he appointed an elisor, Henry H. Scott, to submit nine names to complete the grand jury.[58]

Whether by chance or by design, Wallace chose an individual who, like himself, had a score to settle with Buckley. In 1888, Scott sought and was denied the Democratic nomination for sheriff, and in the campaign of 1890 he appeared as an active participant in the councils of the Reform Democracy. The names which Scott submitted and which Wallace instantaneously approved are no less revealing. At the head of the list stood Barclay Henley (subsequently named foreman of the grand jury) and Jeremiah Lynch, a duo whose hostility toward the Blind Boss already has been considered. Next came James M. McDonald, denied the

226

regular Democratic nomination for mayor in 1890 and humiliatingly defeated as the Reform Democracy's candidate for the same office. In addition, Scott included the names of educator James Denman, former editorial manager of the *Examiner* Dr. Charles C. Cleveland, real estate broker Patrick J. Kennedy, wholesale grocer Reuben Tucker, and wholesale druggist William S. Zeilin, all active in the Reform Democracy during the previous election. In fact, only one individual on Scott's list had not been so involved: printer William H. Cubery, described as an "anti-boss Republican" and coincidentally the publisher of the Reform Democracy's campaign literature. The jurors whom Wallace accepted from the original drawing included five Republicans (among them Henry L. Doge and Lipmann Sachs who had records of active opposition to Buckley), one Democrat, and four individuals described as "not politically active."[59]

A biased judge and elisor and ten (and perhaps more) hostile jurors do not constitute conclusive evidence of collusion or conspiracy against Buckley, but they do at the very least suggest the involvement of something more than coincidence. Indeed, from the announcement of the jury's formation and throughout its brief but stormy existence, many San Franciscans cast a suspicious eye upon the panel. Even before the Wallace jury faced challenges in the courts, Michel De Young and the *Chronicle* charged that it represented nothing more than an ill-disguised scheme by the Reform Democrats to rid themselves permanently of Buckley. William Randolph Hearst and the *Examiner* also raised questions concerning the panel's legitimacy, but like most others in the city concluded that the ends involved were sufficiently meritorious to justify any means employed to attain them. Hearst praised Wallace as "instrumental in getting a grand jury free from all taint of crookedness," perhaps for the first time in the city's history, while others rationalized that Buckley had used similar methods to achieve his goals.[60] The *Examiner's* position typified the attitudes expressed in the city, but there were those who persisted in their criticism—even suggesting that Collis P. Huntington had instigated the scheme in order to embarass Stanford even further and rid himself of the need to deal with the bosses—and opposition proved sufficiently vocal to force Wallace to engage in an extended defense of both the legality of the jury and the purity of his motives.[61]

Despite the controversy, the Wallace jury quickly embarked upon its duties, after selecting Henley chairman and Lynch secretary. The panel apparently considered its function quite universal, for among its committees was one to investigate "dives and social evils" in the city and another to consider the case of a pair of disreputable, bankrupt wine merchants.[62] But early in September it turned to its principal task, the investigation of political corruption, and began to call witnesses, hear testimony, and publish charges. Although he was subpoenaed, Buckley did not appear before the panel; he had departed upon a vacation to Montreal—"for my health," he said—and he remained there, carefully following subsequent developments.[63] The Blind Boss's absence did not deter the jury which quickly handed down indictments, including one against Republican boss Dick Chute for his part in a number of scandals involving the state legislature. Chute, however, elected to challenge the panel in the courts, and in an action which prompted a mass demonstration in Metropolitan Hall, on September 30 Superior Court Judge Daniel J. Murphy declared the Wallace jury illegal and its indictments invalid. Undaunted by the apparent setback, Henley kept the panel in session, and even before the state supreme court reversed Murphy's decision it continued to call witnesses (including attorney Evan S. Pillsbury who also absented himself from the city) and prepare additional charges.[64] Following the high court's decision, new indictments began to appear; Elwood Bruner was charged with selling police force positions and Martin Kelly with attempted murder in connection with an alleged attack on a hack driver several years earlier.[65]

Simultaneously, the grand jury trained its sights on its principal target, Chris Buckley. Unfortunately, transcripts of the proceedings against the Blind Boss no longer exist, but newspaper treatments and other sources make the course of actions reasonably clear.[66] During late October and early November, the jury subpoenaed witnesses and heard testimony, including allegations that the boss used city employees and materials to construct his home at Ravenswood, from a host of Buckley's business and political associates and rivals, and on November 10, 1891 it issued an indictment on a single charge: bribery in connection with a street railway franchise granted in December 1890.[67] The action precipitated petitions to Governor Henry H. Markham to initiate extradition proceedings, but the Blind Boss—like at least one local editor—

expressed contempt for the charge against him and doubts that it could be upheld in court.[68]

The single indictment involved the San Francisco Syndicate and Trust Company which Buckley and several other investors—including Clifton E. Mayne and possibly future mayor Adolph Sutro—formed in 1889 for the purpose of promoting the Metropolitan Electric Street Railway Company. Mayne, whom Buckley called "a kind of financial sharper from the East," arrived in San Francisco in 1889, hoping to repeat the speculative successes which had reaped fortunes in Omaha and Ogden banking and real estate enterprises. Once in California, he invested in the San Francisco Syndicate and Trust Company and urged the Blind Boss to use his influence to secure a street railway franchise for the firm. In December 1890, while Buckley sojourned in Europe, the board of supervisors granted the desired permit over Mayor Pond's veto, along with another equally speculative franchise to Behrend Joost and J. N. Hartzell for the San Francisco and San Mateo County railway line.[69]

Buckley's precise role in acquiring the franchises remains unclear; he may have arranged the matter through his lieutenants before he departed for Europe or, as the boss contended, Mayne may have been solely responsible for whatever bribery occurred.[70] In either circumstance, news of Buckley's in absentia indictment, along with Mayne and Sam Rainey, prompted jubilation among a substantial number of San Franciscans and moved one editor to exult that the boss and his cohorts were now "fugitives from justice, . . . destined to pass the remainder of their lives in exile," that "they can never again return to San Francisco," and that they were "forever dead to the world."[71] Other observers, however, viewed developments with greater caution. There were those who hoped—or feared—that extradition efforts would succeed and that Buckley would be returned to the city to face trial and make further revelations. But many citizens still suspected both the legality of the Wallace jury and the strength of the charges against the boss, and subsequent developments justified their position. On December 12, in a case based upon the complaint of Elwood Bruner, the state supreme court reversed its previous decision and found the Wallace grand jury an illegal body constituted in violation of both the state constitution and the city charter.[72]

Months of the reformer's efforts apparently had gone for naught, but not quite; the episode did have several important consequences. Although the Wallace jury had been "long on denunciation [but] short on documentation" and its exertions produced not one conviction, it did at least call a temporary halt to the worst political abuses in the city and in Sacramento.[73] Indeed, Chris Buckley himself contributed to the same end; although he remained in Canada until early 1892, rumors persisted that he intended to return to San Francisco to reveal what he knew, even about some of the jurors who indicted him. Many—including Pehlan and McNab who took no apparent part in the jury's actions—wished that he would, for they believed the boss to be "an angel of light compared to the men who hired him to buy City Fathers, bribe judges, corrupt legislators, fix juries, and to demoralize things generally."[74] As for the Blind Boss's political future, despite the invalidation of the indictment against him and the lack of a trial or conviction, the affair fulfilled a prediction made just days after charges were leveled against him; the publicity alone proved sufficient to preclude a return to his former position in partisan affairs.[75]

In another way, however, the actions of the grand jury tended to vindicate Buckley and to indict the self-styled reformers who bent the law in their zeal to settle their grievances. The boss mentions no names in his memoirs, but he does discuss a "great jurist," an "ambitious young man of wealth," a "clever man from the northern part of the state," and a popular "young man of affairs" who had requested favors which he could not grant, and the details he includes precisely match the careers of Wallace, Lynch, Henley, and Scott.[76] Possibly, Buckley employed innuendo and unsubstantiated allegations for the purpose of self-vindication and to support his assertion that the grand jury had been rigged against him. But it is equally possible, judging from the composition of the panel and from its subsequent actions, that the boss was right. It would not be the first time that slogans such as "reform" and "political purity" were utilized in order to attain personal ends; nor would it be the last, even in Chris Buckley's career.

10

A Last Hurrah: The Politics of Reform

*T*he controversy, contention, and condemnation surrounding the Wallace grand jury investigation and indictment, together with attendant adverse publicity, terminated Chris Buckley's career in the public affairs of San Francisco and California. They comprised, however, only the immediate episode and by no means constituted the only factors precipitating his downfall or ensuring its permanence. Indeed, neither the jury nor the press revealed substantially more than the urban populace already knew or suspected about the boss's activities or tactics, and exposure contributed to his demise in a significant but strictly limited manner. The elements in the 1891 affair were, in fact, principally symptomatic of continuing changes in the Blind Boss himself, in the city at large, and especially in the nature of a determined and highly organized partisan opposition. Together, these transformations had an impact at least equivalent to that of the Wallace revelations, and Buckley certainly should have recognized their combined significance for him and for his political style. Nevertheless, after a brief period of retirement, he returned to the city and, employing his traditional methods, directed his energies toward recovering his former position during the campaign of 1896, a contest destined to be his last hurrah in San Francisco politics.

Changes in Buckley perhaps blinded him to the futility of the effort. During the closing years of his career, lessons learned behind a horsecar, in The Snug Saloon, under the expert tutelage of Bill Higgins and Al Fritz, and particularly on the hustings in the wards of San Francisco receded from memory, diminishing the sensitivity to the city which had been one of the major keys to his success and rendering him increasingly vulnerable to attack. The Blind Boss became remote from subordinates and constituents alike and lost his intimacy with all but the upper strata of urban society and partisan leadership. As affluence and authority and the demands of business and family increased, Buckley began to move in circles detached from the bases of his strength and to emulate the city's elite in his habits and attitudes. And even though his name never graced the pages of *The San Francisco Blue Book* or other social registers, by 1890 Buckley had become a member of the aristocracy. He relished the status and the amenities it allowed, but it also undermined his effectiveness as a professional politician, depriving him of the "keen sociological intuition" which was one of the principal assets of the nineteenth-century boss and rupturing the lines of communication which had kept him closely attuned to the masses of his fellow San Franciscans and their city.[1] Martin Kelly observed in his own memoirs that, to his constituents, the successful boss must be "at least a real man, a warm-blooded verterbrate [*sic*]" who served his adherents, and that when he lost those qualities, the people "knew . . . how to discipline him."[2] In 1890 and the years following, the public enforced its discipline when neither the Blind Boss nor his organization responded as they once had.

To be sure, a substantial number of the nearly 300,000 San Franciscans who inhabited the peninsula in 1890 opposed Buckley as a consequence of their genuine outrage at the demoralizing influence of his tactics upon the city. Others enlisted in the cause of reform in order to carry out personal vendettas, to assert their own influence, or to eliminate the boss's role as a broker in their business transactions in the city. But a numerically greater element in the population premised its defection upon immediate and pragmatic considerations. The later 1880s and early 1890s brought renewed economic stringency to the state and depression to the city, and hard times increased day-to-day uncertainties for a San Francisco wage-earning class which included permanent and transient members, skilled and unskilled workers, native-born citizens and the largest proportional foreign-born population in any United States city. For many of them—the perennially marginal and the more secure alike—the political machine had constituted a principal bulwark against the persistent material and psychological exigencies of urban life. By 1890, however, Buckley's Democracy apparently had deserted them. Patronage jobs and other forms of economic relief diminished, and precinct and special interest clubs, the mainstays of a loyal and active constituency and sources of recognition and sociability, lost their central position in the partisan organization. As the Blind Boss and his machine became less sensitive, the vital working class—once a most reliable source of votes and estimated at one-third of the city's electorate in 1890—diverted its allegiance to alternate agencies, including the People's (Populist) party or trade unionism, or withdrew entirely from traditional politics.[3]

Simultaneously, San Francisco moved toward a higher degree of social, economic, and cultural metropolitanism. Larger and more productive manufacturing enterprises, financial institutions with assets of millions of dollars, grander public and private buildings, increasingly complex and rationalized transportation and communication networks, more sophisticated entertainment facilities, and a more cosmopolitan population demographically divided along socioeconomic lines provided tangible evidence of the transformation. In addition, expanded business aggregations emerged to influence politics in both the city and the state. Mergers of established firms produced corporate entities such as the Market Street Railway Company and the San Francisco Gas and Electric Company, and numerous associations of businessmen sharing common interests—bankers, merchants, real estate brokers, insurance agents, among others—made their presence felt in municipal affairs.[4]

These transformations, however, proved less significant for Buckley's future than did intimately related intangible changes, including the altered attitudes apparent in a new generation of urban-bred businessmen and professionals in politics who provided a striking contrast to the professional politicians of the Blind Boss's era. Neither less opportunistic than the boss nor more sensitive to the needs of the masses of San Franciscans, they were self-conscious not only of their city's rank among the nation's urban centers but also of their own position in the city. They were, moreover, determined to impose their version of modern metropolitanism on San Francisco and to accomplish their goal by capturing and altering the machinery of partisan politics and municipal government under the rubric of reform.[5]

There is perhaps no better exemplar of both transformed urban conditions and altered municipal perspectives in politics than James Duval Phelan, San Francisco's millionaire reform mayor from 1897 to 1901. Phelan's wealth set him apart from most of his generation of municipal politicians, but he shared with them the essence of an urban experience which influenced both understandings of the city and conceptions of its political life. Born in San Francisco in 1861—just one year prior to Buckley's arrival—Phelan was the son of Irish immigrants, but there ends the similarity in his background and that of the Blind Boss. In contrast to John Buckley, the senior James Phelan was already a successful merchant in the East when he migrated to the gold fields in 1849. In California, he increased his wealth by conducting lucrative merchandising operations in the mining regions and in the city, speculating in mining stocks, urban real estate and agriculture, and founding the First National Gold Bank and other financial institutions. By the year of his son's birth, he had established himself among the local elite. Affluence permitted the son to learn his early lessons behind neither a horsecar nor the bar of a saloon but from hired tutors, from teachers in private schools, and from the Jesuit faculty of Saint Ignatius College (later the University of San Francisco). In 1882, he entered the University of California's Hastings College of Law, intending to prepare for a career as an attorney and to pursue his principal avocation, writing. Under pressures imposed by his father's declining health, however, the young man terminated his legal studies and, following a year-long tour of Europe, assumed a major role in the management of family business affairs.[6]

During his youth, Phelan also formulated the ideas which later guided his understandings of the city, its society, and its politics. His persistent association with the urban elite and education in exclusive schools, for example, effectively insulated him from the kind of frequent and intimate contacts with broad spectrums of the urban populace which had been integral features of Buckley's youth in San Francisco. And his family's residence in equally exclusive hotels and on an isolated estate in the suburbs coupled with increasingly fragmented patterns of urban development combined to reinforce the effect. The young Phelan simultaneously evolved—through both formal and informal educational experiences—social understandings premised upon the Spencerian thought which permeated his age. He read and collected essays elaborating evolutionist theories of society, clipped speeches by the Reverend Henry Ward Beecher and other champions of social Darwinism, and pasted into his scrapbooks numerous articles with such titles as "The Advantages of Early Poverty" and topics equally alien to his experience.[7] Concurrently with his assumption of responsibility for his father's affairs, he affiliated himself with civic, business, and social organizations composed of individuals like himself, and he quickly assumed a place as an officer in the San Francisco Municipal Reform League, the Young Men's Commercial Club, and the Bohemian Club. Thus, Phelan's early experiences and contacts contributed to making him something of an "idealist who loved the city of his birth, had faith in its future, and earnestly desired to help make it one of the most attractive on earth."[8]

The same experiences, however, molded Phelan into what has been termed a "structural reformer" in politics, one more committed to altering the bureaucratic machinery of municipal government, to centralizing political authority, and to transforming the physical aspects of the city than to changing the city's function as a social community.[9] When, for example, Phelan concerned himself with the conditions of life in San Francisco, he focused not upon the tenement districts south of Market Street and elsewhere—where he only rarely had been—but rather upon the kind of monumental developments advocated by the Association for the Improvement and Adornment of San Francisco, the committee to promote the city at the Columbian Exposition in 1893, and the local association organizing the Mid-Winter Fair of 1894. The civic pride of a businessman-booster conditioned his approach, but so too did his youthful visit to Hausmann's Paris and other European cities. He toured and observed continental capitals and, upon his return armed with copious notes, conveyed his admiration of European civic accomplishments to his fellow San Franciscans in a series of speeches and essays. Phelan's political activities and subsequent actions as mayor also reveal the influence of his earlier experiences in shaping his conception of reform in the city. He aligned himself with the Committee of 100 and other associations of "better citizens" in drives for a businesslike charter for San Francisco, extinguished street lights and withheld teachers' salaries in the name of economy, ordered city police to support employers and break a strike of teamsters and waterfront workers and, in the words of his close associate San Francisco *Bulletin* editor Fremont Older,

continued to watch the people's interests, building better streets, better pavements, striking at graft, closely scanning city contracts and keeping the railroad's hands out of the board of supervisors as much as possible.[10]

The accomplishments Older listed were necessary, but they also make it apparent that Phelan's definition of the "people's interests" was a narrow one indeed.

Similar attitudes are revealed in Phelan's conception of politics and political reform. He did not burst suddenly upon the partisan scene in San Francisco as the Democratic candidate for mayor in 1896. In the mid-1880s, he began to take an avid interest in party activities as an observer at the rancorous Stockton convention and as an antimonopolist speaker in the campaign of 1884. During the same contest, it also became apparent that the paths of Phelan and the Blind Boss ultimately would diverge, for the younger man privately criticized Buckley's tactics and candidates. In subsequent campaigns, Phelan vacillated among the regular factions of the party, reformist elements like the Precinct and County Democracy, and various nonpartisan, independent, and ballot reform movements. But in 1890, despite suspicions of Gavin McNab's motives, he aligned himself with the anti-Buckley Reform Democracy and gave that faction the benefit of his considerable prestige and the time and energy of a confirmed bachelor. No evidence links Phelan directly to Wallace's grand jury manipulations in 1891, but his involvement in the organization of the Citizen's Defense Association dedicated to continuing the work of the defunct panel makes his sympathies abundantly clear.[11] Unlike many of his colleagues in the effort to reform the San Francisco Democracy, however, Phelan did not oppose Buckley for reasons of personal animosity or greed for power or material gain. Instead, he sincerely desired to restructure both the party and the municipal government in accordance with his own metropolitan vision, principally through the medium of charter reform, centralized municipal authority, and general civic efficiency.[12]

Despite Phelan's apparent lack of personal hostility toward the Blind Boss, he did share the determination of Democratic reformers, numerous editors, and Wallace jurors still bent on exacting vengeance that the exile should not return from Ravenswood like Napoleon from Elba to regroup scattered forces and reestablish authority in the city.[13] To guard against that eventuality, Phelan joined with McNab, Max Popper, and other partisan leaders who marshalled their forces to prepare a Waterloo for the Blind Boss in the election of 1892, the first contest conducted under the Australian ballot law of 1891.[14] Buckley had been discredited in the eyes of the public, but he nevertheless retained in the San Francisco Democracy a solid coterie of supporters who gave substance to the reformers' anxiety. Much to their relief, however, the boss once again departed for Europe and took no part in the events of 1892. Without his leadership, the remaining lambs suffered a severe primary campaign trouncing. Indeed, the tactics which the well organized opposition employed to ensure the debacle prompted Martin Kelly to lament, "When I saw what was within the scope of a reformers' vision, it was with sadness and humiliation that I realized the narrow limits of my own imagination."[15]

Early in the spring, the anti-Buckley Democrats captured the local party and adopted a new organizational plan which applied the principles of structural reform to the political party well in advance of efforts to impose them upon the municipal government. The reformers all but eliminated the residual influence of the district leaders and precinct clubs which had welded the party into a unified force during Buckley's hegemony, and they centralized control in the hands of a carefully selected and enlarged county committee.[16] During the primary elections, in their zeal to dominate the local organization, the Phelan-McNab forces revealed themselves as apt pupils of their antagonist. The reformers devised a unique "isinglass ticket" printed on paper so thin that several ballots could be pressed together to appear as one and so transparent that they could be read even when folded several times. Their polling places likewise took a page from the bosses' primer and demonstrated considerable ingenuity as well; at one location, the police chief stationed officers to permit only voters with isinglass tickets to enter, at another voters were required to ascend a thirty-foot ladder rocked by a "group of sturdy reformers" in order to register their choices, and at a third they passed ballots through a small opening into the hands of an unseen recipient on the other side of a wall.[17] Needless to say, the reformers led the lambs to slaughter.

In the subsequent campaign and general election, essentially identical tactics and results obtained. At their municipal convention, the new party leadership permitted the nomination of a handful of token lambs, principally opportunistic trimmers placed on the ticket to attract the votes of Buckley's remaining supporters. And during the canvass, although the boss remained in Europe and took no active part, the reformers shrewdly made him an issue in their rhetoric and even in a parodied children's tune in their campaign song book:

The Buckley Man
Air —The Bogie Man

Come all you little Democrats
  And listen unto me,
I'll tell you of a Buckley man
  Who is now across the sea,
He was the shrewdest little man
  Though he could hardly see,
For many a year he boodled here
  The great Democracy.

Hush! hush! hush! here comes a Buckley man.
You'd best look out for there's no doubt
He'll catch you if he can.
Look out you little Democrats,
Here comes a Buckley man.

He wore a dandy suit of clothes,
  Likewise a diamond pin,
And if you wished to see the boss,
  A darky let you in.
He owned a country mansion and
  He drove a spanking pair,
And he put on all the airs and style
  Of a boodle millionaire.

Hush! hush! hush! here comes a Buckley man, etc.[18]

The outcome of the contest, never in serious doubt, confirmed the new Democratic leaders' ability to win by adopting the boss's tactics, recruiting some of his best generals, and employing him as a campaign issue. But their success involved other factors as well. Locally and in the state, a leadership feud involving Daniel Burns, John D. Spreckels, and remnants of the old Higgins organization divided Republican ranks and prompted many adherents of the party to scatter their votes among candidates of nonpartisan and independent movements. The issues in the contest—with the exception of Buckley—were themselves muddied and confused. Indeed, the major local question emerged not in the campaign but rather in the controversy surrounding the new method of casting and counting votes. The first implementation of the Australian ballot in San Francisco fell far short of expectations. Well before the election, Republican leaders challenged the legality of the innovation and carried their fight to the state supreme court, and a local grand jury charged the San Francisco registrar of voters with manipulating the supposedly fool-proof official rolls. On election day, booths too dark to permit adequate vision forced voters to open curtains for light, and poorly designed ballots flapped in plain sight over the edges of inadequate counters, negating the much-heralded secrecy of the Australian ballot. Those who chose to vote under such conditions—and many opted for abstention—found additional impediments in their way when election officials failed to provide sufficient supplies of rubber stamps, ink pads, and ballots. For those ultimately able to mark their choices, the ordeal was not yet ended; containers designed to receive tallies proved too small, and the mishandling of cheese boxes and other receptacles pressed into service precipitated charges of lost ballots, stuffing, and repeating on a grand scale.[19]

Even after the election, confusion persisted throughout a tabulation process more cumbersome than the old, purportedly inefficient system, and challenges which necessitated several recounts postponed publication of official results until February 1893. But despite the confusion, final counts confirmed initial estimates of the outcome, and the new Democratic organization emerged with a respectable victory. The Phelan-McNab machine captured most municipal administrative offices and their patronage, ten positions on the board of supervisors, and six on the school board. Nonpartisans and Independents elected the mayor (Levi R. Ellert), one supervisor, and three school directors, leaving only a few offices to the Republicans. At the state level, Republicans maintained their slim majority in the senate, but Democrats secured sufficient places in the assembly to dominate the legislature and grant Stephen Mallory

White his coveted seat in the United States Senate. Californians also once again gave their electoral votes to Grover Cleveland, rounding off a solid victory for a Democracy which entered the lists without Buckley's leadership for the first time in over a decade.[20]

The Blind Boss followed the 1892 contest from London where his only child, Christopher Augustine, Jr., was born in 1893.[21] By the spring of 1894, however, Buckley made his intention to recover his position in San Francisco Democratic affairs only too apparent for the comfort of the reformers arrayed against him. He returned to California and divided his attention and time between his estate in Livermore and his haunts in San Francisco, frequenting especially the Nob Hill headquarters of the Manhattan Club, soon to be refurbished at the boss's expense and revitalized as the Occidental Club. Simultaneously, he opened a personal headquarters in the Reception Saloon at Sutter and Montgomery Streets and began to confer there with Democratic leaders including Sam Rainey, Max Popper, and Sam Braunhart.[22] Despite the apparent intensity of his early preparations, however, Buckley exerted little real influence in partisan activities. He attended both state and municipal conventions, but only as an observer, and local party leaders summarily rejected his advice to nominate the ultimately successful People's party mayoral candidate Adolph Sutro.[23]

He was, nevertheless, an issue in the campaign, especially as a foil in the hands of enemies who used his reputation to discredit their own adversaries. The strategy, moreover, became increasingly effective—especially for Populists and Republicans—when testimony at Max Popper's trial for improper business conduct drew renewed attention to links between Popper and the boss in street sweeping and contracting firms and in the Mercantile Bank of San Francisco, all of which engaged in transactions with the city. Revelations in the case forced both Popper and McNab, who was indirectly involved in the affair, to resign temporarily their positions on the Democratic County Committee, but they had no appreciable impact upon the election. And for the boss, the 1894 contest had only one tangible result; he found himself once again before Judge William T. Wallace, charged with ballot-box tampering, but subsequently acquitted.[24]

Victorious mayoral candidate Adolph Sutro, a millionaire who opposed railroad monopoly and espoused municipal ownership of utilities and the three-cent fare on street railways, won the 1894 contest with surprisingly universal support. His following "came not from the 'sandlots' but from the meetings of property owners or merchants, and of savings bank depositors," from the San Francisco Afro-American League, from labor, and from business groups such as the Market Street Improvement Club. Opposition to the Populist candidate emanated principally from the Southern Pacific, from entrenched political interests, and from a San Francisco Women's League disenchanted by his refusal to make suffrage a principal issue in his campaign. It was, however, primarily a personal victory for Sutro, and only one other Populist nominee won election in 1894.[25]

A board of supervisors comprised of eight Republicans and four Democrats whom Martin Kelly described as the "hungriest sharks I ever met" collaborated with a contingent of equally rapacious municipal department heads to prevent the mayor from accomplishing any of the reforms advocated during his campaign. Indeed, the coalition San Francisco government of 1895–1896 proved to be among the most corrupt in the city's history. Before its term ended, Superintendent of Streets Thomas Ashworth had been indicted for fraud and threatened with impeachment and members of the board of supervisors had been brought under grand jury investigation and to trial for misusing their offices. Their malfeasances included favoritism in the application of the city tax rate, prize-fight permit frauds, collusion in Southern Pacific efforts to monopolize street railways, permitting the open operation of brothels and gambling dives, and a list of additional violations unmatched in charges brought against Buckley by even his most vindictive antagonists. So blatant, indeed, were the misdeeds of the "Solid Eight" members of the board of supervisors (five Republicans and three Democrats) that both major parties joined the Populists and nonpartisans in publicly denouncing them.[26]

Buckley's recognition of Democratic reformers' entrenched strength discouraged a concerted effort to reassert his authority in 1894, but by 1895 corruption in municipal government and renewed intrapartisan rivalries provided an opportune setting for a potentially successful attempt. Therefore, in mid-1895 he commenced preparations for the 1896 contest which would be the Blind Boss's last hurrah in San Francisco politics. None of the political scandals which rocked the city during

Sutro's administration actually involved Buckley, but the local press, aware of the implications of the boss's increased activity, rarely neglected an opportunity to link him to individuals under investigation, under indictment, or on trial. As Buckley's visits to the city and sequestered conferences with old cronies and new allies became more frequent, local dailies carefully followed his movements and speculated about his intentions, not only reviving allegations from the 1880s and their Napoleon-Elba analogies but also publicizing nonpolitical developments such as a former bodyguard's deranged threats to assassinate the boss and a bizarre incident involving Buckley's partner in the defunct San Francisco Syndicate and Trust Company, Clifton E. Mayne.[27]

In November 1895, a Los Angeles jury convicted Mayne of sexual assaults upon two female minors, and reverberations of the affair provided grist for the anti-Buckley mills grinding in San Francisco. While he awaited sentence, the prisoner accused the boss of engineering both his involvement with the girls and his subsequent conviction. The boss's motives purportedly involved revenge for Mayne's testimony against him before the Wallace grand jury. Evidence to support the allegation remained circumstantial, and affadavits which Mayne's lawyers claimed would document Buckley's influence in the Los Angeles events never came to light. Nevertheless, the San Francisco press—particularly William Randolph Hearst's *Examiner*, now in firm league with the Phelan-McNab reformers—utilized Mayne's accusations in yet another effort to discredit Buckley. At the same time, several members of the Wallace jury vowed to petition the governor on Mayne's behalf if the boss could be linked to his conviction.[28] It was a whirlwind effort, brief and ultimately inconsequential for the boss; but it was significant. The eagerness with which San Francisco Democrats responded to Mayne's accusations underscores their persistent apprehension concerning Buckley's potential for power and their willingness to use the potential threat of his return in their own cause. It was, furthermore, an exercise of doubtful necessity, for a contingent of the Blind Boss's reformist enemies already had engineered a coup which circumscribed his influence even more effectively than the Wallace grand jury had done in 1891. They had, according to spokesman Gavin McNab, relegated the boss to a "political lazaretto."[29]

Despite McNab's confidence, Democratic reformers did have reason for concern about Buckley's threat and the cohesiveness of their ranks. Following the inconclusive election of 1894, the San Francisco party was in disarray. Numerous would-be bosses—McNab, Popper, Ned Lanigan, and Sam Brauhart in addition to Buckley and Sam Rainey—vied for control of the party and for the support of the powerful police and fire departments and the Federal Brigade of government office holders, and the unity which had ensured success in 1892 seemed to be evaporating. On October 2, 1895—a full year in advance of the next campaign —intrapartisan strife culminated in a dramatic test of strength for control of the local governing body, now augmented to 450 members and styled the Democratic General Committee. A committee meeting in Metropolitan Hall reduced itself to a disorderly contest for the committee chairmanship between Buckley's candidate, John O'Brien, and McNab's nominee, Alonzo A. Watkins. Watkins won narrowly, but only after the McNab faction altered party procedures to require printed ballots rather than the traditional voice vote, produced "piles of Watkins tickets" from some mysterious source, and tabulated a vote which substantially exceeded the number of committeemen actually present in the hall. It was an obvious—albeit disputed—victory for McNab and the anti-Buckley forces, but the Scotch Boss moved quickly to further consolidate his faction's control of the party.[30]

A year earlier, delegates to the Democratic municipal convention of 1894 anticipated the potential threat of internal factionalism by authorizing convention chairman Eugene Deuprey to appoint a select committee to reform and reorganize the party. Immediately following the rancorous meeting which placed Watkins at the head of the General Committee, Deuprey carried out his charge, probably at McNab's behest. He named a Committee of Twenty-Five composed of prominent Democrats, and within a week that aggregation invited Chairman Watkins to add another twenty-five members. The resultant Committee of Fifty—which coincidentally included McNab, Watkins, and Deuprey and an overwhelming majority of their followers—quickly became known as the Junta, and its creation successfully ostracized Buckley, his followers, and other potential rivals for power from participation in partisan reorganization.[31] But the reformers were not yet finished with the Blind Boss. Continuing signs of factionalism in the Democracy at large and within the Junta itself prompted the McNab forces to engineer a sophisticated stroke which reduced to rank amateurism the crude tactics employed in 1892 and so warmly admired by Martin Kelly.

At a mid-October meeting of the Committee of Fifty, McNab's close associate, attorney Alex Vogelsang, proposed that the assembled "purity men" appoint (in overt defiance of party rules and traditions) a reliable majority of 250 members to a reconstituted General Committee in order to ensure what the San Francisco *Call* termed a "padlocked Democracy" closed to Buckley and all other opponents of the Junta machine. The Blind Boss and his followers, joined by numerous Democrats who had no abiding loyalty to Buckley but resented McNab's maneuvers, did not submit willingly to their exclusion. They organized themselves as the Regular Democracy, claimed to be the legitimate arm of the party in San Francisco, condemned the Junta as a collection of incompetent demagogues and their tactics as an intrapartisan revolution, and appealed to the State Central Committee for recognition. They were, however, no match for McNab's forces who quickly moved to reinforce their already solid position. On November 15, the Committee of Fifty called a General Committee meeting for the following evening and delayed notification of the Regular Democrats until virtually the eleventh hour, allowing them little opportunity for preparation. In reality, additional time would have made little difference, for McNab and the Junta laid their plans with meticulous care. The reformers' 250 hand-picked delegates dominated the Metropolitan Hall gathering which opened and closed in tumult. Following traditional preliminaries, which included several fistic exchanges and a visit by the police, the Junta implemented its prearranged scheme. From the floor came motions (but no audible seconds) to adjourn the General Committee *sine die*. Chairman Watkins called for the vote (but only the ayes), declared the motion carried, and hastily departed from the hall as the gaslights went out. The jubilant McNab forces immediately dispersed, contending that the General Committee had dissolved itself and set the stage for the creation of an entirely new, Junta-dominated Democratic governing body in San Francisco.[32]

Not all of the Democrats present in Metropolitan Hall either sanctioned or accepted the Junta's manipulated victory. Attorney Joseph Rothschild, vice chairman of the General Committee and a Buckley associate since the 1880s, attempted to keep the dissident partisans assembled and managed to secure the passage of a second motion to adjourn the committee for only one week. But the action of Rothschild's rump session had no real effect; nor did the Regular Democrats' subsequent effort to establish themselves as the recognized Democracy in San Francisco. Early in 1896, McNab's faction received the sixty-one to seven vote sanction of an obviously sympathetic State Central Committee and forthwith named a solid Junta delegation—McNab, Phelan, Watkins, Deuprey, Popper, William Sullivan, and Marion Biggs—to represent the city party in state affairs. Through a series of adept, calculated, and highly successful strokes, Democratic reformers simultaneously reinforced their own position, created an opportunity to name their own General Committee, and relegated not only the Blind Boss but also other opponents to political oblivion in the councils of the local and state party. The tactics employed outraged many San Francisco Democrats, and even the *Examiner* temporarily turned on McNab and his contingent. At a more pragmatic level, however, the events of late 1895 and early 1896 left little doubt concerning the Junta's control, and their obvious success proved sufficient to entice most defectors and contenders for power—including Buckley's old partner Sam Rainey—into the reformers' fold.[33]

Thus, by the time the Mayne accusations agitated San Francisco in the fall of 1895, McNab's coup had completed what the Wallace grand jury began five years earlier. Ironically, a Committee of Fifty numerically and socioeconomically analogous to the group which in 1882 placed the reins of the Democracy in Buckley's hands unhorsed him in 1895. In the process, they accomplished his virtually complete isolation from positions of power within the party, a fact which Collis P. Huntington acknowledged by rescinding the few remaining lambs' railroad passes. And they were few indeed, for most of the Democrats who had joined in the struggle with the Junta had, by early 1896, expeditiously deserted the vanquished boss and joined ranks with the victorious opposition. Nevertheless, despite the odds against him, Chris Buckley was not yet finished with San Francisco politics; nor were San Francisco politicians finished with him.

The Blind Boss's political intuition should have informed him of the futility of continued conflict with the Junta. Still, in 1896 he mounted his most energetic campaign to recover power in the party, an effort which one *Examiner* reporter dubbed the "steam beer handicap."[34] If

245

Buckley did not recognize the precariousness of his position, San Franciscans did, and they sought explanations for his seemingly suicidal determination to persist. One rumor placed the boss in the pay of John D. Spreckels who had ambitions to place his associate, Samuel L. Shortridge, in the Senate of the United States. But that allegation is hardly tenable in view of Spreckels' vituperative assaults upon Buckley in the pages of his San Francisco *Call*. Another prevalent suspicion involved collusion with Collis P. Huntington and the Southern Pacific, but that too seems unlikely since the shrewd railroad czar already had made clear his contempt for Buckley's diminished power. Further speculations allied the boss with Populist senatorial hopeful Thomas V. Cator, purportedly in exchange for the patronage of any offices which People's party captured in the city and state, and Buckley's subsequent infiltration of the Populist municipal convention gave belated credence to the presumption, but little real confirmation.[35]

Additional rumors asserted that the Blind Boss remained in the campaign for plunder rather than power and that the Regular Democrats were but a piece club assembled to extort funds from legitimate candidates in return for promises of phantom votes. Buckley's motives for such a strategy in 1896 allegedly involved efforts to compensate for $5000 annual deficits accrued in the operation of his estate and winery at Livermore. But like other explanations of his activities, the piece club speculation is plausible but highly improbable. Regular Democrats made no overtures to either of the major parties during the campaign, and the energies initially committed to their own canvass suggest not a diversion or sham but a genuine effort to win. References to Buckley's financial difficulties likewise have little substance; for Livermore newspapers simultaneously reported highly productive and profitable viticultural operations at Ravenswood.[36]

Indeed, it is entirely possible that the search for tangible motives for Buckley's activities in 1896 was as futile as the activities themselves and that the most convincing explanation involves the Blind Boss himself rather than complicity with Spreckels, Huntington, or Cator or the organization of a piece club for monetary gain. San Francisco and its politics, after all, had been his profession and his major concern for more than a quarter of a century, and had, in many ways, given meaning to his life. To be sure, he savored his bucolic retreat at Ravenswood, but it is unlikely that the existence of a gentleman farmer and vintner, despite his protestations to the contrary, could for long satisfy his ambitions or appetites for political activity or power. Therefore, it may not be amiss to suggest that, like a retired wheelhorse answering a firebell in the night, he entered and ran an obviously overmatched sweepstake in 1896 out of habit or compulsion or simply out of a desire to participate in what had been his life for a generation.[37]

Whatever the reasons, Buckley and his Regular Democrats commenced and conducted their early campaign in a spirit of gravity, confidence, and determination, despite a series of calculated impediments which McNab and the Junta placed in their path. Early in March 1896, elements of a rejuvenated organization began to appear, numbering in its ranks not only remnants of the old push and lambs from the halcyon days of the 1880s but also local and state officeholders, businessmen, attorneys, and physicians whose abiding distaste for McNab and his tactics led them to affiliate with the boss. Many of these gentlemen of property and standing, however, reconsidered their position when the Regulars failed to achieve their first goal: recognition by a State Central Committee packed with Junta sympathizers and Stephen Mallory White's country delegates. It would be but the first of many frustrations, but the obviously unintimidated remaining Regulars denounced the state officers' actions and, under the leadership of their own General Committee chairman Joseph Rothschild, prepared to achieve their second goal: admission to the state party convention to be held in Sacramento in June. Despite vigorous efforts which included a statewide campaign for support, however, the second assault on a clearly hostile state organization was no more successful than the first, and defeat further eroded the Regular Democrats' support. Still, Buckley and his remaining followers determined to remain in the contest, held mass meetings to vent their displeasure with the state party, threatened to take the matter to the courts and to the Democratic national convention in Chicago, and began preparations for the local campaign in San Francisco.[38]

There Buckley found yet another obstacle standing in his way when a Junta-dominated Board of Election Commissioners refused to permit Regular Democrats to participate in the selection of precinct election officials. The Blind Boss could only protest, add one more to his lengthening list of defeats, and proceed with plans for primary elections and a municipal convention. Following a summer flurry of activity, the Regulars organized their convention in B'nai B'rith Hall on September 3 and, to the disappointment of local journalists, the gathering was relatively decorous and uneventful. With dispatch, the Buckley party endorsed the candidates and programs of the state and national Democratic conventions and formulated a platform which denounced McNab's rival party and outlined the Regular Party's stand on municipal issues: for reduced municipal expenditures and fiscal responsibility, the dollar-limit, reduced utility rates, efficient public schools, improved streets, and the right to carry bicycles as baggage on the street railways; against the American Protective Association and its campaign to limit teaching in California to those educated in public schools. In addition, the convention emulated their Republican and Democratic counterparts by nominating a typical Buckley slate of businessmen—headed by Joseph I. Dimond, one of only four incumbent supervisors not currently under indictment—to run for municipal office.[39]

Almost as the gathering adjourned, however, two more obstacles confronted the Blind Boss and his party. On September 16, the state supreme court ruled that, on the basis of a 1893 law, no county officials could be elected in California in 1896, a particularly significant ruling in San Francisco where county contests comprised nearly half of the local slate. Ten days later, the Junta-affiliated San Francisco Registrar of Voters denied the Regular Democrats a place on the official ballot. The boss responded first with a writ of mandate to compel his candidates' inclusion and then with a suit which he carried to the state supreme court. Still, Buckley apparently anticipated a negative decision; for when the court ruled against him in mid-October, he already was prepared with another stratagem to keep himself and his party in the race.[40] Indeed, even earlier in the month he had launched a petition drive, and by the time the court handed down its decision, he had gathered enough signatures to ensure a place on the ballot under the rubric of the Anti-Charter Democratic party. The new organization proclaimed Jeffersonian principles, adherence to the platform and candidates of the defunct Regular Democracy, and opposition to the proposed city charter of 1896.[41]

Two years earlier, the San Francisco Merchants' Association—formed in 1893 to improve economic and sanitary conditions in the city—

248

turned its attention to civic affairs and inaugurated a drive for a new, modern charter to supplant the village system of government prevailing under the Consolidation Act of 1856. In the election of 1894, voters responded by approving yet another Board of Freeholders to draft a new organic law for the city. Initially, support emanated from nearly all sectors of the urban population: a Civic Federation of businessmen and professionals, labor leaders, the reform wings of both major parties, and even representatives of the Populist party. As ties between the Freeholders, the Merchants' Association, and the Civic Federation became firmer, however, and the probable "class" nature of the charter became apparent, opposition surfaced long before Buckley organized his Anti-Charter Democracy. The San Francisco Labor Council resented its exclusion from the charter-making process and the obvious antilabor biases of those who were involved, and it condemned the absence of provisions for municipal ownership and the elimination of corruption from a "charter strong on centralization, civil service, and corporate principles."[42]

Father Peter Yorke, the articulate spokesman for the city's numerous Irish-Catholic citizens, soon joined the opposition. Yorke found traces of nativism, anti-Catholicism, and American Protective Association influence in the charter and made his position known in the pages of his weekly *Monitor*. And many San Francisco teachers, distressed by the charter's educational provisions, dropped their support. An active campaign conducted by the Merchants' Association, the Civic Federation, and the San Francisco Charter Association headed by James D. Phelan failed to overcome popular resistance, and the reform suffered a narrow defeat in a November election in which only half of the more than 60,000 who went to the polls voted on the proposed charter.[43]

The boss's opposition party, formed only a month before the election, had little bearing upon the failure; nor did it appreciably influence San Franciscans on other matters before them in 1896. National issues permeated the rhetoric of the local contest: the Panic of 1893 and its aftermath, expansive industrialism and its regulation, Populism and the silver question, overseas expansion and the tariff, urban-rural tensions and the strains of modernism.[44] And points of local contention, in addition to the charter, added both sound and fury: Oriental exclusion, the railroad funding issue,[45] municipal ownership of utilities, women's suffrage, bossism and corruption, the anti-Catholic American Protective

Association, internecine partisan warfare, and even appeals to the city's newest organized political bloc, bicycle riders or "wheelmen." Before the campaign reached its climax, factionalism disrupted both major parties and no fewer than eleven full or partial tickets appeared in the field.[46] For Buckley, however, these were not the principal concerns; his goal involved the establishment of sufficient strength to recapture something of his former position in partisan affairs in the city. And in pursuit of that goal, he embarked upon what was the most incongruous phase of his campaign by attempting to infiltrate the San Francisco People's party.

Populism retained some strength in California in 1896, and the People's party commenced preparations for the contest early in the spring.[47] In the city itself, the Populist Central Committee organized for primary elections and a mid-September municipal convention to be held in a massive tent at Martin and Larkin Streets. In recognition of the party's minority status, early in the campaign Populist leaders contemplated fusion with sympathetic state and local Democratic candidates, but San Francisco Populists—unlike their counterparts in Alameda county across the bay—rejected the strategy and elected instead to hold a separate convention and to support individual candidates loyal to William Jennings Bryan and the cause of silver. Still, fusion ultimately would characterize the People's party municipal ticket, but neither as they anticipated nor on their terms. Capitalizing upon the lack of Populist cohesion in the city, Buckley entered Anti-Charter Democrats in People's party municipal primaries, and forty-three of his lambs became delegates to the Populist municipal convention, much to the horror of "simon-pure" partisans like Thomas V. Cator and Burnett G. Haskell. And at a tumultuous convention, with Buckley giving orders from the gallery, Anti-Charter Democrats—including Joseph I. Dimond who won the mayoral candidacy by a vote of seventy-four to thirty—captured sixty percent of the places on the Populist municipal ticket.[48]

Buckley's triumph at the People's party convention inspired considerable jocular comment, including an *Examiner* cartoon captioned "BUCKLEY WOULD NOW A FARMER BE."[49] But it also seemed to terminate the campaign for the Blind Boss. In sharp contrast to the energy and enthusiasm which characterized its beginning, the closing

BUCKLEY WOULD NOW A FARMER BE.
Parody of Buckley's 1896 excursion into Populist politics.

weeks of the contest seemed apathetic, almost as if Buckley recognized the political bankruptcy of his organization—matched by its financial insolvency—and resigned himself to defeat. If such were the case, the results of the November 2 election confirmed his pessimism. After a remarkable ninety percent voter turnout, throngs of eager San Franciscans watched as the *Chronicle* and the *Examiner* projected results on the walls of buildings. Most of the tabulations surprised no one. William McKinley won the presidential contest in the city, but by a narrow margin, and the proposed charter suffered defeat. James D. Phelan succeeded in the mayoral contest, and remaining municipal offices were nearly evenly divided among major party candidates, many of whom ran with the additional endorsement of nonpartisan or independent associations. Only a single Populist–Anti-Charter nominee, school director Thomas R. Carew, emerged victorious, and he carried the anomolous support of two anti-charter parties and that of the Nonpartisan movement which sponsored the reform. No other Buckleyite or Populist polled even ten percent of the votes cast.[50] For the Blind Boss, the defeat hardly could have been more decisive, but it should not have been unanticipated.

Martin Kelly observed that the 1890s marked the "beginning of the change from the ancient order of things" for bosses in San Francisco and that "1896 was . . . fateful in introducing a new and important character [James D. Phelan] into local politics." But Phelan—"young, capable, ambitious and, if for no other reason than his vast wealth, incorruptible"—did not constitute the whole of the portentous transformation.[51] A combination of developments, perhaps principally perceptible in historical retrospect, virtually assured Buckley's defeat in 1896 and the end of the era of the saloon boss in the city. Like other nineteenth-century urban centers, San Francisco changed dramatically in the decades following Buckley's arrival and initial forays into municipal politics, and the transition from a boisterous and uninhibited boomtown to a sophisticated and cosmopolitan metropolis rendered the political style of a previous age both inappropriate and, to many, unacceptable. Simultaneously, the evolution of the city also altered the Blind Boss; he became an urban aristocrat whose apparent attitudes provided potential supporters with few discernible alternatives between him and his adversaries. It was, however, principally Buckley's adversaries and their influence upon municipal politics which assured not only his demise but also its permanence. A contingent of dynamic and aggressive leaders, most of them bred in the milieu of the metropolis, combined to alter both the Democratic party and the city and to oust the boss from municipal politics in the name of reform. Kelly would term them "Hannibals."

According to the Republican boss's concept of ancient history, the Carthaginian conquered Rome when he "gathered together his army mules, tied firecrackers to their tales [*sic*], red lights to their ears and tacked pinwheels on their collars, . . . touched the fireworks off and headed the procession toward the Roman rockrollers" occupying the Alpine heights above him. Hannibal represented "far-seeing intelligence, self interest, big business"—reformers. The "Roman rockrollers" were the common people, and the pyrotechnic-laden mules were diversions, most often the specious moral issues which constituted the "last resort of cornered Hannibals" bent on distracting the public from their true intentions. Furthermore, according to Kelly, reforming Hannibals shared with the bosses whom they sought to depose a single goal: the power to control the city and its politics.[52] Although Kelly's allegorical analysis mentions few specific incidents, it is entirely feasible that Buckley's experiences between 1891 and 1896 provided at least a portion of his inspiration. For, contrary to traditional interpretation, neither Stephen Mallory White nor a disenchanted state party leadership disposed of the Blind Boss.[53] Instead, a determined coalition of San Francisco Democrats terminated his career, and they accomplished their victory by adopting the tactics of Kelly's Hannibal. The effort to eliminate Buckley from the San Francisco political arena, moreover, specifically relates events in the city to scholarly analyses of the frequent discrepancy between the rhetoric and the reality of municipal reform in the late nineteenth century.[54]

In the name of political purity and legality, in 1891 Judge William T. Wallace unabashedly violated the law which he was sworn to uphold in order to achieve his own ends and those of the jurors he appointed. During the primary elections of the following year, the Reform Democracy headed by Phelan and McNab simultaneously made Buckley and his methods a moral issue and adopted the very tactics which they so vociferously denounced. In 1895 and 1896, ostensibly in the name of reform and civic improvement, the Junta utilized sophisticated methods—not those of the saloon boss but nevertheless machine politics, adapted to novel urban conditions and new political objectives—and manipulated traditional policies of the local Democracy in the quest for power in the city.

Neither the Junta's partisan contrivances nor its exploitation of Buckley as a moral issue aimed exclusively at the Blind Boss. He was, however, consistently the most apparent target, for he represented in more than a symbolic way a serious impediment to both Junta control of the party and genuine municipal reform. Buckley had been discredited, but two elements in partisan affairs made him a continuing threat: "those who [would] actively support him and those who [would] endure him."[55] Active supporters included principally adherents from the halcyon days of the 1880s. But more importantly, respectable San Franciscans—opponents of business involvement in politics, advocates of the old dollar-limit, job-seekers thrown out of work by the depression of the 1890s, doubters of the Junta's experience and ability, ethnic and labor interests opposed to the 1896 charter, and protesters against McNab's tactics—found it temporarily expedient to endure Buckley as the sole Democratic alternative to the Junta.[56]

Therefore, the reformers' Hannibal-like assaults represented neither a wholly personal attack upon the Blind Boss nor an entirely impersonal onslaught against bossism. Instead, they involved calculated efforts to shatter a not inconsiderable contingent of potential opponents driven into the boss's camp by suspect Junta tactics and policies. And since Buckley's leadership had been primarily personal rather than ideologically partisan, he could be publicly censured without besmirching the party itself. In its attacks upon the boss and other opponents, however, the Junta accepted and employed precisely those tactics which it had denounced as immoral and unethical. San Francisco Democratic reformers between 1891 and 1896 changed the rules of the political game when it was convenient and even circumvented the law in order to accomplish their goals. When Buckley manipulated the political system, he was a scoundrel. Rumors of his efforts to dissolve the General Committee or infiltrate the State Central Committee branded him as a charlatan. His attempts to mobilize the federal brigade, the police and fire departments, and other sources of mass support amounted to chicanery. Rigging election procedures made him a political parasite. Yet the Junta utilized all of these tactics and more in the name of good government, doing considerable violence to democratic procedures, and confirming scholarly analyses of contradictions between what reformers said and what they did.[57]

Because the Junta consisted of a mixed lot—businessmen, professionals, officeholders at various levels of government, would-be bosses like McNab and Popper, and genuine reformers like Phelan—interests and motivations for political involvement varied widely. Indeed, no systematically articulated program emerged from the coalition, except in the proposed reform charters of 1896 and 1898. Reformers did, however, share at least two common traits: abiding suspicion of Buckley and fear (either real or contrived) of his power and a desire to exert their authority by controlling the local Democracy and through it San Francisco. In their quest for power, they confirmed not only their willingness to use the Blind Boss as an issue in their campaigns but also the validity of Martin Kelly's warning: "When anything especially mysterious occurs, the French have a saying, 'Cherchez la dame,' which means 'Chase the dame,' or something like that. I would suggest as a substitute, 'Look out for Hannibal.' "[58] Unfortunately for Chris Buckley, the caveat came two decades too late.

11

Epilogue

Had Martin Kelly delivered his warning to Chris Buckley in 1895 rather than to the readers of editor Fremont Older's San Francisco *Bulletin* in 1917, it would have altered matters little. A transformed city and a new generation of partisan leadership already had rendered both the Blind Boss and his methods practically ineffective if not entirely obsolete. The Wallace jury had discredited Buckley, followers of James D. Phelan and Gavin McNab had seized the local Democracy and centralized their control over it, and the Junta had reinforced the bastions circumscribing the influence of the boss and other intrapartisan adversaries. At the same time, state legislation further inhibited the potential efficacy of Buckley's methods with the Australian ballot law of 1891 and a campaign practices law in 1893, and these would be followed by laws regulating the selection of convention delegates in 1901 and eliminating local nominating conventions in 1909.[1] Unlike many of his contemporaries in both major parties—including Kelly and McNab—Buckley either could not or would not adapt to novel conditions. He seemed to sense that the first rays of the twentieth century appearing over the horizon signaled the setting of his political sun, and his final appearances in the San Francisco partisan arena in 1898 and 1899 were perfunctory at best and orchestrated principally by his opponents.

For Buckley, 1896 constituted an unmitigated disaster, but for James D. Phelan and others involved in the drive for charter reform it was both a victory and a defeat. To be sure, a respectable majority of the city's voters gave Phelan the office of mayor and installed Junta candidates and independents in most other municipal offices. The charter which the mayor so avidly supported, however, encountered apathy and rejection. Therefore, Phelan and his determined allies—including Democrats, Republicans, nonpartisans, and especially members of the San Francisco Merchants' Association—regrouped for another effort to extend the principle of centralization beyond party organization to the municipal government itself. Early in 1897, the mayor named a committee of 100 prominent citizens to draft a new organic law, the fifth attempt since 1880. In subsequent months, Phelan and his committeemen applied sufficient pressure in Sacramento to secure state legislation permitting charter questions to be decided at special elections. The first of these in San Francisco occurred in December 1897 when barely one-third of the urban electorate chose a Committee of 100 slate as a Board of Freeholders empowered to complete a charter proposal and present it to the public. The second special election took place less than six months later in May 1898 when the same fraction of the city's voters, by a narrow plurality of 2364 affirmative ballots, approved a modern, efficient, businesslike municipal charter.[2]

In its principal characteristics—centralization and bureaucracy—San Francisco's new charter closely resembled similar documents promoted by structural reformers in cities across the nation in the late nineteenth and early twentieth centuries.[3] A strong-mayor charter, it increased the administrative latitude and appointive authority of the city's chief executive and made heads of municipal departments responsible directly to that office. It provided for a board of supervisors increased from twelve to eighteen members and elected from the city at large rather than by individual wards, and it applied similar principles to the school department by augmenting the authority of an elected, professional superintendent and limiting that of an appointed (and paid) school board reduced to four members. Other features of the 1898 charter regularized franchise and licensing procedures in an effort to reduce the manipulation of the system, enhance the economic climate of the city, and place municipal operations on a businesslike basis. To reduce partisanship in local affairs and reduce the use of patronage as a political weapon, it also mandated that municipal elections be held in odd-numbered years and introduced the rudiments of a civil service system. Finally, the charter provided for eventual municipal ownership of utilities and transportation facilities and expanded home rule, giving the city substantially greater control over its own affairs and reducing its dependence upon the state.[4]

Despite the hopes of its sponsors, the new charter did not eliminate partisan politics from the government of the city. Nor did it terminate bossism in San Francisco politics; Martin Kelly and Gavin McNab remained and, whether or not he was a boss in the traditional sense, Abraham Ruef was yet to come.[5] Nevertheless, the organic law of 1898 reflected the goals and attitudes of its sponsors—Junta reformers and their business-oriented allies in both political parties—and institutionalized their vision of the city in the municipal decision-making process. It also responded to the impulse toward modernism which took the city out of the age of saloon bosses like Buckley and thrust it into the era of the professional in politics.

Although the Blind Boss opposed the new charter, he remained aloof from the controversies surrounding its formulation and adoption and from the subsequent municipal election campaign. Indeed, his role in 1898 remained the essentially passive one of a straw man constructed by John D. Spreckels and his San Francisco *Call*. Emulating the Junta's successful tactics of 1895 and 1896, Spreckels' editors and reporters implied the existence of ties between Buckley, Phelan, and the charter in an effort to defeat the proposed reform and discredit the mayor and the Democracy in the eyes of the public.[6] The strategy failed when voters approved the charter in May and returned Phelan to office in November, but just one year later Buckley assumed a similar function in the municipal elections of 1899, the first held under the aegis of the new organic law. Although the boss's activities were more energetic and apparent than they had been during the previous contest, his greater visibility served principally to make him an even more tempting target. Not only

Spreckels' *Call* but also Michel De Young's *Chronicle* and William Randolph Hearst's *Examiner* touched off Hannibal-like pyrotechnics attempting to link the Blind Boss with the publishers' various adversaries.[7] As they had in 1898, however, the Phelan-McNab forces—with Hearst's vigorous support—emerged victorious in both primary and general elections, once again confirming what had become apparent as early as 1892: Buckley no longer constituted a factor in the politics of his city or his party. His retirement was both permanent and complete.

Recurrent defeat failed to diminish the constancy of Buckley's affection for San Francisco. In one of the few unguarded passages in his memoirs, he commented: "From the moment I arrived, . . . I have loved the old town and its people and love both still. It is the only place on earth that seems like home to me."[8] Even the debacle of 1896 did not alter his sentiment, and shortly after his ouster at the hands of the Junta, he purchased an O'Farrell Street mansion, formerly the home of silver baron John W. Mackay, installed his family in it, and diverted his attention from politics and toward a variety of business interests and real estate investments in the city and elsewhere.[9] At the same time, he retained his affection for life on the land at Ravenswood, and during the years after 1896 he divided his time between San Francisco and his rural retreat where he became a popular, respected citizen and "truly the lord of Livermore."[10] During previous years, the boss expanded the residence and the winery on his property and improved the vineyards and gardens surrounding them so that by 1896 his estate provided both a pleasant sanctuary characterized by sturdy, unpretentious Victorian elegance and a potentially lucrative business enterprise.[11] With publisher Henry S. Crocker and local vintners—including the Wente, Concannon, and Cresta Blanca interests—he helped to found the cooperative California Winemakers' Corporation and participated enthusiastically in its efforts to promote local vintages. He also became as avid a student of viticulture as he had been of politics and took unreserved pride in the quality of the wines and brandies produced on his lands.[12]

Simultaneously, retirement from politics and especially life at Livermore permitted Buckley, perhaps for the first time, to indulge his gregarious nature by entertaining old friends and political allies, prominent theatrical and literary figures, and such luminaries as Jack Sharkey who sojourned with the boss prior to his 1899 bout with Jim Jeffries in San

Ravenswood, 1899.

Ravenswood, 1978, restored and designated as a
California Historical Site.

Francisco. With avid interest, local journals followed the parade of visitors traversing Arroyo Road on their way to Ravenswood and the movements of the Buckley family between the valley and the city and on excursions abroad. Livermore residents also responded to the boss's sense of humor and affinity for practical jokes, and they repeated tales—often with considerable embellishment—of the Ravenswood mule which Alex

Greggains instructed in the fine art of pugilism and of the holdup which Buckley staged to terrify guests arriving by tally-ho from the local train depot.[13]

But for the Blind Boss, the opportunity to hear friends and family read to him from the books he loved and to spend time with the wife and son he adored provided the greatest pleasures of bucolic leisure. Daily walks and domestic chats with Annie Marie in the rose gardens surrounding their country home became a habit, as did pampering young Christopher, Jr., the "lord of the manor." In San Francisco, Buckley employed private tutors for the boy, sent him to Saint Ignatius School, and acted the part of a "stern martinet, . . . a real boss" who demanded academic excellence, perhaps in an effort to prepare his son to "do anything, anything but politics." At Ravenswood, however, he lavished affection upon the child, showered him with gifts, and made him the center of his life. The lad also became the inspiration for Buckley's renewed but ultimately futile quest to recover his sight and for the lament, "I would give $100,000 to look for one minute at my boy."[14]

The earthquake and fire of 1906 destroyed Buckley's city home and much of his urban investment property and rendered his residence at Ravenswood more permanent. He increased his participation in local activities at Livermore, appeared with his family in parades and at other community functions, sent his son to the public high school, contributed to numerous charitable causes, and during World War I put the town's Liberty Bond drive "over the top" with a single purchase of $8000.[15] During the same years, the Blind Boss maintained a series of homes and an office in his beloved San Francisco and devoted substantial attention to investments which included properties in the city, Los Angeles, and San Diego, Kern County land purchased prior to the oil boom in the region and subsequently sold at a substantial profit, the United States Wireless Printing Telegraph Company and the Burlingame Typewriting Telegraph Company, both engaged in the development of teletype processes, and support for experiments with a rectifier system to expand the potential use of electrical power. Following the world war, Christopher, Jr.—graduated from the University of California in 1914 and Boalt Hall College of Law in 1916 and fresh from a hitch in the navy—joined his father in the management of the family's interests, and the boss passed his final years enjoying his wealth, dispensing his charity lavishly, and traveling the world in the company of his family.[16]

Despite Buckley's erratic presence in the city, even in retirement he rarely escaped the scrutiny of the San Francisco public. Newspapers apprised their readers of his movements, his business activities, and his personal affairs (including even the purchase of a family crypt), and they revived him as an issue in virtually every local election campaign. Thus, when the seventy-six-year-old boss died of a "severe attack of indigestion" on April 20, 1922—in his Clay Street home with his family and the ubiquitous Greggains at his bedside—it was not a total stranger, even to younger and newer San Franciscans, who passed from the local scene and whose demise precipitated an "uncanny metamorphosis of opinion" among both journalists and the public.[17]

Editors who had excoriated Buckley during his public career lavished praise upon him, and the man who in life had been the scourge of San Francisco became in death a benevolent despot, a "figure of romance, legend, and strange glamour" who "developed a genius for organization and mastery of detail that lifted him, through sheer force of personal talents, to the undisputed dictatorship" of the city and the state. His reign, previously denounced as the nadir of political life in San Francisco, suddenly became a "kindly, just, and generous dispensation," and for three days editorials and obituaries eulogized Buckley with anecdotes from the past, comments on the loyalty of his friends and beneficiaries, evidences of the constancy of his word, and stories of the colorful figures involved in his career. Finally, on the foggy morning of April 24, a host of San Franciscans—private citizens, steadfast friends and former enemies, municipal and state dignitaries, and a smattering of the merely curious—crowded into Saint Dominic's Church and followed the funeral cortege to Holy Cross Cemetery in suburban Colma to pay final respects and to observe the interment of the Blind Boss.[18]

The metamorphosis of opinion evident in both attendance at Buckley's funeral and the public adulation which preceded it was, perhaps, neither so strange nor so uncanny as it initially seems. Both reactions included, to be sure, a substantial element of antiquarian nostalgia, and they also involved an outpouring of genuine grief from among the Blind Boss's scores of friends and hundreds of acquaintances, not only in the city and the state but also across the nation and throughout the world. They included, too, sincere expressions of gratitude from among the many recipients of his charity.[19] Responses to the boss's death, however, also may have involved a less apparent or tangible ingredient, specifically a belated recognition that Buckley was not the demonic monster devoid of personal morality portrayed in political cartoons and that his hegemony in San Francisco was not an entirely negative period in the history of the city.

Had Buckley acquired his fame and fortune in business rather than in politics, contemporaries and historians might have labeled him a hero of the nineteenth century, a self-made man.[20] They also might have tolerated in him practices allowed to speculators and entrepreneurs. When, for example, legislators diverted substantial sums of public funds to enhance the values of properties belonging to William Ralston and John Middleton, articulate San Franciscans—including some displaced by the promoters' projects—accepted the schemes with only mild protests.[21] But in situations involving analogous principles, allegations that the Blind Boss used municipal labor and materials to improve his residences and revelations of his partnership in enterprises contracting with the city provoked charges of corrupt manipulation and confirmed the existence of different standards of public morality for the politician and the businessman. Buckley remained the target of similar accusations for a quarter of a century as he worked at his profession, mastered it, and emerged from the obscurity of the immigrant working classes to a position of positive affluence and substantial renown before his fortieth birthday. For him and for talented contemporaries of similar backgrounds, politics furnished an avenue of social and economic mobility, an alternate to more traditional routes.[22] But politics—particularly in the cities—also involved implicit pejorative connotations which minimized accomplishments and frequently cast them in an entirely negative light. The term *boss,* moreover, conjured up (and continues to do so) sinister images reminiscent of Lord James Bryce's depiction of the municipal politico who "generally avoids publicity, preferring the substance to the pomp of power, and is all the more dangerous because he sits, like a spider, hidden in the midst of his web."[23]

Throughout his public career, however, the Blind Boss found evasion of the limelight impossible. His adversaries mercilessly attacked his character and vigorously denied that he possessed even rudimentary moral or ethical principles. Yet available evidence renders their accusations difficult to support. At the personal level, throughout his life Buckley remained a steadfast communicant of the Roman Catholic Church and equally devoted to his family which included not only his wives and his son but also parents, nephews, nieces, and distant cousins. Despite his succession of marriages, no hint of infidelity, domestic scandal, or impropriety ever was unearthed, even by his most vitriolic critics or determined investigators. Nor were they able, despite yeoman efforts and persistent allegations, to link the boss to such enterprises as prostitution and gambling. Appearances in courts—some of them remote from his influence or presided over by his enemies—failed to substantiate charges of involvement in vice activities. Similarly, repeated civil and criminal actions brought by a succession of political adversaries, business associates and competitors, and occasional envious family members produced not a single conviction. Indeed, even a grand jury created for the specific purpose in 1891 could find sufficient evidence to indict Buckley on but a single charge, a minor one in comparison to the nature and quantity of the culpable offenses attributed to him during his career.[24] Failure to convict or lack of evidence do not, of course, constitute grounds for blanket exoneration; but neither do unfounded accusations —despite their volume—provide a basis for universal condemnation.

Neither Buckley nor his counterparts should be romanticized as political Robin Hoods who took from the rich and gave to the poor.[25] In fact, they took from rich and poor alike and retained much of what they obtained. By his own frank admission, the Blind Boss accepted for himself and his party substantial remunerations and participated in both honest and dishonest graft. He extracted fees for services rendered to the business community and others, he expected and received partisan contributions from elected city officials and holders of patronage appointments, and he used his position to amass a substantial personal fortune based upon enterprises conducting business with the city and investments involving the kind of inside information which made them "certainties."[26] And it is apparent that these and other activities for which Buckley's enemies denounced him—patronage, favoritism, manipulation of the electoral process, and the like—were detrimental to the city in both moral and fiscal terms.

But it is equally evident that, despite charges by his critics, Chris Buckley did not corrupt municipal polity in San Francisco. It already had been corrupted, if not by individuals certainly by the historical processes of urbanization which rendered government under the Consolidation Act of 1856 and its maze of amendments both ineffectual and obsolete. The Blind Boss and his organization, like their counterparts in countless United States cities, brought a rough form of rudimentary order to the chaos existing in municipal affairs and provided an interim—if extralegal—government that perhaps facilitated otherwise impossible civic development. The candidates elected on Buckley's tickets were not all or even principally political hacks; mayors and other officials provided competent administration, by nineteenth-century standards, despite scandals which repeatedly rocked the school system and the board of supervisors. Under their guidance, work progressed on civic projects, tax rates and the municipal debt remained low (perhaps too low to provide adequate services), and the city's books were kept in balance throughout the Buckley years. The boss and his organization also undertook the management of economic and social conflict in the city, acting as brokers among various competing business enterprises and as arbiters among the multitude of potentially divisive interests in the city's wards and neighborhoods. Finally, the latent functions of the Democratic machine in San Francisco furnished to the urban working classes services which official agencies were unprepared to render: relief, employment, sociability, and alleviation of the anomie characteristic of life in the industrial city.

Services to varied elements in the urban community created a symbiosis between the masses of voters in nineteenth-century cities and the political organizations which kept bosses like Buckley in power, and failure to provide those services frequently resulted in their downfall.[27] When the Blind Boss lost touch with his constituency and when it became apparent that he had overstepped the traditionally tolerated bounds of political chicanery, San Franciscans turned against him. But they did not vote unequivocally for reform. In 1898, for example, only one-third of those eligible registered an opinion on the charter question and less than twenty percent cast an affirmative ballot.[28] Indeed, the structural reformers who displaced Buckley offered no tenable alternatives to the machine's services, and it is in contrast to his successors that Buckley's contribution to the history of his city becomes apparent.

Reformers provided a more modern framework of government, eliminated some of the worst abuses of the partisan system, and perhaps set the stage for San Francisco's twentieth-century development. But whether, as a group, they were appreciably more honest, altruistic, and sincerely concerned with improving the city and the lot of its residents or less bent upon the acquisition of personal power than Buckley is open to serious question. Likewise, their performance in office is subject to criticism, especially in terms of the commitment to economy which was a principal ingredient in their rhetoric. Municipal budgets, debts, tax rates, assessment rolls, and capital expenditures all increased annually under reform governments, even prior to 1906 and the necessity for rebuilding after the earthquake and fire. Reformers also articulated support for the expansion of democracy in municipal affairs, but performance belies that commitment as well. Their urban view—in contrast to the boss's originally broad, pluralistic understanding—was a holistic one which precluded specific attention to many of the elements comprising the urban community. They denied, for example, the validity of ward representation in municipal government and partisan activities and institutionalized that ideology, first by dismantling the Democracy's club system of organization and finally by providing for at-large elections in the 1898 charter. They also took the political organization out of the employment and welfare business, but they offered no official programs or policies to replace these critical functions of the machine.

Structural reformers in San Francisco erected a bureaucratic system, "a silent, unseen, underground machine," in place of the personal and informal government which Buckley and his lieutenants in the ward and neighborhood clubs had provided.[29] Somewhat ironically, the reformers' attacks on the clubs—beginning with the precinct reorganization of 1886—may have precluded their establishment of real control over the local Democracy. Without the ward-level power base which they helped to demolish, neither James Duval Phelan nor even "Scotch Boss" Gavin McNab was able to exercise the authority which had been Buckley's. On the other hand, elimination of the Blind Boss's system of organization also may have prevented in San Francisco the revival of machine-style politics which characterized the post-reform experience of many other cities, most notably New York. Without an existing power base to capture, no subsequent politico—not even Abraham Ruef whose credentials as a boss have been questioned—managed to dominate local partisan organizations.[30] But whatever the case, either by chance or design (and perhaps both) reform programs did tend to reduce citizens' identification with and participation in municipal government and politics, for better or worse.

Martin Kelly observed, "It is hard to canonize a boss"; but the Republican leader considered it virtually impossible even to beatify reformers whom he described, perhaps unfairly, as "an assortment of cranks, idealists, monomaniacs, psalm-singers, [and] exploiting sky pilots."[31] And so long as there exist differing definitions of political morality and ethics and contrasting conceptions of the proper functions of municipal government, the question of the relative benefits to the city of machine and reform politics is not likely to be resolved. There can be no doubt, however, that both Chris Buckley and those who supplanted him were not only makers but also products of the history of their city. Phelan and his associates emerged in a sophisticated urban setting and by determined effort imposed their views of the city upon its government. The Blind Boss, on the other hand, arrived in a burgeoning, adolescent boomtown and employed his own unique talents to capitalize upon existing opportunities or "certainties." He provided the city, at least for a time, with precisely what it required: a focus of authority to reduce the confusion resulting from archaic political systems and a means to fit a multitude of frequently abrasive and irregular fragments into the mosaic of a maturing metropolis. In sum, to paraphrase Voltaire, if a Christopher Augustine Buckley had not existed, it would have been necessary for nineteenth-century San Francisco to create one.

NOTES

ABBREVIATIONS USED IN NOTES

1. *Newspapers and Periodicals*

Jolly Giant	*Thistleton's Jolly Giant* (San Francisco)
LA *Times*	Los Angeles *Times*
Liv. *Echo*	Livermore (Calif.) *Weekly Echo*
Liv. *Herald*	Livermore (Calif.) *Herald*
NY *Times*	New York *Times*
Oak. *Trib.*	Oakland (Calif.) *Tribune*
Sac. *Bee*	Sacramento (Calif.) *Bee*
SF *Alta*	San Francisco *Daily Alta California*
SF *Argonaut*	San Francisco *Argonaut*
SF *Bull.*	San Francisco *Bulletin* and *Evening Bulletin*
SF *Circular*	*San Francisco Real Estate Circular* and *Carter's Real Estate Circular*
SF *Call*	San Francisco *Morning Call* and *Call*
SF *Chron.*	San Francisco *Chronicle*
SF *Exam.*	San Francisco *Daily Examiner* and *Examiner*
SF *Newsletter*	*San Francisco Newsletter and California Advertiser*

SF *Post*	San Francisco *Evening Post*
SF *Wasp*	San Francisco *Wasp*
SF *Wave*	San Francisco *Wave*
Val. *Chron.*	Vallejo (Calif.) *Evening Chronicle*

2. *Scholarly Journals*

AH	*Agricultural History*
AHR	*American Historical Review*
AQ	*American Quarterly*
CHQ	*California Historical Quarterly* and *California Historical Society Quarterly*
JAH	*Journal of American History*
JUH	*Journal of Urban History*
JW	*Journal of the West*
MVHR	*Mississippi Valley Historical Review*
OM	*Overland Monthly*
PHR	*Pacific Historical Review*
PNQ	*Pacific Northwest Quarterly*
PSQ	*Pacific Science Review*
SCQ	*Southern California Quarterly* and *Historical Society of Southern California Quarterly*

3. *Other Abbreviations*

BL	Bancroft Library, University of California, Berkeley
Buckley interviews	Interviews with Christopher A. Buckley, Jr., Pebble Beach, Calif., August, September, November 1974
Buckley, "Reminiscences"	Christopher A. Buckley, "The Reminiscences of Christopher A. Buckley," San Francisco *Bulletin*, 31 Aug.–9 Oct. 1918; 23 Dec. 1918–5 Feb. 1919
DAB	*Dictionary of American Biography,* ed. Dumas Malone (New York, 1962)
JCA	*Journal of the California Assembly*
JCS	*Journal of the California Senate*
"Martin Kelly's Story"	Martin Kelly, "Martin Kelly's Story," San Francisco *Bulletin,* 1 Sept.–26 Nov. 1917
Ruef, "The Road I Traveled"	Abraham Ruef, "The Road I Traveled: An Autobiographical Account of My Career from the University to Prison, with an Intimate Recital of

White Papers the Corrupt Alliance between Big Business and Politics in San Francisco," San Francisco *Bulletin,* 21 May–5 Sept. 1912

Stephen Mallory White Papers, Bender Room, Stanford University Library

PREFACE

1. Alexander B. Callow, Jr., "San Francisco's Blind Boss," *PHR,* 25 (August 1956): 261–279; Alexander B. Callow, Jr., *The Tweed Ring* (New York, 1965); Alexander B. Callow, Jr. (ed.), *The City Boss in America* (New York, 1976).
2. Buckley interviews.
3. For comparative purposes, three anthologies are especially useful: Callow (ed.), *City Boss in America;* Bruce M. Stave (ed.), *Urban Bosses, Machines, and Progressive Reformers* (Lexington, Mass., 1972); Blaine A. Brownell and Warren E. Stickles (eds.), *Bosses and Reformers* (Boston, 1973).

CHAPTER ONE

1. Rudyard Kipling, *American Notes* (New York, 1891), 51; Rudyard Kipling, *Rudyard Kipling's Letters from San Francisco* (San Francisco, 1949), 46–48; Robert Louis Stevenson and Lloyd Osbourne, *The Wrecker* (New York, 1907), 167; Jeremiah Lynch, *Buckleyism* (San Francisco, 1889); SF *Exam.,* 11 April 1889. Lynch's portrayal of Buckley influenced historians as well as Kipling and Stevenson; see Callow, "San Francisco's Blind Boss," 262–264; John P. Young, *San Francisco* (San Francisco, 1912), II 563–564; Edith Dobie, *The Political Career of Stephen Mallory White* (Stanford, 1927), 19; R. Hal Williams, *The Democratic Party and California Politics, 1880–1896* (Stanford, 1974), 23–24. Other characterizations of Buckley appear in Amelia Ransome Neville, *The Fantastic City* (Boston, 1932), 258; Julius Wangenheim, "An Autobiography," *CHQ,* 35 (June 1956): 144.
2. For clarification of the Chinese phrase, I am grateful to my colleague, Professor David B. Chan.
3. Buckley interviews; SF *Exam.,* 22, 27 April 1922; SF *Chron.,* 21 April 1922; Buckley, "Reminiscences," 31 Aug.–9 Oct. 1918; 23 Dec. 1918–5 Feb. 1919; "Martin Kelly's Story," 1 Sept.–26 Nov. 1917.
4. Insights into San Francisco in the nineteenth century are found in Young, *San Francisco;* Gunther Barth, *Instant Cities* (New York, 1975); Roger W. Lotchin, *San Francisco, 1846–1856* (New York, 1974); Doris Muscatine, *Old San Francisco* (New York, 1975); Douglas Daniels, "Afro-San Franciscans: A History of Urban Pioneers, 1860–1930" (Ph.D. thesis, University of California, Berkeley, 1974); Neil Larry Shumsky, "Tar Flat and Nob Hill: A Social

History of Industrial San Francisco in the 1870s" (Ph.D. thesis, University of California, Berkeley, 1972); Martyn J. Bowden, "The Dynamics of City Growth: An Historical Geography of the San Francisco Central District" (Ph.D. thesis, University of California, Berkeley, 1967); Neil L. Shumsky, "San Francisco's Workingmen Respond to the Modern City," *CHQ,* 55 (Spring 1976): 46–57; Roger Olmsted, "The Sense of the 'Seventies: California 100 Years Ago," *CHQ,* 50 (June 1971): 131–160; Frank Mazzi, "Harbingers of the City: Men and Their Monuments in Nineteenth Century San Francisco," *SCQ,* 55 (Summer 1973): 141–162; and Alvin Averbach, "San Francisco's South of Market District, 1850–1950; The Emergence of a Skid Row," *CHQ,* 53 (Fall 1973): 197–223.

5. Roy Swanstrom, "The Reform Administration of James D. Phelan, Mayor of San Francisco" (M.A. thesis, University of California, Berkeley, 1949), 23–26.

6. Buckley interviews; Callow, "Blind Boss," 261–262; Callow, *Tweed Ring,* 64; Williams, *Democratic Party,* 23–24; Rita Kramer, "Well, What Are You Going to Do about It?" *American Heritage,* 24 (February 1973): 18; SF *Chron.,* 21, 22, 25 April 1922; SF *Bull.,* 21, 22, 24 April 1922; SF *Exam.,* 24 July 1899, 21, 22, 25 April 1922; Liv. *Herald,* 22 April 1922; Burial Records, Holy Cross Cemetery, Colma, Calif; Kevin Starr, *Americans and the California Dream, 1850–1915* (New York, 1973), 46–48 and passim.

7. Burial Records, Holy Cross Cemetery, Colma, Calif.; Rodman W. Paul, *California Gold* (Cambridge, 1947), Chap. 2; Rodman W. Paul, *Mining Frontiers in the Far West, 1848–1880* (New York, 1963), Chaps. 4–5; Robert L. Kelley, *Gold vs. Grain* (Glendale, Calif., 1959), 21–56; Muscatine, *Old San Francisco,* 384; Starr, *California Dream,* 94, 179, 191–192; Franklin Walker, *San Francisco's Literary Frontier* (Seattle, 1969), 97; Hugh Quigley, *The Irish Race in California and on the Pacific Coast* (San Francisco, 1878), 135.

Few Irishmen achieved the goal of landownership in California; nor were they entirely free of persecution. See Peyton Hurt, "The Rise and Fall of the 'Know-Nothings' in California," *CHQ,* 9 (March 1930): 16–49, (June 1930): 99–128; John Higham, "The American Party, 1886–1891," *PHR,* 19 (February 1950): 37–47.

Since William Buckley and his brother John, Jr. died within months of one another in 1864 (in February and April respectively), it is possible that both were involved in military service. The frequency of the appearance of similar names in military records, however, makes confirmation impossible. If they were in the Union Army, John Buckley, Sr. and Christopher would have been exempt from the Conscription Act of 1863, but it is also possible that the older brothers served the Confederacy.

8. Buckley interviews; SF *Directories, 1863–1871;* Mazzi, "Harbingers of the City," 149–152; William F. Heintz, *San Francisco's Mayors, 1850–1880* (Woodside, Calif., 1975), 57; Callow, "Blind Boss," 261; Bowden, "Dynamics

of City Growth," Chap. 1; Muscatine, *Old San Francisco,* 111–112, 118–119; Averbach, "San Francisco's South of Market District," 198–200; SF *Bull.,* 21 Oct. 1864.

9. Heintz, *San Francisco's Mayors,* 50; Barth, *Instant Cities,* 209–212, 222–224; SF *Directory, 1875;* 20; James E. Vance, Jr., *Geography and Urban Evolution in the San Francisco Bay Area* (Berkeley, 1964), 15–26. SF *Directories* provide information on street railways, their routes, and occasional maps. For attitudes toward street railways, see Joel A. Tarr, "From City to Suburb: The 'Moral' Influence of Transportation Technology," in Alexander B. Callow, Jr. (ed.), *American Urban History* (New York, 1973), 202–212; and for the impact of transportation technology upon urban patterns, see Sam Bass Warner, Jr., *Streetcar Suburbs* (Cambridge, Mass., 1962); George Rogers Taylor, "The Beginning of Mass Transportation in Urban America," *Smithsonian Journal of History,* 1 (Fall 1966): 35–49.

10. Muscatine, *Old San Francisco,* 112–113, 115, 127, 177; Sherman L. Ricards and Gregory M. Blackburn, "The Sydney Ducks: A Demographic Analysis," *PHR,* 42 (February 1973): 20–31; Daniels, "Afro-San Franciscans," Chap. 1; Lotchin, *San Francisco,* 120; Barth, *Instant Cities,* 131, 135, 160; Averbach, "San Francisco's South of Market District," 199–200; Thomas Pedemonte, "Italy in San Francisco: 'Old Wine in New Bottles' " (M.A. thesis, California State College, Hayward, 1971), 17–18, 23; Doris M. Wright, "The Making of Cosmopolitan California: An Analysis of Immigration, 1848–1870," *CHQ,* 20 (December 1940): 339–340; Thomas F. Prendergast, *Forgotten Pioneers* (San Francisco, 1942), 23–27; Shumsky, "Tar Flat and Nob Hill," 109–151, passim.

11. Gunther Barth, "Metropolism and Urban Elites in the Far West," in Frederic C. Jaher (ed.), *The Age of Industrialism in America* (New York, 1968), 162–163; Asbury Harpending, *The Great Diamond Hoax and other Stirring Incidents in the Life of Asbury Harpending* (Norman, Okla., 1958), 81; Starr, *California Dream,* 74, 347, 354; Muscatine, *Old San Francisco,* 111, 362–363; Lotchin, *San Francisco,* 11, 16–17, 25–26, 28, 127; Albert E. Shumate, *A Visit to Rincon Hill and South Park* (San Francisco, 1963), 3, 8–10.

12. Barth, "Metropolism and Urban Elites," 160–161; Barth, *Instant Cities,* 156–159; Muscatine, *Old San Francisco,* 112–113, 164, 347; Buckley, "Reminiscences," 11 Sept. 1918; Starr, *California Dream,* 239; Lotchin, *San Francisco,* 277–279; Bradford Luckingham, "Benovolence in Emergent San Francisco: A Note on Immigrant Life in the Urban Far West," *SCQ,* 55 (Winter 1973): 431–443; Bradford Luckingham, "Immigrant Life in Emergent San Francisco," *JW,* 12 (October 1973): 600–617.

13. Harpending, *Diamond Hoax,* 75–76.

14. SF *Alta,* 24 June 1862; Charles A. Fracchia, "The Founding of the San Francisco Mining Exchange," *CHQ,* 48 (March 1969): 3–18; Joseph L. King, *History of the San Francisco Stock and Exchange Board* (San Francisco, 1910),

3–12; Clyde G. Chenoweth, "The San Francisco Stock Exchange and Its History" (Ph.D. thesis, Stanford University, 1932), Chap. 1; Buckley, "Reminiscences," 16 Sept. 1918; Lotchin, *San Francisco,* 73; Barth, *Instant Cities,* 142, 144–145, 169; Muscatine, *Old San Francisco,* 118–119, 129–134, 142–150, 288, 366; Heintz, *San Francisco's Mayors,* 49, 52, 55; Mazzi, "Harbingers of the City," 142.

15. Buckley, "Reminiscences," 31 Aug. 1918.

16. Ibid., 2, 3 Sept. 1918.

17. Lois Fuller Rodecape, "Tom Maguire, Napoleon of the Stage," *CHQ,* 20 (December 1941): 292–297, 299–301; Muscatine, *Old San Francisco,* 144; Lotchin, San Francisco, 219–223. For Maguire's previous and subsequent careers, see Lois Fuller Rodecape, "Tom Maguire, Napoleon of the Stage," *CHQ,* 21 (March 1942): 39–72, (June 1942): 141–182, (September 1942): 239–275.

18. Rodecape, "Tom Maguire," (September 1942): 297–300, 305–308; Muscatine, *Old San Francisco,* 144–146; Mazzi, "Harbingers of the City," 149; Buckley, "Reminiscences," 7 Sept., 8 Oct. 1918; Jere D. Wade, "The San Francisco Stage, 1859–1869" (Ph.D. thesis, University of Oregon, 1972), Chap. 1 and passim.

19. Buckley, "Reminiscences," 31 Aug. 1918; Pauline Jacobsen, "Playhouses of the Pioneers," SF *Bull.,* 12 Aug. 1916; Rodecape, "Tom Maguire," (December 1942): 308, (March 1942): 40; Idwal Jones, *Ark of Empire* (New York, 1951).

20. Buckley, "Reminiscences," 31 Aug. 1918.

21. Walker, *San Francisco's Literary Frontier,* ix.

22. Ibid., 132–133, 150–152, 185–187, 189–195; Muscatine, *Old San Francisco,* 166; Barth, *Instant Cities,* 148, 193; Starr, *California Dream,* 49–50.

23. Walker, *San Francisco's Literary Frontier,* 63–69, 78–82, 150–152, 198–202, 238–242, 295, 360; Muscatine, *Old San Francisco,* 172; Barth, *Instant Cities,* 219; Starr, *California Dream,* 115–116, 133–141, 242, 248.

24. Buckley, "Reminiscences," 11 Sept. 1918; Buckley interviews.

25. Buckley, "Reminiscences," 5, 7, 8, 9, 10, 18 Sept. 1918; Walker, *San Francisco's Literary Frontier,* 159–161, 167–170; Rodecape, "Tom Maguire," (March 1942): 58–59; Muscatine, *Old San Francisco,* 146, 172; Wade, "San Francisco Stage," Chap. 2.

26. Buckley, "Reminiscences," 23, 24 Sept. 1918; SF *Chron.,* 2 July 1870; Muscatine, *Old San Francisco,* 169.

27. Buckley, "Reminiscences," 31 Aug. 1918; Rodecape, "Tom Maguire," (December 1941): 308.

28. SF *Exam.,* 22 Aug. 1889; SF *Chron.,* 22 Aug. 1889; "Martin Kelly's Story," 5 Sept. 1917; Callow, "Blind Boss," 262; Mazzi, "Harbingers of the City," 149.

29. SF *Exam.,* 22 Aug., 1889, 24 July 1899; SF *Chron.,* 22 Aug. 1889; SF

Alta, 22 Aug. 1889; Buckley, "Reminiscences," 25 Dec. 1918, 7 Jan. 1919; "Martin Kelly's Story," 5 Sept. 1917; George R. Stewart, *Committee of Vigilance* (New York, 1964), 245–246, 255–256.

30. SF *Directory, 1867,* 109–110; SF *Directory, 1868,* 116; Buckley, "Reminiscences," 23 Jan. 1919.

31. Buckley, "Reminiscences," 6, 10 Sept. 1918; SF *Directory, 1869,* 124; SF *Directory, 1870,* 130.

32. Buckley, "Reminiscences," 10 Sept., 15 Oct. 1918.

33. Rodecape, "Tom Maguire," (June 1942): 150–155, 167; Mazzi, "Harbingers of the City," 154; Buckley, "Reminiscences," 4, 14, 16 Sept. 1918; Bowden, "Dynamics of City Growth," Chaps. 2–3; SF *Chron.,* 10 July 1870; *SFMR, 1867–68,* 630–631.

34. Paul, *Mining Frontiers,* 57–60, 74–75; Ward McAfee, *California's Railroad Era, 1850–1911* (San Marino, Calif., 1973), 47–56, 99–100; Walton Bean, *California* (New York, 1973), 228–232; Mel Scott, *The San Francisco Bay Area* (Berkeley, 1959), 57–70; Vance, *Geography and Urban Evolution,* 33–41; SF *Alta,* 15 Jan. 1871; SF *Bull.,* 22 May, 26 Oct. 1871; Hubert Howe Bancroft, *History of California* (San Francisco, 1890), VII, 685–687; SF *Circular,* 2 (September 1868): 3.

35. Scott, *San Francisco Bay Area,* 57.

36. Ibid., 57–60; McAfee, *California's Railroad Era,* 58, 77–78, 91–96, 99; Sac. *Bee,* 5 Jan., 22, 23 March 1871; Val. *Chron.,* 3, 5 July 1871.

37. SF *Alta,* 19 May 1871; *Solano County Advertiser,* 13 Feb. 1869; Val. *Chron.,* 7, 19, 25 July, 16 Aug., 18 Oct., 11 Nov. 1871; *Articles of Association, Acts of Incorporation, And By-Laws of the Vallejo City Homestead Association* (Sacramento, 1869); John S. Hittell, *The Prospects of Vallejo* (Vallejo, 1871); Henry George, "What the Railroad Will Bring Us," *OM,* 1 (October 1868): 299.

38. Scott, *San Francisco Bay Area,* 67; McAfee, *California's Railroad Era,* 104.

39. Burial Records, Holy Cross Cemetery, Colma, Calif.; SF *Exam.,* 1 Aug. 1870; SF *Chron.,* 2 Aug. 1870.

40. Callow, "Blind Boss," 262; *Great Register, County of Solano, State of California* (Vallejo, 1872), reg. numbers 609, 612, 3859; *Vallejo City Directory, 1870* (Vallejo, 1870), 177; SF *Directory, 1869,* 261; Val. *Chron.,* 22, 24 July, 29 Aug., 8 Sept. 1871, 2 Jan. 1872; Theresa Barthé, "Early Days in Vallejo" (Typescript, Solano County Public Library), 7–9.

41. "Martin Kelly's Story," 5 Sept. 1917; Callow, "Blind Boss," 262; Winfield J. Davis, *History of Political Conventions in California, 1849–1892* (Sacramento, 1893), 5, 55, 59, 70, 100, 624; Val. *Chron.,* 28, 29 Aug., 18 Oct., 8 Sept. 1871, 25 July, 25 Sept. 1872.

42. Val. *Chron.,* 7, 13, 15, 18 Nov., 14 Dec. 1871; "Charter Members of Engine Company #2, Organized November 17, 1871," California Historical Society Photograph Collection.

43. McAfee, *California's Railroad Era,* 99–104; Val. *Chron.,* 8 July, 14 Aug. 1871, 16 July 1872, 10 Feb. 1873; SF *Alta,* 17 Sept., 18 Oct. 1872, 3 Jan. 1873.

44. Val. *Chron.,* 11 Feb. 1873; *Ward Register: Fifth Ward of the City and County of San Francisco* (San Francisco, 1875), 5; SF *Exam.,* 12 Oct. 1898; SF *Chron.,* 12 Oct. 1898.

CHAPTER TWO

1. "Martin Kelly's Story," 5 Sept. 1917.

2. Ibid., 4, 5 Sept. 1917; Anon., *History of Solano County* (Vallejo, 1879), 118–119; Davis, *Political Conventions,* 312.

3. See, for example, Frank Soulé, John Gihon, and James Nisbet, *The Annals of San Francisco* (New York, 1855), 97, 192, 787–789, and passim; Benjamin Lloyd, *Lights and Shades in San Francisco* (San Francisco, 1876), 202–203, and passim; Neville, *Fantastic City;* Herbert Asbury, *The Barbary Coast* (New York, 1968); Curt Gentry, *The Madames of San Francisco* (New York, 1964); Joseph Henry Jackson, *San Francisco Murders* (New York, 1947); Ronald A. St. Laurence, "The Myth and the Reality: Prostitution in San Francisco, 1880–1913" (M.A. thesis, California State University, Hayward, 1974).

4. The work of two scholars, Gunther Barth and Neil Larry Shumsky, provides a perceptive analysis of the transformation of San Francisco in the 1870s. See Barth, *Instant Cities;* Barth, "Metropolism and Urban Elites," 158–187; Shumsky, "Tar Flat and Nob Hill"; and Shumsky, "San Francisco's Workingmen," 46–57.

5. In general, scholars define the metropolis and its attributes in relation to their own disciplines. Compare, for example, the approach of geographer Gideon Sjoberg, "The Origin and Evolution of Cities," *Scientific American,* 213 (September 1965): 54–63, with that of economist and planner Hans Blumenfeld, ibid., 64–74. Some urbanologists, including Lewis Mumford in *The City in History* (New York, 1961), reject the validity of the concept in favor of terms such as "conurbation," while pioneer urban demographer Adna Ferrin Weber in *The Growth of Cities in the Nineteenth Century* (New York, 1899) treats the metropolis as little more than a large industrial city. Historians employ the term with little greater precision; see Sam Bass Warner, Jr., *The Private City* (Philadelphia, 1968), which places metropolitanism essentially in the context of the twentieth century, and his *Streetcar Suburbs,* which places its origins in the nineteenth. Also compare approaches in Warner's *The Urban Wilderness* (New York, 1972); Zane L. Miller, *The Urbanization of Modern America* (New York, 1973); Richard C. Wade, "Urbanization," in C. Vann Woodward (ed.), *The Comparative Approach to American History* (New York, 1968), 187–205; and Robert M. Fogelson, *The Fragmented Metropolis* (Cambridge, Mass., 1967).

6. Wade, "Urbanization," 191–194; Zane L. Miller, *Boss Cox's Cincinnati* (New York, 1968), 3–8; Warner, *Streetcar Suburbs,* 15–21.

7. Miller, *Urbanization of Modern America,* 79; Warner, *Streetcar Suburbs,* 3.

Notes to Pages 29–34

8. Miller, *Urbanization of Modern America,* 75.

9. Warner, *Private City,* 79–82, 163–164, 169–190, 202–204, 214–216; Miller, *Urbanization of Modern America,* 75–77, 80, 83–87; Wade, "Urbanization," 191–199; Fogelson, *Fragmented Metropolis,* 3–7, and passim.

10. Buckley, "Reminiscences," 25 Dec. 1918.

11. Ibid.; Edgar M. Kahn, "Andrew Smith Hallidie," *CHQ,* 19 (June 1940): 150; Hubert Howe Bancroft, *History of California,* VII, 691; Andrew S. Hallidie, "Manufacturing in San Francisco," *OM,* 11 (June 1888): 636–638; Barth, *Instant Cities,* 210–212, 223–224, 217–221; Heintz, *San Francisco's Mayors,* 52, 58–59, 63, 78; Muscatine, *Old San Francisco,* 11, 223, 292; Mazzi, "Harbingers of the City," 154; Averbach, "San Francisco's South of Market District," 198–199; *SFMR, 1866–67,* 475; *SFMR, 1872–73,* 490–493; Harpending, *Diamond Hoax,* 75, 99–100; SF *Call,* 30 March 1870; Buckley, "Reminiscences," 16 Sept., 25 Dec. 1918; Peter R. Decker, *Fortunes and Failures* (Cambridge, Mass., 1978), 196–230, and passim.

12. Harpending, *Diamond Hoax,* 74.

13. Ibid., 17–27, 48–53; Heintz, *San Francisco's Mayors,* 50–60, 68–69; Starr, *California Dream,* 103–104; Davis, *Political Conventions,* 29–34, 39–42, 54–57, 70–74, 85–92, 96–97, 99–100, 111–124, 165–172, 196–201; Benjamin F. Gilbert, "The Confederate Minority in California," *CHQ,* 20 (June 1941): 154–170; Earl Pomeroy, "California, 1846–1860: Politics of a Representative Frontier State," *CHQ,* 32 (December 1953): 291–302.

14. Shumsky, "Tar Flat and Nob Hill," 67, 99–100; Bancroft, *History of California,* VII, 593–594, 690–692; George, "What the Railroad Will Bring Us," 298–300; Cross, *Labor Movement,* 30–31; Barth, *Instant Cities,* 217–219; Harpending, *Diamond Hoax,* 74–75, 99–100; Heintz, *San Francisco's Mayors,* 49–52, 64, 88; Walker, *San Francisco's Literary Frontier,* 3–5.

15. See, for example, Hittell, *Commerce and Industries,* 49–53.

16. Shumsky, "Tar Flat and Nob Hill," 42–44; SF *Bull.,* 4 Oct. 1864; Averbach, "San Francisco's South of Market District," 198–200; Heintz, *San Francisco's Mayors,* 14, 63, 68, 78; Muscatine, *Old San Francisco,* 111, 188–192; Barth, *Instant Cities,* 210–212, 217–220, 223–224; Hallidie, "Manufacturing in San Francisco," 636–648; Barth, "Metropolism and Urban Elites," 166–168; SF *Alta,* 13 May 1861; California State Agricultural Society, *Transactions of the California State Agricultural Society during the Year 1859* (Sacramento, 1860); SF *Directory, 1863–64,* 34; Cecil G. Tilton, *William Chapman Ralston, Courageous Builder* (Boston, 1935), 86.

17. Muscatine, *Old San Francisco,* 111, 200, 223; Barth, "Metropolism and Urban Elites," 166–168; Heintz, *San Francisco's Mayors,* 63, 68, 78; SF *Circular,* 2 (May 1868): 2–4; Tilton, *Ralston,* 86–87, 158–159; Martyn J. Bowden, "Dynamics of City Growth," 212–222; Louis R. Miller, "The History of the San Francisco and San Jose Railroad" (M.A. thesis, University of California, Berkeley, 1947), 68–69; Shumsky, "Tar Flat and Nob Hill," 45–104.

18. Heintz, *San Francisco's Mayors,* 68, 78.

19. Arthur Calder-Marshall (ed.), *The Bodley Head Jack London* (London, 1963), 192–193.

20. Rodman Paul, *Mining Frontiers,* 50–51, 67–69; John S. Hittell, *The History of the City of San Francisco and Incidentally of the State of California* (San Francisco, 1878), 276–278; Shumsky, "Tar Flat and Nob Hill," 37–40.

21. The literature on California agricultural development is voluminous; for a convenient summary see Richard J. Orsi (comp.), *A List of References for the History of Agriculture in California* (Davis, Calif., 1974).

22. Shumsky, "Tar Flat and Nob Hill," 34–36; SF *Alta,* 23 April 1864.

23. U.S. Department of the Treasury, *Income Tax Assessment Records, Division One, State of California, 1862–66* (Microfilm, Federal Archives and Record Center, San Bruno, Calif.), reels 1–16; *Population Schedules of the Ninth Census of the United States, 1870,* City of San Francisco, Ward Four (Washington, D.C., 1956), Microfilm Roll 80, p. 124.
John Buckley's income was substantial by contemporary standards; see Stephan Thernstrom, *Poverty and Progress* (Cambridge, Mass., 1964), 117–131 and passim.

24. Hittell, *History of San Francisco,* 381–404; Robert A. Burchell, "The Loss of a Reputation; or, the Image of California in Britain before 1875," *CHQ,* 53 (Summer 1974): 128; U. S. Bureau of the Census, *Population of Cities Having 25,000 Inhabitants or More in 1900, at Each Census: 1790–1900* (Washington, D.C., 1901), 430–432; U.S. Department of the Interior, *The Statistics of the Population of the United States, 1870* (Washington, D.C., 1872), 318, 386–390. The foreign-born population in 1870 included 25,864 Irish, 13,602 Germans, 11,703 Chinese, 5166 English, 3543 French, 1687 Scots, 1622 Italians, and smaller groups of other nationalities.

25. Shumsky, "Tar Flat and Nob Hill," 21–22, 37–47, 49–53, 80–81; Shumsky, "San Francisco's Workingmen," 46–48; SF *Directory, 1876,* 12; Cross, *Labor Movement,* 61–65, 83; Alexander P. Saxton, *The Indispensible Enemy* (Berkeley 1971), 62–66; Gunther Barth, *Bitter Strength* (Cambridge, Mass., 1964), 118–119.

26. Bruno Fritzche, "San Francisco, 1846–1848: The Coming of the Land Speculators," *CHQ,* 51 (Spring 1972): 17; King, *San Francisco Stock Exchange,* 3, 136, 285; Lotchin, *San Francisco,* 175; Bancroft, *History of California,* VII, 672; Lloyd, *Lights and Shades,* 40; Shumsky, "Tar Flat and Nob Hill," 29–30; Walker, *San Francisco's Literary Frontier,* 177; Barth, *Instant Cities,* 111–112, 121, 144–145; Muscatine, *Old San Francisco,* 108; Mazzi, "Harbingers of the City," 142.

27. See, for example, *A "Pile," or, a Glance at the Wealth of the Monied Men of San Francisco and Sacramento City* (San Francisco, 1851); SF *Call,* 6 Aug. 1871; SF *Bull.,* 21 July 1877; Douglas S. Watson, "The San Francisco McAllisters," *CHQ,* 11 (June 1932): 124–128.

28. Frankfort (Germany) *Gazette,* cited in Barth, *Instant Cities,* 169; Oscar Lewis, *The Big Four* (New York, 1938); *The Silver Kings* (New York, 1959).

29. Barth, *Instant Cities,* 169; Muscatine, *Old San Francisco,* 148, 304–305, 361–362; Buckley, "Reminiscences," 16 Sept. 1918. Shumsky, "Tar Flat and Nob Hill," 153–198, provides an extensive discussion of the acquisition of wealth in the 1860s and 1870s and its implications for San Francisco.

30. Shumsky, "Tar Flat and Nob Hill," 26–29.

31. Ibid., 30–32; Hittell, *History of San Francisco,* 454–455, 461; King, *San Francisco Stock Exchange,* 3–12.

32. Decker, *Fortunes and Failures,* 170–188 and passim; King, *San Francisco Stock Exchange,* 23–37; Heintz, *San Francisco's Mayors,* 49, 52, 55; Shumsky, "Tar Flat and Nob Hill," 30–32; *A Review of the Commercial, Financial and Mining Interests of the State of California,* 1876 (San Francisco, 1877), 29.

33. King, *San Francisco Stock Exchange,* 33, 37, 49–50, 74–76; Heintz, *San Francisco's Mayors,* 57, 64, 79, 86; SF *Bull.,* 16 Sept. 1869. Mining companies usually sold shares on the basis of tunnel footage rather than capital valuation.

34. Shumsky, "Tar Flat and Nob Hill," 37–38, 54–55. Decker, *Fortunes and Failures,* 70–80, 87–105, 170–195 and passim, shows that in the 1850s through the 1870s merchant success in San Francisco rarely matched expectations or the claims of boosters; the most successful were those who turned to alternate fields such as finance, real estate speculation, and industry.

35. Shumsky, "Tar Flat and Nob Hill," 55–57; *DAB,* VIII, 333–334; Tilton, *Ralston,* 15, 21–32, 38–51, 70, 94–96; David S. Lavender, *Nothing Seemed Impossible* (Palo Alto, Calif., 1975), 17–38, 97–110, 123–130, 165–182, and passim; Bancroft, *History of California,* VII, 674–675; Muscatine, *Old San Francisco,* 290ff.; Heintz, *San Francisco's Mayors,* 58–59; Shumate, *Visit to Rincon Hill,* 10; Harpending, *Diamond Hoax,* 75–76.

36. Shumsky, "Tar Flat and Nob Hill," 55–57, 99–100; Tilton, *Ralston,* 159–170; Lavender, *Nothing Seemed Impossible,* 203, 236–239; Harpending, *Diamond Hoax,* 86; Muscatine, *Old San Francisco,* 292; Mazzi, "Harbingers of the City," 154; Bancroft, *History of California,* VII, 675–677; SF *Directory, 1867–68,* 14; SF *Directory, 1868–69,* 16–17.

37. Shumsky, "Tar Flat and Nob Hill," 21–23; U.S. Bureau of the Census, *Wealth and Industry of the United States at the Ninth Census, 1879* (Washington, D.C., 1872), 495–496.

38. Geoffrey P. Mawn, "Framework for Destiny: San Francisco, 1847," *CHQ,* 51 (Summer 1972): 165–178; Fritzche, "San Francisco, 1846–1848," 17–32; Lotchin, *San Francisco,* 175; Barth, *Instant Cities,* 111, 121.

39. Barth, "Metropolism and Urban Elites," provides a close examination of the Second Street Cut episode and its implications. Also see Muscatine, *Old San Francisco,* 362–363; Harpending, *Diamond Hoax,* 104; Shumate, *Visit to Rincon Hill,* 13–15; King, *San Francisco Stock Exchange,* 355; George Groh, *Gold Fever* (New York, 1966), 4–5.

40. *JCA, 1867–68,* 17th Sess., 491; *Statutes of California, 1867–68,* 17th Sess., 594–599; The People of the State of California *ex rel.* John Ferguson *v.* the Board of Supervisors of the City and County of San Francisco, 39 *California Reports,* 595.

41. Barth, "Metropolism and Urban Elites," 164.

42. Selby quoted in ibid., 169; Harpending, *Diamond Hoax,* 104.

43. Barth, "Metropolism and Urban Elites," 166.

44. Ibid., 171–172; Muscatine, *Old San Francisco,* 291–292; Tilton, *Ralston,* 182–186; Lavender, *Nothing Seemed Impossible,* 238, 244–245.

45. *SFMR, 1864–65,* 374; *SFMR, 1866–67,* 475, 484; *SFMR, 1867–68,* 630–631; Heintz, *San Francisco's Mayors,* 58–59; Harpending, *Diamond Hoax,* 75–77, 84; Tilton, *Ralston,* 367; SF *Circular,* 5 (June 1871): 1.

46. Harpending, *Diamond Hoax,* 75, 82, 105–108, 111; Harpending *v.* Haight, 39, *California Reports,* 189; Tilton, *Ralston,* 238, 243–247; Lavender, *Nothing Seemed Impossible,* 242, 246–250.

47. Tilton, *Ralston,* 236, 241–245; *SFMR, 1870–71,* 519–521; Barth, *Instant Cities,* 220–221.

48. *SFMR, 1863–64,* 346; *SFMR, 1870–71,* 519–526; *SFMR, 1872–73,* 480–483; *Statutes of California, 1869–70,* 18th Sess., 481–501; Buckley, "Reminiscences," 16 Sept. 1918; Harpending, *Diamond Hoax,* 78–82; SF *Exam.,* 26 March 1870; 16 July 1897; SF *Chron.,* 25 March, 10 July 1870; SF *Alta,* 11, 31 March, 5 April 1870; SF *Call,* 30 March 1870; Barth, *Instant Cities,* 220–221; Rodecape, "Tom Maguire," (June 1942): 167; Bowden, "Dynamics of City Growth," 275ff.; SF *Circular,* 2 (January 1869): 3, 4 (November 1869): 2, 5 (September 1871): 1, 6 (September 1872), 3; Tilton, *Ralston,* 239–241; Lavender, *Nothing Seemed Impossible,* 361–365.

The Montgomery Street Real Estate Co. associates acquired only enough property to push New Montgomery Street two blocks southward. It has never been extended. Nevertheless, other company properties became the sites for some of the most impressive new buildings in the city, including the Palace Hotel and the Harpending Block of business offices. Increased values of their properties along Market Street altered patterns of city growth and handsomely repaid investments in both land and political favors.

49. Tilton, *Ralston,* 247; Neville, *Fantastic City,* 191; SF *Circular,* 4 (February 1870): 2, 4 (April 1870): 3.

50. Muscatine, *Old San Francisco,* 330–331; Tilton, *Ralston,* 170, 260–261; SF *Directory, 1864,* 40; Averbach, "San Francisco's South of Market District," 200–201.

The Buckley family resided at 530 Tehama Street in the South of Market district until 1867 when they moved to 1136 Pacific Street, a more amenable working class neighborhood a few blocks west of Montgomery Street. In 1870, they moved again to 911 Stockton Street in the same area. When Buckley returned from Vallejo, he lived at a series of addresses in the older boarding house areas a few blocks north of Market Street. See SF *Directory, 1863–64,* 83; SF *Directory, 1867,* 109–110; SF *Directory, 1870,* 130; SF *Directory, 1874,* 129; SF *Directory, 1875,* 157; SF *Directory, 1876,* 166.

51. See especially Joel A. Tarr, "From City to Suburb: The 'Moral' Influences of Transportation Technology," in Callow (ed.),, *American Urban History,* 204–205; Hugo A. Meier, "American Technology and the Nineteenth Century World," *AQ,* 10 (Spring 1958): 116–130; Glen E. Holt, "The Changing Perception of Urban Pathology: An Essay on the Development of Mass Transit in the United States," in Kenneth T. Jackson and Stanley K. Schultz (eds.), *Cities in American History* (New York, 1972), 324–342.

CHAPTER THREE

1. Barth, *Instant Cities,* 157, 177; Lotchin, *San Francisco,* 122–123; Luckingham, "Immigrant Life," 600–601.

2. SF *Directories, 1866–1873* document increasing numbers and varieties of associations ranging in size from a half-dozen members to over 100 and dedicated to causes as diverse as the population of San Francisco itself.

3. SF *Directory, 1873,* 881–884; Frederick J. Bowlen, "Firefighters of the Past: A History of the Old Volunteer Fire Department of San Francisco from 1849 to 1866," unpublished manuscript (BL), 164ff.; *The Exempt Firemen of San Francisco, Their Unique and Gallant Record, Together with a Resumé of the San Francisco Fire Department and Its Personnel* (San Francisco, 1900), 12–16; Luckingham, "Immigrant Life," 609–610.

4. SF *Directory, 1873,* 855–866.

5. Ibid., 841–853; Starr, *California Dream,* 97–107; Muscatine, *Old San Francisco,* 117; Walker, *San Francsico's Literary Frontier,* 90; Hittell, *History of San Francisco,* 444–445.

6. SF *Directory, 1873,* 876–877; Muscatine, *Old San Francisco,* 156, 182–184; Heintz, *San Francisco's Mayors,* 81.

7. SF *Directory, 1873,* 871–875, 877–881; Muscatine, *Old San Francisco,* 351; Walker, *San Francisco's Literary Frontier,* 352; Heintz, *San Francisco's Mayors,* 52; Starr, *California Dream,* 246; Jon M. Kingsdale, "The 'Poor Man's Club': Social Functions of the Urban Working Class Saloon," *AQ,* 25 (October 1973): 472–489; Buckley, "Reminiscences," 11 Sept. 1918; Barth, *Instant Cities,* 177–178.

8. Barth, *Instant Cities,* 156–159.

9. Walker, *San Francisco's Literary Frontier,* 177.

10. Charles A. Fracchia, "The Founding of the San Francisco Mining Exchange," *CHQ,* 48 (March 1969): 4–5; King, *San Francisco Stock Exchange,* 4; Shumsky, "Tar Flat and Nob Hill," 99–103.

11. Lotchin, *San Francisco,* 73; Barth, *Instant Cities,* 142; Bancroft, *History of California,* VII, 667–670; Fracchia, "Founding of the San Francisco Mining Exchange," 3–18; J. H. Liggett (ed.), *Industries of San Francisco* (San Francisco,

1889), 32–33; King, *San Francisco Stock Exchange,* 4–5, 49, 90; Muscatine, *Old San Francisco,* 118, 288, 366.

12. SF *Directory, 1873,* 871–875; SF *Chron.,* 6 July 1870; Cross, *Labor Movement,* 31–35, 37–39.

13. King, *San Francisco Stock Exchange,* 7, 56; Cross, *Labor Movement,* 53–55, 134–140; *Statutes of California, 1867–68,* 17th Sess., 63.

14. SF *Bull.,* 11 Jan. 1865, 16 Sept. 1869, 3 Jan. 1871; Heintz, *San Francisco's Mayors,* 57, 64; Tilton, *Ralston,* 107–108; Cross, *Labor Movement,* 29, 62–63; U.S. Director of the Mint, *Report of the Director of the Mint on the Production of Precious Metals in the United States During the Calendar Year 1889* (Washington, D.C., 1890), 222; SF *Circular,* 3 (October 1869): 3, 5 (January 1871): 3.

15. King, *San Francisco Stock Exchange,* 73; Heintz, *San Francisco's Mayors,* 79, 86; SF *Bull.,* 20 May 1872; SF *Circular,* 7 (January 1873): 1.

16. Bancroft, *History of California,* VII, 674–677; King, *San Francisco Stock Exchange,* 101–113; Cross, *Labor Movement,* 69; Tilton, *Ralston,* 142–148, 324–331; Lavender, *Nothing Seemed Impossible,* 337–339, and passim; SF *Circular,* 9 (September 1875): 1; SF *Bull.,* 27 Aug. 1875; SF *Alta,* 27 Aug. 1875. Also see George D. Lyman, *Ralston's Ring* (New York, 1945).

17. Tilton, *Ralston,* 355–357; Lavender, *Nothing Seemed Impossible,* 379.

18. Cross, *Labor Movement,* 55, 61–65, 69–70, 83; SF *Circular,* 7 (April 1873): 1; SF *Directory, 1876,* 12.

19. Shumsky, "Tar Flat and Nob Hill," 115; SF *Chron.,* 6 July 1870; Starr, *California Dream,* 133; Asbury, *Barbary Coast,* 150–164; Alexander P. Saxton, *The Indispensable Enemy* (Berkeley, 1971), 71–78, and passim; Cross, *Labor Movement,* 83–87.

20. *Jolly Giant,* 9 (1 Dec. 1873): 6; SF *Bull.,* 12, 22 Jan. 1870; Heintz, *San Francisco's Mayors,* 80.

21. Shumsky, "Tar Flat and Nob Hill," 251ff.; Cross, *Labor Movement,* 71–72; Shumsky, "San Francisco's Workingmen," 46–57. Also see a series of articles on unemployment in SF *Post,* 3 Aug.-7 Sept. 1878, probably written by Henry George.

22. Gertrude Atherton, *California* (New York, 1914), Chap. 19, is the first use of the phrase "terrible 'seventies."

23. Buckley, "Reminiscences," 25 Dec. 1918; Barth, *Instant Cities,* 155–156, 166.

24. Bernard Moses, *The Establishment of Municipal Government in San Francisco* (Baltimore, 1889), 24–60.

Lt. Washington A. Bartlett should not be confused with the Washington Bartlett who served as mayor of San Francisco from 1883 to 1887; see Robert W. Righter, "Washington Bartlett: Mayor of San Francisco, 1883–1887," *JW,* 3 (January 1964): 102–114.

25. Moses, *Municipal Government,* 62; Lotchin, *San Francisco,* 137.

26. Moses, *Municipal Government*, 79–83; Lotchin, *San Francisco*, 138–139.
27. *Statutes of California, 1856*, 7th Sess., 145–176; SF *Directory, 1863*, 436–486; SF *Directory, 1873*, 763–769.
28. Lotchin, *San Francisco*, 140–141; SF *Directory, 1863*, 436–437; SF *Directory, 1873*, 763–769.
29. Bancroft, *History of California*, VI, 768–772; Lotchin, *San Francisco*, 141.
30. SF *Director, 1873*, 763–770; Lotchin, *San Francisco*, 140, 247, 318; *SFMR, 1863–64*, 353–357; *SFMR, 1865–66*, 403–404.
31. *SFMR, 1863–64*, 346–347; *SFMR, 1864–65*, 21, 212–215; *SFMR, 1865–66*, 376–377; *SFMR, 1866–67*, 411; Muscatine, *Old San Francisco*, 249–251; Heintz, *San Francisco's Mayors*, 50, 57–58; William A. Bullough, *Cities and Schools in the Gilded Age* (New York, 1974), 65–67.
32. *SFMR, 1865–66*, 395; *SFMR, 1866–67*, 474; *SFMR, 1867–68*, 551; SF *Alta*, 18 Nov. 1865, 18 July 1867, 23 June 1868; SF *Bull.*, 23 May 1868.
33. *SFMR, 1866–67*, 464–473; *SFMR, 1868–69*, 562–567, 580–581; SF *Circular*, 2 (January 1868): 2, 2 (March 1868): 3, Heintz, *San Francisco's Mayors*, 62–63, 69–70.
34. *SFMR, 1863–64*, 332; *SFMR, 1865–66*, 367.
35. Heintz, *San Francisco's Mayors*, passim.
36. Ibid., 50–52, 72.
37. *Statutes of California, 1865–76*, 16th–21st Sessions.
38. Gerald D. Nash, *State Government and Economic Development* (Berkeley, 1964), 106–108; Lamberta M. Voget, "The Waterfront of San Francisco, 1863–1930: A History of Its Administration by the State of California" (Ph.D. thesis, University of California, Berkeley, 1943), Chap. 1; *SFMR, 1862–63*, 202; *SFMR, 1863–64*, 205–207; *SFMR, 1866–67*, 505–507; SF *Alta*, 24 April 1863; SF *Bull.*, 13 May 1863; SF *Chron.*, 4 Nov. 1868.
39. In 1873, the SF *Directory* required just six pages to reproduce the Consolidation Act but fifty-seven pages to print supplements and amendments. Almost ten years later, a recharter advocate complained that in an 1876 recodification "thirty-one pages contain all that is left of the original Act, while the Amendments and special Acts cover 251 pages." Still later, another observer commented that "amendments extending over forty years have so confused matters that is was difficult to facilitate government." See Frank W. Blackmar, "San Francisco's Struggle for Good Government," *The Forum*, 26 (January 1899): 569; SF *Exam.*, 6 Oct. 1882. Also see Buckley, "Reminiscences," 25 Dec. 1918; Hittell, *History of San Francisco*, 463–465; Williams, *Democratic Party*, 5.
40. Buckley, "Reminiscences," 3, 17 Jan., 5 Feb. 1919.
41. Compare *Great Register of the City and County of San Francisco* (San Francisco, 1872), 48; *Great Register. County of Solano, State of California* (Vallejo, 1872), reg. #609; *Great Register of the City and County of San Francisco* (San

Francisco, 1873), 49. One entry subsequently was expunged; see *Ward Register. Fifth Ward of the City and County of San Francisco* (San Francisco, 1875), 5.

42. Buckley, "Reminiscences," 26 Dec. 1918, 17 Jan. 1919; "Martin Kelly's Story," 4, 8 Sept. 1917; Ruef, "The Road I Traveled," 24 May, 4 June 1912; Callow, "Blind Boss," 264–268; Eric F. Petersen, "The Struggle for the Australian Ballot in California," *CHQ,* 51 (Fall 1972): 227–230; Walton Bean, *Boss Ruef's San Francisco* (Berkeley, 1952), 1–11; William A. Bullough, "The Steam Beer Handicap: Chris Buckley and the San Francisco Municipal Election of 1896," *CHQ,* 54 (Fall 1975): 246–247.

43. See Buckley, "Reminiscences," 25, 26 Dec. 1918, 3 Jan. 1919; "Martin Kelly's Story," 3, 4, 5, 6, 8 Sept. 1917; Ruef, "The Road I Traveled," 22, 23, 24, 29 May, 1, 8, 19 June 1912; Bean, *Boss Ruef;* James P. Walsh, "Abe Ruef Was No Boss: Machine Politics, Reform, and San Francisco," *CHQ,* 51 (Spring 1972): 3–16; Sam Leake, "When King Mazuma Reigned," SF *Bull.,* 16 March–26 April 1917.

44. Buckley, "Reminiscences," 17 Jan. 1919.

45. Ibid., 26 Dec. 1918; "Martin Kelly's Story," 9 Sept. 1917; Ruef, "The Road I Traveled," 23 May, 1, 3, 4 June 1912; Shumsky, "Tar Flat and Nob Hill," 143–144; Kingsdale, "Poor Man's Club," 482–484.

46. Buckley, "Reminiscences," 17 Jan. 1919; Ruef, "The Road I Traveled," 24, 25, 27 May 1912; Robert K. Merton, *Social Theory and Social Structure* (New York, 1957), 71–82. Roy V. Peel, *The Political Clubs of New York City* (New York, 1935) provides a useful comparison.

47. Buckley, "Reminiscences," 3 Jan., 5 Feb. 1919; "Martin Kelly's Story," 9 Sept. 1917; Ruef, "The Road I Traveled," 8, 19 June 1912.

48. Ruef, "The Road I Traveled," 19 June 1912; Buckley, "Reminiscences," 27 Jan. 1919; "Martin Kelly's Story," 4 Sept. 1917.

49. Buckley, "Reminiscences," 17 Jan. 1919; Petersen, "Struggle for the Australian Ballot," 228.

50. Buckley, "Reminiscences," 8 Jan. 1919.

51. Ibid., 7, 17 Jan. 1919; Ruef, "The Road I Traveled," 6 April, 23 May 1912; "Martin Kelly's Story," 8, 9 Sept. 1912; Petersen, "Struggle for the Australian Ballot," 228–229.

52. Buckley, "Reminiscences," 24 Jan. 1919.

53. Ibid., 26 Dec. 1918.

54. Williams, *Democratic Party,* 5.

55. Callow, "Blind Boss," 269; Ruef, "The Road I Traveled," 6 April 1912; Barth, *Instant Cities,* 177–178.

56. William L. Riordon, *Plunkitt of Tammany Hall* (New York, 1963), ix.

57. "Martin Kelly's Story," 5 Sept. 1917; Callow, "Blind Boss," 262–263; Lynch, *Buckleyism,* 8–9.

On national and state partisan realignments during the Gilded Age, see especially Williams, *Democratic Party,* 59–62, 132–133, 146, 245–251, and passim; R. Hal Williams, *Years of Decision* (New York, 1978); Lewis L. Gould, "The Republican Search for a National Majority," in H. Wayne Morgan (ed.), *The Gilded Age* (Syracuse, 1971), 171–187; H. Wayne Morgan, *From Hayes to McKinley* (Syracuse, 1969); Robert D. Marcus, *Grand Old Party* (New York, 1971); Paul J. Kleppner, *The Cross of Culture* (New York, 1970); Richard J. Jensen, *The Winning of the West* (Chicago, 1971); Robert Wiebe, *The Search for Order, 1877–1920* (New York, 1967).

58. Buckley, "Reminiscences," 25, 26, 27, 28 Dec. 1918. Prior to 1882, San Francisco held municipal elections in September of odd-numbered years. The California Constitution of 1879 required that state and local contests occur in November of even-numbered years, to coincide with national practice, but challenges and litigation postponed implementation of the change until 1882. See SF *Chron.*, 8 May, 5, 16 June 1881; SF *Alta*, 25 April, 16 June 1881; SF *Exam.*, 13 April, 16, 17 May, 4 June 1881.

59. See Ralph Kauer, "The Workingmen's Party of California," *PHR*, 12 (September 1944): 275–291; Henry George, "The Kearney Agitation in California," *Popular Science Monthly*, 17 (August 1880): 433–453; Cross, *Labor Movement*, 73–129; Ira B. Cross (ed.), *Frank Roney* (Berkeley, 1931), 261–316; Shumsky, "San Francisco's Workingmen," 46–57.

60. Young, *San Francisco*, II, 563, 699; Lynch, *Buckleyism*, 12; Callow, "Blind Boss," 272; SF *Exam.*, 24 July 1899; Dobie, *S. M. White*, 36, 48, 110.

61. SF *Exam.*, 24 July 1899; "Martin Kelly's Story," 5 Sept. 1917; Williams, *Democratic Party*, 22–24; *Historical Souvenir of San Francisco, Cal.* (San Francisco, 1887), 14–17; Mazzi, "Harbingers of the City," 141–162; Averbach, "San Francisco's South of Market District," 199–202; Muscatine, *Old San Francisco*, 250; *SFMR*, 1863–64, 357; SF *Directory, 1875*, 182; SF *Directory, 1876*, 166; SF *Directory, 1877*, 186, 230; SF *Directory, 1879*, 165; SF *Directory, 1880*, 167; SF *Alta*, 24 Oct. 1885.

62. Davis, *Political Conventions*, 4, 176; Callow, "Blind Boss," 262–263.

63. SF *Exam.*, 27, 28 May 1881; SF *Chron.*, 27, 28 May 1881; Callow, "Blind Boss," 263; Buckley, "Reminiscences," 23 Jan. 1919; "Martin Kelly's Story," 4, 5 Sept. 1917; SF *Directory, 1880*, 1112; SF *Directory, 1884*, 109.

64. Callow, "Blind Boss," 263–264; Lynch, *Buckleyism*, 14–15; SF *Chron.*, 1 Oct. 1895, 26 Nov. 1903; "Martin Kelly's Story," 4, 5, 10 Sept. 1917; Young, *San Francisco*, II, 564; SF *Exam.*, 24 July 1899, 26 Nov. 1903.

65. Callow, "Blind Boss," 263; Buckley, "Reminiscences," 26 Dec. 1918, 23 Jan. 1919; SF *Call*, 12 Nov. 1891, 25 July 1899; Lynch, *Buckleyism*, 7; "Martin Kelly's Story," 4, 5 Sept. 1917; Davis *Political Conventions*, 644; Heintz, *San Francisco's Mayors*, 95–108.

The term "Chivalry Democrats" was used rather loosely in contemporary literature. The California party had been factionalized even before the Civil War, divided into "Tammany" supporters of Senator David C. Broderick and the "Southern" or "Chivalry" set surrounding Senator William Gwin. Even when issues which caused original divisions were no longer relevant, the local press persisted in the use of the phrase "Chivalry Democrats" to identify members of the old Gwin-Breckenridge faction and their successors. See Davis, *Political Conventions,* 50–356; Lotchin, *San Francisco,* 213–244; Bean, *California,* 177–181; Earl Pomeroy, "California, 1846–1860: Politics of a Representative Frontier State," *CHQ,* 32 (December 1953): 291–320.

66. Buckley, "Reminiscences," 23 Jan. 1919; Davis, *Political Conventions,* 617.

67. Davis, *Political Conventions,* 417; Williams, *Democratic Party,* 22; Averbach, "San Francisco's South of Market," 200–202; SF *Exam.,* 24 July 1899; Young, *San Francisco,* II, 563; Lynch, *Buckleyism,* 9–11; "Martin Kelly's Story," 9 Sept, 1917; Callow, "Blind Boss," 264; Wangenheim, "Autobiography," 144; Buckley interviews.

Conversations with physicians regarding the Buckley medical history suggest that latent diabetes may have been a factor in the boss's blindness. Christopher A. Buckley, Jr. indicates that the ability to recognize individuals may have been less impressive than presumed; bodyguards like Alex Greggains often identified those approaching the boss.

68. Irving McKee, "The Shooting of Charles De Young," *PHR,* 16 (August 1947): 271–284.

69. SF *Exam,* 13 Feb, 2 Sept., 8, 20 Oct. 1880.

70. Davis, *Political Conventions,* 389–402; Carl B. Swisher, *Motivation and Political Technique in the California Constitutional Convention, 1878–1879* (Claremont, Calif., 1930); Dudley T. Moorehead, "Sectionalism and the California Constitution of 1879," *PHR,* 12 (September 1943): 278–293; SF *Exam.,* 12 March, 3 July, 3, 9 Sept. 1880; Buckley, "Reminiscences," 27 Dec. 1918.

71. Buckley, "Reminiscences," 27 Dec. 1918; SF *Exam.,* 13 Feb., 12 March, 9, 11 Sept., 9 Oct. 1880; Davis, *Political Conventions,* 429, 432; SF *Chron.,* 14, 17, 18, 25, 26 Feb., 2, 4, 9, 13 March 1880.

72. Dobie, *S. M. White,* 32; SF *Exam.,* 11 Sept. 1880; Bean, *California,* 242; SF *Chron.,* 14, 17, 24 Feb. 1880.

73. Ferdinand Lundberg, *Imperial Hearst* (New York, 1936), 20; W. A. Swanberg, *Citizen Hearst* (New York, 1961), 22.

74. SF *Exam.,* 26 March, 9, 22 April 1881; SF *Chron.,* 22 April, 8 May 1881; SF *Alta,* 22 April 1881; Buckley, "Reminiscences," 27 Dec. 1918.

75. SF *Chron.,* 30 April, 3, 6, 8 May 1881; SF *Exam.,* 1, 3, 5, 6, 7, 8, 10 May 1881; SF *Alta,* 3, 8 May 1881; Buckley, "Reminiscences," 26 Dec. 1918, 3 Jan. 1919; "Martin Kelly's Story," 4 Sept. 1917.

76. SF *Chron.,* 8 May 1881.

77. Ibid., 16 June 1881; SF *Exam.,* 28 April 1881.

78. SF *Chron.,* 8 May 1881; SF *Exam.,* 3, 7, 10 May 1881.

CHAPTER FOUR

1. Lynch, *Buckleyism,* 11–12.

2. Buckley interviews; Neville, *Fantastic City,* 258; Wangenheim, "Autobiography," 144; SF *Bull.,* 21 April 1922; SF *Exam.,* 21 April 1922; Liv.

Herald, 22 April 1922; SF *Chron.,* 21 April 1922; SF *Call,* 14 Nov. 1922; Buckley, "Reminiscences," 9 Oct. 1918.

3. See Morton Keller, *The Art and Politics of Thomas Nast* (New York, 1968); Harold Zink, *City Bosses in the United States* (Durham, N.C., 1931); Kenneth M. Johnson, *The Sting of the Wasp* (San Francisco, 1976); and especially *Jolly Giant* (holdings at the San Francisco Public Library).

4. Until relatively recently, scholarly investigations of bosses and political machines focused upon either the immorality of the bosses or the defects in municipal governmental structures. Currently, perhaps stimulated by Merton's now-standard theory of the "latent functions of the machine" in *Social Theory and Social Structure,* investigators are examining the interaction between the characteristics of boss politics, the process of urbanization itself, and changing political styles—including reform—in the city. For convenient summaries of varying interpretations, see Callow (ed.), *City Boss in America;* Stave (ed.), *Urban Bosses, Machines, and Progressive Reformers;* Brownell and Stickle (eds.), *Bosses and Reformers;* Bruce M. Stave, "Urban Bosses and Reform," in Raymond A. Mohl and James F. Richardson (eds.), *The Urban Experience* (Belmont, Calif., 1973), 182–195.

5. Merton, *Social Theory and Social Structure,* 72, 74; Buckley, "Reminiscences," 28 Jan. 1919.

6. "Martin Kelly's Story," 5 Sept. 1917; Buckley, "Reminiscences," 23 Jan. 1919; SF *Exam.,* 27, 28 May 1881; SF *Chron.,* 27, 28 May 1881; Callow, "Blind Boss," 264.

7. SF *Alta,* 25 April, 16 June 1881; SF *Chron.,* 8, 11 May, 5, 16 June 1881; SF *Exam.,* 23, 24 April, 6, 8, 16, 17 May, 16 June 1881.

8. SF *Chron.,* 5 June 1881.

9. Ibid., 20, 27 May 1881; SF *Alta,* 27 May 1881; SF *Exam.,* 20, 27 May 1881.

10. SF *Exam.,* 17 June 1881.

11. Ibid., 9, 17, 28, 30 June 1881; SF *Chron.,* 5, 19, 24, 28, 30 June, 1 July 1881; SF *Alta,* 30 June 1881; Williams, *Democratic Party,* 47–51; Davis, *Political Conventions,* 422–424.

12. Swanstrom, "Reform Administration of Phelan," 23–28.

13. SF *Chron.,* 1 July 1881; SF *Exam.,* 30 June 1881.

14. Buckley, "Reminiscences," 17 Jan. 1919.

15. SF *Chron.,* 1 July 1881; SF *Alta,* 2 July 1881; SF *Exam.,* 1, 2 July 1881.

16. SF *Alta,* 2 July 1881; SF *Chron.,* 10, 12, 16, 17 July 1881; SF *Exam.,* 12 July 1881.

17. SF *Chron.,* 19, 21, 23, 24, 26, 27, 28 July 1881; SF *Exam.,* 21, 24, 28 July, 2 Aug. 1881; SF *Alta,* 25 July, 2 Aug. 1881.

18. SF *Exam.,* 29, 30 July, 1, 2 Aug. 1881; SF *Chron.,* 29 July, 1, 2 Aug. 1881; SF *Alta,* 29 July, 1 Aug. 1881.

19. SF *Exam.,* 3, 4 Aug. 1881; SF *Chron.,* 3, 4 Aug. 1881; SF *Alta,* 3 Aug. 1881.

20. SF *Chron.*, 6, 11, 12, 13, 14 Aug. 1881; SF *Exam.*, 7, 9, 10, 11 Aug. 1881; SF *Alta*, 11 Aug. 1881.

21. SF *Exam.*, 14, 16, 17, 18, 19, 20 Aug. 1881; SF *Chron.*, 20, 21 Aug. 1881.

22. Dobie, *S. M. White*, 34, 45, 51, 126; Callow, "Blind Boss," 273; Buckley, "Reminiscences," 27 Dec. 1917.

23. SF *Alta*, 8 Sept. 1881; SF *Exam.*, 28, 30 Aug., 1, 5, 7, 8 Sept. 1881; SF *Chron.*, 7, 8, 9, 11 Sept. 1881; Buckley, "Reminiscences," 27 Dec. 1918.

24. Buckley, "Reminiscences," 28 Dec. 1918; Shumsky, "Tar Flat and Nob Hill," 251–291; Shumsky, "San Francisco's Workingmen," 46–57.

25. Elmer C. Sandmeyer, "California Anti-Chinese Legislation and the Federal Courts: A Study in Federal Relations," *PHR*, 5 (May 1936): 192–211; Rodman W. Paul, "The Origins of the Chinese Question in California," *MVHR*, 25 (September 1938): 181–196; Alexander P. Saxton, *The Indispensable Enemy* (Berkeley, 1971), 113–200, and passim; Gerald W. Nash, "The California Railroad Commission, 1876–1911," *SCQ*, 44 (December 1962): 265–279; David B. Griffiths, "Anti-Monopoly Movements in California, 1873–1898," *SCQ*, 52 (June 1970): 93–121; Robert L. Kelley, "The Mining Debris Question in the Sacramento Valley," *PHR*, 25 (November 1956): 331–346; Williams, *Democratic Party*, 19–24, 136–140; Dobie, *S. M. White*, 32–37; Robert W. Righter, "Washington Bartlett: Mayor of San Francisco, 1883–1887," *JW*, 3 (January 1964): 102–114.

26. SF *Exam.*, 30 Nov., 3, 7, 12, 15, 26 Dec. 1881; SF *Alta*, 2, 15 Dec. 1881; SF *Chron.*, 3, 23 Dec. 1881.

27. Buckley, "Reminiscences," 28 Dec. 1918; SF *Exam.*, 23 Dec. 1881, 10 Jan., 24 March 1882; SF *Alta*, 23 Dec. 1881; SF *Chron.*, 23 Dec. 1881.

28. Members of the Committee of Fifty of 1881 included a cross-section of the local business and professional community. Occupations are those given in SF *Directories, 1881–1882*. Factional affiliations are indicated by Y (Yosemite Club) or M (Manhattan Club).

Attorneys

Thomas B. Bishop	Joseph P. Hoge, M
James Vincent Coffey, Y	Judge Frank W. Lawler, M
Michael Mooney	Leander Quint, M
Judge Robert Ferral, Y	Edward B. Stonehill, Y
Walker C. Graves, Y	Francis J. Sullivan, Y
Solomon Heydenfeldt	

Business, Commerce, and Finance

Thomas Ashworth, M (capitalist)
James H. Barry, Y (printing firm)
Colin M. Boyd, Y (insurance broker)
Charles K. Breeze (provision merchant)
William J. Bryan (wholesale pharmaceuticals)
William T. Coleman, M (wholesale liquor, shipping)

William Cronan (roofing contractor)
William Dunphy (wholesale cattle dealer)
Isadore Gutte, M (insurance broker)
James Humphrey (grocery and liquor dealer)
Michael Kane, Y (wine and liquor dealer)
Jeremiah Lynch, M (investor)
Frank McCoppin (capitalist)
Martin V. Taylor (real estate broker)
James F. Tichenor, Y (speculator)
Henry Wangenheim (flour mill owner)
Alonzo A. Watkins, M (importer)
Raphael Weill, Y (drygoods emporium)

Public Officeholders

Frank M. Clough, Y (justice of the peace)
Edward P. Drum (city health inspector)
Joseph W. Jourdan, Y (tax collector's clerk)
L. J. Welch (tax collector's cashier)

Working Class

Dennis Gunn (ironmolder)	John J. Reichenbach (clerk)
Washington Irving (special policeman)	Thomas T. Tully (boxmaker)
Lawrence Masterson (watchman)	John B. Walters (plasterer)

Other

Samuel Deal, Y (detective)	William P. Frost, Y (journalist)
Arthur K. Hawkins (mining)	James L. Jones (mining)
J. Campbell Shorb, M (physician)	

Identification Uncertain

James D. Carr	James Duffy	J. Higgins
John Connors	Thomas Duffy	T. W. Murphy

29. SF *Alta,* 10 Jan. 1882; SF *Exam.,* 9, 10, 14, 16 Jan. 1882; SF *Chron.,* 10, 17 Jan. 1882. Members of the Subcommittee on Plans included William P. Frost, Frank McCoppin, James Duffy, James L. Jones, Charles K. Breeze, Edward B. Stonehill, Frank J. Sullivan, Martin V. Taylor, James H. Barry, Thomas B. Bishop, Walker C. Graves, Frank M. Clough, and L. J. Welch.

30. SF *Chron.,* 29 Jan. 1882.

31. See Committee of Fifty, *Addresses to the People* (San Francisco, [1882?]); and Democratic Party, *Plan for the Reorganization of the Democracy of the City and County of San Francisco adopted by the Committee of 50 and Approved by the State and County Central Committees, April 6, 1882* (San Francisco, 1882). Both are in the Pamphlets on San Francisco Collection (BL).

32. Subcommittee members with ties to Buckley included Frost, Stonehill, Sullivan, Barry, Graves, Clough, and McCoppin.

33. SF *Exam.,* 24 March 1882; SF *Chron.,* 24 March 1882; SF *Alta,* 24 March 1882.

34. SF *Exam.,* 29 March 1882; SF *Alta,* 29 March 1882; SF *Chron.,* 29 March 1882. Buckleyites who voted against the plan included Frank M. Clough, Walker C. Graves, Robert Ferral, Joseph W. Jourdan. Other opponents included J. Duffy, Bishop, Irving, Drumm, Welch, Lawler, and Bryan.

35. Buckley, "Reminiscences," 28 Dec. 1918.

36. Democratic Party, *Plan for Reorganization,* 14–22; SF *Exam.,* 15 April 1882. Maps appear in the SF *Exam.*

37. Democratic Party, *Plan for Reorganization,* 4–6.

38. Ibid., 6–8.

39. Ibid., 6, 7.

40. Ibid., 9–14.

41. Ibid., 7–8, 9, 12–14.

42. SF *Exam.,* 29 March, 21, 25, 27, 29 April, 4, 6, 10, 12 May 1882; Buckley, "Reminiscences," 28 Dec. 1918.

43. SF *Exam.,* 21, 25, 27, 29 April, 4, 6, 10, 12, 20 May 1882; Buckley, "Reminiscences," 28 Dec. 1918.

44. SF *Exam.,* 18 Jan., 5, 11, 16, 20, 23 March, 5, 7, 9, 13 April, 7 Oct. 1882; SF *Chron.,* 4, 17, 18, 23, 24 Jan., 3 Feb., 3, 5, 11, 21 March, 5 April 1882; SF *Alta,* 2 Jan., 24 March, 5 April, 1, 2 July, 1, 5, 18, 22, 25 Aug., 12 Sept. 1882; SF *Call,* 24, 25 Oct. 1882; SF *Bull.,* 30 Oct. 1882; Righter, "Washington Bartlett," 102–105; Bean, *California,* 226–228; Buckley, "Reminiscences," 30 Dec. 1918.

45. SF *Exam.,* 23, 25, 26, 30 May, 2 June 1882; SF *Call,* 2 June 1882. For Buckley's role in the 1882 convention and in the conflicting gubernatorial claims of Stoneman and Hearst, see Young, *San Francisco,* II, 697–698; Callow, "Blind Boss," 272–273; Williams, *Democratic Party,* 22–27; Dobie, *S. M. White,* 32–37; Davis, *Political Conventions,* 431–438; Curtis E. Grassman, "Prologue to California Reform: The Democratic Impulse, 1886–1898," *PHR,* 42 (November 1973): 521.

46. SF *Chron.,* 4 Feb., 1, 3, 36 Oct. 1882; SF *Exam.,* 10, 17, 23, 24 March, 1 May, 5, 21 June, 27 July, 27 Sept., 1, 20 Oct. 1882; SF *Alta,* 14, 25, 29 July, 28 Aug., 27, 30 Sept., 14, 26 Oct. 1882.

47. SF *Alta,* 2 July, 30 Aug., 21 Sept. 1882; SF *Exam.,* 9 July, 9, 26 Aug., 1, 6, 17 Sept., 17, 18 Oct. 1882; SF *Chron.,* 1 Oct. 1882.

48. SF *Call,* 21 June 1882; SF *Argonaut,* 7 July 1882.

49. SF *Exam.,* 21 Sept., 8 Oct. 1882; Democratic Party, *Plan for Reorganization,* 7–8.

50. SF *Chron.,* 4, 6, 10, 11, 12, 13, 17, 18 Oct. 1882; SF *Alta,* 6, 11, 12, 13, 14, 15, 17, 18 Oct. 1882; Grassman, "Prologue to Reform," 521; Righter,

"Washington Bartlett," 103; Callow, "Blind Boss," 273. The Republican "ringer" was William T. Sesnon, candidate for county clerk; see "Martin Kelly's Story," 6 Sept. 1917.

51. "Martin Kelly's Story," 6 Sept. 1917; SF *Chron.,* 2, 8 Nov. 1882; SF *Alta,* 8, 11 Nov. 1882; SF *Exam.,* 8, 9, 11 Nov. 1882; SF *Argonaut,* 2 Nov. 1882; Williams, *Democratic Party,* 24.

52. Neither contemporaries nor historians dispute Buckley's authorship of the club plan, and at least one political opponent credited him with devising the system and guiding it to success; see "Martin Kelly's Story," 5 Sept. 1917.

With the exception of returns for superior court judges, assemblymen, and congressmen, none of the precinct election records which might document specific sources of partisan strength in the city survived the earthquake and fire of 1906. A comparison of published Assembly District and Ward results with manuscript census records, however, provides a rough but reasonably satisfactory substitute. Throughout the 1880s, the Democracy's most impressive and consistent pluralities occurred in those regions, especially south of Market Street (the 30th, 37th, and 46th Assembly Districts, according to 1890 designations) and along the waterfront (the 29th, 32nd, and 33rd districts) which provided homes for the immigrants and working classes and for the disproportionate numbers of single males characteristic of San Francisco and other frontier cities. Newspaper reports also suggest a higher degree of club activity in those same regions. Such conclusions, however, must be drawn only tentatively in view of the size of Assembly Districts and Wards and the heterogeneity of San Francisco's population.

Professor William Issel of San Francisco State University generously provided the results of his analyses of the composition of San Francisco Assembly Districts. Also see U.S. Bureau of the Census, *Population Schedules of the Ninth Census of the United States, 1870;* U.S. Bureau of the Census, *Population Schedules of the Tenth Census of the United States, 1880;* San Francisco election returns by precinct, California State Archives, Sacramento; Blake McKelvey, *American Urbanization* (Glenview, Ill., 1973), 101.

53. Callow, "Blind Boss," 272; "Martin Kelly's Story," 19 Sept. 1917; Ruef, "The Road I Traveled," 31 May 1912.

54. SF *Chron.,* 24 March 1882; Shumsky, "San Francisco's Workingmen," 53–55; Buckley, "Reminiscences," 28 Jan. 1919, and passim.

55. Walker, *San Francisco's Literary Frontier,* 9.

CHAPTER FIVE

1. U.S. Bureau of the Census, *Statistics of Manufactures of the United States at the Tenth Census, 1880* (Washington, D.C., 1883), 380 and passim; Shumsky, "Tar Flat and Nob Hill," 23–24; Muscatine, *Old San Francisco,* 187–197; Barth, *Instant Cities,* 142–143, 210; SF *Exam.,* 1 Jan 1884, 21 July 1888; SF *Chron.,* 1 Jan. 1884, 20 July 1888; SF *Alta,* 20 July 1888; *Historical Souvenir of*

San Francisco, Cal. (San Francisco, 1887), 12, 17–18, 22, 28; *Bancroft Scraps* (BL), vol. 48, "California Manufacturing Industries."

2. California Bureau of Labor Statistics, *First Biennial Report* (Sacramento, 1884), 11, 211–214; Peter Varcados, "Labor and Politics in San Francisco" (Ph.D. thesis, University of California, Berkeley, 1969), 34–37, 40–58; Saxton, *Indispensable Enemy*, 159–160, 165, 226–227; Cross, *Labor Movement*, 143–147.

3. Cross, *Labor Movement*, 132–135; Saxton, *Indispensable Enemy*, 157, 164, 215, 218–221; Oscar Lewis, *San Francisco* (Berkeley, 1966), 167; Cross (ed.), *Frank Roney*, 356 and passim.

4. Saxton, *Indispensable Enemy*, 166–168, 171–177, 180–184, 214; Cross, *Labor Movement*, 135–136, 139–141; Young, *San Francisco*, II, 682–683; SF *Exam.*, 8 Jan. 1882.

5. Saxton, *Indispensable Enemy*, 168, 219–224; Cross, *Labor Movement*, 141.

6. U.S. Bureau of the Census, *Tenth Census of the United States, 1880. Statistics of Cities* (Washington, D.C., 1887), Part II, 769; U.S. Bureau of the Census, *Population of Cities, 1790–1900,* 430–432; Allyn C. Loosely, "Foreign Born Population of California, 1848–1920" (M.A. thesis, University of California, Berkeley, 1927), 10, 15, 18; Barth, *Instant Cities,* 131, 135, 146, 175; Walker, *San Francisco's Literary Frontier,* 8; Cross, *Labor Movement,* 135; Williams, *Democratic Party,* 87–91.

7. Neville, *Fantastic City,* 164; Starr, *California Dream,* 201; Muscatine, *Old San Francisco,* 422; SF *Exam.,* 27 Feb. 1886; SF *Chron.,* 21 Feb. 1886.

8. Shumate, *Visit to Rincon Hill,* 12–13, 16–17; Neville, *Fantastic City,* 191; Kipling, *Letters,* 5; James Bryce, *The American Commonwealth* (New York, 1904), II, 428.

9. U.S. Bureau of the Census, *Population Schedules of the Ninth Census of the United States, 1870,* San Francisco City (Washington, D.C., 1956), microfilm, rolls 79–83; U.S. Bureau of the Census, *Population Schedules of the Tenth Census of the United States, 1880,* San Francisco City (Washington, D.C., 1956) microfilm, rolls 73–77; SF *Directories,* 1880–1889; SF *Exam.,* 7 Jan. 1884, 1 Jan. 1886; Neville, *Fantastic City,* 178–192; Decker, *Fortunes and Failures,* 196–249.

A survey and comparison of the manuscript census schedules for each San Francisco ward in 1870 and 1880 provides insights into changing patterns of population distribution and land use in the city. In lieu of the 1890 census data, ninety percent of which was burned in the 1920s, SF *Directories,* SF *Circular,* and New Year's Day editions of local newspapers furnish some basic insights and comprehensive summaries of real estate activities.

10. Kipling, *Letters,* 12.

11. *SFMR, 1883–84,* 104–139; Muscatine, *Old San Francisco,* 194; SF *Chron.,* 1 Jan. 1884; Righter, "Washington Bartlett," 106; "Martin Kelly's Story," 6, 7 Sept. 1917; Young, *San Francisco,* II, 577–579; Grassman, "Prologue to Reform," 520.

12. Young, *San Francisco*, II, 577; Heintz, *San Francisco's Mayors*, 61–65.
13. Julia C. Altrocchi, *The Spectacular San Franciscans* (New York, 1949), 217–220; Decker, *Fortunes and Failures*, 232–245.
14. Altrocchi, *Spectacular San Franciscans*, 222–227, 237–239; Neville, *Fantastic City*, 70, 72–73, 131–134, 180, 210, 216, 226, 252–256; Muscatine, *Old San Francisco*, 363–364, 367, 373–374.
15. Neville, *Fantastic City*, 153, 255–256; Kipling, *Letters*, 4, 54–60; Muscatine, *Old San Francisco*, 234; Constance Gordon-Cummin, *Granite Crags* (London, 1886), 23; Ralph Springer, "Golden Gate Park," *OM*, 69 (February 1917): 101–108.
16. Neville, *Fantastic City*, 83; SF *Exam.*, 17 Jan. 1884.
17. Muscatine, *Old San Francisco*, 205, 238, 242–243, 345; Shumate, *Visit to Rincon Hill*, 3; Neville, *Fantastic City*, 73, 237–239.
18. Altrocchi, *Spectacular San Franciscans*, 245–248; Muscatine, *Old San Francisco*, 346, 414–415; Neville, *Fantastic City*, 239–240, 242, 247–248.
19. Altrocchi, *Spectacular San Franciscans*, 245–248; Neville, *Fantastic City*, 162–163, 227–228, 231–236; Muscatine *Old San Francisco*, 368–372; Starr, *California Dream*, 248; SF *Exam.*, 10 March 1884; SF *Call*, 12 March 1884.
20. Muscatine, *Old San Francisco*, 413–414; Neville, *Fantastic City*, 223–224, 244–245; Altrocchi, *Spectacular San Franciscans*, 218–222; SF *Chron.*, 20 Oct. 1884; Stevenson and Osbourne, *The Wrecker.*
21. Kipling, *Letters*, 15–17; Daniels, "Afro-San Franciscans," Chap. 5; Saxton, *Indispensable Enemy*, 214–216.
22. Muscatine, *Old San Francisco*, 298–301, 336–337; Neville, *Fantastic City*, 125–126; Robert H. Kroninger, *Sarah and the Senator* (Berkeley, 1964).
23. Barth, *Instant Cities*, 151–152; Muscatine, *Old San Francisco*, 359; McKee, "Shooting of Charles De Young," 271–284; SF *Chron.*, 20 Nov. 1884; SF *Exam.*, 20 Nov. 1884; Herbert Asbury, *The Barbary Coast* (New York, 1968), 211–231.
24. "Martin Kelly's Story," 8 Sept. 1917; SF *Exam.*, 28, 30 Sept. 1888; SF *Chron.*, 28 Sept. 1888.
25. Buckley, "Reminiscences," 24, 31 Jan. 1919.
26. Muscatine, *Old San Francisco*, 204–208; Asbury, *Barbary Coast*, 163–184, 233–268; St. Laurence, "Myth and Reality," 98–110.
27. See, for example, Lincoln Steffens, *The Shame of the Cities* (New York, 1904); Bryce, *American Commonwealth;* Callow, *Tweed Ring;* Seymour J. Mandelbaum, *Boss Tweed's New York* (New York, 1965); Merton, *Social Theory;* Josiah Strong, *Our Country* (New York, 1891).
28. Quoted in Brownell and Stickles (eds.), *Bosses and Reformers,* ix; italics in original.
29. Robert H. Wiebe, *The Search for Order, 1877–1920* (New York, 1967), 13, 30–31, 44–75, and passim. In 1883, the San Francisco mayor appointed members of thirteen standing committees of the board of supervisors: Judiciary,

Finance and Auditing, Fire Department, Streets and Wharves, Public Buildings, Water and Water Supplies, Health and Police, License and Orders, Hospital, Printing and Salaries, Industrial School, Street Lighting, and Outside Lands. Frequently, half or more of the committees were called upon to deal with a single proposed ordinance. See *SFMR, 1882–83,* 2.

30. Callow, *Tweed Ring,* 5–6.

31. *SFMR, 1881–82,* 218–220; *SFMR, 1882–83,* 382–384, 441, 449–450, 479; SF *Directory, 1883,* 81÷93.

32. Merton, *Social Theory,* 74–76; Riordon, *Plunkitt of Tammany Hall,* 90–98; "Martin Kelly's Story," 3 Sept. 1917.

33. Buckley, "Reminiscences," 28 Jan. 1919.

34. Callow, "Blind Boss," 270–271.

35. Ibid.

36. "Martin Kelly's Story," 6, 7, 9 Sept. 1917; Callow, *Tweed Ring,* 83, 131, 184–188; *Boss Ruef,* 89–90, 112–118, 140–142; Miller, *Boss Cox's Cincinnati,* 170–171, 176; Dorsett, *Pendergast Machine,* 4–5.

37. Merton, *Social Theory,* 75–77; Callow, "Blind Boss," 269–271; Bullough, *Cities and Schools,* 65–71; Eric L. McKitrick, "The Study of Corruption," *PSQ,* 62 (December 1957): 502–514; Kipling, *American Notes,* 51.

38. Buckley, "Reminiscences," 24 Jan. 1919.

39. SF *Exam.,* 30 Jan. 1897; Callow, "Blind Boss," 270. When he died in 1922, Buckley's estate included Spring Valley Water Company first mortgage bonds in the amount of $25,000 and California Gas and Electric Company first mortgage bonds valued at $75,000; see San Francisco County Clerk, Probate File Number 34037.

40. Buckley, "Reminiscences," 28 Jan. 1919.

41. "Martin Kelly's Story," 3 Sept. 1917.

42. Callow, *Tweed Ring,* 164–165; Bean, *Boss Ruef,* 85–95, 100–107, 131–137, 199–212.

No evidence, even that uncovered in grand jury investigations, supports the frequent allegations that Buckley maintained intimate connections with the underworld. Most such charges may be traced to two principal sources: Jeremiah Lynch's 1889 attack on Buckley and journalistic charges, especially following the assassination of the Chinese hoodlum Little Pete (Fung Jing Toy) in 1897. Both sources contain inaccuracies. See Lynch, *Buckleyism,* 28; Callow, "Blind Boss," 271; SF *Exam.,* 30 Jan 1897, 24 July 1899; SF *Call,* 25 Jan. 1897; Asbury, *Barbary Coast,* 193, 270; Dobie, *S. M. White,* 19, 34; Young, *San Francisco,* II, 563–565, 696–699.

43. Riordon, *Plunkitt of Tammany Hall,* 3–6; Buckley, "Reminiscences," 28 Jan. 1919.

Buckley came to consider himself equally a businessman and a politician; see SF County Clerk, Probate File Number 34037; SF *Directory, 1889,* 290; Buckley, "Reminiscences," 28 Jan. 1919; Buckley interviews.

44. "Martin Kelly's Story," 19 Sept. 1917.

45. *SFMR, 1882–83*, 80–83; Howard B. Melendy and Benjamin F. Gilbert, *The Governors of California* (Georgetown, Calif., 1965), 219–220; Righter, "Washington Bartlett," 104; SF *Argonaut*, 2 Nov. 1882; "Martin Kelly's Story," 6 Sept. 1917; Buckley, "Reminiscences," 1 Jan. 1919; SF *Exam.*, 8, 9, 11 Nov. 1882, 1, 2 Jan. 1883; SF *Chron.*, 8, 9 Nov. 1882; SF *Alta*, 8, 11 Nov. 1882; Bancroft, *History of California*, VII, 421, fn. 26.

I am indebted to William F. Heintz who permitted access to his research notes and unpublished manuscript materials related to San Francisco mayors after 1880; hereafter cited as Heintz manuscript. Also see Robert W. Righter, "The Life and Career of Washington Bartlett" (M.A. thesis, San Jose [Calif.] State College, 1963).

46. Heintz manuscript.; SF *Chron.*, 13, 31 Oct. 1882; Davis, *Political Conventions*, 325–326, 525, 602–603, 607; Melendy and Gilbert, *Governors of California*, 219–225; Righter, "Washington Bartlett," 102–104; Bancroft, *History of California*, VII, 434; Theodore H. Hittell, *History of California* (San Francisco, 1897), IV, 700–721; California Society of Pioneers, *Memorial of the Life and Services of Washington Bartlett* (San Francisco, 1888); Felix P. Wierzbicki, *California as It Is and as It Might Be; or, a Guide to the Gold Region* (San Francisco, 1849).

Washington and Columbus Bartlett made substantial investments in property in Oakland and elsewhere in Alameda County in the early 1880s; see Alameda (Calif.) County Recorder, *Index of Deeds*, Numbers 26–28.

47. See, for example, SF *Chron.*, 2 Nov. 1882; Righter, "Washington Bartlett," 103; Callow, "Blind Boss," 273–274.

48. SF *Newsletter*, 14 Oct. 1882.

49. SF *Directory, 1880*, passim; SF *Directory, 1884*, 58–59 and passim. Most ethnic and national groups—with the exception of blacks, Chinese, and Latins—were represented on the ticket, albeit not proportionately. The phrase "Tammany Hall West" is quoted from a conversation with Professor James P. Walsh of San Jose State University.

50. SF *Alta*, 11, 12 Oct. 1882; SF *Directory, 1883*, 57 and passim; *Population Schedules, Tenth Census*, passim.

Board of Supervisors (by ward)

1. J. T. Sullivan, merchant
2. John J. Reichenbach, merchant
3. John Shirley, real estate
4. Charles H. Burton, capitalist
5. J. Henley Smith, merchant
6. Edward B. Pond, capitalist
7. John D. Griffin, boat builder
8. Fleet F. Strother, real estate
9. John B. Lewis, real estate
10. Herman Ranken, saloon keeper
11. Jefferson G. Ames, livestock
12. Thomas Ashworth, capitalist

Pond would succeed Bartlett as mayor. Sullivan and Reichenbach had been members of the Committee of Fifty. The fact that Ames represented the Eleventh Ward (the still sparsely settled Mission District to the south of the city) explains his practice of an occupation somewhat unique for a municipal official. All of the supervisors resided in the wards they represented.

School Directors

Robert P. Hastings, attorney	John M. Foard, journalist
Frank Conklin, merchant	Charles E. Travers, attorney
James M. Eaton, M.D.	Isidor Danielwitz, attorney
Lee O. Rodgers, M.D.	J. Appleton Melcher, insurance
Ernest Brand, attorney	Raphael Weill, merchant
James Cahalin, salesman	Charles D. Cleaveland, M.D.

Weill had been a member of the Committee of Fifty. Cleaveland in 1883 became the publisher of George Hearst's *Examiner;* in 1896 he was a free silver advocate and a Populist nominee for supervisor.

51. SF *Directory, 1880,* passim; SF *Directory, 1884,* 58–59 and passim; Oscar T. Shuck, *History of Bench and Bar in California* (Los Angeles, 1901); *Population Schedules, Tenth Census,* passim.

Judicial Officials (all attorneys)

Jeremiah F. Sullivan	Frank M. Clough
James G. Maguire	Robert Ferral
Frank W. Lawler	James Lawlor
James Vincent Coffey	J. C. Pennie

City Officers

City and County Attorney: William Craig, attorney
District Attorney: Jeremiah D. Sullivan, attorney
Police Chief: Patrick Crowley, stock broker
County Clerk: William Sesnon, law student
Sheriff: Patrick Connolly, police officer
Recorder: William J. Bryan, wholesale pharmaceuticals
Auditor: William M. Edgar, deputy county auditor
Assessor: Louis F. Holtz, stationery dealer
Tax Collector: John H. Grady, furniture finisher
City and County Surveyor: George H. Rogers, contractor
Superintendent of Streets: Timothy J. Lowney, carriage making firm
Superintendent of Schools: Andrew J. Moulder, secretary Pacific Stock Exchange
City and County Coroner: Marc Levingston, M.D.

Lawler, Coffey, Clough, Ferral, and Bryan had been members of the Committee of Fifty. Crowley was appointed by the police commission.

52. Varcados, "Labor and Politics," 129.

53. Heintz, *San Francisco's Mayors,* passim; Heintz manuscript.

54. Buckley, "Reminiscences," 1 Feb. 1919; SF *Newsletter,* 9 Sept. 1882; Shuck, *Bench and Bar,* 404–405; Neville, *Fantastic City,* 82–83; Davis, *Political Conventions,* passim.

55. Richard Hofstadter, *The Age of Reform* (New York, 1955), 131–174 and passim. Also see George E. Mowry, "The California Progressive and His Rationale: A Study in Middle Class Politics," *MVHR*, 36 (September 1949): 239–250.

56. Merton, *Social Theory*, 74–78.

57. Neville, *Fantastic City*, 57–58, 82–83; William A. Bullough, "Hannibal versus the Blind Boss: The 'Junta,' Chris Buckley, and Democratic Reform Politics in San Francisco," *PHR*, 46 (May 1977): 181–206; Bullough, "Steam Beer Handicap," 245–262; Buckley interviews.

Social memoirs such as Neville, *Fantastic City* and Altrocchi, *Spectacular San Franciscans,* society sections of local newspapers, and volumes such as *Elite Directory of San Francisco, 1879* (San Francisco, 1879) and *A Social Manual for San Francisco and Oakland* (San Francisco, 1884) reveal a strong strain of elitism and snobbery in the city during the 1880s.

58. Merton, *Social Theory*, 74–78. San Francisco did have an examination system for teachers, but its administration by elected school directors and the superintendent kept teaching positions deeply embroiled in the patronage process and partisan politics; see Lee S. Dolson, Jr., "The Administration of San Francisco Public Schools, 1847–1947" (Ph.D. thesis, University of California, Berkeley, 1964), 138–150, 237–240.

59. Buckley, "Reminiscences," 28 Jan. 1919.

60. *Population Schedules, Tenth Census,* City of San Francisco, Ward Five, Roll 74, Enumeration District 45, p. 8 and passim.

61. SF *Directory, 1880,* 167. Since most of the records of the City and County of San Francisco were destroyed by fire in 1906 and local newspapers are silent on the subject, the circumstances surrounding Buckley's first marriage are obscure. His wife's fate is similarly uncertain. Given the Roman Catholic Church's proscription and the fact that Buckley's second marriage received church sanction, it is unlikely that divorce was involved. Sallie Buckley, like so many young women in nineteenth-century San Francisco, probably died prematurely.

62. SF *Directory, 1884,* 284; *Population Schedules, Tenth Census,* City of San Francisco, Ward Twelve, Roll 76; *Realty Directory of San Francisco* (San Francisco, 1896), 41.

63. SF *Chron.,* 10 Jan. 1884; SF *Exam.,* 10 Jan. 1884; SF *Call,* 11 Jan. 1884; Buckley interviews.

64. Buckley interviews; Buckley family sources. Neither San Francisco nor Boston records refer to the marriage to Elizabeth Hurley.

In the spring of 1884, the estate of a John Buckley, possibly the Boss's father, was settled in an amount slightly over $20,000 and may have been the basis for Buckley's 1885 property purchase in Livermore; see SF *Call,* 19 April 1884.

65. Alameda (Calif.) County Recorder, *Index of Deeds,* Number 28, entry 6/8503; Liv. *Herald,* 25 Jan. 1896; Oakland (Calif.) *Enquirer,* 13 Dec. 1897;

Idwal Jones, *Vines in the Sun* (New York, 1949), 168–170; Idwal Jones, "At Ravenswood," *Westways,* 40 (March 1948), 6–7; SF *Exam.,* 23 Sept. 1891; Frona R. Waite, *Wines and Vines of California* (San Francisco, 1889), 157.
  66. Buckley, "Reminiscences," 4 Feb. 1919; Buckley interviews.

CHAPTER SIX

  1. Wangenheim, "Autobiography," 144; Neville, *Fantastic City,* 258; Kipling, *Letters from San Francisco,* 46–48; Stevenson and Osbourne, *The Wrecker,* 167; SF *Exam.,* 12 Sept., 27 Oct. 1885; SF *Alta,* 24 Oct. 1885; Sac. *Bee,* 23 Oct. 1885; SF *Chron.,* 23 Oct. 1885; Buckley interviews and family photographs.
  2. See John G. Sproat, *"The Best Men"* (New York, 1968), 67–69, 171–172, 184–185, 215–216, and passim.
  3. SF *Chron.,* 5 Feb., 5 July, 16 Oct. 1884; SF *Exam.,* 8, 9, 10 Jan. 1883, 3 Jan., 5 Feb. 1884; SF *Newsletter,* 27 Jan., 3 Feb. 1883; SF *Directory, 1881,* 352; SF *Directory, 1882,* 746; SF *Directory, 1883,* 758; SF *Directory, 1884,* 58–59, 271, 835; SFMR, *1882–83,* 80–83; SFMR, *1884–85,* 691; Callow, "Blind Boss," 267–269.
John Buckley was unable to enjoy his position for long; appointed to the street department in January 1883, he died in January 1884 at the age of seventy-nine years and nine months.
  4. SF *Chron.,* 6, 9, 12, 13 Jan. 1883; SF *Exam.,* 9, 11 Jan. 1883; Bullough, *Cities and Schools,* 67–68; David B. Tyack, *The One Best System* (Cambridge, Mass., 1974), 98–100.
  5. SF *Exam.,* 4, 23 April 1883; SF *Chron.,* 21 March, 4, 18 April 1883; SF *Newsletter,* 24 March, 16 June 1883; SF *Wasp,* 7, 21 April 1883; Bullough, *Cities and Schools,* 68–69; Lee S. Dolson, Jr., "The Administration of San Francisco Public Schools, 1847–1957" (Ph.D. thesis, University of California, Berkeley, 1964), 237–240; "Martin Kelly's Story," 6 Oct.–5 Nov. 1917.
  6. SF *Chron.,* 11, 24 April 1883, 10 Jan., 16 Oct. 1884; SF *Newsletter,* 28 April 1883; SF *Exam.,* 16 Jan. 1883.
  7. Dolson, "Administration," 240–244.
  8. Buckley, "Reminiscences," 27 Jan. 1919 ; Callow, "Blind Boss," 269; Buckley interviews.
  9. Callow, "Blind Boss," 269; Lynch, *Buckleyism,* 17; Dolson, "Administration," 171, 239–240, 252; SFMR, *1884–85,* 665–666, 674–675; SF *Chron.,* 12, 28 April, 1, 3, 5, 8, 12 July 1884. Also see Ellwood P. Cubberly, "The School Situation in San Francisco," *Educational Review,* 14 (April 1901): 364–381.
  10. Righter, "Washington Bartlett," 107; SF *Chron.,* 8 Nov. 1884; SF *Exam.,* 8 Nov. 1884; SF *Call,* 8 Nov. 1884.
For Buckley's involvement with Grover Cleveland and federal patronage, see Williams, *Democratic Party,* 53–58, 113–116; Dobie, *S. M. White,* 55–60.

11. SF *Alta,* 6, 8 Oct. 1882; SF *Exam.,* 6, 7, 10 Oct. 1882; SF *Chron.,* 4, 6, 7 Oct. 1882, 15 June 1883; SF *Call,* 24, 25 Oct. 1882; SF *Bull.,* 30 Oct. 1882; SF *Wasp,* 10 Feb. 1883; *Statutes of California, 1877–78,* 22nd Sess., 111–113, 333–334; Buckley, "Reminiscences," 24 Dec. 1918, 1 Jan. 1919; Davis, *Political Conventions,* 639; "Martin Kelly's Story," 3 Sept. 1917; Righter, "Washington Bartlett," 104–105; *SFMR, 1882–83,* 80–83.

12. *SFMR, 1882–83,* 80–83.

13. Ibid., 94–100; Righter, "Washington Bartlett," 104; SF *Wasp,* 10, 17 Feb. 1883; SF *Alta,* 28 Feb. 1883; SF *Exam.,* 17 Feb., 3 April 1883.

14. Righter, "Washington Bartlett," 104; *SFMR, 1882–83,* 100–104, 107, 115–116; SF *Exam.,* 8 Jan., 28 Feb. 1883; SF *Alta,* 28 Feb. 1883; SF *Newsletter,* 17 March, 19 May 1883; SF *Chron.,* 3 April 1883.

15. *SFMR, 1882–83,* 106–107, 109, 112; SF *Chron.,* 7 March, 10 April 1883; SF *Newsletter,* 7 April 1883; Righter, "Washington Bartlett," 105.

16. *SFMR, 1882–83,* 107, 115–116; SF *Wasp,* 3, 10 March 1883.

17. *SFMR, 1882–83,* 118–119, 132, 134–135; Righter, "Washington Bartlett," 106; SF *Alta,* 19 June 1883; SF *Exam.,* 20 June 1883; Heintz manuscript.

18. SF *Bull.,* 24 Aug. 1883; SF *Chron.,* 15 June 1883; SF *Alta,* 16 June 1883; SF *Exam.,* 17 June 1884; Bancroft, *History of California,* VII, 690–691; *SFMR, 1884–90,* especially Treasurer's, Assessor's, and Tax Collector's reports. Preliminary findings in the work of Professor Terrence J. McDonald of San Francisco State University tend to corroborate Buckley's claim that taxation and bonded indebtedness remained at relatively low levels during his regimes.

19. Righter, "Washington Bartlett," 105–109; SF *Circular,* 19 (December 1884): 3; SF *Exam.,* 3 April 1883; SF *Chron.,* 15 June 1883, 8 Nov. 1884; SF *Alta,* 3 April 1883; Buckley, "Reminiscences," 2 Jan. 1919.

20. Buckley, "Reminiscences," 28 Jan. 1919; "Martin Kelly's Story," 3 Sept. 1917; Righter, "Washington Bartlett," 106; Grassman, "Prologue to Reform," 520.

21. "Martin Kelly's Story," 6 Sept. 1917.

22. *Bancroft Scraps* (BL), "San Francisco Miscellany," II, 228–237; Young, *San Francisco,* II, 577; SF *Chron.,* 11 March 1878; SF *Exam.,* 1 Jan. 1886; *Statutes of California, 1877–78,* 22nd Sess., 18; Buckley, "Reminiscences," 24 Dec. 1918.

23. "Martin Kelly's Story," 6 Sept. 1917.

24. Ibid.; *SFMR, 1883–84,* 104–139; Young, *San Francisco,* II, 577–579; Changni Young, "The Market Street Railway System in San Francisco" (Ph.D. thesis, Harvard University, 1949), 86–113, and passim. More than forty franchises were granted between 1877 and 1879; see *SFMR, 1883–84,* 104–139; *SFMR, 1887–88,* 136–177.

25. *SFMR, 1883–84,* 124–125.

26. Ibid., 113; "Martin Kelly's Story," 6 Sept. 1917; Callow, "Blind Boss," 270–271; *Historical Souvenir,* 24–26; Righter, "Washington Bartlett," 106–111; Young, *San Francisco,* II, 759–761; SF *Alta,* 2 Oct. 1883.

27. *SFMR, 1883–84,* 104–105, 119–120, 124–125, 135–139; *SFMR, 1887–88,* 137, 149; SF *Newsletter,* 6 Oct., 8 Dec. 1883; SF *Chron.,* 1 July 1884; San Francisco Board of Park Commissioners, *Souvenir Programme, Golden Gate Park, S.F.* (San Francisco, 1883); Cable Railway Company, *In Reply to the Pamphlet Issued by the Market Street Cable Company* (San Francisco, [1884]), 1, 4–5.

28. *SFMR, 1883–84,* 104–139; *SFMR, 1887–88,* 136–177; *SFMR, 1889–90,* 184–191; Callow, "Blind Boss," 270–271; SF *Alta,* 17 Nov. 1885; SF *Chron.,* 1 Jan. 1884, 6 Feb. 1889; *Historical Souvenir,* 23–24, 26–27; "Martin Kelly's Story," 7, 21, 27 Sept. 1917; Young, "Market Street Railway System," 47–63.

29. Muscatine, *Old San Francisco,* 194; "Martin Kelly's Story," 21, 22, 24, 25 Sept. 1917.

30. "Martin Kelly's Story," 25, 27, 28, 29 Sept. 1917.

31. Ibid., 24 Sept. 1917.

32. Ibid., 7 Sept. 1917; Ruef, "The Road I Traveled," 21 June 1912; Buckley, "Reminiscences," 4 Jan. 1919; Callow, "Blind Boss," 270–271; Bean, *Boss Ruef,* 7–8.

33. Buckley's portfolio contained substantial blocks of utility and transportation company first mortgage bonds as well as major real estate holdings in the city and elsewhere. See SF County Clerk, Probate File Number 34037; *Realty Directory of San Francisco* (San Francisco, 1896), 41; *San Francisco Block Book* (San Francisco, 1906), 86, 573; *Mery's Block Book of San Francisco* (San Francisco, 1909), 164, 678; Buckley interviews; SF *Alta,* 10 June 1886, 6 Jan., 8 March 1888; SF *Chron.,* 1 Jan., 8 March 1888; 5 Aug. 1890, 2 Nov. 1892.

34. M. M. O'Shaughnessy, *Hetch-Hetchy* (San Francisco, 1934), 45, 50–51, 64, and passim.

35. Young, *San Francisco,* II, 586; SF *Newsletter,* 3 Feb. 1883; SF *Wasp,* 10 Feb., 1883; SF *Alta,* 12 Feb. 1883; *SFMR, 1882–83,* 78–79.

36. SF *Wasp,* 3 March 1883; SF *Exam.,* 9 March 1883.

37. *SFMR, 1882–83,* 151–163, *SFMR, 1883–84,* 77, 92; SF *Chron.,* 13 March 1883; SF *Alta,* 16 March 1883; SF *Bull.,* 23 March 1883.

38. *SFMR., 1883–84,* 81–85.

39. Ibid., 80–81, 83–85, 94–96; SF *Chron.,* 8, 28 Feb., 11, 18 March 1884; SF *Exam.,* 10, 12, 28 Feb., 11, 18 March 1884; SF *Alta,* 18 March 1884; SF *Call,* 19 March 1884.

40. Buckley, "Reminiscences," 6 Jan. 1919.

41. "Martin Kelly's Story," 8 Sept. 1917.

42. *SFMR, 1884–85,* 83.

43. Ibid., 106–108, 122–124; SF *Alta,* 18 March, 30 June 1885.

44. *SFMR, 1885–86,* 12–13; *SFMR, 1886–87,* 105–119; *SFMR, 1887–88,* 102–111; *SFMR, 1888–89,* 226–228; *SFMR, 1889–90,* 105–167; *SFMR, 1890–91,* 106–118; Ruef, "The Road I Traveled," 6 June 1912; Buckley, "Reminiscences," 14 Jan. 1919.

45. Buckley, "Reminiscences," 14 Jan. 1919.

46. San Francisco County Clerk, Probate File Number 34037; Buckley interviews.
47. Ibid. Buckley's estate included California Gas and Electric Co. bonds valued at $75,000 and San Francisco Gas and Electric Co. bonds valued at $22,000.
48. Barth, *Instant Cities,* 198, 223–225; Lotchin, *San Francisco,* 170–172; Muscatine, *Old San Francisco,* 111; Young, *San Francisco,* II, 582–584; SF *Newsletter,* 23 Dec. 1882; SF *Wasp,* 5 May 1883; "Martin Kelly's Story," 11 Sept. 1917; SF *Exam.,* 17 July 1888; SF *Chron.,* 17 Jan. 1888.
49. *SFMR, 1883–84,* 140–149; *SFMR, 1885–86,* 95–106; *SFMR, 1887–88,* 112–120, 220–238; *SFMR, 1888–90,* 199–204; SF *Chron.,* 8, 15, 22, 29 April 1884; SF *Exam.,* 15, 22 April 1884.
50. "Martin Kelly's Story," 8, 19 Sept. 1917; Callow, "Blind Boss," 270; SF *Exam.,* 30 Jan. 1897; SF *Bull.,* 7 May 1889; SF *Wave,* 22 Aug. 1891; SF *Call,* 21 Nov. 1891; Young, *San Francisco,* II, 689.
51. SF *Alta,* 10 June 1886, 6, 31 Jan., 8 March 1888; SF *Chron.,* 10 June 1886, 1 Jan., 8 March 1888, 5 Aug., 2 Nov. 1890, 9, 12 Sept. 1894, 11 Feb. 1909, 21 March 1911; Sac. *Bee,* 11 Feb. 1909; SF *Call,* 3, 5, 12 Sept. 1894, 21 April 1901, 12 Feb. 1909; Williams, *Democratic Party,* 150–151.
52. Young, *San Francisco,* II, 697; Righter, "Washington Bartlett," 103, 112; Buckley, "Reminiscences," 4, 13, 16 Jan. 1919.
53. See, for example, Rush Welter, *Popular Education and Democratic Thought in America* (New York, 1962); Stanley K. Schultz, *The Culture Factory* (New York, 1973); Selwyn K. Troen, *The Public and the Schools* (Columbia, Mo., 1975); Marvin Lazerson, *Origins of the Urban School* (Cambridge, Mass., 1971); Tyack, *The One Best System,* 72–78; Bullough, *Cities and Schools,* 3–14.
54. SF *Bull.,* 28 Nov. 1878; San Francisco Board of Education, *The School Scandal of San Francisco* (San Francisco, 1878), passim; SF *Newsletter,* 24, 31 March, 7, 14, 21 April, 16, 23 June, 18 Aug. 1883; SF *Chron.,* 13, 16, 20, Jan. 1883, 6 Feb. 1884; SF *Call,* 13 Jan. 1883; SF *Wasp,* 7 April 1883; Dolson, "Administration," 144–148.
55. Bullough, *Cities and Schools,* 15–28; Tyack, *The One Best System,* 30–38, 137–139, 154–155; U.S. Commissioner of Education, *Annual Reports* (Washington, D.C., 1880–1890). Data relating to San Francisco public schools are compiled in William A. Bullough, "Urban Education in the Gilded Age, 1876–1906" (Ph.D. thesis, University of California, Santa Barbara, 1970), 421–422.
56. SF *Newsletter,* 5 July 1884; SF *Chron.,* 4, 17, 26 Jan.; 18 April; 8 July; 16 Oct.; 19 Nov. 1884; SF *Exam.,* 5 Sept. 1882; 15, 16 Jan.; 12 Feb.; 7 May 1884; Dolson, "Administration," 155–156, 161–163; *SFMR, 1884–85,* 665–666, 674–675.
57. SF *Chron.,* 3 Jan., 12 April, 1, 3, 5, 8, 10, 11, 12 July, 2 Nov. 1884; SF *Exam.,* 3, 26 Jan. 1884; SF *Alta,* 5, 9, 12 July 1884.
58. SF *Chron.,* 22 Feb., 21 June, 24 Oct. 1884; SF *Exam.,* 2 April 1884.

59. SF *Newsletter,* 11 Aug., 24 Nov., 8 Dec. 1883.

60. SF *Exam.,* 15, 18, 19 Jan. 1885, 24 Jan., 1 Dec. 1895, 17 July 1896, 28 Jan. 1897; SF *Chron.,* 19 Oct., 28 Dec. 1895, 5 Jan. 1900; SF *Bull.,* 24, 25 Sept. 1895; SF *Call,* 28 April 1892; Dolson, "Administration," 295–300; Ruef, "The Road I Traveled," 27 May, 19 June 1912.

61. See, for example, SF *Bull.,* 7 May 1889; SF *Wave,* 22 Aug. 1891, 2 Jan. 1892; SF *Call,* 21 Nov. 1891, 25 Jan. 1897; SF *Exam.,* 24 July 1899; Lynch, *Buckleyism,* 17–18.

62. Dolson, "Administration," 235–242.

CHAPTER SEVEN

1. Buckley, "Reminiscences," 4 Jan. 1919; Dobie, *S. M. White,* 44–45; Callow, "Blind Boss," 277; Petersen, "Struggle for the Australian Ballot," 230–231; SF *Newsletter,* 7 April 1883; SF *Exam.,* 4 April, 20, 22 May 1884; SF *Chron.,* 3 April 1883, 20 March, 1 April, 20 May, 19, 20 June 1884; SF *Call,* 1 June 1884; Democratic Party, *Plan for Reorganization,* 3–4; Davis, *Political Conventions,* 455–463; Williams, *Democratic Party,* 46–56.

2. *Statutes of California, 1883,* 25th Sess., 85–93; Democratic Party, *Plan of Reorganization,* 14; SF *Exam.,* 14 Feb. 1884; SF *Chron.,* 22 Feb. 1884.

3. SF *Exam.,* 14, 19 Feb., 13 March 1884; SF *Chron.,* 19, 22 Feb., 2, 12 March 1884; James D. Phelan Papers (BL), "Scrapbooks," Vol. 68.

4. Dobie, *S. M. White,* 35, 49; Williams, *Democratic Party,* 25–26; Callow, "Blind Boss," 272–273; Grassman, "Prologue to Reform," 519, 521; Young, *San Francisco,* II, 697–698; SF *Exam.,* 10 April 1881; SF *Chron.,* 22 Feb., 2 March 1884.

5. SF *Chron.,* 2, 12, 28 March, 1, 3, 19 April 1884; SF *Exam.,* 13, 22, 23, 28 March, 3, 4, 15 April 1884.

6. SF *Exam.,* 23 March 1884; SF *Chron.,* 1, 25 April, 20, 22, 24, 27 May 1884; SF *Newsletter,* 20 Sept., 25 Oct. 1884; SF *Wasp,* 1 Nov. 1884.

7. SF *Argonaut,* 7 July 1882.

8. See *Statutes of California, 1883–1890;* Davis, *Political Conventions,* 623; SF *Chron.,* 20 Jan., 2 March 1883; SF *Newsletter,* 20, 27 Jan. 1883; *Bancrofts Scraps* (BL) "San Francisco Charters," Vol. 69; White Papers, S. M. White to C. A. Buckley, 26 Nov. 1886, 13 July, 9 Nov. 1888, C. A. Buckley to S. M. White, 9 May 1888, 20 July 1889.

The scope of Buckley's activity as a political agent for the railroad is not clear, due principally to the lack of documentary evidence. There can be little doubt, despite Huntington's denial that he was acquainted with the boss, that Buckley was involved with the Southern Pacific and other corporations, but his precise role remains highly speculative. It is, moreover, apparent that the political influence of the railroad in California was neither as consistent nor as impregnable as it once was presumed to be. For clarification of this point, I am indebted to my colleague Professor Richard J. Orsi who has given me the benefit of his extensive research in Southern Pacific Company papers at Syracuse University and at the Huntington Library in San Marino, California. Also see Williams, *Democratic Party*, 169–172, 206–209, and passim; SF *Call*, 4 May, 27 Oct. 1894, 23 June, 1 Aug. 1899; "Martin Kelly's Story," 5 Sept. 1917.

9. Young, *San Francisco*, II, 697–699; Buckley, "Reminiscences," 13 Jan. 1919; Callow, "Blind Boss," 272–273; Grassman, "Prologue to Reform," 519–521; Dobie, *S. M. White*, 32–35, 41–42, 45–49; Williams, *Democratic Party*, 22–24, 50–51; SF *Call*, 21 June 1882, 2 Sept. 1886; SF *Newsletter*, 1 July 1882; Davis, *Political Conventions*, 431–437.

10. Williams, *Democratic Party*, 40–46; Dobie, *S. M. White*, 33–37, 41, 46, 49–51, 53, 70–80; Young, *San Francisco*, II, 697–698; Callow, "Blind Boss," 274; SF *Chron.*, 12 March, 1, 9, 10 April 1884; SF *Exam.*, 8, 10 March 9, 20 April, 16 May 1884; SF *Newsletter*, 24 March 1883, 22 March, 19 April 1884; SF *Argonaut*, 15 March 1884; SF *Bull.*, 31 March 1884.

11. Williams, *Democratic Party*, 18–27, 46–56, and passim; Dobie, *S. M. White*, 44–55, 104–105, and passim; Young, *San Francisco*, II, 697–698; Callow, "Blind Boss," 272–273; SF *Newsletter*, 1 July 1882; SF *Call*, 21 June 1882; Davis, *Political Conventions*, 431–438, 455–463; Buckley, "Reminiscences," 4 Jan. 1919.

Future reform mayor James D. Phelan attended the Stockton convention in support of the congressional candidacy of his close friend Frank Sullivan. It was probably at this time—partially as a consequence of Sullivan's rejection in favor of one of the Blind Boss's lambs—that he first became aware of Buckley's role in local politics and began to develop an animosity toward him. See James Phelan Correspondence (BL), James D. Phelan to James Phelan, 11, 14, 17 June 1884.

12. Buckley, "Reminiscences," 4, 16 Jan. 1919.

13. Williams, *Democratic Party*, 21–24, 50–51; "Martin Kelly's Story," 5, 7 Sept. 1917; Buckley, "Reminiscences," 30 Dec. 1918, 4, 6 Jan. 1919; Young, *San Francisco*, II, 526, 649–650; Callow, "Blind Boss," 274–275; Righter, "Washington Bartlett," 112; SF *Chron.*, 22 June, 10 Aug. 1884; SF *Exam.*, 23 May 1884.

14. Buckley, "Reminiscences," 4, 6 Jan. 1919; SF *Exam.*, 16 Feb., 8 April 1884; SF *Chron.*, 19 Jan., 16 Feb., 8 April, 31 Aug., 1 Oct. 1884; SF *Newsletter*, 2 Sept 1882, 6 Jan., 19 May 1883, 5 Jan. 1884; SF *Wasp*, 26 May 1884.

15. During the year prior to the opening of the 1884 campaign, Buckley moved from the Fifth Ward to the Western Addition, buried his father, and married Boston socialite Elizabeth Hurley.

16. See SF *Chron.*, 22 June, 10 Aug., 24 Sept. 1884; SF *Exam.*, 23 May 1884.

17. SF *Chron.*, 14, 15, 16 Oct. 1884; SF *Newsletter*, 25 Oct. 1884; SF *Wasp*, 1 Nov. 1884; SF *Alta*, 14, 15 Oct. 1884.

18. SF *Alta*, 28 Sept. 1884; SF *Bull.*, 4 Oct. 1884; SF *Chron.*, 28 Sept. 1884; Righter, "Washington Bartlett," 107.

19. SF *Newsletter,* 18, 25 Oct. 1884; SF *Chron.,* 19 Jan., 1, 2 Oct. 1884; Varcados, "Labor and Politics," 130–131; Cross (ed.), *Frank Roney,* 419–422; Heintz manuscript.
20. *SF Chron.,* 30 Sept., 1, 2, 3 Oct. 1884; SF *Alta,* 30 Sept., 1, 2, 3 Oct. 1884; SF *Exam.,* 30 Sept., 1, 2, 3 Oct. 1884.
21. Williams, *Democratic Party,* 51–56; SF *Chron.,* 7, 24 Oct. 1884; SF *Newsletter,* 7 June, 20 Sept., 11 Oct. 1884; SF *Circular,* 18 (October 1884): 10; Cross, *Labor Movement,* 145–150, 168–169; James D. Phelan Papers (BL), "Scrapbooks," Vol. 69; White Papers, S. M. White to B. Henley, 26 Dec. 1885, S. M. White to Editor SF *Exam.,* 10 Jan. 1885.
22. SF *Exam.,* 5, 7 Nov. 1884; SF *Chron.,* 5, 7, 8 Nov. 1884; SF *Alta,* 7, 16 Nov. 1884; SF *Bull.,* 7 Nov. 1884; "Martin Kelly's Story," 6 Sept. 1917; Bancroft, *History of California,* VII, 425–426; Williams, *Democratic Party,* 51–56; Buckley, "Reminiscences," 6 Jan. 1919; White Papers, S. M. White to B. Henley, 23 Nov. 1884.
23. Williams, *Democratic Party,* 51–56; Callow, "Blind Boss," 274–275; Varcados, "Labor and Politics," 26; California Society of Pioneers, *Washington Bartlett,* 29; Dobie, *S. M. White,* 52–55.
24. SF *Alta,* 6 Jan. 1885.
25. Buckley, "Reminiscences," 6, 20, 22 Jan. 1919.
26. Dobie, *S. M. White,* 55–60; Williams, *Democratic Party,* 57–63, 80–81; White Papers, S. M. White to W. D. English, 7 Feb., 30 Sept. 1885, S. M. White to D. M. Delmas, 14 Feb. 1885, S. M. White to B. Henley, 23 Nov. 1884, W. D. English to S. M. White, 10 Jan. 1885; SF *Call,* 21 April 1885; SF *Alta,* 22 April 1885; Sac. *Bee,* 1 March 1886; SF *Newsletter,* 19 June 1886; Buckley, "Reminiscences," 10 Jan. 1919; Bancroft, *History of California,* VII, 375, fn. 6; Davis, *Political Conventions,* 658; Weaverville (Calif.) *Trinity Journal* files; SF *Exam.,* 30 May 1886.
27. SF *Exam.,* 30 Sept. 1884; SF *Chron.,* 30 Sept. 1884; SF *Alta,* 30 Sept. 1884.
28. Buckley, "Reminiscences," 24 Dec. 1918, 13 Jan. 1919.
29. Liv. *Herald,* 25 Jan 1896; Alameda (Calif.) County Recorder, Index of Deeds, Number 28, entry number 6/8503; Buckley interviews. The Livermore sale was concluded on 8 April 1885 and recorded on 18 May 1885.
30. SF *Exam.,* 24 Oct. 1885; SF *Alta,* 24 Oct. 1885; SF *Chron.,* 23 Oct. 1885; Sac. *Bee,* 23 Oct. 1885.
31. San Francisco County Clerk, Probate File Number 34037; SF *Chron.,* 10 June 1886, 8 March 1888, 2 Nov. 1890, 9 Sept. 1894; SF *Alta,* 10 June 1886, 31 Jan. 1888; SF *Call,* 3 Sept. 1894, 24 July 1895, 3 Oct. 1897, 15 April, 15 Nov. 1902; Buckley interviews; Buckley, "Reminiscences," 28 Jan. 1919; *SFMR, 1887–88,* 121.
32. Bonnet *v.* City and County of San Francisco, 1 *Pacific* Reporter, 815; Parker *v.* City and County of San Francisco, 1 *Pacific Reporter,* 816; *In re* Buckley, 10 *Pacific Reporter,* 69–87; Supreme Court of the State of California,

"In the Matter of the Proceedings to Punish Christopher A. Buckley for Contempt." Transcript, Docket Number 20136 (California State Archive, Sacramento).

33. Superior Court of the State of California in and for the City and County of San Francisco, "Bonnet v. Taylor," Transcript (California State Archive, Sacramento), 35–36, 49; SF *Exam.*, 2, 13, 20 Sept., 11, 17 Oct. 1885; SF *Chron.*, 2, 3, 12, 20 Sept. 1885; Sac. *Bee,* 17 Oct. 1885; SF *Alta,* 21 Sept., 10, 17, Oct. 1885; SF *Newsletter,* 3 Oct. 1885.

34. *In re* Buckley, 69–87; "Proceedings to Punish Christopher A. Buckley," 34–52; Sac. *Bee,* 27 Oct. 1885; SF *Alta,* 21 Sept. 1885, 2 March 1886; SF *Chron.*, 3, 20 Sept., 27, 28 Oct. 1885, 4 March 1886; SF *Exam.*, 13, 20 Sept., 27, 28 Oct. 1885, 28 Feb. 1886; SF *Newsletter,* 21 Nov. 1885.

35. "Proceedings to Punish Christopher A. Buckley," 18–19, 122–123; SF *Chron.*, 4 March 1886; SF *Alta,* 2 March 1886; SF *Exam.*, 28 Feb. 1886; *In re* Cowdery, 10 *Pacific Reporter,* 47; *In re* Whittemore, 10 *Pacific Reporter,* 48.

36. Buckley, "Reminiscences," 7 Jan. 1919; "Martin Kelly's Story," 8 Sept. 1917; Ruef, "The Road I Traveled," 24, 25, 27 May 1912.

37. Buckley, "Reminiscences," 10 Jan. 1919.

38. Righter, "Washington Bartlett," 108–110; SF *Chron.*, 4, 13 Sept. 1886; SF *Newsletter,* 27 June 1885, 17 April 1886; SF *Bull.*, 24 Aug. 1886.

39. SF *Newsletter,* 4 July 1885; SF *Exam.*, 18 May, 20, 22 June 1886; SF *Chron.*, 8 Sept. 1885, 18 May 1886; SF *Bull.*, 24 Aug. 1886; Buckley, "Reminiscences," 14 Jan. 1919.

40. *SFMR, 1886–87,* 105–119; San Francisco Board of Supervisors, *Report of Professor George Davidson upon a System of Sewerage for the City of San Francisco* (San Francisco, 1886), 5–8, and passim; SF *Alta,* 5 May, 12 June, 2, 10, 30 July, 22 Aug. 1886; SF *Chron.*, 1 May, 18, 21 June, 13 July, 22 Aug. 1886; SF *Exam.*, 1 May, 9 July, 22 Aug. 1886.

41. Young, *San Francisco,* II, 516; "Martin Kelly's Story," 7 Sept. 1917; Righter, "Washington Bartlett," 108; SF *Exam.*, 26, 27 Oct. 1885, 18, 27, 30 April, 4, 16 May, 9 June, 7 July 1886; SF *Alta,* 21 Oct. 1885, 9 June, 8 July 1886; SF *Chron.*, 14, 15, 22, 29 Sept. 1885, 9, 13, 20, 29 April, 13 May, 3, 9 June, 1, 8, 15 July 1886; SF *Newsletter,* 19 April 1884, 20 June 1885, 19 June, 18 Sept. 1886; Sac. *Bee,* 10 Oct. 1885.

42. "Martin Kelly's Story," 5, 8 Sept. 1917; Ruef, "The Road I Traveled," 6 April, 24, 25, 27 May 1912; Buckley, "Reminiscences," 7, 10 Jan. 1919; Williams, *Democratic Party,* 103–105; Dobie, *S. M. White,* 75–77; Bean, *Boss Ruef,* 2–5, and passim; SF *Chron.*, 18, 19 Feb. 1886; SF *Exam.*, 27 Feb. 1886; SF *Newsletter,* 7 Oct. 1885.

43. Ruef, "The Road I Traveled," 24 May 1912; "Martin Kelly's Story," 8 Sept. 1917; Bean, *Boss Ruef,* 3–4; SF *Exam.*, 23, 27 March, 2, 3, 6, 27 April 1886; SF *Alta,* 3, 6, 9, 10, 16 April, 8, 12, 27 May 1886; SF *Chron.*, 6, 8, 13, 14, 25, 27 April, 8, 12 May 1886.

44. "Martin Kelly's Story," 8 Sept. 1917; Buckley, "Reminiscences," 7 Jan. 1919; Ruef, "The Road I Traveled," 22, 23, 25, 27 May 1912; SF *Chron.,* 18 Feb., 25 July, 7 Aug., 14, 15, 16, 21 Sept. 1886; SF *Exam.,* 9, 10, 24 July, 7, 14, 15 Aug. 1886; SF *Alta,* 5 June, 10 July, 7, 12, 13, 15, 22, 23 Aug., 14, 15, 16, 22, 24, 25 Sept., 7 Oct. 1886.

45. John Higham, "American Party," 37–46; Cross, *Labor Movement,* 168–189; Saxton, *Indispensable Enemy,* 205–213, 219–228; SF *Chron.,* 6 July 1886; SF *Exam.,* 6 July 1886; SF *Alta,* 8 July 1886.

46. Higham, "American Party," 39; Williams, *Democratic Party,* 104; Davis, *Political Conventions,* 526–533.

47. Higham, "American Party," 40–43; Buckley, "Reminiscences," 10 Jan. 1919; SF *Chron.,* 30 Oct., 4, 7 Nov. 1886; SF *Exam.,* 13 Sept., 6, 7 Nov. 1886; SF *Alta,* 30 Oct., 5, 6, 7, Nov. 1886; SF *Call,* 6 Nov. 1886.

48. SF *Alta,* 4 April 1886; SF *Chron.,* 27 April, 4 May 1886; SF *Exam.,* 21 April, 4 May 1886.

49. SF *Alta,* 8, 11, 19 May, 4 June 1886; SF *Chron.,* 8, 12, 19 May, 4 June 1886; SF *Exam.,* 11, 12, 19, 26, 30 May, 4 June 1886.

50. SF *Exam.,* 18, 26, 30 May 1886; SF *Alta,* 25 May, 10 June, 3 July 1886; SF *Chron.,* 19, 25 May, 4, 10 June 1886; Davis, *Political Conventions,* 321, 361, 364, 415, 422; SF *Newsletter,* 12, 26 June 1886.

51. SF *Exam.,* 8, 10, 13, 18, 21, 22 July 1886; SF *Alta,* 15, 17, 18, 22 July 1886; SF *Chron.,* 15, 22 July 1886; SF *Newsletter,* 24 July 1886.

52. SF *Alta,* 23, 24, 29, 31 July, 12 Aug. 1886; SF *Exam.,* 10, 24, 30, 31 July, 1, 5 Aug. 1886; SF *Chron.,* 25, 29, 30 July, 1, 5, 12 Aug. 1886.

53. SF *Alta,* 12, 13, 14, 20, 23, 24 Aug. 1886; SF *Chron.,* 12, 13, 15, 20, 27 Aug. 1886; SF *Exam.,* 13, 20, 22, 27 Aug. 1886.

54. SF *Alta,* 27, 28, 30 Aug.; 1 Sept. 1886; SF *Chron.,* 31 Aug., 1 Sept. 1886.

55. SF *Chron.,* 19, 28 Aug. 1886; SF *Alta,* 19, 27 Aug. 1886.

56. Williams, *Democratic Party,* 107; Dobie, *S. M. White,* 70.

57. Williams, *Democratic Party,* 23, 94–96, 101–103, 106–108; Dobie, *S. M. White,* 75; White Papers, W. D. English to S. M. White, 22 Sept. 1885, S. M. White to W. D. English, 18 Feb. 1886.

58. Williams, *Democratic Party,* 101–103, 105, 108–109; Dobie, *S. M. White,* 64–65; 67–74; Crassman, "Prologue to Reform," 522; Davis, *Political Conventions,* 518–524; White Papers, S. M. White to D. M. Delmas, 23 March 1886, S. M. White to G. Stoneman, 16 March 1886, S. M. White to W. D. English, 18 Feb., 26 Nov. 1886.

59. Buckley, "Reminiscences," 14 Jan. 1919.

60. Petersen, "Struggle for the Australian Ballot," 229; Cross, *Labor Movement,* 186; SF *Alta,* 3, 8, 21, 25 Sept., 1, 8, 9 Oct. 1886; SF *Chron.,* 7, 21, 25 Sept., 9, 14 Oct. 1886; SF *Exam.,* 9 Oct. 1886; SF *Newsletter,* 25 Sept., 2 Oct. 1886.

61. SF *Chron.,* 16, 22, 25 Sept. 1886; SF *Alta* 22, 25 Sept., 24, 30 Oct. 1886; SF *Exam.,* 25 Sept., 13 Oct. 1886.
62. SF *Chron.,* 3, 5, 6, 7 Oct. 1886, 23 April 1890; SF *Alta,* 3, 5, 7, 8, 17 Oct. 1886; SF *Exam.,* 3, 5, 6, 7, 8, 9, 10, 13 Oct. 1886; Varcados, "Labor and Politics," 137–138; Davis, *Political Conventions,* 611, 637, 649, 654.
63. Varcados, "Labor and Politics," 137–138; SF *Exam.,* 17 Oct. 1886; SF *Chron.,* 18 Feb., 4, 21 Sept., 14, 29 Oct., 2 Nov. 1886; SF *Alta,* 9, 14, 29 Oct., 2 Nov. 1886.
64. SF *Exam.,* 3, 6 Nov. 1886; SF *Alta,* 3, 4, 5, 6, 7 Nov. 1886; SF *Chron.,* 13 Oct., 4, 5, 7, 14, 18, 19, 20, 21, 23 Nov. 1886; SF *Call,* 18 Nov. 1886; Williams, *Democratic Party,* 105; Davis, *Political Conventions,* 532–533; *SFMR, 1886–87* 434; Callow, "Blind Boss," 275; Varcados, "Labor and Politics," 145–146; White Papers, S. M. White to W. D. English, n.d. [Nov. 1886], 22 Nov. 1886.

CHAPTER EIGHT

1. SF *Call,* 18 Nov. 1886, 31 July 1887; SF *Alta,* 31 July 1887; Springfield (Mass.) *Republican,* 18 June 1887; Buckley, "Reminiscences," 16 Jan. 1919; Buckley interviews.
2. Buckley, "Reminiscences," 13 Jan. 1919.
3. Williams, *Democratic Party,* 107; Dobie, *S. M. White,* 77, 88–89, 98–99; *JCS, 1887,* 27th Sess., 41–42; SF *Exam.,* 7 Nov. 1886; SF *Alta,* 9 April, 4, 7 Nov. 1886; *SFMR, 1886–87,* 101; Grassman, "Prologue to Reform," 523–525, 527–528.
4. Williams, *Democratic Party,* 65, 107–108; Dobie, *S. M. White,* 62–67; SF *Alta,* 6, 15 April 1885; White Papers, S. M. White to B. Henley, 23 Nov. 1884, 29 Sept. 1890, S. M. White to W. D. English, 18 Feb., 26 Nov. 1886, S. M. White to G. Stoneman, 16 March 1886, S. M. White to D. M. Delmas, 23 March 1886.
5. Swanberg, *Citizen Hearst,* 3–7, 26–27, 43–48, Lundberg, *Imperial Hearst,* 21, 28. Tweed quoted in Callow, *Tweed Ring,* 254.
6. Swanstrom, "Reform Administration of Phelan," 23–28, and passim; Starr, *California Dream,* 249; Muscatine, *Old San Francisco,* 405; Grassman, "Prologue to Reform," 527–528; SF *Alta,* 1 Nov. 1884, 14 April 1887; Petersen, "Struggle for the Australian Ballot," 230–231; James Phelan Correspondence (BL), J. D. Phelan to J. Phelan, 11 June 1884; James D. Phelan Papers (BL), "Scrapbooks," Vol. 69; White Papers, S. M. White to W. D. English, 25 Sept. 1887; Williams, *Democratic Party,* 105, 153; Dobie, *S. M. White,* 86, 91–96.
7. Righter, "Washington Bartlett," 102–103, 110–112; *SFMR, 1882–83,* 136–139; *SFMR, 1886–87,* 131; SF *Exam.,* 23 Jan. 1880; SF *Alta,* 4 Jan. 1887; SF *Chron.,* 11 Feb., 24 July 1879, 9 Sept. 1880; SF *Bull.,* 10 Dec. 1879, 9 Sept. 1880; SF *Call,* 10 Dec. 1879, 20 May 1880; *Bancroft Scraps*

(BL), "San Francisco Charter," Vol. 69; Bancroft, *History of California,* VII, 413; John P. Young, *Journalism in California* (San Francisco, 1915), 161–162.

8. Heintz, *San Francisco's Mayors,* 81; Righter, "Washington Bartlett," 102; Young, *San Francisco* II, 561; SF *Alta,* 25 March 1874; SF *Bull.,* 18 Jan. 1876, 10 Dec. 1879; SF *Newsletter,* 22 May 1886.

9. Buckley, "Reminiscences," 23 Dec. 1918, 24 Jan. 1919.

10. Petersen, "Struggle for the Australian Ballot," 230–231, and passim; Grassman, "Prologue to Reform" 520–521, and passim; SF *Exam.,* 23 Jan. 1880, 6, 15, 17, 18 Oct. 1882, 10, 12, 13, 16 Jan., 3 Feb. 1883; SF *Call,* 10 Dec. 1879, 20 May 1880; SF *Bull.,* 18 Jan. 1876, 10 Dec. 1879, 10 Jan. 1883; SF *Chron.,* 11 Feb., 24 July 1879, 6 Oct. 1882, 19 May, 13 Sept., 22 Oct., 16 Nov. 1886; SF *Newsletter,* 10 March 1882, 6, 13 Jan 1883, 22 May, 18 Sept. 1886; SF *Alta,* 25 March 1874, 15, 18 Oct. 1882, 2 March 1883, 19 May, 12 Sept., 22 Oct. 1886; *SFMR, 1882–83,* 136–139; *SFMR, 1886–87,* 129–131; *Bancroft Scraps* (BL) "San Francisco Charter," Vol. 69; Young, *Journalism in California,* 16; Blackmar, "San Francisco's Struggle for Good Government," 566–568.

11. Ibid.

12. *SFMR, 1882–83,* 136–138; *SFMR, 1886–87,* 129–131; Righter, "Washington Bartlett," 103; Bancroft, *History of California,* VII, 413–414; Young, *Journalism in California,* 162; Young, *San Francisco,* II, 561.

13. SF *Exam.,* 13, 16 Jan. 1883; SF *Wasp,* 3 Feb., 3 March 1883; SF *Alta,* 14 April 1887; Blackmar, "San Francisco's Struggle for Good Government," 568.

Allegedly, the proposed charter of 1887 was the product of a Buckley-Higgins conspiracy and for this reason Hearst directed *Examiner* editorial policy against it, thereby ensuring its defeat. This seems unlikely in view of Buckley's subsequent actions and the recency of Hearst's acquisition of the newspaper.

14. SF *Chron.,* 24 July 1879, 13 Sept. 1886; SF *Exam.,* 12, 13, 16 Jan. 1883; SF *Alta,* 2 March 1883; Blackmar, "San Francisco's Struggle for Good Government," 566; Righter, "Washington Bartlett," 103, 108, 110, 112; Young, *Journalism in California,* 161–162; Young, *San Francisco,* II, 556, 561; *Bancroft Scraps* (BL), "San Francisco Charter," Vol. 69.

15. Barth, *Instant Cities,* 131, 135; Bion J. Arnold, *Report on the Improvement and Development of the Transportation Facilities of San Francisco* (San Francisco, 1913), 83–92; *Historical Souvenir of San Francisco,* 28–29; *SFMR, 1887–88,* 220–238; Grassman, "Prologue to Reform," 520; Buckley, "Reminiscences," 25 Dec. 1918; SF *Alta,* 17 July 1888; SF *Chron.,* 17, 19 Jan., 17 July 1888; SF *Exam.,* 1 Jan. 1886, 17 July 1888, 15 April 1890; U.S. Bureau of the Census, *Tenth Census of the United States, 1880,* I, 471, 536–540; U.S. Bureau of the Census, *Eleventh Census of the United States, 1890,* I, xcii-xciii, cli.

16. Cross, *Labor Movement,* 181–195; Saxton, *Indispensable Enemy,* 213–228.

17. SF *Alta,* 13, 16 July 1887, 4, 28 Feb., 3, 4, 6 April, 8, 12 May, 8

June, 1, 17, 22, 24 July, 10 Sept. 1888; SF *Chron.,* 10, 17, 19 Jan., 1, 22, 28 Feb., 6 March, 13 April, 10 Sept. 1888; SF *Exam.,* 1 Jan. 1887, 10 Jan., 3, 28 Feb., 6 March, 3, 4, 10 May, 1, 17, 24, 27 July, 10 Sept. 1888; SF *Argonaut,* 10 March 1888; *SFMR, 1887–88,* 220–238.

18. SF *Exam.,* 19 Jan., 1, 3, 4, 5 Feb., 29 April, 19 May, 11, 24 July, 27 Sept., 20 Oct. 1888; SF *Chron.,* 1 Jan., 7 March, 19 May, 24 July, 27 Sept., 20 Oct. 1888; SF *Alta,* 20 April, 12 July 1887, 6, 31 Jan., 4 Feb., 3 April, 1 June, 1, 11, 24 July, 22, 27 Sept. 1888; SF *Call,* 28 April 1887; SF *Weekly Star,* 23 July 1887.

19. *SFMR, 1887–88,* 467–468; *SFMR, 1888–89,* 323–324; SF *Chron.,* 2, 8 Feb. 1888.

20. *SFMR, 1887–88,* 467–472; *SFMR, 1888–89,* 323–324; SF *Wasp,* 28 Jan. 1888; SF *Chron.,* 5, 12, 15 Jan. 1888; SF *Alta,* 1, 3, 4, 11, 12, 20, 25, 26, 28 Jan. 1888; SF *Exam.,* 5 Jan., 1 Feb. 1888.

21. SF *Alta,* 1, 11, 12, 20, 25, 26, 28 Jan., 8 Feb. 1888; SF *Chron.,* 12, 16, 24 Jan. 1888; SF *Exam.,* 20, 21 Jan. 1888; SF *Wasp,* 28 Jan. 1888.

22. SF *Alta,* 3, 4, 9, 20, 25, 26, 28 Jan. 1888; SF *Exam.,* 5, 14, Jan., 1 Feb. 1888; SF *Chron.,* 5, 15 Jan. 1888.

23. SF *Chron.,* 5, 16, 25, 26 Jan., 8, 9, 11 Feb., 7 March 1888; SF *Alta,* 14, 20, 25, 26, 28 Jan., 30 April 1888; SF *Exam.,* 14 Jan., 8 Feb., 7 April 1888.

24. *SFMR, 1887–88,* 467–472; *SFMR, 1888–89,* 323–324; SF *Exam.,* 8, 27, 31 Jan., 10 Feb., 27 Oct. 1888; SF *Alta,* 31 Jan., 11 Feb. 1888; SF *Chron.,* 7, 16, 17 March 1888.

25. Sam Bass Warner, Jr., *The Private City* (Philadelphia, 1968), 3–4, 205.

26. Arnold, *Transportation Facilities,* 418–425; *SFMR, 1891–92,* 281–288; Buckley, "Reminiscences," 24 Dec. 1918; 13 Jan. 1919; Callow, "Blind Boss," 269; "Martin Kelly's Story," 7, 11, 13, 19, 20, 22, 24 Sept. 1917; Young, *San Francisco,* II, 557; Nash, *State Government and Economic Development,* 177–181; James D. Phelan Papers (BL), "Scrapbooks," Vols. 68–69; SF *Exam.,* 29 Oct. 1888.

27. San Francisco Board of Supervisors, *System of Sewerage,* Buckley, "Reminiscences," 16 Jan. 1919; *SFMR, 1887–88,* 220–238; SF *Chron.,* 10 Jan., 6, 7 March, 16 May, 17 July, 27 Sept. 1888; SF *Exam.,* 1, 10 Jan., 28 Feb., 6 March, 28, 29 April, 27 Sept. 1888; SF *Alta,* 4, 28 Feb., 3 April, 1, 8 June, 11, 13 July 1888.

28. Democratic Party, *Plan for Reorganization,* 3; SF *Call,* 13 Dec. 1895; SF *Chron.,* 15 Jan., 3 April 1888; SF *Alta,* 23 Feb., 3 April, 15 Aug. 1888; SF *Exam.,* 9 March, 3 April, 15 Aug., 27 Sept. 1888.

29. SF *Call,* 13 Dec. 1895; SF *Alta,* 20 March, 3, 31 Aug. 1888; SF *Chron.,* 31 Aug. 1888.

30. SF *Alta,* 21 April 1887, 16, 20 March, 23 Aug. 1888; SF *Exam.,* 9, 17 March, 11 April, 4 July 1888; SF *Chron.,* 9, 16 March, 23 Aug. 1888.

31. SF *Chron.*, 21 Aug. 1888; SF *Alta*, 2, 31 Oct. 1888; SF *Exam.*, 4 July, 21 Aug., 12, 27, 28 Sept. 1888.

32. SF *Exam.*, 22 Feb., 1, 9 March, 11 April, 3, 4 July 1888; SF *Alta*, 22, 23 Feb., 7 March 1888.

33. SF *Chron.*, 22, 23 Feb., 3 April 1888; SF *Alta*, 3 April 1888; SF *Exam.*, 7, 24 Jan., 3 Feb., 16 March, 3 April 1888.

34. SF *Alta*, 10 Feb., 28 March 1888; SF *Exam.*, 7, 31 Jan., 10 Feb., 28 March 1888; SF *Chron.*, 7 Jan., 1, 10 Feb., 28 March 1888.

35. SF *Exam.*, 4, 11, 12, 13, 17, 21, 22, 26, 27, 28 April, 3, 9 May 1888; SF *Alta*, 4, 7, 11, 12, 13, 17, 21, 22, 26, 27, 28 April, 3, 9 May 1888; SF *Chron.*, 4, 11, 12, 18, 21, 26, 27 April, 9 May 1888.

36. White Papers, C. A. Buckley to S. M. White, 9, 11 May 1888, S. M. White to C. A. Buckley, 9, 10 May 1888, S. M. White to H. Schwartz, 11 May 1888; LA *Times*, 10, 12, 14, 15, 19, 25 May 1888; SF *Exam.*, 19 May 1888; SF *Chron.*, 10 May 1888; SF *Alta*, 10 May 1888; SF *Post*, 10 May 1888; Dobie, *S. M. White*, 88.

37. SF *Post*, 10 May 1888.

38. Williams, *Democratic Party*, 92, 113–116, 124–125, 127; Dobie, *S. M. White*, 88–89; Grassman, "Prologue to Reform," 522–523, 525; White Papers, S. M. White to J. F. Sullivan, 8 Nov. 1888.

39. Dobie, *S. M. White*, 81–82; Williams, *Democratic Party*, 113–116, 127–128; White Papers, S. M. White to W. D. English, 30 Sept. 1885; SF *Exam.*, 7 Dec. 1887; SF *Chron.*, 11 Jan. 1888.

40. Williams, *Democratic Party*, 120–124; White Papers, S. M. White to W. D. English, 18 Sept. 1888; SF *Exam.*, 26 June, 21 Aug., 6 Sept., 2 Oct. 1888; SF *Alta*, 2 Oct. 1888; SF *Chron.*, 24 June, 2 Oct. 1888.

41. LA *Times*, 14 May 1888.

42. Ibid., 14, 15 May 1888; SF *Alta*, 14, 15 May 1888; Williams, *Democratic Party*, 117–118; Dobie, *S. M. White*, 87–89; Davis, 543–544.

43. Davis, *Political Conventions*, 543–546.

44. Ibid., 546–547; SF *Exam.*, 13, 16, 17, 18 May 1888; LA *Times*, 16, 17, 18 May 1888; SF *Alta*, 16, 17, 18 May 1888; SF *Chron.*, 17, 18 May 1888; Dobie, S. M. White, 85–86.

45. White did not sever his connections with the Southern Pacific until October 1889, after he had served nearly two years in the state senate. See White Papers, S. M. White to C. Haymond, 8 Dec. 1883, 18 March 1887, 27 July 1888, 17 Aug. 1889; Dobie, *S. M. White*, 102; Williams, *Democratic Party*, 108–109.

46. Young, *San Francisco*, II, 699.

47. Williams, *Democratic Party*, 108; Grassman, "Prologue to Reform," 524–526; Dobie, *S. M. White*, 88–89, 98–99.

48. Dobie, *S. M. White*, 87; White Papers, S. M. White to W. D. English, 8 Dec. 1888.

49. LA *Times*, 16 May 1888; SF *Chron.*, 17 May 1888; Dobie, *S. M. White*, 85–86.

50. Buckley, "Reminiscences," 1 Feb. 1919.

51. U.S. Bureau of the Census, *Population Schedules, 1880*, San Francisco City, Ward Eight, Roll 75, Enumeration District 83, p. 24; SF *Directories, 1880–1890*, passim; SF *Exam.*, 21 Aug. 1891; SF *Chron.*, 23 Aug. 1891, 8 June 1917; Young, *Journalism in California*, 289–290; Dobie, *S. M. White*, 138.
Lynch's works include *Egyptian Sketches* (New York, 1890); *The Life of David C. Broderick, a Senator of the Fifties* (New York, 1911); and *Three Years in the Klondike* (London, 1904).

52. Buckley, "Reminiscences," 1, 3 Feb. 1919; Dobie, *S. M. White*, 138; Davis, *Political Conventions*, 546.

53. Lynch, *Buckleyism;* SF *Exam.*, 11 April 1889, 21 Aug. 1891; SF *Chron.*, 23 Aug. 1891; Williams, *Democratic Party*, 151–152; Leake, "King Mazuma," 17, 18, April 1917; Bullough, "Hannibal versus the Blind Boss," 187–191.

54. SF *Alta*, 20 April, 16 July 1887, 6, 31 Jan., 1, 24, July, 22, 27 Sept. 1888; SF *Chron.*, 1 Jan., 22, 28 Feb., 8 March, 19 May, 24 July 1888; SF *Exam.*, 1, 3 Feb., 28 April, 1, 11, 24 July, 20 Oct. 1888; SF *Call*, 28 April 1888; SF *Weekly Star*, 23 July 1887; SF *Argonaut*, 10 March 1888; Buckley, "Reminiscences," 13 Jan. 1919.

55. Buckley, "Reminiscences," 16, 24, 31 Jan. 1919.

56. SF *Chron.*, 15 Jan., 31 Aug. 1888; SF *Alta*, 22, 23 Feb., 3 Aug. 1888; SF *Exam.*, 22 Feb., 9 March 1888.

57. SF *Alta*, 18, 19, 20, 24 July, 4, 12 Aug. 1888; SF *Exam.*, 4 July, 4, 12 Aug. 1888; SF *Chron.*, 19 July, 2, 4 Aug. 1888; Williams, *Democratic Party*, 116–118; Dobie, *S. M. White*, 86–87.

58. SF *Alta*, 5 Aug. 1888; SF *Exam.*, 5 Aug. 1888; SF *Chron.*, 5 Aug. 1888.

59. SF *Alta*, 2, 4, 7, 9, 10, 15, 16 Aug., 31 Oct., 1 Nov. 1888; SF *Exam.*, 2, 7, 15 Aug., 8 Sept., 29 Oct., 1 Nov. 1888; SF *Chron.*, 2 Aug. 1888; Cross, *Labor Movement*, 191–197; Cross (ed.), *Frank Roney*, 521.

60. SF *Exam.*, 26 Aug. 1888; SF *Chron.*, 26 Aug. 1888; SF *Alta*, 26 Aug. 1888.

61. SF *Exam.*, 19, 27 April 1888; SF *Chron.*, 20, 27 March, 19, 26 April 1888; SF *Alta*, 4, 27 March, 19, 27 April 1888.

62. LA *Times*, 5 May 1888; SF *Chron.*, 2 July, 12, 23, 28, 29 Sept. 1888; SF *Alta*, 5 May, 7, 12, 28, 29, 30 Sept. 1888; SF *Exam.*, 5 May, 10 July, 7, 12, 28, 29, 30 Sept. 1888.

63. Davis, *Political Conventions*, 537–542, 550–551; SF *Alta*, 9 Oct. 1888; SF *Chron.*, 9 Oct. 1888; SF *Exam.*, 28 Sept., 9, 13, Oct., 1 Nov. 1888.

64. SF *Chron.*, 27 July 1888; SF *Exam.*, 3 July, 16 Aug. 1888; SF *Alta*, 5, 27, 31 July, 16 Aug. 1888; SF *Argonaut*, 17 March, 3, 10 Sept., 29 Oct.

1888; Davis, *Political Conventions,* 547–550; Higham, "American Party," 42–45.

65. SF *Alta,* 23 Aug. 1888.

66. Ibid., 11, 18, 19, 24 Oct. 1888; SF *Exam.,* 9, 17, 18, 19 Oct. 1888; SF *Argonaut,* 29 Oct. 1888.

Independents attempted to nominate a slate of municipal candidates by fusing with Nonpartisans, the Citizens' League, the Public School Reform Association, the Union party, and even the American party, but without success. Phelan apparently returned to Democratic ranks early in the campaign.

67. SF *Chron.,* 6, 22, 29 Sept. 1888; SF *Exam.,* 31 Aug., 1, 6, 12, 25, 20 Sept., 3 Oct. 1888; SF *Alta,* 6, 7, 13, 23, 30 Sept. 1888.

68. SF *Chron.,* 5, 6, 9, 10, 11 Oct. 1888; SF *Alta,* 6, 9, 10, 11 Oct. 1888; SF *Exam.,* 6, 9, 11 Oct. 1888; SF *Directory, 1888,* passim.

69. SF *Alta,* 3, 8, 9 Nov. 1888; SF *Exam.,* 3, 7, 8, 9, 10 Nov. 1888; SF *Chron.,* 18 Oct., 8, 9, 10 Nov. 1888; SF *Argonaut,* 12 Nov. 1888; Williams, *Democratic Party,* 126–127; Davis, *Political Conventions,* 552–553; Buckley, "Reminiscences," 17, 20 Jan. 1919.

70. SF *Alta,* 8, 9 Nov. 1888; SF *Exam.,* 8, 9, 10 Nov. 1888; SF *Chron.,* 8, 9, 10 Nov. 1888; SF *Argonaut,* 12 Nov. 1888; Williams, *Democratic Party,* 128–129; Dobie, *S. M. White,* 88, 251; White Papers, S. M. White to W. D. English, 21 Sept. 1888, S. M. White to C. A. Buckley, 9 Nov. 1888, C. A. Buckley to S. M. White, 9, 28 Nov. 1888; S. M. White to A. Caminetti, 16 Nov. 1888; S. M. White to A. F. Jones, 13 Nov. 1888.

71. SF Chron., 22 Sept. 1888; SF *Exam.,* 4 May, 13, 29, 31 Oct., 8, 9 Nov. 1888; SF *Alta,* 3 April, 4 May, 16 Aug., 11, 19 Oct., 9 Nov. 1888; Williams, *Democratic Party,* 127–130.

72. Buckley, "Reminiscences," 20 Jan. 1919.

CHAPTER NINE

1. SF *Exam.,* 8 July 1890; SF *Call,* 24 July, 13 Dec. 1895; *Handy Block-Book of San Francisco* (San Francisco, 1894), 55.

2. SF *Exam.,* 3, 4 April 1888, 9 July 1890; SF *Alta,* 3, 4 April, 23 Aug. 1888; Springfield (Mass.) *Republican,* 18 June 1887; SF *Chron.,* 3, 4 April 1888; SF *Call,* 28 Feb. 1894; SF *Wave,* 11 July 1891; Liv. *Echo,* 29 Aug., 5 Sept., 17 Oct., 21 Nov., 5 Dec. 1889, 1 Jan., 13 Feb., 9 Oct. 1890.

3. SF *Exam.,* 9 July 1890; Buckley, "Reminiscences," 9 Oct. 1918, 20 Jan. 1919; White Papers, S. M. White to W. D. English, 12 July 1890, emphasis in the original.

4. Lynch, *Buckleyism,* 17–21, 27–29, and passim; SF *Exam.,* 11 April 1889; Lundberg, *Imperial Hearst,* 28–29; Swanberg, *Citizen Hearst,* 48–50; SF *Alta,* 4, 14 Oct. 1888; SF *Chron.,* 4 Oct. 1888.

5. SF *Exam.,* 27 June, 8 July, 10 Oct. 1890.

6. SF *Bull.,* 7 May 1889.

7. SF *Wave,* 2 Aug. 1890; SF *Exam.,* 27 June 1890; SF *Chron.,* 26, 27 June, 5 Aug., 17 Oct. 1890.

8. SF *Chron.,* 21 Dec. 1889; SF *Exam.,* 20 Dec. 1889, 17 June 1890; SF *Call,* 17 June 1890; SF *Alta,* 17 June 1890; Commonwealth of Massachusetts, Registry of Vital Records and Statistics, *Records of Marriage, 1890,* Vol. 408, p. 179.

9. SF *Exam.,* 27 May, 17, 25, 20, 27 June 1890; SF *Chron.,* 26, 27 June 1890; SF *Alta,* 27 May, 17 June 1890.

10. SF *Exam.,* 6, 8, 10, June 1890; SF *Chron.,* 6, 7, 10 June 1890; SF *Alta,* 7, 8, 12, 13 June 1890.

11. SF *Chron.,* 5 Aug., 17 Oct. 1890.

12. Ibid., 15 May 1890; SF *Alta,* 7, 11 May 1889; 15 May 1890; SF *Argonaut,* 6 Jan. 1890; *SFMR, 1888–89,* 226–268; *SFMR, 1889–90,* 205–232.

13. SF *Alta,* 6 June 1890; SF *Exam.,* 6, 7 June 1890; SF *Bull.,* 7 May 1889.

14. SF *Chron.,* 29 April, 14, 22, May, 5 June 1890; SF *Exam.,* 2, 8, 14, 22 May 1890; SF *Alta,* 29 April, 2, 7, 8, 22 May, 5 June 1890.

15. SF *Exam.,* 21 May 1890; SF *Alta,* 21 May 1890; SF *Chron.,* 21 May 1890.

16. SF *Chron.,* 13, 14, 16, 17 Aug. 1890; SF *Alta,* 2, 3, Aug. 1890; SF *Wave,* 2 Aug. 1890; White Papers, C. A. Buckley to S. M. White, [?] April 1890. Buckley and White remained on overtly cordial terms; see C. A. Buckley to S. M. White, 20 July 1889.

17. Williams, *Democratic Party,* 140–143; Oscar Lewis, *The Big Four* (New York, 1938), 188–191; SF *Exam.,* 10, 12, 13 April, 19 Oct. 1890; SF *Argonaut,* 19 May, 2 June, 29 Sept. 1890; SF *Chron.,* 10, 11, 12 April 1890; SF *Alta,* 10 April 1890; Bean, *California,* 300.

18. White Papers, S. M. White to W. D. English, 13 April 1890; Williams, *Democratic Party,* 143.

19. White Papers, S. M. White to W. D. English, 15 Sept. 1889.

20. Ibid., 25 May 1890; SF *Exam.,* 7, 18 Oct. 1890.

21. Williams, *Democratic Party,* 144–145; Dobie, *S. M. White,* 113–115; SF *Argonaut,* 16 June 1890; SF *Exam.,* 19, 20 Aug. 1890; SF *Chron.,* 19 Aug. 1890.

22. Williams, *Democratic Party,* 135–140; Harold E. Taggart, "Thomas Vincent Cator: Populist Leader of California," *CHQ,* 27 (December 1948): 311–318; 28 (March 1949): 47–55; Donald E. Walters, "The Feud between California Populist T. V Cator and Democrats James Maguire and James Barry," *PHR,* 27 (August 1958): 283–285, 287; Cross, *Labor Movement,* 201–209; Varcados, "Labor and Politics," 98–142; SF *Chron.,* 10 April 1890.

23. SF *Alta,* 17, 19, 20, 21 Aug. 1890; SF *Chron.,* 19, 20, 21 Aug. 1890; SF *Exam.,* 19, 20, 21 Aug. 1890; Davis, *Political Conventions,* 565–570; Dobie, *S. M. White,* 113–115; Petersen, "Struggle for the Australian Ballot," 232.

24. White Papers, S. M. White to W. D. English, 25 May 1890; SF *Alta,* 16 Aug. 1890; SF *Exam.,* 29 May 1890; Dobie, *S. M. White,* 115.

25. SF *Chron.,* 22 Aug. 1890; SF *Alta,* 22 Aug., 1890; SF *Exam.,* 22 Aug. 1890; Davis, *Political Conventions,* 568–569; Dobie, *S. M. White,* 114–115.

26. SF *Newsletter,* 22 March 1884; SF *Exam.,* 10 March 1884; SF *Chron.,* 12 March 1884; SF *Argonaut,* 15 March 1884; SF *Bull.,* 31 March 1884; Dobie, *S. M. White,* 41; Davis, *Political Conventions,* 660.

27. SF *Exam.,* 16, 19, 22, 23 Aug. 1890; SF *Alta,* 16, 23 Aug. 1890; SF *Chron.,* 17, 23 Aug. 1890; SF *Call,* 26, 28 Aug. 1890; Davis, *Political Conventions,* 569; Buckley, "Reminiscences," 1 Feb. 1919.

28. Dobie, *S. M. White,* 114–115, 123; Buckley, "Reminiscences," 1 Feb. 1919; SF *Call,* 21, 22, 23 Aug. 1890.

29. SF *Exam.,* 29 Dec. 1927; SF *Bull.,* 28 Dec. 1927; SF *Chron.,* 4 Oct. 1895; Callow, "Blind Boss," 277.

30. Dobie, *S. M. White,* 115; Williams, *Democratic Party,* 149–150; Callow, "Blind Boss," 277; SF *Exam.,* 24 Aug. 1890; SF *Argonaut,* 22 Sept. 1890; SF *Alta,* 16, 27 July 1890; Petersen, "Struggle for the Australian Ballot," 230–231.

Officers of the Reform Democracy included James D. Phelan, Thomas F. Barry, James M. McDonald, George Faylor, A. J. Donovan, Joseph Leggett, Dr. R. Beverly Cole, J. W. Craig, and Dr. C. D. Cleaveland. Barry, McDonald, Faylor, Craig, and Cleaveland had previous ties to Buckley.

31. SF *Alta,* 16 July, 5 Aug. 1890; SF *Exam.,* 16, 25, 27 July 1890; SF *Chron.,* 16, 27 July 1890.

32. SF *Argonaut,* 22 Sept. 1890; SF *Chron.,* 22, 23, 24, 25, 30 Sept. 1890; SF *Exam.,* 22, 23, 24, 25, 30 Sept. 1890; SF *Alta,* 23, 24, 25, 29 Sept. 1890; Democratic Party, *Regular (Reform) Democratic Party of the City and County of San Francisco Platform* (San Francisco, 1890).

33. SF *Chron.,* 25 Sept., 25, 28 Oct. 1890; SF *Exam.,* 9, 10, 15 Oct. 1890; SF *Alta,* 1, 10 Oct. 1890.

34. SF *Chron.,* 10 Oct. 1890; SF *Alta,* 26, 30 Sept. 1890; SF *Exam.,* 26 Sept., 3 Nov. 1890.

35. SF *Chron.,* 22 Aug. 1889, 5, 9 Oct. 1890; SF *Exam.,* 22 Aug. 1889, 8, 16 July, 5, 7 Oct. 1890; SF *Alta,* 2 Aug. 1889, 8, 15, 16 July, 5, 7 Oct. 1890; "Martin Kelly's Story," 11, 12, 13, 15 Sept. 1917; Callow, "Blind Boss," 262.

36. SF *Alta,* 3, 6 July, 5, 17, 24 Aug., 24, 27 Sept., 2 Oct. 1890; SF *Exam.,* 27 May, 3, 6 July, 5 Aug., 28 Sept., 1, 2, 5 Oct. 1890; SF *Chron.,* 5 Aug., 2 Oct. 1890; SF *Wave,* 2 Aug. 1890.

37. SF *Alta,* 8, 9, 10, 11, 12, 14 Oct. 1890; SF *Chron.,* 8, 9, 10, 11, 12, 14 Oct. 1890; SF *Exam.,* 2 Aug., 24 Sept., 8, 10, 11, 13, 14 Oct. 1890.

38. SF *Alta,* 6, 8, 14 Oct. 1890; SF *Chron.,* 8, 14 Oct. 1890; SF *Exam.,* 8, 14 Oct. 1890.

39. SF *Chron.*, 17, 18, 23 Oct., 2 Nov. 1890.

40. Dobie, *S. M. White*, 116–120; Williams, *Democratic Party*, 144–145.

41. SF *Chron.*, 22, 25, 28, 31 Oct., 2 Nov. 1890.

42. Ibid., 15, 17, 18, 21, 23 Oct., 2 Nov. 1890; SF *Alta*, 31 Oct., 1 Nov. 1890; SF *Exam.*, 17 Oct., 3 Nov. 1890; Petersen, "Struggle for the Australian Ballot," 233.

43. Buckley, "Reminiscences," 22 Jan. 1919; Williams, *Democratic Party*, 145–147; Dobie, *S. M. White*, 116–120; Callow, "Blind Boss," 277; Petersen, "Struggle for the Australian Ballot," 234; SF *Exam.*, 6, 7 Nov. 1890; SF *Alta*, 5, 6, 7, 8 Nov. 1890; SF *Chron.*, 5, 6, 7 Nov. 1890; Davis, *Political Conventions*, 570–571.

44. SF *Exam.*, 6 Nov. 1890.

45. Ibid., 6, 7, Nov. 1890; SF *Alta*, 5 Nov. 1890; Buckley, "Reminiscences," 22 Jan. 1919; White Papers, S. M. White to J. P. Irish, 12 Nov. 1890, S. M. White to E. B. Pond, 19 Nov. 1890.

46. SF *Exam.*, 22, 25, 26 Sept., 7 Oct., 6, 7, Nov. 1890; SF *Alta*, 5 Nov. 1890.

47. Williams, *Democratic Party*, 147, 149–150; SF *Exam.*, 6 Nov. 1890; Varcados, "Labor and Politics," 26; White Papers, W. J. Tinnin to S. M. White, 12 Nov. 1890; Grassman, "Prologue to Reform," 535.

48. Buckley, "Reminiscences," 22 Jan. 1919.

49. White Papers, E. B. Pond to S. M. White, 17 Nov. 1890, S. M. White to E. B. Pond, 19 Nov. 1890; Dobie, *S. M. White*, 120; Williams, *Democratic Party*, 149–150; Callow, "Blind Boss," 276; Bullough, "Hannibal versus the Blind Boss," 188–189.

50. No hard evidence supports charges of a Buckley-Stanford alliance, but many Democratic leaders suspected its existence, even before the 1890 election. See White Papers, S. M. White to J. P. Irish, 12 Nov. 1890, W. J. Tinnin to S. M. White, 12 Nov. 1890, S. M. White to W. J. Tinnin, 14 Nov. 1890, E. B. Pond to S. M. White, 17 Nov. 1890, S. M. White to E. B. Pond, 19 Nov. 1890, J. H. Barry to S. M. White, 14 Nov. 1890; SF *Call*, 14, 26 May, 1, 12 June 1890; SF *Exam.*, 11 July 1891; Dobie, *S. M. White*, 106, 116–120, 123–127; Williams, *Democratic Party*, 148–149.

51. White Papers, S. M. White to W. J. Tinnin, 14 Nov. 1890, S. M. White to J. P. Irish, 12 Nov. 1890; Ruef, "The Road I Traveled," 8 June 1912; Dobie, *S. M. White*, 110, 126.

52. Williams, *Democratic Party*, 149–150; White Papers, S. M. White to W. J. Tinnin, 14 Nov. 1890, S. M. White to T. V. Cator, 10 Jan. 1891, S. M. White to J. P. Irish, 11 Jan. 1891; SF *Exam.*, 1, 2 July 1891; Callow, "Blind Boss," 277; Dobie, *S. M. White*, 124–127; Buckley, "Reminiscences," 4 Feb. 1919; Grassman, "Prologue to Reform," 529–530.

53. SF *Wave*, 11 July, 22 Aug. 1891.

54. Alexander B. Callow, Jr., "The Legislature of a Thousand Scandals," *SCQ*, 39 (December 1957): 342–344; "Martin Kelly's Story," 16, 17 Sept.

1917; Williams, *Democratic Party,* 150–151; SF *Exam.,* 1 March 1891; SF *Chron.,* 1 March 1891; Leake, "King Mazuma," 13 April 1917.

The "Wastepaper Basket Affair" began on 17 March 1891 when state librarian W. S. Leake reported to U.S. Senate hopeful Morris M. Estee that he had found wrappers from fifteen $500 money bundles in the library trash and that the only people in that part of the building had been supporters of Estee's rival for the senate seat, Charles Felton. Before the episode ended in Felton's election, it involved allegations of bribery (probably true) but never in concrete proof that the senate seat was purchased in the library.

55. Buckley, "Reminiscences," 1 Feb. 1919; Leake, "King Mazuma," 14, 16 April 1917; SF *Newsletter,* 1 Aug. 1891.

56. Buckley, "Reminiscences," 1, 3 Feb. 1919; "Martin Kelly's Story," 28 Sept., 3 Oct. 1917; Leake, "King Mazuma," 17, 18 April 1917.

57. SF *Directory, 1873,* 765, 775; *California Consitution, 1879,* Art. I, Sec. 8; SF *Exam.,* 17 Nov. 1891.

58. SF *Chron.,* 18, 23 Aug. 1891; Leake, "King Mazuma," 19 March, 17 April 1917; SF *Exam.,* 18, 21, Aug. 1891; Williams, *Democratic Party,* 151–152.

59. SF *Directories, 1890, 1891, 1892,* passim; SF *Chron.,* 12 March, 21, 23, Aug. 1891; SF *Exam.,* 10 March, 9 April 1884; 21 Aug., 1 Oct. 1891; Leake, "King Mazuma," 17 April 1917; Buckley, "Reminiscences," 1 Feb. 1919; Davis, *Political Conventions,* 324–325, 569, 630–631; Williams, *Democratic Party,* 43, 55, 65–66, 107–108; Dobie, *S. M. White,* 41, 62–67; R. Hal Williams to W. A. Bullough, 24 April 1975; Bullough, "Hannibal versus the Blind Boss," 189–190.

60. SF *Exam.,* 21 Aug., 7 Oct. 1891; SF *Chron.,* 23 Aug. 1891; SF *Argonaut,* 7 Dec. 1890, 5, 26 Oct. 1891; SF *Newsletter,* 3 April 1886, 31 Oct., 14, 21 Nov. 1891; SF *Wave,* 10 Oct. 1891.

61. SF *Wave,* 10 Oct. 1891; Leake, "King Mazuma," 18, 19 April 1917; "Martin Kelly's Story," 28 Sept. 1917; *Report of the Grand Jury of the City and County of San Francisco* (San Francisco, 1892), 12–24.

62. SF *Exam.,* 18 Aug., 21 Oct., 18 Nov. 1891; SF *Chron.,* 18, 21, 23 Aug. 1891; *Report of the Grand Jury,* 2–3.

63. SF *Exam.,* 26 Sept., 1, 2, 16, 31 Oct., 10, 12, 13, 17, 25 Nov., 13 Dec. 1891; SF *Wave,* 10 Oct. 1891; LA *Times,* 25 Nov. 1891; SF *Newsletter,* 21 Nov., 26 Dec. 1891.

64. SF *Exam.,* 1, 2, 3, 7, 8, 9, 14 Oct. 1891; SF *Chron.,* 1, 3, 7 Oct. 1891; SF *Argonaut,* 5 Oct. 1891; SF *Wave,* 10 Oct. 1891; Leake, "King Mazuma," 18 April 1917; People *ex rel.* Attorney General *v.* Wallace, 27 *Pacific Reporter,* 767; *Ex Parte* Haymond, 27 *Pacific Reporter,* 859.

65. SF *Exam.,* 16, 17, 20, 21, 22, 29 Oct. 1891; SF *Argonaut,* 26 Oct. 1891; SF *Newsletter,* 31 Oct. 1891; SF *Chron.,* 16, 21, 22 Oct. 1891; "Martin Kelly's Story," 28 Sept. 1917.

66. The Wallace grand jury records were turned over to the Citizens' De-

fense Association cofounded by James D. Phelan. All transcripts and other documents apparently burned in 1906. See SF *Exam.*, 6, 8 Dec. 1895, 19 Sept. 1896; Swanstrom, "Reform Administration of Phelan," 25, 55, 62.

67. SF *Exam.*, 23 Sept., 17, 20, 21 Oct., 7, 10, 11, 12, 13, 14 Nov. 1891, 24 July 1899; SF *Chron.*, 10, 12 Nov. 1891; SF *Call*, 11, 12 Nov. 1891; SF *Wave*, 14 Nov. 1891; SF *Newsletter*, 14 Nov. 1891; Williams, *Democratic Party*, 151; Callow, "Blind Boss," 276.

68. SF *Exam.*, 12, 13, 14 Nov. 1891; SF *Newsletter*, 14 Nov. 1891; LA *Times*, 25 Nov. 1891; Sac. *Bee*, 20 Nov. 1891; Buckley, "Reminiscences," 1, 3 Feb. 1919.

69. Buckley, "Reminiscences," 1 Feb. 1919; "Martin Kelly's Story," 27 Sept. 1917; Clifton E. Mayne, "Dictations and other Related Biographical Materials, 1888–1890" (BL); SF *Exam.*, 20, 21 Oct., 11 Nov. 1891, 1, 3, 6, 7, 8 Dec. 1895; SF *Chron.*, 28 Feb. 1894, 8 Nov. 1895; SF *Call*, 11 Nov. 1891, 28 Feb. 1894; SF *Wave*, 14 Nov. 1891; SF *Alta*, 18 Nov., 3, 10, 24 Dec. 1890; LA *Times*, 8 Nov. 1895; Williams, *Democratic Party*, 151; Callow, "Blind Boss," 276; *SFMR, 1891–92*, 286–288; Arnold, *Transportation Facilities*, 418, 420–421.

70. Buckley, "Reminiscences," 1 Feb. 1919.

71. SF *Wave*, 14 Nov. 1891.

72. Bruner *v.* Superior Court of the City and County of San Francisco, 28 *Pacific Reporter*, 341–354; *Report of the Grand Jury*, 4, 13; SF *Exam.*, 17, 18 Nov., 13 Dec. 1891; SF *Call*, 21 Nov. 1891; LA *Times*, 25 Nov. 1891; SF *Newsletter*, 26 Dec. 1891; Callow, "Blind Boss," 276–277; Williams, *Democratic Party*, 151–152; Liv. *Echo*, 17 Dec. 1891.

73. Callow, "Legislature of a Thousand Scandals," 248.

74. SF *Newsletter*, 21 Nov., 26 Dec. 1891.

75. Ibid., 14 Nov. 1891.

76. Buckley, "Reminiscences," 1, 3 Feb. 1919.

CHAPTER TEN

1. Merton, *Social Theory*, 74. Portions of the material in Chapter Ten are adapted from two previously published articles: "The Steam Beer Handicap: Chris Buckley and the San Francisco Municipal Election of 1896," and "Hannibal versus the Blind Boss: Chris Buckley, the 'Junta,' and Democratic Reform Politics in San Francisco." They are used here by permission.

2. "Martin Kelly's Story," 26 Nov. 1917.

3. Averbach, "San Francisco's South of Market District," 202–204; William Issel, "Class and Ethnic Conflict in San Francisco: The Reform Charter of 1898," *Labor History*, 18 (Summer 1977): 342–343; SF *Directory, 1890*, 1433; SF *Directory, 1892*, 65–68; SF *Directory, 1899*, 1901–1902; U.S. Bureau of the Census, *Population of Cities, 1790–1900*, 430–432; U.S. Bureau of the Census,

Eleventh Census of the United States, 1890 (Washington, D. C., 1894), I, xcii–xciii, cli; Barth, *Instant Cities,* 131–135; Alexander P. Saxton, "San Francisco Labor and the Populist and Progressive Insurgencies," *PHR,* 34 (November 1965): 421–438; Cross, *Labor Movement,* 214–220.

4. Arnold, *Transportation Facilities,* 418–421; *SFMR, 1891–92,* 286–288; SF *Alta,* 14 April 1887; SF *Exam.,* 30 Jan. 1897; Nash, *State Government and Economic Development,* 176–187, and passim; Mansel G. Blackford, *The Politics of Business in California, 1890–1920* (Columbus, Ohio, 1977), 129–145, 161–172, and passim.

5. Barth, "Metropolism and Urban Elites," 158–187.

6. Phelan's career merits careful investigation as an exemplar of the progressive mentality in municipal politics in the 1880s and 1890s. Two unpublished studies provide biographical data and some insights into his early years: Roy Swanstrom, "The Reform Administration of James D. Phelan, Mayor of San Francisco," 19–25, and passim; Robert E. Hennings, "James D. Phelan and the Wilson Progressives on California," 1–15, and passim. Also see George E. Mowry, *The California Progressives* (Berkeley, 1951), 23–25; Muscatine, *Old San Francisco,* 223–224, 288, 362, 405, 419, 433–436; Starr, *California Dream,* 249–252.

The James D. Phelan Papers (BL) contain little correspondence which antedates 1900, but Phelan's "Scrapbooks" furnish insights into his early activities and interests, as do letters in the James Phelan Correspondence (BL).

7. Swanstrom, "Reform Administration of Phelan," 24–26, and passim; Hennings, "Phelan and Progressives," Chap. 1, and passim; SF *Directories, 1870–1880;* James D. Phelan Papers (BL) "Scrapbooks," Vols. 27, 68, 70.

8. Swanstrom, "Reform Administration of Phelan," 26. Compare Starr, *California Dream,* 252; Older, *My Own Story,* 23.

9. For a brief and incisive discussion of the concept of structural reform, see Holli, *Reform in Detroit,* 157–183.

For analyses of the relationship between the urban experience and conceptions of the city and reform, see three articles by Samuel P. Hays: "The Changing Political Structure of the City in Industrial America," *JUH,* 1 (November 1974): 6–38; "The Politics of Reform in Municipal Government in the Progressive Era," *PNQ,* 55 (October 1964): 157–169; "The Social Analysis of American Political History, 1880–1920," *PSQ,* 80 (September 1965): 373–393.

10. Muscatine, *Old San Francisco,* 405, 419, 433–436; Swanstrom, "Reform Administration of Phelan, 24–26; James D. Phelan Papers, "Scrapbooks," Vols. 68–70; James D. Phelan, "The New San Francisco: Address at the Opening of the Mechanics' Institute Fair, Sept. 1, 1896"; SF *Exam.,* 29 Oct. 1888; *DAB,* VII, 523; Starr, *California Dream,* 249–250; Holli, *Reform in Detroit,* 167; Older, *My Own Story,* 22–23; Issel, "Class and Ethnic Conflict," 345. On Older, see Evelyn Wells, *Fremont Older.*

11. Swanstrom, "Reform Administration of Phelan," 24–28, 77–80, 83–86, and passim; Holli, *Reform in Detroit,* 167; Older, *My Own Story,* 27–31, 65; Mowry, *California Progressives,* 23–25; Bean, *Boss Ruef,* 8–9, 16–17, 23; James Phelan Correspondence (BL), James D. Phelan to James Phelan, 11, 13, 17 June 1884; James D. Phelan Papers (BL), untitled manuscript, box 74; "Scrapbooks," Vol. 69; James D. Phelan, *Corruption and Bribery in Elections* (San Francisco, 1889); Petersen, "Struggle for the Australian Ballot," 230–231.

12. James D. Phelan Papers (BL), "Scrapbooks," Vols. 1, 5–7; James D. Phelan, *Municipal Conditions and the New Charter* (San Francisco, 1896); James D. Phelan, "Municipal Conditions and the New Charter," *OM,* 28 (July 1896): 104–111; James D. Phelan, "Municipal Conditions in San Francisco," *Arena,* 17 (June 1897): 989–995; Issel, "Class and Ethnic Conflict," 342–350.

13. SF *Wave,* 11 July, 22 Aug. 1891, 2 Jan., 13 Feb. 1892; SF *Exam.,* 30 June 1890, 8 Dec. 1895; SF *Call,* 18 Nov. 1895; SF *Chron.,* 18 Sept. 1894.

14. Williams, *Democratic Party,* 153; Dobie, *S. M. White,* 141; "Martin Kelly's Story," 3 Oct. 1917; Callow, "Legislature of a Thousand Scandals," 342; Petersen, "Struggle for the Australian Ballot," 328–329; Grassman, "Prologue to Reform," 529–531.

15. "Martin Kelly's Story," 3 Oct. 1917.

16. Democratic Party, *Plan of Organization of the Democratic Party of the City and County of San Francisco, as Amended April 22, 1892* (San Francisco, 1892); White Papers, S. M. White to J. D. Phelan, 9 Sept. 1892.

17. "Martin Kelly's Story," 3 Oct. 1917; Callow, "Blind Boss," 277.

18. Harrison Reid, *A Campaign Songster* (San Francisco, 1892), 23.

19. SF *Chron.,* 8, 9, 10, 11 Nov. 1892; SF *Exam.,* 12, 21, 24, 27, 28 Oct., 8, 17 Nov. 1892.

20. SF *Exam.,* 29, 30 Dec. 1892, 19 Jan., 2, 24 Feb. 1893; SF *Chron.,* 12 Nov. 1892; Harold F. Taggart, "The Senatorial Election of 1893 in California," *CHQ,* 19 (March 1940): 59–60, 73; "Martin Kelly's Story," 2 Oct. 1917.

21. Buckley interviews; SF *Chron.,* 1 Jan. 1894.

22. SF *Exam.,* 2 June 1894; SF *Call,* 4 May, 29 June 1894; SF *Chron.,* 1 Jan., 29, 30 June 1894; SF *Directory, 1891,* 1091, 1151.

23. Buckley, "Reminiscences," 4 Feb. 1919; SF *Call,* 22 Sept. 1894; SF *Exam.,* 22 Sept. 1894; SF *Chron.,* 16 Aug., 18, 20, 21 Sept. 1894; Robert and Mary Stewart, *Adolph Sutro* (Berkeley, 1962) 204–210; A. H. J. Townsend, "Adolph Sutro, Mayor Elect of San Francisco: a Capitalist Fight against Monopoly," *Reviews of Reviews,* 10 (December 1894): 628–629; Oak. *Trib.,* 8 Nov. 1894.

24. SF *Exam.,* 11 Nov. 1894; SF *Chron.,* 16 Aug., 3, 4, 12, 13, 19, 25 Sept. 1894; SF *Call,* 3, 4, 5 Sept., 26, 27 Oct., 24 Nov., 4, 7, Dec. 1894; SF *Bull.,* 20 Oct. 1894.

25. SF *Exam.,* 1, 11, 16 Oct., 2, 6 Nov. 1894; SF *Chron.,* 4 Nov. 1894;

Townsend, "Adolph Sutro," 629; Oak. *Trib.,* 8 Nov. 1894; Stewart and Stewart, *Adolph Sutro,* 209–210.

26. "Martin Kelly's Story," 6 Nov. 1917; Ruef, "The Road I Traveled," 24 June 1912.

27. SF *Exam.,* 15 Dec. 1895; SF *Chron.,* 11 April, 1, 2, 5 Oct. 1895; SF *Call,* 4, 17 March, 10 April, 5, 9 Oct. 18 Nov., 9, 13, 18 Dec. 1895.

28. Bullough, "Hannibal versus the Blind Boss," 190–193.

29. Ibid., 193–194.

30. Ibid., 195–197.

31. Ibid., 197–200. Identifiable members of the Junta included ten holders of government offices, thirteen attorneys, twenty businessmen, one physician, and only one member of the wage-earning classes. For names and occupations, see Bullough, "Hannibal versus the Blind Boss," 193–194, fn. 34.

32. Ibid., 199–202.

33. Ibid., 201–203; SF *Exam.,* 13, 14, 15 March, 14 July 1896; SF *Chron.,* 15 July 1896; SF *Bull.,* 16 July 1896.

34. SF *Exam.,* 11 Sept. 1896.

35. Bullough, "Steam Beer Handicap," 247–249; Buckley, "Reminiscences," 17 Jan. 1919.

36. Buckley, "Reminiscences," 16 Jan., 4 Feb. 1919.

37. Bullough, "Steam Beer Handicap," 249–252.

38. Ibid., 253–255; SF *Call,* 14, 15, 19, 20 March 1896; SF *Chron.,* 16 May 1896.

39. Bullough, "Steam Beer Handicap," 254; SF *Chron.,* 6 Sept. 1896; SF *Exam.,* 6 Sept. 1896.

40. Bullough, "Steam Beer Handicap," 254; Ruef, "The Road I Traveled," 24, 25 June 1912; "Martin Kelly's Story," 7 Nov. 1917; Issel, "Class and Ethnic Conflict," 349.

41. Bullough, "Steam Beer Handicap," 254–255.

42. Issel, "Class and Ethnic Conflict," 345.

43. Ibid., 346; James D. Phelan Papers (BL), "Scrapbooks," Vol. 1; Good Government Club of San Francisco, *Publication Number Two: Report on Charter Reform* (San Francisco, 1896), 2–3, and passim; Williams, *Democratic Party,* 200; Swanstrom, "Reform Administration of Phelan," 30–32; Hennings, "Phelan and Progressives," Chap. 2; SF *Exam.,* 9 Sept. 1895, 10, 13 July 1896; SF *Chron.,* 4, 5, 7 July 1896; *SFMR, 1897–98,* 300–304.

44. See Micahel P. Rogin and John L. Shover, *Political Change in California* (Westport, Conn., 1970), Chap 1.; Wiebe, *Search for Order,* Chaps. 4–6; Paul Kleppner, *The Cross of Culture* (New York, 1970), Chaps. 4–5; Paul W. Glad, *McKinley, Bryan, and the People* (New York, 1964), Chaps. 1–2, 4; J. Rogers Hollingsworth, "The Historian, Presidential Elections, and 1896," *Mid-America,* 45 (July 1963): 184–192.

45. Original federal subsidies to railroads had been secured by thirty-six-year

bonds at six percent interest. In the 1890s, lobbyists in Washington began to press for a funding bill which would replace original agreements with ninety-nine-year bonds at one-half percent interest, a proposal which became a major issue in California politics.

46. SF *Exam.*, 15 Oct. 1896. The parties included Republican, Democratic, National Republican, Nonpartisan, Populist, Socialist-Labor, National (Gold) Democrats, Citizens' Republican, Anti-Charter Democratic, Citizen's Independent (affiliated with the American Protective Association), and Prohibitionist.

47. SF *Exam.*, 26 April, 11 May 1896; SF *Chron.*, 12, 14 May 1896; SF *Bull.*, 11, 12, 13 May 1896. Donald E. Walters, "Populism in California, 1889–1900" (Ph.D. thesis, University of California, Berkeley, 1952); Saxton, "Populist and Progressive Insurgencies," 421–438; Taggart, "T. V. Cator," (December 1948): 311–318, (March 1949): 47–55.

48. Bullough, "Steam Beer Handicap," 255–256.

49. SF *Exam.*, 2 Oct. 1896.

50. Ibid., 3, 5, 6 Nov. 1896; SF *Bull.*, 5 Nov. 1896; SF *Chron.*, 3, 5, 6, 7 Nov. 1896; "Steam Beer Handicap," 257–259; Ruef, "The Road I Traveled," 3 June 1912.

Of 72,359 registered voters in the city, 65,178 cast ballots. Ticket splitting in the municipal election seems to indicate that San Francisco was an exception to the solidly Republican "System of 1896" postulated for the state in Rogin and Shover, *Political Change*, 2–6 and passim. A quantitative analysis of precinct voting records would be helpful in this regard, but the San Francisco Registrar of Voters reports that all such records were destroyed in the fire of 1906.

51. "Martin Kelly's Story," 3 Oct., 9 Nov. 1917; Buckley, "Reminiscences," 5 Feb. 1919.

52. "Martin Kelly's Story," 26 Sept. 1917.

53. Dobie, *S. M. White*, 124–127; Grassman, "Prologue to Reform," 522.

54. See Hays, "Politics of Reform"; Hays, "Changing Political Structure"; Hays, "Social Analysis"; Richard M. Bernard and Bradley R. Rice, "Political Environment and the Adoption of Progressive Municipal Reform," *JUH*, 1 (February 1975): 149–174; James Weinstein, *The Corporate Ideal in the Liberal State* (Boston, 1968) 92–116; James Weinstein, "Organized Business and the Commission and Manager Movements," *Journal of Southern History*, 28 (May 1962): 167–181.

55. SF *Call*, 4 Oct., 1895.

56. Ibid., 6, 23 Oct., 5 Nov. 1895; SF *Chron.*, 11 Oct., 18 Nov. 1895; SF *Bull.*, 15 Nov. 1895.

57. For a more detailed analysis, see Bullough, "Hannibal versus the Blind Boss," 202–206, and passim.

58. "Martin Kelly's Story," 26 Nov. 1917.

CHAPTER ELEVEN

1. Petersen, "Struggle for the Australian Ballot," 240; Jerrold G. Rusk, "The Effect of Australian Ballot Reform on Split Ticket Voting, 1876–1908," *American Political Science Review,* 64 (December 1970): 1220–1238.

2. See Issel, "Class and Ethnic Conflict," 350–359; *SFMR, 1897–98,* 302–304; "Martin Kelly's Story," 9 Nov. 1917; Charter Convention of 100, *Reports of the Committees* (San Francisco, 1897); Swanstrom, "Reform Administration of Phelan," 77–80, 83, 85–86; Phelan, "Municipal Conditions in San Francisco," 989–995; Blackmar, "San Francisco's Struggle for Good Government," 567–577; Cubberly, "School Situation in San Francisco," 364–381; Older, *My Own Story,* 21–25, 67, and passim; SF *Exam.,* 8, 9, 14 Sept., 18 Oct. 1898.

3. For comparison, see Clifford W. Patton, *The Battle for Municipal Reform* (Washington, D.C., 1940); Mansel G. Blackford, "Reform Politics in Seattle during the Progressive Era, 1902–1916," *PNQ,* 59 (October 1968): 177–185; Augustus Cerillo, Jr., "The Reform of Municipal Government in New York City: From Seth Low to John Purroy Mitchell," *New York Historical Society Quarterly,* 57 (January 1973): 51–71; Albert H. Clodius, "The Quest for Good Government in Los Angeles, 1890–1910" (Ph.D. thesis, Claremont Graduate School, 1953); Charles Garrett, *The La Guardia Years: Machine and Reform Politics in New York City* (New Brunswick, N.J., 1961); Louis G. Geiger, "Joseph W. Folk v. Edward Butler: St. Louis, 1902," *JSH,* 28 (November 1962): 438–449; Holli, *Reform in Detroit;* Marjorie Hornbein, "Denver's Struggle for Home Rule," *Colorado Magazine,* 48 (Fall 1971): 337–354; Roy Lubove, "The Twentieth Century City: The Progressive as Municipal Reformer," *Mid-America,* 41 (October 1959): 195–209; J. Paul Mitchell, "Boss Speer and the City Functional: Boosters and Businessmen versus Commission Government in Denver," *PNQ,* 63 (October 1972): 155–164; Charles H. Parkhurst, *Our Fight with Tammany* (New York, 1970 [1895]); Frank M. Stewart, *A Half-Century of Municipal Reform: The History of the National Municipal League* (Berkeley, 1950).

4. See above, notes 2 and 3.

5. On the matter of Ruef's role as boss, compare Bean, *Boss Ruef,* and James P. Walsh, "Abe Ruef Was No Boss: Machine Politics, Reform, and San Francisco," *CHQ,* 51 (Spring 1972): 3–16.

6. SF *Call,* 26 May, 1, 15, Sept., 1 Oct. 1898; SF *Exam.,* 29 May, 28 Oct. 1898; Swanstrom, "Reform Administration of Phelan," 33–34.

7. SF *Call,* 18 April, 6 May, 7, 23 June, 25, 26, 27 July, 1, 6 Aug. 1899; SF *Exam.,* 7, 24, 25 July, 6, 7, 8, 9 Aug. 1899; SF *Chron.,* 20, 28 July 1899.

8. Buckley, "Reminiscences," 16 Jan. 1919.

9. Buckley interviews.

10. SF *Call,* 3 Oct. 1897.

11. *Faulkner's Handbook and Directory of Murray Township* (Livermore, Calif., 1886), 65, 106; Liv. *Echo,* 28 Nov. 1889, 27 Aug. 1891, 15 June 1893; Liv. *Herald,* 25 Jan. 1896; Oakland (Calif.) *Enquirer,* 13 Dec. 1897; SF *Exam.,* 23 Sept. 1891, 3 Sept., 15 Dec. 1895; SF *Call,* 30 April 1896; Wait, *Wines and Vines,* 157; Jones, *Vines in the Sun,* 169; Jones, "At Ravenswood," 6–7; Buckley interviews.

12. Wait, *Wines and Vines,* 157; Jones, "At Ravenswood," 6–7; Jones, *Vines in the Sun,* 168; Liv. *Herald,* 17, 31 July, 21, 24 Aug., 23 Oct., 11, 25 Dec. 1897, 15 July 1899; Oakland (Calif.) *Enquirer,* 13 Dec. 1897; SF *Exam.,* 23 Sept. 1891, 3 Sept. 1895; SF *Call,* 3 Oct. 1897; Buckley interviews. Buckley continued to sell part of his grape crop to Wente Brothers Winery until at least 1911; Ernest A. Wente to W. A. Bullough, 14 April 1975.

13. Liv *Echo,* 28 Nov. 1889, 17 Feb. 1898; Liv. *Herald,* 16 Jan., 20 Feb., 20 March, 15 May, 12, 26 June, 31 July, 14, 24 Aug., 16 Oct., 25 Dec. 1897, 8, 29 July, 12, 19 Aug., 9 Sept. 1899; Buckley interviews and family photographs.

14. SF *Call,* 30 April 1897; SF *Exam.,* 15 Dec. 1895; Liv. *Herald,* 25 Jan. 1896, 16, 24 July 1897, 8 July 1899; Liv. *Echo,* 3 Oct. 1897; Buckley interviews.

15. Buckley interviews; Liv. *Herald,* 20 April 1918.

16. Buckley interviews; San Francisco County Clerk, Probate File Number 34037; SF *Exam.,* 21 Nov. 1916; SF *Chron.,* 11 Feb., 22 May, 24 June 1909, 21 March 1911; SF *Call,* 15 April, 28 Nov. 1902, 12 Feb. 1909; Sac. *Bee,* 11 Feb. 1909; SF *Directory, 1900,* 340; SF *Directory, 1909,* 329; *Mery's Block Book of San Francisco* (San Francisco, 1909), 164, 505, 565, 678; *San Francisco Block Book* (San Francisco, 1906), 86, 573.

17. Callow, "Blind Boss," 261.

18. Ibid., 261–262; SF *Chron.,* 21, 22, 25 April 1922; SF *Bull.,* 21, 22, 24 April 1922; SF *Exam.,* 21, 22, 25 April 1922; SF *Call,* 21 April 1922; Liv. *Herald,* 22 April 1922; Buckley interviews.

19. Ibid.; SF *Exam.,* 15 Nov. 1922; Callow, "Blind Boss," 272, fn. 51; San Francisco County Clerk, Probate File Number 34037. Buckley's will included bequests to family and friends and to numerous charities, Catholic, Protestant, Jewish, and secular. Less than six months after the probate of his will, his widow appealed to the courts for an increase in her monthly trust allowance in order to meet charitable commitments; the court granted her request.

20. See John G. Cawelti, *Apostles of the Self-Made Man* (Chicago, 1965); Moses Rischin (ed.), *The American Gospel of Success* (Chicago, 1965); Irvin G. Wyllie, *The Self-Made Man in America* (New Brunswick, N.J., 1954).

21. Shumate, *Visit to Rincon Hill,* 13–15; Barth, "Metropolism and Urban Elites," 164–166.

22. Merton, *Social Theory,* 76–78.

23. James Bryce, *The American Commonwealth* (New York, 1904), II, 109.

24. Buckley, "Reminiscences," 4, 13, 16, 24 Jan. 1919; "Martin Kelly's Story," 3 Sept. 1917.

25. Harvey Wheeler, "Yesterday's Robin Hood: The Rise and Fall of Baltimore's Trenton Democratic Club," *AQ,* 7 (Winter 1975): 332—344.

26. Riordon, *Plunkitt of Tammany Hall,* 3—6, and passim; Buckley, "Reminiscences," 24, 28 Jan. 1919.

27. Although somewhat dated in interpretation, Zink, *City Bosses* (1931) remains useful for comparative purposes.

28. Issel, "Class and Ethnic Conflict," 354; "Martin Kelly's Story," 26 Sept. 1917.

29. "Martin Kelly's Story," 26 Nov. 1917. Apparently, after more than three-quarters of a century, modern San Franciscans have concluded that the old political system indeed had something to offer. As this was being written, residents of the city voted in favor of a return to district representation on their board of supervisors and in November 1977, for the first time since 1898, elected board members representative of specific constituencies.

30. Walsh, "Abe Ruef." I am indebted to Professor Martin Shefter of Cornell University for suggesting the possible relationship between the dismantling of the clubs, Buckley's demise, the reformers' failures to dominate the party, and the absence of resurgent bossism from twentieth-century San Franciso history.

31. "Martin Kelly's Story," 1 Sept., 26 Nov. 1917.

BIBLIOGRAPHY

PRIMARY SOURCES

1. Manuscript Collections and Archives

Hubert Howe Bancroft Papers. Bancroft Library. University of California, Berkeley.

Clifton E. Mayne, Dictations and other Related Biographical Materials, 1888–1890. Bancroft Library. University of California, Berkeley.

James Phelan Correspondence. Bancroft Library. University of California, Berkeley.

James Duval Phelan Papers. Bancroft Library. University of California, Berkeley.

Stephen Mallory White Papers. Bender Collection. Stanford University Library.

California State Archive. Sacramento, California.

National Archive and Record Center. Bayonne, New Jersey.

National Archive and Record Center. San Bruno, California.

2. Newspapers and Periodicals

Livermore (California) *Herald*.

Livermore (California) *Weekly Echo*.

Los Angeles *Times*.

Oakland *Enquirer*.

Oakland *Tribune*.

Sacramento *Bee*.

San Francisco *Argonaut*.

San Francisco *Bulletin*.

San Francisco *Call.*
San Francisco *Chronicle.*
San Francisco *Daily Alta California.*
San Francisco *Examiner.*
San Francisco Newsletter and California Advertiser.
San Francisco Real Estate Circular.

San Francisco. *Thistleton's Jolly Giant.*
San Francisco. *The Wasp.*
Solano County Advertiser.
Vallejo *Evening Chronicle.*
Vallejo *Evening Register.*
Weaverville (California) *Trinity Journal.*

3. *Memoirs and Reminiscences*

Altrocchi, Julia Cooley. *The Spectacular San Franciscans.* New York: Dutton, 1949.

Buckley, Christopher A. "The Reminiscences of Christopher A. Buckley." San Francisco *Bulletin.* 31 August–9 October 1918, 23 December 1918–5 February 1919.

Buckley, Christopher A., Jr. Interviews. August–November 1974. Pebble Beach, California.

Harpending, Asbury. *The Great Diamond Hoax and Other Stirring Incidents in the Life of Asbury Harpending.* Norman: University of Oklahoma Press, 1958.

Kelly, Martin. "Martin Kelly's Story." San Francisco *Bulletin.* 1 September–26 November 1917.

Leake, Sam. "When King Mazuma Reigned." San Francisco *Bulletin.* 16 March–26 April 1917.

Neville, Amelia Ransome. *The Fantastic City: Memoirs of the Social and Romantic Life of Old San Francisco.* Boston: Houghton-Mifflin, 1932.

Older, Fremont. *My Own Story.* New York: Macmillan, 1926.

Ruef, Abraham. "The Road I Traveled: An Autobiographic Account of My Career from the University to Prison, with an Intimate Recital of the Corrupt Alliance between Big Business and Politics in San Francisco." San Francisco *Bulletin.* 6 April–5 September 1912.

Wangenheim, Julius. "An Autobiography." *California Historical Society Quarterly,* 35 (March 1956): 19–44, (September 1956): 253–274, (December 1956): 345–366; 36 (March 1957): 63–78, (June 1957): 149–164.

4. *Government Records and Reports*

Alameda County Recorder. *Deed Book Number 282.*
———. *Index of Deeds Number 28.*

Arnold, Bion J. *Report on the Improvement and Development of the Transportation Facilities of San Francisco.* San Francisco: n.p., 1913.

California Reporter.

San Francisco. Board of Education. *The School Scandal of San Francisco.* San Francisco: San Francisco News Co., 1878.

———. Board of Park Commissioners. *Souvenir Programme, Golden Gate Park, San Francisco.* San Francisco: n.p., 1888.

———. Board of Supervisors. *Municipal Reports.*

————. Board of Supervisors. *Report of Professor George Davidson upon a System of Sewerage for the City of San Francisco.* San Francisco: F. Eastman, 1886.

————. *Great Register of the City and County of San Francisco, 1872.* San Francisco: A. L. Bancroft, 1872.

————. *Great Register of the City and County of San Francisco, 1873.* San Francisco: A. L. Bancroft, 1873.

————. County Clerk. Probate File Number 34037.

————. *Report of the Grand Jury of the City and County of San Francisco.* San Francisco: Carson, 1892.

————. *Ward Register of the Fifth Ward of the City and County of San Francisco, 1875.* San Francisco: L. G. Richmond, 1875.

Solano County (California). *Great Register, County of Solano, State of California.* Vallejo: Chronicle Co., 1872.

State of California. *Journal of the California Assembly.*

————. *Journal of the California Senate.*

————. *Statutes of California.*

————. Bureau of Labor Statistics. *First Biennial Report.* Sacramento: State Printer, 1884.

Superior Court of the State of California in and for the City and County of San Francisco. "Bonnet *v.* Taylor." Transcript. California State Archive, Sacramento.

Supreme Court of the State of California. "In the Matter of the Proceedings to Punish Christopher A. Buckley for Contempt." Transcript. Docket Number 20136. California State Archive, Sacramento.

U.S. Bureau of the Census. *Eleventh Census of the United States, 1890.* Vol. I. *Population.* Washington, D.C.: Government Printing Office, 1894.

————. *Tenth Census of the United States, 1880.* Vol. I. *Population.* Washington, D.C.: Government Printing Office, 1883.

————. *Tenth Census of the United States, 1880. Statistics of Cities.* Washington, D.C.: Government Printing Office, 1887.

————. *Population of Cities Having 25,000 Inhabitants or More in 1900, at Each Census: 1790–1900.* Washington, D.C.: Government Printing Office, 1901.

————. *Population Schedules of the Ninth Census of the United States, 1870. City of San Francisco, Ward Four.* Washington, D.C.: National Archives Microfilm Publications, 1956.

————. *Population Schedules of the Tenth Census of the United States, 1880. San Francisco City.* Washington, D.C.: National Archives Microfilm Publications, 1956.

————. *Statistics of Manufactures of the United States at the Tenth Census, 1880.* Washington, D.C.: Government Printing Office, 1883.

————. *Wealth and Industry of the United States at the Ninth Census, 1870.* Washington, D.C.: Government Printing Office, 1872.

U.S. Department of the Interior. *Statistics of the Population of the United States, 1870.* Washington, D.C.: Government Printing Office, 1872.

U.S. Department of the Treasury. *Income Tax Assessment Records, Division One, State of California, 1862–1866.* Microfilm. Federal Archives and Record Center, San Bruno, California.

U.S. Director of the Mint. *Report of the Director of the Mint on the Production of Precious Metals in the United States during the Calendar Year 1889.* Washington, D.C.: Government Printing Office, 1890.

5. *Directories and Guidebooks*

Cooke and LeCount. *A Pile, or a Glance at the Wealth of the Monied Men of San Francisco and Sacramento City.* San Francisco: Cooke and LeCount, 1851.

Elite Directory of San Francisco, 1879. San Francisco: Argonaut, 1879.

Faulkner's Business and Residence Directory of Murray Township. Livermore, Calif.: Herald Co., 1887.

Faulkner's Handbook Directory of Murray Township. Livermore, Calif.: Herald Co., 1886.

Handy Block-Book. San Francisco: Hicks-Judd, 1894.

Historical Souvenir of San Francisco, Cal. San Francisco: C. P. Heininger, 1887.

Mery's Block Book of San Francisco. San Francisco: California Block Book and Map. Co., 1909.

Rasmussen, Louis J. *San Francisco Ship Passenger Lists.* Vol. I. San Francisco: Record and Genealogy Bulletin, 1965.

Realty Directory of San Francisco. San Francisco: Realty Directory Co., 1896.

A Review of the Commercial, Financial and Mining Interests of the State of California, 1876. San Francisco: Commercial Herald, 1877.

San Francisco Block Book. San Francisco: Hicks-Judd, 1906.

San Francisco City Directories, 1862–1922. Various titles and publishers.

San Francisco Office Building and Business Directory. San Francisco: Spaulding-Bonestall, 1905.

A Social Manual for San Francisco and Oakland. San Francisco: City Publishing Co., 1884.

Vallejo City Directory, 1870. Vallejo, Calif.: Kelly and Prescott, 1870.

6. *Contemporary Books and Pamphlets*

Bryce, James. *The American Commonwealth.* 3rd ed. 2 vols. New York: Macmillan, 1904.

Gordon-Cummin, Constance. *Granite Crags.* London: Blackwood, 1886.

Hackett, Fred H. (ed.) *The Industries of San Francisco; Her Rank, Resources, Advantages, Trade, Commerce and Manufactures.* San Francisco: Payot and Co., 1884.

Hittell, John S. *The Commerce and Industries of the Pacific Coast of North America.* San Francisco: A. L. Bancroft, 1884.

Kipling, Rudyard. *American Notes.* New York: Ivers, 1891.

Liggett, J. H. (ed.). *Industries of San Francisco.* San Francisco: Cosmopolitan Co., 1889.

Lloyd, Benjamin E. *Lights and Shades in San Francisco.* San Francisco: A. L. Bancroft, 1875.

Lynch, Jeremiah. *Buckleyism: The Government of a State.* San Francisco: n.p., 1889.

MacGregor, William L. *Hotels and Hotel Life at San Francisco, California, in 1876.* San Francisco: News Co., 1877.

Olmsted, Vaux and Company. *Preliminary Report in Regard to a Plan of a Public Pleasure Grounds for the City of San Francisco.* New York: W. C. Bryant, 1866.

[Pendleton, Harry C.?]. *The Exempt Firemen of San Francisco, Their Unique and Gallant Record, Together with a Resumé of the San Francisco Fire Department and Its Personnel.* San Francisco: Commercial Co., 1900.

Phelan, James D. *Municipal Conditions and the New Charter.* San Francisco: Commercial Co., 1896.

Quigley, Father Hugh. *The Irish Race in California and on the Pacific Coast.* San Francisco: A. Roman, 1878.

Soulé, Frank, James H. Gihon, and James Nisbet. *The Annals of San Francisco.* New York: Appleton, 1855.

Stedman, J. C. and R. A. Leonard. *The Workingmen's Party of California: An Epitome of Its Rise and Progress.* San Francisco: Bacon Co., 1878.

Wait, Frona R. *Wines and Vines of California.* San Francisco: A. L. Bancroft, 1889.

Wierzbicki, Felix P. *California As It Is and As It Might Be; Or, A Guide to the Gold Region.* San Francisco: Washington Bartlett, 1849.

7. *Contemporary Articles*

Blackmar, Frank W. "San Francisco's Struggle for Good Government." *Forum,* 26 (January 1899): 567–577.

Cubberly, Ellwood P. "The School Situation in San Francisco." *Educational Review,* 14 (April 1901): 364–381.

George, Henry. "The Kearney Agitation in California." *Popular Science Monthly,* 17 (August 1880): 433–453.

———. "What the Railroad Will Bring Us." *Overland Monthly,* 1 (October 1868): 297–310.

Hallidie, Andrew A. "Manufacturing in San Francisco." *Overland Monthly,* 11 (June 1888): 636–648.

Hittell, John S. "The Prospects of Vallejo; Or Evidences that Vallejo Will Become a Great City." *Vallejo Evening Chronicle,* March–July 1871.

Phelan, James D. "Municipal Conditions and the New Charter." *Overland Monthly,* 28 (July 1896): 104–111.

———. "Municipal Conditions in San Francisco." *Arena,* 17 (June 1897): 989–995.

Townshend, A. H. J. "Adolph Sutro: Mayor Elect of San Francisco; A Capitalist Fight against Monopoly." *Review of Reviews,* 10 (December 1894): 628.

Vassault, F. I. "Why the Political 'Boss' Is a Factor." *Overland Monthly*, 17 (April 1891): 362–368.

8. *Miscellaneous*

Articles of Association, Acts of Incorporation, and By-Laws of the Vallejo City Homestead Association, Incorporated February 24, 1869. Sacramento: H. S. Crocker, 1869.

Cable Railway Company. *In Reply to the Pamphlet Issued by the Market Street Cable Company.* San Francisco: n.p., [1884].

California Society of Pioneers. *Memorial of the Life and Services of Washington Bartlett.* San Francisco: The Society, 1888.

California State Agricultural Society. *Transactions, 1859.* Sacramento: C. T. Botts, 1860.

Charter Convention of 100. *Reports of the Committees.* San Francisco: n.p., 1897.

Committee of Fifty. *Addresses by the Committee of Fifty to the People.* San Francisco: n.p., [1882].

Democratic Party. *Plan of Organization of the Democratic Party of the City and County of San Francisco, as Amended April 22, 1892.* San Francisco: J. H. Barry, 1892.

———. *Plan for the Reorganization of the Democracy of the City and County of San Francisco Adopted by the Committee of 50 and Approved by the State Central and County Committees, April 6, 1882.* San Francisco: Donovan and Shahan, 1882.

———. *Regular (Reform) Democratic Party of the City and County of San Francisco Platform.* San Francisco: Cubery, 1890.

Good Government Club of San Francisco. *Publication Number Two: Report on Charter Reform.* San Francisco, n.p., 1895.

History of Solano County. Vallejo, Calif.: Wood, Alley Co., 1879.

Holy Cross Cemetery Burial Records. Colma, California.

Reid, Harrison. *A Campaign Songster.* San Francisco: Booth and Coffey, 1892.

SECONDARY WORKS

1. *Books*

Allswang, John M. *Bosses, Machines, and Urban Voters: An American Symbiosis.* New York: Kennikat, 1977.

Asbury, Herbert. *The Barbary Coast: An Informal History of the San Francisco Underworld.* New York: Capricorn, 1968.

Atherton, Gertrude. *California: An Intimate History.* New York: Harpers, 1914.

Bancroft, Hubert Howe. *History of California.* 7 vols. San Francisco: History Co., 1884–1890.

Barth, Gunther. *Bitter Strength: A History of the Chinese in the United States.* Cambridge: Harvard University Press, 1964.

———. *Instant Cities: Urbanization and the Rise of San Francisco and Denver.* New York: Oxford University Press, 1975.

Bean, Walton, *Boss Ruef's San Francisco: The Story of the Union Labor Party, Big*

Business, and the Graft Prosecution. Berkeley: University of California Press, 1952.

———. *California: An Interpretive History.* 2nd ed. New York: McGraw-Hill, 1973.

Blackford, Mansell. *The Politics of Business in California, 1890–1920.* Columbus: Ohio State University Press, 1977.

Brownell, Blaine A. and Warren E. Stickles (eds.). *Bosses and Reformers: Urban Politics in America, 1880–1920.* Boston: Houghton-Mifflin, 1973.

Bullough, William A. *Cities and Schools in the Gilded Age: The Evolution of an Urban Institution.* New York: Kennikat, 1974.

Callow, Alexander B., Jr. (ed.), *American Urban History: An Interpretive Reader with Commentaries.* 2nd ed. New York: Oxford University Press, 1973.

———. *The City Boss in America: An Interpretive Reader.* New York: Oxford University Press, 1976.

———. *The Tweed Ring.* New York: Oxford University Press, 1965.

Cawelti, John G. *Apostles of the Self-Made Man.* Chicago: University of Chicago Press, 1965.

Coblentz, Edmond D. (ed.). *William Randolph Hearst: A Portrait in His Own Words.* New York: Simon and Schuster, 1952.

Cross, Ira B. (ed.). *Frank B. Roney: Irish Rebel and California Labor Leader.* Berkeley: University of California Press, 1931.

———. *A History of the Labor Movement in California.* Berkeley: University of California Press, 1935.

Dana, Julian. *The Man Who Built San Francisco: A Study of Ralston's Journey with Banners.* New York: Macmillan, 1936.

Davis, Winfield J. *A History of Political Conventions in California, 1849–1892.* Sacramento: California State Library, 1893.

Decker, Peter R. *Fortunes and Failures: White-Collar Mobility in Nineteenth-Century San Francisco.* Cambridge: Harvard University Press, 1978.

Dobie, Edith. *The Political Career of Stephen Mallory White: A Study of Party Activities under the Convention System.* Stanford: Stanford University Press, 1927.

Dorsett, Lyle W. *The Pendergast Machine.* New York: Oxford University Press, 1968.

Fogelson, Robert M. *The Fragmented Metropolis: Los Angeles, 1850–1930.* Cambridge: Harvard University Press, 1967.

Frisch, Michael H. *Town into City: Springfield, Massachusetts and the Meaning of Community, 1840–1880.* Cambridge: Harvard University Press, 1972.

Gentry, Curt. *The Madames of San Francisco.* New York: Doubleday, 1964.

Glad, Paul. *McKinley, Bryan and the People.* New York: Lippincott, 1964.

Hauser, Philip M. and Leo F. Schnore (eds.) *The Study of Urbanization.* New York: Wiley, 1965.

Heintz, William F. *San Francisco's Mayors, 1850–1880.* Woodside, Calif.: Gilbert Richards, 1975.

Hittell, John S. *The History of the City of San Francisco and Incidentally of the State of California.* San Francisco: A. L. Bancroft, 1878.

Hittell, Theodore H. *History of California.* 4 vols. San Francisco: N. J. Stone, 1897.

Hofstadter, Richard. *The Age of Reform: From William Jennings Bryan to FDR.* New York: Knopf, 1955.

Holli, Melvin. *Reform in Detroit: Hazen Pingree and Urban Politics.* New York: Oxford University Press, 1969.

Jackson, Joseph Henry. *San Francisco Murders.* New York: Duell, Sloane, and Pearce, 1947.

Jensen, Richard J. *The Winning of the Midwest: Social and Political Conflict, 1888–1896.* Chicago: University of Chicago Press, 1971.

Johnson, Kenneth M. *The Sting of the Wasp: Political and Satirical Cartoons from the Truculent San Francisco Weekly.* San Francisco: Book Club of California, 1967.

Jones, Idwal. *Ark of Empire: San Francisco's Montgomery Block.* New York: Doubleday, 1951.

———. *Vines in the Sun.* New York: Morrow, 1949.

Keller, Morton. *The Art and Politics of Thomas Nast.* New York: Oxford, 1968.

Kelley, Robert L. *Gold vs. Grain: The Hydraulic Mining Controversy in California's Sacramento Valley.* Glendale, Calif.: Arthur H. Clarke, 1959.

King, Joseph L. *History of the San Francisco Stock and Exchange Board.* San Francisco: The Author, 1910.

Kipling, Rudyard. *Rudyard Kipling's Letters from San Francisco.* San Francisco: Colt Press, 1949.

Kleppner, Paul J. *The Cross of Culture: A Social Analysis of Midwestern Progressive Politics, 1850–1922.* New York: Free Press, 1970.

Kroninger, Robert H. *Sarah and the Senator.* Berkeley: Howell-North, 1964.

Lavender, David S. *Nothing Seemed Impossible: William C. Ralston and Early San Francisco.* Palo Alto, Calif.: American West, 1975.

Lazerson, Marvin. *Origins of the Urban School: Public Education in Massachusetts, 1870–1915.* Cambridge: Harvard University Press, 1971.

Lewis, Oscar. *The Big Four: The Story of Huntington, Stanford, Hopkins and Crocker and the Building of the Central Pacific.* New York: Knopf, 1938.

———. *San Francisco: Mission to Metropolis.* Berkeley: Howell-North, 1966.

———. *The Silver Kings.* New York: Knopf, 1959.

London, Jack. *The Bodley Head Jack London.* Ed. Arthur Calder-Marshall. London: Bodley Head, 1963.

Lotchin, Roger W. *San Francisco, 1846–1856: From Hamlet to City.* New York: Oxford University Press, 1974.

Lundberg, Ferdinand. *Imperial Hearst: A Social Biography.* New York: Equinox, 1936.

Lyman, George D. *Ralston's Ring: Plunderers of the Comstock Lode.* New York: Scribner's, 1945.

McAfee, Ward. *California's Railroad Era, 1850–1911.* San Marino, Calif.: Golden West Books, 1973.

McCabe, Bob and James E. Henly. *Ravenswood.* Livermore, Calif.: Livermore Heritage Guild, 1976.

Mandelbaum, Seymour. *Boss Tweed's New York.* New York: Wiley, 1965.

Marcus, Robert D. *Grand Old Party: Political Structure in the Gilded Age, 1880–1896.* New York: Oxford University Press, 1971.

Mechanics' Institute. *One Hundred Years of the Mechanics' Institute in San Francisco.* San Francisco: The Institute, 1955.

Melendy, Howard B. and Benjamin F. Gilbert. *The Governors of California: Peter Burnett to Edmund G. Brown.* Georgetown, Calif.: Talisman, 1965.

Merton, Robert K. *Social Theory and Social Structure.* Rev. ed. New York: Free Press, 1957.

Mighels, Ella S. *The Story of the Files: A Review of California Writers and Literature.* San Francisco: Cooperative Printing Co., 1893.

Miller, Zane L. *Boss Cox's Cincinnati: Urban Politics in the Progressive Era.* New York: Oxford University Press, 1968.

———. *The Urbanization of Modern America.* New York: Harcourt Brace Jovanovich, 1973.

Morgan, H. Wayne. *From Hayes to McKinley: National Party Politics, 1877– 1896.* Syracuse: Syracuse University Press, 1969.

———, (ed.). *The Gilded Age: A Reappraisal.* Rev. ed. Syracuse: Syracuse University Press, 1970.

Moses, Bernard. *The Establishment of Municipal Government in San Francisco.* Baltimore: Johns Hopkins University Press, 1889.

Mowry, George E. *The California Progressives.* Berkeley: University of California Press, 1951.

Muscatine, Doris. *Old San Francisco: The Biography of a City from Early Days to the Earthquake.* New York: Putnam's, 1975.

Nash, Gerald D. *State Government and Economic Development: A History of Administrative Policies in California.* Berkeley: University of California Press, 1964.

O'Shaughnessy, M. N. *Hetch-Hetchy: Its Origins and History.* San Francisco: Recorder Co., 1934.

Parkhurst, Charles H. *Our Fight with Tammany.* New York: Arno, 1970 [1895].

Patton, Clifford W. *The Battle for Municipal Reform: Mobilization and Attack, 1875–1900.* Washington, D.C.: American Council on Public Affairs, 1940.

Paul, Rodman W. *California Gold.* Cambridge: Harvard University Press, 1947.

———. *Mining Frontiers of the Far West, 1848–1880.* New York: Holt, Rinehart and Winston, 1963.

Peel, Roy V. *The Political Clubs of New York City.* New York: Putnam's, 1935.

Prendergast, Thomas F. *Forgotten Pioneers: Irish Leaders in Early California.* San Francisco: Trade Pressroom, 1942.

Riordon, William, *Plunkitt of Tammany Hall.* New York: Dutton, 1963.

Rischin, Moses (ed.). *The American Gospel of Success: Individualism and Beyond.* Chicago: Quadrangle, 1965.

Rogin, Michael P. and John L. Shover. *Political Change in California, 1890– 1966.* Westport, Conn.: Greenwood, 1970.

Saxton, Alexander P. *The Indispensable Enemy: Labor and the Anti-Chinese Movement in California.* Berkeley: University of California Press, 1971.

Schmitt, Peter. *Back to Nature: The Arcadian Myth in Urban America.* New York: Oxford University Press, 1969.

Schultz, Stanley K. *The Culture Factory: Boston Public Schools, 1789–1869.* New York: Oxford University Press, 1973.

Scott, Mellier G. *The San Francisco Bay Area: A Metropolis in Perspective.* Berkeley: University of California Press, 1959.

Shuck, Oscar T. *History of Bench and Bar in California.* Los Angeles: Commercial Printing House, 1901.

Shumate, Albert E. *A Visit to Rincon Hill and South Park.* San Francisco: E Clampus Vitus, 1963.

Sproat, John G. *"The Best Men": Liberal Reformers in the Gilded Age.* New York: Oxford University Press, 1968.

Starr, Kevin. *Americans and the California Dream, 1850–1915.* New York: Oxford University Press, 1973.

Stave, Bruce M. (ed.). *Urban Bosses, Machines, and Progressive Reformers.* Lexington, Mass.: D. C. Heath, 1972.

Steffens, Lincoln. *The Shame of the Cities.* New York: McClure, Phillips, 1904.

Stevenson, Robert Louis and Lloyd Osbourne. *The Wrecker.* New York: Scribner's, 1907.

Stewart, Frank M. *A Half-Century of Municipal Reform: The History of the National Municipal League.* Berkeley: University of California Press, 1950.

Stewart, George R. *Committee of Vigilance: Revolution in San Francisco, 1851.* New York: Houghton-Mifflin, 1964.

Stewart, Robert E. and Mary F. Stewart. *Adolph Sutro: A Biography.* Berkeley: Howell-North, 1962.

Strong, Josiah. *Our Country: Its Possible Future and Its Present Crisis.* New York: Baker and Taylor, 1891.

Swanberg, W. A. *Citizen Hearst: A Biography of William Randolph Hearst.* New York: Scribner's, 1961.

Swisher, Carl B. *Motivation and Political Technique in the California Constitutional Convention, 1878–1879.* Claremont, Calif.: Huntington Library, 1930.

Taper, Bernard (ed.). *Mark Twain's San Francisco.* New York: McGraw-Hill, 1963.

Tarr, Joel A. *A Study of Boss Politics: William Lorimer of Chicago.* Urbana: University of Illinois Press, 1971.

Thernstrom, Stephan. *Poverty and Progress: Social Mobility in a Nineteenth Century City.* Cambridge: Harvard University Press, 1964.

Tilton, Cecil G. *William Chapman Ralston, Courageous Builder.* Boston: Christopher House, 1935.

Troen, Selwyn K. *The Public and the Schools: Shaping the St. Louis System, 1838–1920.* Columbia: University of Missouri Press, 1975.

Tyack, David B. *The One Best System: A History of American Urban Education.* Cambridge: Harvard University Press, 1974.

Vance, James E. *Geography and Urban Evolution in the San Francisco Bay Area.* Berkeley: University of California Institute of Governmental Studies, 1964.

Walker, Franklin. *San Francisco's Literary Frontier.* Seattle: University of Washington Press, 1969.

Warner, Sam Bass, Jr. *The Private City: Philadelphia in Three Periods of Its Growth.* Philadelphia: University of Pennsylvania Press, 1968.

———. *Streetcar Suburbs: The Process of Growth in Boston, 1870–1900.* Cambridge: Harvard University Press, 1962.

———. *The Urban Wilderness: A History of the American City.* New York: Harper and Row, 1972.

Weber, Adna F. *The Growth of Cities in the Nineteenth Century: A Study in Statistics.* New York: Macmillan, 1899.

Weinstein, James. *The Corporate Ideal in the Liberal State.* Boston: Beacon Press, 1968.

Wells, Evelyn. *Fremont Older.* New York: Appleton-Century, 1936.

Welter, Rush. *Popular Education and Democratic Thought in America.* New York: Columbia University Press, 1962.

White, Morton and Lucia White. *The Intellectual versus the City: From Thomas Jefferson to Frank Lloyd Wright.* Cambridge: Harvard University Press, 1962.

Wiebe, Robert H. *The Search for Order, 1877–1920.* New York: Hill and Wang, 1962.

Williams, R. Hal. *The Democratic Party and California Politics, 1880–1896.* Stanford: Stanford University Press, 1973.

———. *Years of Decision: American Politics in the 1890s.* New York: Wiley, 1978.

Winkler, John K. *W. R. Hearst: An American Phenomenon.* New York: Simon and Schuster, 1928.

Wirt, Frederick M. *Power in the City: Decision-Making in San Francisco.* Berkeley: University of California Press, 1974.

Wyllie, Irvin G. *The Self-Made Man in America: The Myth of Rags to Riches.* New Brunswick, N.J.: Rutgers University Press, 1954.

Young, John P. *Journalism in California.* San Francisco: Chronicle Co., 1915.

———. *San Francisco: A History of the Pacific Coast Metropolis.* 2 vols. San Francisco: S. J. Clarke, 1912.

Zink, Harold. *City Bosses in the United States.* Durham, N.C.: Duke University Press, 1930.

334

2. Articles

Averbach, Alvin. "San Francisco's South of Market District, 1850–1950; The Emergence of a Skid Row." *California Historical Quarterly,* 53 (Fall 1973): 197–223.

Barth, Gunther. "Metropolism and Urban Elites in the Far West." In *The Age of Industrialism in America: Essays in Social Structure and Cultural Values.* Ed. Frederic C. Jaher. New York: Free Press, 1968. 158–187.

Bernard, Richard M. and Bradley R. Rice. "Political Environment and the Adoption of Progressive Municipal Reform." *Journal of Urban History,* 1 (February 1975): 149–174.

Blackford, Mansel G. "Reform Politics in Seattle during the Progressive Era, 1902–1916." *Pacific Northwest Quarterly,* 59 (October 1968): 177–185.

Blumenfeld, Hans. "The Modern Metropolis." *Scientific American,* 213 (September 1965): 64–74.

Buenker, John D. "The Urban Political Machine and the Seventeenth Amendment." *Journal of American History,* 56 (September 1969): 305–322.

Bullough, William A. "Hannibal versus the Blind Boss: Chris Buckley, The 'Junta,' and Democratic Reform Politics in San Francisco." *Pacific Historical Review,* 46 (May 1977): 181–206.

———. "'It Is Better to Be a Country Boy': The Lure of the Country in Urban Education in the Gilded Age." *The Historian,* 35 (February 1973): 183–195.

———. "The Steam Beer Handicap: Chris Buckley and the San Francisco Municipal Election of 1896." *California Historical Quarterly,* 54 (Fall 1975): 245–262.

Burchell, Robert A. "The Loss of a Reputation; Or, The Image of California in Britain before 1875." *California Historical Quarterly,* 53 (Summer 1974): 115–130.

Callow, Alexander B., Jr. "The Legislature of a Thousand Scandals." *Historical Society of Southern California Quarterly,* 39 (December 1957): 332–344.

———. "San Francisco's Blind Boss." *Pacific Historical Review,* 25 (August 1956): 261–279.

Cerillo, Augustus, Jr. "The Reform of Municipal Government in New York City: From Seth Low to John Purroy Mitchell." *New York Historical Society Quarterly,* 57 (January 1973): 51–71.

Davis, William H. "Emerson the Lecturer in California." *California Historical Society Quarterly,* 20 (March 1941): 1–11.

Fracchia, Charles A. "The Founding of the San Francisco Mining Exchange." *California Historical Society Quarterly* (March 1969): 3–18.

Fritzche, Bruno, "San Francisco, 1846–1848: The Coming of the Land Speculator." *California Historical Quarterly,* 51 (Spring 1972): 17–32.

Geiger, Louis G. "Joseph W. Folk v. Edward Butler: St. Louis, 1902." *Journal of Southern History,* 28 (November 1962): 438–449.

335

Gilbert, Benjamin F. "The Confederate Minority in California." *California Historical Society Quarterly*, 20 (June 1941): 154–170.

Griffith, David B. "Anti-Monopoly Movements in California, 1873–1898." *Southern California Quarterly*, 52 (June 1970): 93–121.

Grassman, Curtis E. "Prologue to California Reform: The Democratic Impulse, 1886–1898." *Pacific Historical Review*, 42 (November 1973): 518–536.

Hays, Samuel P. "The Changing Political Structure of the City in Industrial America." *Journal of Urban History*, 1 (November 1974): 6–38.

——. "The Politics of Reform in Municipal Government in the Progressive Era." *Pacific Northwest Quarterly*, 55 (October 1964): 157–169.

——. "The Social Analysis of American Political History, 1880–1920." *Political Science Quarterly*, 80 (September 1965): 373–393.

Higham, John. "The American Party, 1886–1891." *Pacific Historical Review*, 19 (February 1950): 37–47.

Hollingsworth, J. Rogers. "The Historian, Presidential Elections, and 1896." *Mid-America*, 45 (July 1963): 184–192.

Holt, Glen E. "The Changing Perception of Urban Pathology: An Essay on the Development of Mass Transit in the United States." In *Cities in American History*. Eds. Kenneth T. Jackson and Stanley K. Schultz. New York: Knopf, 1972. 324–343.

Hornbein, Marjorie. "Denver's Struggle for Home Rule." *Colorado Magazine*, 48 (Fall 1971): 337–354.

Hurt, Peyton. "The Rise and Fall of the 'Know-Nothings' in California." *California Historical Society Quarterly*, 9 (March 1930): 16–49, (June 1930): 99–128.

Issel, William. "Class and Ethnic Conflict in San Francisco Political History: The Reform Charter of 1898." *Labor History*, 18 (Summer 1977): 341–359.

Jacobson, Pauline, "Playhouses of the Pioneers." San Francisco *Bulletin* (12 August 1916), p. 11.

Jones, Idwal. "At Ravenswood." *Westways*, 40 (May 1948): 6–7.

Kahn, Edgar M. "Andrew Smith Hallidie." *California Historical Society Quarterly*, 19 (June 1940): 144–156.

Kalisch, Philip. "The Black Death in Chinatown: Plague and Politics in San Francisco, 1900–1904." *Arizona and the West*, 14 (Summer 1972): 113–136.

Kauer, Ralph. "The Workingmen's Party of California." *Pacific Historical Review*, 12 (September 1944): 275–291.

Kelley, Robert L. "The Mining Debris Controversy in the Sacramento Valley." *Pacific Historical Review*, 25 (November 1956): 331–346.

Kingsdale, Jon M. "The 'Poor Man's Club': Social Functions of the Urban Working Class Saloon." *American Quarterly*, 25 (October 1973): 472–489.

Lubove, Roy. "The Twentieth Century City: The Progressive as Municipal Reformer." *Mid-America*, 41 (October 1959): 195–209.

Luckingham, Bradford F. "Benovolence in Emergent San Francisco: A Note on Immigrant Life in the Urban Far West." *Southern California Quarterly*, 55 (Winter 1973): 431–443.

———. "Immigrant Life in Emergent San Francisco." *Journal of the West*, 12 (October 1973): 600–617.

McAfee, Ward M. "A Constitutional History of Railroad Rate Regulation in California, 1879–1911." *Pacific Historical Review*, 37 (August 1968): 265–279.

McKee, Irving. "The Shooting of Charles De Young." *Pacific Historical Review*, 16 (August 1974): 271–284.

McKitrick, Eric L. "The Study of Corruption." *Political Science Quaterly*, 62 (December 1957): 502–514.

Mawn, Geoffrey P. "Framework for Destiny: San Francisco, 1847." *California Historical Quarterly*, 51 (Summer 1972): 165–178.

Mazzi, Frank. "Harbingers of the City: Men and Their Monuments in Nineteenth Century San Francisco." *Southern California Quarterly*, 55 (Summer 1973): 141–162.

Meier, Hugo A. "American Technology and the Nineteenth Century World." *American Quarterly*, 10 (Spring 1958): 116–130.

Mitchell, J. Paul, "Boss Speer and the City Functional: Boosters and Businessmen versus Commission Government in Denver." *Pacific Northwest Quarterly*, 63 (October 1972): 155–164.

Moorehead, Dudley T. "Sectionalism and the California Constitution of 1879." *Pacific Historical Review*, 12 (September 1943): 278–293.

Mowry, George E. "The California Progressive and His Rationale: A Study in Middle Class Politics." *Mississippi Valley Historical Review*, 36 (September 1949): 239–250.

Nash, Gerald D. "The California Railroad Commission, 1876–1911." *Southern California Quarterly*, 44 (December 1962): 287–306.

Olmsted, Roger. "The Sense of the 'Seventies: California 100 Years Ago." *California Historical Society Quarterly*, 50 (June 1971): 131–160.

Orsi, Richard J. "*The Octopus* Reconsidered: The Southern Pacific and Agricultural Modernization in California, 1865–1915." *California Historical Quarterly*, 54 (Fall 1975): 197–220.

Paul, Rodman W. "The Origin of the Chinese Issue in California." *Mississippi Valley Historical Review*, 25 (August 1938): 181–196.

———. "The Wheat Trade between California and the United Kingdom." *Mississippi Valley Historical Review*, 45 (December 1958): 391–412.

Pease, Otis A. "Urban Reformers in the Progressive Era: A Reassessment." *Pacific Northwest Quarterly*, 62 (April 1972): 150–154.

Petersen, Eric F. "End of an Era: California's Gubernatorial Election of 1894." *Pacific Historical Review*, 38 (May 1969): 141–156.

337

———. "The Struggle for the Australian Ballot in California." *California Historical Quarterly*, 51 (Fall 1972): 227–242.

Pomeroy, Earl. "California, 1846–1860: Politics of a Representative Frontier State." *California Historical Society Quarterly*, 32 (December 1953): 291–302.

Ricards, Sherman L. and Gregory M. Blackburn. "The Sydney Ducks: A Demographic Analysis." *Pacific Historical Review*, 42 (February 1973): 20–31.

Righter, Robert W. "Washington Bartlett: Mayor of San Francisco, 1883–1887." *Journal of the West*, 3 (January 1964): 102–114.

Rischin, Moses. "Immigration, Migration, and Minorities in California: A Reassessment." *Pacific Historical Review*, 41 (February 1972): 71–90.

Rodecape, Lois Fuller. "Tom Maguire, Napoleon of the Stage." *California Historical Society Quarterly*, 20 (December 1941): 289–314, 21 (March 1942): 39–74, (June 1942): 141–182, (September 1942): 239–275.

Rusk, Jerrold G. "The Effect of Australian Ballot Reform on Split Ticket Voting, 1876–1908." *American Political Science Review*, 64 (December 1970): 1220–1238.

Sandmeyer, Elmer C. "California Anti-Chinese Legislation and the Federal Courts: A Study in Federal Relations." *Pacific Historical Review*, 5 (May 1936): 192–211.

Saxton, Alexander P. "San Francisco Labor and the Populist and Progressive Insurgencies." *Pacific Historical Review*, 34 (November 1965): 421–438.

Schiesl, Martin J. "Progressive Reform in Los Angeles under Mayor Alexander, 1909–1913." *California Historical Quarterly*, 54 (Spring 1975): 37–56.

Shumsky, Neil L. "San Francisco's Workingmen Respond to the Modern City." *California Historical Quarterly*, 55 (Spring 1976): 46–57.

Sjoberg, Gideon. "The Origin and Evolution of Cities." *Scientific American*, 213 (September 1965): 54–62.

Springer, Ralph. "Golden Gate Park." *Overland Monthly*, 69 (February 1917): 101–108.

Stave, Bruce M. "The New Deal, the Last Hurrah, and the Building of an Urban Machine: Pittsburgh Committeemen, a Case Study." *Pennsylvania History*, 33 (October 1966): 460–483.

———. "Urban Bosses and Reform." In *The Urban Experience*. Eds. Raymond A. Mohl and James F. Richardson. Belmont, Calif.: Wadsworth, 1973. 182–195.

Taggart, Harold F. "The Party Realignment of 1896 in California." *Pacific Historical Review*, 8 (December 1939): 435–452.

———. "Thomas Vincent Cator: Populist Leader of California." *California Historical Society Quarterly*, 27 (December 1948): 311–318, 28 (March 1949): 47–55.

Tarr, Joel A. "From the City to Suburb: The Moral Influences of Transportation Technology." In *American Urban History*. Ed. Alexander B. Callow, Jr. New York: Oxford, 2d ed., 1973. 202–212.

Taylor, George Rogers. "The Beginning of Mass Transportation in Urban America." *Smithsonian Journal of History,* 1 (Fall 1966): 35–49.

Walsh, James P. "Abe Ruef Was No Boss: Machine Politics, Reform, and San Francisco." *California Historical Quarterly,* 51 (Fall 1972): 3–16.

Wade, Richard C. "Urbanization." In *The Comparative Approach to American History.* Ed. C. Vann Woodward. New York: Basic Books, 1968. 187–205.

Walters, Donald E. "The Feud between California Populist T. V. Cator and Democrats James Maguire and James Barry." *Pacific Historical Review,* 27 (November 1958): 281–298.

Watson, Douglas S. "The San Francisco McAllisters." *California Historical Society Quarterly,* 11 (June 1932): 124–128.

Weinstein, James. "Organized Business and the Commission and Manager Movements." *Journal of Southern History,* 28 (May 1962): 167–181.

Wheeler, Harvey. "Yesterday's Robin Hood: The Rise and Fall of Baltimore's Trenton Democratic Club." *American Quarterly,* 7 (Winter 1955): 332–344.

Wiebe, Robert. "Business Disunity and the Progressive Movement." *Mississippi Valley Historical Review,* 44 (March 1958): 664–685.

Wiltsee, Ernest A. "The City of New York of the Pacific." *California Historical Society Quarterly,* 12 (March 1933): 25–33.

Wright, Doris M. "The Making of Cosmopolitan California: An Analysis of Immigration, 1848–1870." *California Historical Society Quarterly,* 20 (December 1940): 65–79.

3. Unpublished Works

Barthé, Theresa. "Early Days in Vallejo." Typescript. Solano County (California) Public Library.

Blackford, Mansell G. "The Politics of Business in California, 1890–1920." Ph.D. thesis. University of California, Berkeley, 1972.

Bowden, Martyn J. "The Dynamics of City Growth: Historical Geography of the San Francisco Central District, 1850–1931." Ph.D. thesis. University of California, Berkeley, 1967.

Bowlen, Frederick J. "Firefighters of the Past: A History of the Old Volunteer Fire Department of San Francisco from 1849 to 1866." Typescript. Bancroft Library. University of California, Berkeley.

Bullough, William A. "Urban Education in the Gilded Age, 1876–1906." Ph.D. thesis. University of California, Santa Barbara, 1970.

Chenoweth, Clyde G. "The San Francisco Stock Exchange and Its History." Ph.D. thesis. Stanford University, 1932.

Clodius, Albert H. "The Quest for Good Government in Los Angeles, 1890–1910." Ph.D. thesis. Claremont Graduate School, 1953.

Daniels, Douglas. "Afro-San Franciscans: A Social History of Urban Pioneers, 1860–1930." Ph.D. thesis. University of California, Berkeley, 1975.

Dolson, Lee S., Jr. "The Administration of San Francisco Public Schools, 1847–1947." Ph.D. thesis. University of California, Berkeley, 1964.

Foster, Mark S. "The Decentralization of Los Angeles during the 1920s." Ph.D. thesis. University of Southern California, 1971.

Grassman, Curtis E. "Prologue to Progressivism: Senator Stephen M. White and the California Reform Impulse, 1875–1905." Ph.D. thesis. University of California, Los Angeles, 1970.

Heintz, William F. Notes and unpublished manuscripts.

Hennings, Robert E. "James D. Phelan and the Wilson Progressives of California." Ph.D. thesis. University of California, Berkeley, 1961.

Loosely, Allyn C. "Foreign Born Population of California, 1848–1920." M.A. thesis. University of California, Berkeley, 1927.

Luckingham, Bradford E. "Associational Life on the Urban Frontier: San Francisco, 1848–1856." Ph.D. thesis. University of California, Davis, 1968.

Miller, Louis R. "The History of the San Francisco and San Jose Railroad." M.A. thesis. University of California, Berkeley, 1947.

Pedemonte, Thomas A. "Italy in San Francisco: 'Old Wine in New Bottles.'" M.A. thesis. California State College, Hayward, 1971.

Petersen, Eric F. "California Politics, 1870–1894." Ph.D. thesis. University of California, Los Angeles, 1968.

Righter, Robert W. "The Life and Career of Washington Bartlett." M.A. thesis. San Jose (California) State College, 1963.

St. Laurence, Ronald A. "The Myth and the Reality: Prostitution in San Francisco, 1880–1913." M.A. thesis. California State University, Hayward, 1974.

Shumsky, Neil L. "Tar Flat and Nob Hill: A Social History of Industrial San Francisco in the 1870s." Ph.D. thesis. University of California, Berkeley, 1972.

Swanstrom, Roy A. "The Reform Administration of James D. Phelan, Mayor of San Francisco." M.A. thesis. University of California, Berkeley, 1949.

Varcados, Peter. "Labor and Politics in San Francisco, 1880–1892." Ph.D. thesis. University of California, Berkeley, 1968.

Voget, Lamberta M. "The Waterfront of San Francisco, 1863–1930: A History of Its Administration by the State of California." Ph.D. thesis. University of California, Berkeley, 1943.

Wade, Jere D. "The San Francisco Stage, 1859–1869." Ph.D. thesis. University of Oregon, 1972.

Walters, Donald E. "Populism in California, 1889–1900." Ph.D. thesis. University of California, Berkeley, 1952.

Young, Changni. "The Market Street Railway System in San Francisco." Ph.D. thesis. Harvard University, 1946.

INDEX

Designer: Al Burkhardt
Compositor: Typesetting Services of California
Printer: Thomson-Shore
Binder: Thomson-Shore
Text: VIP Garamond
Display: Typositor Normandia
Cloth: Kivar 5 Cocoa
& Process Materials Elephant Hide
Paper: 55lb P&S offset Regular A69